Domestic Manners of the Americans

FRANCES TROLLOPE (1780–1863) is now best remembered as the mother of Anthony Trollope. She turned to writing in a desperate attempt to support her family. *Domestic Manners of the Americans*, her first and most famous book, was written when she was over 50. She produced over forty books: novels, travel books, and poetry. Her novels made her one of the most popular authors of her time and in works like *Michael Armstrong* she attacked various social evils. She founded one of the greatest writing families of the century.

RICHARD MULLEN was born in New Jersey. After gaining his doctorate in history at the University of Oxford, he has taught British and American history in the Universities of Oxford and London. He has written documentaries for the BBC on Mrs Trollope as well as on her son Anthony.

Domestic Manners of the Americans

By
Frances Trollope

Edited by
RICHARD MULLEN

On me dit que pourvu que je ne parle ni de l'autorité, ni du culte,
ni de la politique, ni de la morale, ni des gens en place, ni de
l'opéra, ni des autres spectacles, ni de personne qui tienne à
quelque chose, je puis tout imprimer librement.

BEAUMARCHAIS, *Mariage de Figaro.*

Oxford   New York
OXFORD UNIVERSITY PRESS
1984

Oxford University Press, Walton Street, Oxford OX2 6DP

London New York Toronto
Delhi Bombay Calcutta Madras Karachi
Kuala Lumpur Singapore Hong Kong Tokyo
Nairobi Dar es Salaam Cape Town
Melbourne Auckland

and associated companies in
Beirut Berlin Ibadan Mexico City Nicosia

Oxford is a trade mark of Oxford University Press

First published 1832
This (fifth) edition published 1839 by Richard Bentley
First issued as an Oxford University Press paperback 1984

British Library Cataloguing in Publication Data
Trollope, Frances
Domestic manners of the Americans.
1. United States—Description and travel
—1783–1848
I. Title   II. Mullen, Richard
917.3'0455   E165
ISBN 0-19-281464-8

Library of Congress Cataloging in Publication Data
Trollope, Frances Milton, 1780–1863.
Domestic manners of the Americans.
Reprint. Originally published: 5th ed. London:
R. Bentley, 1839. With new introd.
1. United States—Social life and customs—1783–1865.
I. Mullen, Richard.   II. Title.
E165.T84 1984   973   84–7905
ISBN 0-19-281464-8 (pbk.)

Printed in Great Britain by
Richard Clay (The Chaucer Press) Ltd.
Bungay, Suffolk

Contents

	PAGE
INTRODUCTION BY RICHARD MULLEN - - -	IX
NOTE ON THE TEXT	xxxii
PREFACES BY FRANCES TROLLOPE	xxxiii

CHAPTER ONE
Entrance of the Mississippi—Balize - - - 1

CHAPTER TWO
New Orleans—Society—Creoles and Quadroons—Voyage up the Mississippi - - - - - - 4

CHAPTER THREE
Company on Board the Steam-Boat—Scenery of the Mississippi —Crocodiles—Arrival at Memphis—Nashoba - - 13

CHAPTER FOUR
Departure from Memphis—Ohio River—Louisville—Cincinnati 26

CHAPTER FIVE
Cincinnati—Forest Farm—Mr Bullock - - - 35

CHAPTER SIX
Servants—Society—Evening Parties - - - 44

CHAPTER SEVEN
Market—Museum—Picture Gallery—Academy of Fine Arts— Drawing School—Phrenological Society—Miss Wright's Lecture - - - - - - - 50

CHAPTER EIGHT
Absence of Public and Private Amusement—Churches and Chapels —Influence of the Clergy—A Revival - - - 59

V

Contents

CHAPTER NINE

PAGE

Schools—Climate—Water-Melons—Fourth of July—Storms—Pigs—Moving Houses—Mr Flint—Literature - - 67

CHAPTER TEN

Removal to the Country—Walk in the Forest—Equality - 78

CHAPTER ELEVEN

Religion - - - - - - - 89

CHAPTER TWELVE

Peasantry, Compared to that of England—Early Marriages—Charity — Independence and Equality—Cottage Prayer-Meeting - - - - - - - 96

CHAPTER THIRTEEN

Theatre—Fine Arts—Delicacy—Shaking Quakers—Big-Bone Lick—Visit of the President - - - - 108

CHAPTER FOURTEEN

American Spring—Controversy between Messrs Owen and Campbell —Public Ball—Separation of the Sexes—American Freedom —Execution - - - - - - - 120

CHAPTER FIFTEEN

Camp-Meeting - - - - - - 137

CHAPTER SIXTEEN

Danger of Rural Excursions—Sickness - - - 145

CHAPTER SEVENTEEN

Departure from Cincinnati—Society on Board the Steamboat—Arrival at Wheeling—Bel Esprit - - - 150

CHAPTER EIGHTEEN

Departure for the Mountains in the Stage—Scenery of the Alleghany—Haggerstown - - - - - 159

CHAPTER NINETEEN

Baltimore—Catholic Cathedral—St Mary's College—Sermons—Infant Schools - - - - - - 170

Contents

CHAPTER TWENTY

PAGE

Voyage to Washington—Capitol—City of Washington—Congress Indians—Funeral of a Member of Congress - - 180

CHAPTER TWENTY-ONE

Stonington—Great Falls of the Potomac - - - 199

CHAPTER TWENTY-TWO

Small Landed Proprietors—Slavery - - - - 202

CHAPTER TWENTY-THREE

Fruits and Flowers of Maryland and Virginia—Copper-Head Snake —Insects—Elections - - - - - 213

CHAPTER TWENTY-FOUR

Journey to Philadelphia—Chesapeake and Delaware Canal— City of Philadelphia—Miss Wright's Lecture - - 220

CHAPTER TWENTY-FIVE

Washington Square—American Beauty—Gallery of Fine Arts— Antiques—Theatres—Museum - - - - 225

CHAPTER TWENTY-SIX

Quakers—Presbyterians—Itinerant Methodist Preacher—Market —Influence of Females on Society - - - 233

CHAPTER TWENTY-SEVEN

Return to Stonington—Thunder-Storm—Emigrants—Illness— Alexandria - - - - - - 245

CHAPTER TWENTY-EIGHT

American Cooking — Evening Parties— Dress —Sleighing — Money-Getting Habits—Tax-Gatherer's Notice—Indian Summer—Anecdote of the Duke of Saxe-Weimar - - 254

CHAPTER TWENTY-NINE

Literature—Extracts—Fine Arts—Education - - - 267

CHAPTER THIRTY

Journey to New York—Delaware River—Stage-Coach—City of New York—Collegiate Institute for Young Ladies— Theatres—Public Garden—Churches—Morris Canal— Fashions—Carriages - - - - - 293

vii

Contents

CHAPTER THIRTY-ONE

PAGE

Reception of Captain Basil Hall's Book in the United States   313

CHAPTER THIRTY-TWO

*Journey to Niagara—Hudson—West Point—Hyde Park—
Albany—Yankees—Trenton Falls—Rochester—Genesee
Falls—Lockport* - - - - - - 323

CHAPTER THIRTY-THREE

*Niagara—Arrival at Forsythes—First Sight of the Falls—Goat
Island—The Rapids—Buffalo—Lake Erie—Canandaigua—
Stage-Coach Adventures* - - - - 336

CHAPTER THIRTY-FOUR

Return to New York—Conclusion - - - - 355

Editor's Notes - - - 365

Mark Twain's Comments - - - 369

Introduction

IN the summer of 1832 a young British officer, E. T. Coke, visited New York to gather information for a book about the United States. While he was there copies began to arrive of another English travel book and soon an American edition appeared. 'The commotion it created is truly inconceivable. At every corner a large placard met the eye with "For Sale: *Domestic Manners of the Americans* by Mrs Trollope". At every hotel table, on board of every steamboat, in every stage coach, and in all societies, the first question was, "Have you read Mrs Trollope?"'[1]

During the nineteenth century there was something of a minor industry in writing travel books about America. Most share the fate of E. T. Coke's and are forgotten. Only a few have survived. Of these few, none has ever achieved and retained the fame or notoriety of Frances Trollope's *Domestic Manners of the Americans*, first published in March 1832. It has survived because first and foremost it is a good book, the product of a lively and colourful pen. Whether the book delights or annoys, it is always amusing. Even if many of the customs Mrs Trollope records have disappeared or perhaps changed, the book is still full of a perceptive, if incomplete, analysis of American society. The book has also survived because it is part of an incredible adventure which launched one of the greatest writing families of the nineteenth century, the Trollopes. *Domestic Manners* is so bound up with Mrs Trollope's life that it is essential to know something of her background.

In 1809, Frances, daughter of the Revd William Milton,

1 E. T. Coke, *A Subaltern's Furlough* (London, 1833), pp. 167-8.

married Thomas Anthony Trollope, a barrister descended from a long line of baronets and country clergy. At first they settled in London but shortly after the birth of their youngest son, Anthony, in 1815, the family moved to a mansion they built at Harrow, then a quiet village near London. Thomas Anthony was a talented man, but one possessed of an ungovernable temper. His eldest son, Thomas Adolphus, recalled 'No one of all the family circle was happy in his presence.'[2] He carried his rages into business as well, for he could never resist telling attorneys that they were blockheads. Naturally this was not good for business. He attempted to cure his frequent migraines with huge doses of calomel, to which he became addicted. This is why, perhaps, Mrs Trollope was so concerned at the ease with which American doctors prescribed that drug.

The move to Harrow was not only designed to give the rapidly growing family more room and better air. It was also to allow Thomas Anthony to indulge in the risky life of a gentleman farmer. It was perhaps only to be expected that such a man would take up such a pursuit at the very moment when English agriculture plunged into depression. At least he had the consolation of conducting an acrimonious correspondence with his landlord. For the next dozen years the family's finances tumbled steadily downhill. Harrow had, however, one great advantage: families who lived in the parish could send their sons to Harrow School without paying the normal fees. A public school education was an absolute necessity for a family so devoted to the concept of gentility as the Trollopes: a family that boasted a liveried footman, even if it meant economising on candles. To Mr Trollope Harrow School was nothing but 't'other school' but at least it offered virtually free education for his sons until they could follow in his footsteps to Winchester and Oxford.

To Mrs Trollope Harrow provided an introduction to many similar families with whom she could indulge her passions for

2 The family background is best observed in Thomas Adolphus Trollope, *What I Remember* (London, 1887) and Anthony Trollope, *An Autobiography* (London, 1883).

Introduction

literary talk and amateur theatricals. Harrow was still full of memories of her literary hero, Lord Byron. His former master was a friend of hers. She exploded with righteous anger when the evangelical vicar of Harrow refused to allow Lord Byron's illegitimate daughter, Allegra, to have a headstone in the churchyard for fear it would corrupt the boys. Soon her friends were delighting in a clever and spiteful poem that she wrote and circulated, attacking the vicar.[3] Here, already, was a theme she was to develop in *Domestic Manners*: a fierce hatred of evangelical clergy who attempted to stifle culture. In her later writings she would develop this type of pompous hypocrisy in *The Vicar of Wexhill*. Her youngest son, Anthony, would carry the type to its literary perfection in *Barchester Towers*: this is just one of his many literary inheritances from his mother.

Fanny Trollope (as she was known) delighted in literary society, and the absence of it on the American frontier was to be among her great losses. Her literary fascinations led directly to her American adventure. Her oldest friends were the Garnett sisters, who, like herself, came from Somerset; but their father had taken the whole family to America. The Garnetts told Mrs Trollope of a young Scotswoman whom they had befriended: Fanny Wright, the orphaned daughter of a wealthy merchant. One day while browsing in the library of her aunt's country house, she had stumbled across a history of the American Revolution in Italian. Fanny Wright was able to read the foreign language but she was not certain if this new country existed until she found an atlas. Her reading awoke in her the feeling she was never to abandon, that 'there existed a country consecrated to freedom'.[4] She was eventually able to realize her dream when she visited America, where she stayed for almost two years. In 1821 she published *Views of Society and Manners in America*, an enthusiastic account of the veritable perfection of the young Republic: a land where porters refused tips and

3 For the poem see N. John Hall (ed.), *Salamagundi, Byron, Allegra, and the Trollope Family* (Pittsburgh, Penn., 1975).

4 Frances Wright, *Biography, Notes, and Political Letters of Frances Wright D'Arusmont* (Dundee, 1844), p. 8.

where even the horses seemed happier in the air of liberty. Shortly after this she became friendly with the Trollopes. Although Mrs Trollope was fifteen years older, she fell completely under the spell of the Scotswoman. Soon the Trollopes joined Fanny Wright in Paris where Mrs Trollope met American writers such as Washington Irving and James Fennimore Cooper. Fanny Wright arranged a visit to La Grange, the château of the elderly 'hero of two continents', the Marquis de Lafayette. He had been delighted by the Wright book and soon blossomed forth as Fanny Wright's 'adopted father'.

Although Fanny Wright had not devoted much attention to it in her book, she believed that the United States had one glaring fault: slavery. After brooding about it, she determined to do something. Using her fortune she bought some land and slaves in Tennessee where she set up an experimental community called Nashoba (the modern 'commune' would be a better word). Here she hoped to educate the slaves for gradual emancipation. If this experiment worked, it might encourage slaveholders to follow her example. In 1827 Fanny Wright was once again in England on a visit. Already rumours were drifting across the Atlantic that Nashoba was a dangerous place where doctrines of atheism were preached and outrages of free love practised. Both the Trollopes were vaguely liberal in politics, having 'a leaning to sedition', as Mrs Trollope exaggerated it once she had changed her views. But it was not political theories or rumours that motivated Mrs Trollope. For here there was only one consideration: unjust talk was attacking that 'angel' Fanny Wright.

The 'angel's' planned return to Nashoba coincided with several crises in the Trollope family. The family's fortunes had slipped even further. Years before they had been forced to let their elegant new mansion (to none other than the despised evangelical vicar). Fanny Trollope's great abilities in decoration had made the next house almost as elegant, but now her husband told her that they must abandon it for a farmhouse outside Harrow. At the same time, the middle son, Henry, was failing in an attempt to become a banker in Paris. The idle Henry seemed possessed of only one enthusiasm: Fanny Wright and her causes. These trials made Mr Trollope's temper even worse. Mrs Trollope confided this to one of the Garnetts: 'He is a good, honourable man—but his temper is dreadful— every year increases his irritability—and also its lamentable effect upon the children.'[5] If Mrs Trollope accompanied the 'angel' to America she could escape from some of these problems *and* have a thrilling adventure. It is not exactly clear whether the Trollopes planned to set up Henry in some 'commercial speculation' in the expanding nation, but it seems likely that this played some part in the decision to go. In any case, Mrs Trollope only made up her mind some five days before the ship sailed and perhaps her hasty decision contributed to her rapid disillusionment.

Fanny Wright tried to persuade her to give up the trip. Nevertheless, in December 1827, Mrs Trollope (already 48 years old) and three of her five surviving children, 16-year-old Henry, 11-year-old Cecilia, and 9-year-old Emily boarded the ship *Edward* at Tower Stairs in London. She was also accompanied by her maid and manservant, for even in Utopia she required some comfort. The final member of the already exotic party came aboard separately and secretly. It was the children's drawing master, a young French artist.

August Jean Hervieu was the son of one of Napoleon's officers who had died amid the horrors of the Russian campaign.[6] The young Hervieu dabbled in revolution in Spain and then settled in England. He lived for some time in the Trollope house while they tried to promote his artistic career, without much success. Fanny Wright said that he could teach the slaves at Nashoba to paint, as well as to speak French. It is

5 Helen Heineman, *Mrs Trollope* (Athens, Ohio, 1979), p. 63. This is now the best study of Mrs Trollope. See also Cecilia Payne-Gaposchkin, 'The Nashoba Plan . . .' in the *Harvard Library Bulletin*, No. 23 (1975).

6 On Hervieu see John Francis McDermott, 'Mrs Trollope's Illustrator: Auguste Hervieu in America, 1827–31', *Extrait de la Gazette des Beaux-Arts* (March 1958), pp. 169–90.

not precisely clear why the slaves required these two polite accomplishments. Although it is virtually certain that Mrs Trollope's relations with Hervieu were perfectly proper, she realized that it would be best to keep his presence discreetly quiet. Undoubtedly this somewhat strange travelling companion shocked many of Mrs Trollope's American acquaintances. It may have denied her invitations to better homes. Nevertheless, it was only due to Hervieu that she survived. Time and time again in the next three years it was only his portraits of frontier worthies that kept the Trollopes from actual starvation. He contributed twenty-four drawings to the original edition of *Domestic Manners* and Mrs Trollope believed they played a considerable role in its great success.

Already on the voyage Mrs Trollope began to have doubts about the 'angel', who busied herself writing an address to the revolutionary youth of France and reading to sailors while patching their breeches. Such few illusions as she still cherished fled when she saw the primitive huts of Nashoba. One night spent in a leaky cabin with Fanny Wright convinced Mrs Trollope that Nashoba was no place for her. Radical theories that were so delightful in a London drawing-room or a French château vanished amid the rain-soaked reality of a Tennessee forest. Fanny Wright, generous as ever, advanced enough money—$300—for the Trollope family to find some place 'in the Western world' better suited for them. It is interesting to note the increasing acerbity of Mrs Trollope's comments about Fanny Wright in *Domestic Manners* although, actually, she cut some of her nastier remarks out of her first draft. Fallen angels have never been popular.

Within a few days Mrs Trollope was on a steam-boat going up the Ohio River, on her way to Cincinnati. It was her silliness that had brought her with three children, two servants, and one French artist to America. It would take all her noble determination to survive.

Domestic Manners of the Americans consists of two sections. The first contains Mrs Trollope's reaction to Cincinnati, while the second consists of more general reflections based upon her

Introduction

travels in some of the eastern states. It was the first sixteen chapters, which dealt with Cincinnati, that gave the most offence to contemporary American readers. Yet today we can see them as an entertaining and truthful account of life in a frontier town.

Cincinnati, Ohio, was at the very centre of the American frontier in the 1820s. Its location on the Ohio River on the border between North and South, as well as between East and West, made it the crossroads of the expanding nation. It called itself the 'Queen City of the West' but it was also known as 'Porkopolis' because of the hordes of pigs that passed through the city from steamboat to slaughterhouse. The city had grown from virtually nothing at the beginning of the century to a city of 20,000 inhabitants by the time of Mrs Trollope's arrival. Its growing importance was symbolized by a recent visit by Mrs Trollope's friend, the Marquis de Lafayette. Somehow one feels that many a Cincinnati matron must have been regaled with accounts of Mrs Trollope's visit to his château.

When Mrs Trollope arrived in Cincinnati on 10 February 1828 her plan was to await the arrival of her husband. Months went by without any response to the numerous letters she sent him but the haphazard organization of transatlantic mail was probably more to blame than the lethargy of that eccentric gentleman. As her funds drifted away she began to look about for some means to support herself. Henry had been sent to a progressive school in New Harmony, Indiana. But that poor lad seemed to have inherited his father's luck and he returned from this wretched place where the Utopian education had consisted of little save toiling in the fields and virtual starvation. Henry then turned to that ready resort of any educated Englishman in distress: he advertised his services as a tutor. The Cincinnati press sported advertisements that Henry Trollope offered to teach Latin to 'gentlemen at their own houses . . . in a much shorter space of time than has hitherto been considered necessary'. Unfortunately the gentlemen of Cincinnati were not anxious to abandon their ploughs or their pigs to learn Latin, even quickly at fifty cents an hour.

Henry's linguistic skills were soon put to another use when the proprietor of the Western Museum persuaded Mrs Trollope to exploit her love of amateur dramatics. She drew no doubt on her recollection of a popular London attraction, 'The Invisible Girl: The Oracle of Leicester Square' and provided a similar show for Cincinnati. Soon the local press was advertising:

THE INVISIBLE GIRL, AT THE WESTERN MUSEUM corner of Main and Columbia Streets, is now ready to deliver her RESPONSES to visitors . . . The light is admitted *through transparencies* painted by MR HERVIEU.

Parties of twelve were admitted and could ask the 'Invisible Girl' any question, provided it was decent. The Delphic reply came back in a mixture of English, French, Greek, and Latin: the 'Invisible Girl' was none other than Henry Trollope.

Soon Mrs Trollope turned to another project. When Mr Trollope and their eldest son, Tom, arrived in September 1828 Mrs Trollope convinced her husband that there was a possibility of making a good investment in the bustling city. She decided to build a large bazaar which would provide a place for entertainment and the purchase of selected European luxury goods. Mr Trollope returned to England to organize finance and supplies. Soon an absurd structure began to rise in the city. A later British traveller who despised Mrs Trollope, the shrewish Harriet Martineau, described it: 'The Bazaar is the great deformity of the city . . . It is built of brick, and has Gothic windows, Grecian pillars, and a Turkish dome . . . Originally ornamented with Egyptian devices.'[7] The bazaar—in many ways the ancestor of modern American shopping malls—was financed mainly by a timely inheritance from Mrs Trollope's father. Unfortunately, Mrs Trollope fell into the hands of a crooked builder and eventually the sheriff seized all her property for non-payment of debts. Perhaps the most apt comment on the whole affair was made by the local poet, Timothy Flint, in his review of *Domestic Manners*: 'As

7 Harriet Martineau, *Retrospect of Western Travels* (London, 3 vols., 1838), II. 54.

incapable as an infant of such a project in her own country, in America her ruin was more complete than that of infantine folly.'

Mrs Trollope left Cincinnati in March 1830, after a stay of just over two years. She did not return to England at once, having already decided to write a book about America. Not long after her arrival in Cincinnati she had started to see writing as a possible way to make money and she asked her New York banker, Charles Wilkes, to try to get her a publisher there, but apparently without success.[8] She had been much impressed by the tremendous interest in Cincinnati in a book by another British traveller, Captain Basil Hall. Mrs Trollope thought she already had the materials for a book founded on her own adventures of living in, rather than travelling through, America. To her family in England she had written, 'I amuse myself by making notes and hope some day to manufacture them into a volume' about 'this remote corner of the world'. However, she felt it would be necessary to travel in some other parts of America to gather more information. The difficulty was that she was virtually out of funds and Mr Trollope did not reply to her urgent appeals. She became totally dependent upon the faithful Hervieu. She and Hervieu set out for Washington with the hope that Congress would buy his large picture of Lafayette landing in Cincinnati, but once again their hopes were dashed. Mrs Trollope found some refuge with an old friend, Mrs Stone, one of the Garnett sisters, who lived near Washington. Seated on her verandah overlooking the broad and beautiful Potomac, with the comforting sounds of Mozart in the background on the pianoforte, Mrs Trollope set to work frantically on her book. Even the second major illness she suffered in America did not long delay the rapid strokes of her indignant pen.

Eventually she was able to drag enough money from her husband for their voyage back to England. Henry had already been sent home, for his health had broken under the strain of his experiences in America. Mrs Trollope arrived back in

8 Parrish Collection, Princeton University Library, Princeton, New Jersey, AM 20408, dated 18 June 1828.

England on 5 August 1831, having spent over three and a half years in America. When she reached the dreary farmhouse she found her husband's health worse than ever and the family finances even worse than that. Mrs Trollope's book was their last hope and she set to work with tremendous determination. By the end of the month she had completed the book. She sought the advice of her old friend, that delightful essayist Mary Mitford, who gave her a recommendation to a publisher and some advice as well: 'A first work must be given away to make a reputation but then will afterward bring money.'[9]

Mrs Trollope's luck turned even before the actual publication of *Domestic Manners* in March 1832. Whitakers, her publisher, sent the manuscript to Basil Hall for his opinion. Far from being a jealous rival, he recommended the book and, it is said, suggested the title. The title undoubtedly helped make its fame, as it made clear that this was no tome about politics, economics, or slavery, but an account of ordinary life. Perhaps Mrs Trollope, with her wry sense of humour, was not unmindful that her erstwhile friend, Fanny Wright, had used the word 'Manners' in the title of her book on America some ten years before. Most of all, Mrs Trollope was fortunate in her timing. The book appeared in the midst of the final crisis over the Reform Bill of 1832. If Britain were about to adopt a wider franchise, surely the condition of America could offer some indication of what democracy might produce. It is difficult now to comprehend the passions that were aroused by this first step towards universal suffrage. Indeed, a tablet at Harrow Parish Church bears witness to this by recording the death of a judge, John Henry North, who, at the age of 44, had 'sunk beneath the efforts of a mind too great for his earthly frame, in opposing the revolutionary invasion of the Religion and Constitution of England on the 29th of September, 1831.' Although Mrs Trollope avoided lengthy discussions of politics as being unseemly for a lady, her book is full of warnings to Englishmen of the dangers of democracy. The warnings were all the more

9 Mitford MSS, Berkshire County Library. Letter dated 18 September 1831.

effective coming from one who had gone out to America professing radical sentiments and who had been converted to Toryism by her experience.

Reviewers, therefore, tended to react to the book according to party attitudes. This was quite common, for, as John Stuart Mill said, every travel book about America was a 'party pamphlet'.[10] The *Quarterly Review*, the flagship of Toryism, greeted the book with a review of over forty pages and praised Mrs Trollope as 'an English *lady* of sense and acuteness' who had been misled into the trip by that 'fanatical female', Fanny Wright. The reviewer compared *Domestic Manners* to that other excellent work by Captain Basil Hall. 'We have now before us the story of a lady who also carried with her to the New World the most exaggerated notions of liberalism, and who seems to have returned, if possible, a stouter enemy of all such notions than the gallant Captain himself.' The author of the anonymous review was none other than the 'gallant Captain himself'. This long review selected the most hostile quotations from the book and gave rise to the idea that Mrs Trollope's book was nothing but a tirade against America.

Mrs Trollope revelled in her success. To one of her sons she wrote—echoing Byron—that 'I awoke one morning and found myself famous.' More importantly, she began to earn money from her writing, far greater and far sooner than Mary Mitford had suggested. She now saw a career unfolding by which she could support her family. For herself there was little indulgence in luxury. With her royalties she bought two things she had missed in America: half a pound of good butter and a quarter-pound of green tea. Though she was already busy on other writing, she took some time off to attend those London parties she had so missed on the frontier; but now she was the centre of attention. Lady Charlotte Lindsay 'implored' her to write more, while Lady Louisa Stuart told her she 'had quite

10 Mill's comment is in his review of the second volume of Alexis de Tocqueville's *Democracy in America* in the *Westminster Review*, reprinted in the 1961 New York edition of *Democracy in America*, Vol. II, p. vi.

Richard Mullen

put English out of fashion, and that everyone was talking Yankee talk'. (Lady Charlotte and Lady Louisa were the daughters of Lord North and Lord Bute, the two most reviled statesmen in colonial America, and thus they had good reason for enjoying Mrs Trollope's book.) 'In short,' said the triumphant Mrs Trollope, 'I was *overpowered*.'[11] She must have been even more overpowered when word reached her that Wordsworth and Southey had praised the book.

Coleridge, however, felt differently and, sturdy Tory though he was, he urged moderation in writing books about America: 'The possible destiny of the United States of America, as a nation ... stretching from the Atlantic to the Pacific, living under the laws of Alfred, and speaking the language of Shakespeare and Milton, is an august conception.' When this prediction was realized (it was still twenty years away), 'America would then be England viewed through a solar microscope; Great Britain in a state of glorious magnification!' Coleridge therefore lamented the hostile spirit which some English travel books showed towards America. 'They hate us, no doubt, just as brothers hate; but they respect the opinion of an Englishman concerning themselves ten times as much as that of a native of any other country on earth.' He called for a 'little humouring of their prejudices, and some courtesy of language'.[12] The Whig *Edinburgh Review*, holding similar views, launched a broadside at Mrs Trollope. They criticized this 'elderly personage' for devoting so much attention to Cincinnati. It was as if an American had written a book about Britain which concentrated on the Orkneys. The journal at least admitted that the book was enjoyable: 'Mrs Trollope describes better than she thinks.'

Such criticism was as nothing to the barrage from across the Atlantic. American publishers did not recognize English

11 Frances E. Trollope, *Frances Trollope* (London, 2 vols., 1895), I. 161. This biography, by her daughter-in-law, contains much family correspondence.

12 H. N. Coleridge (ed.), *Table Talk of Samuel Taylor Coleridge* (n.d.), p. 195; 10 April 1833.

copyright and Mrs Trollope's book was republished in America with no royalty payment to her. This piracy of English books promoted bad feeling throughout the nineteenth century and was responsible for much hostility toward America by English authors such as Charles Dickens. Insult was added to injury when *Domestic Manners* was reprinted in New York in June 1832 with only eight of the original Hervieu drawings instead of the twenty-four that appeared in the English edition. This New York edition carried a contribution by the 'American editor' about 'the real name and character of the author'. 'She makes her first appearance sailing up the Mississippi. Nobody knows where she is going, or what brought her to this country . . . she pretends to have a husband.' The 'editor' throws out strong hints about Hervieu's role in the party: 'Whom she travelled with, or why she travelled at all, is an inscrutable mystery. She must, admitting her to be what she pretends, she must have had a protector.' She was then attacked for a 'want of delicacy in style and sentiment'. Actually, this was to be a frequent criticism of all of Mrs Trollope's writings as she often used words that the growing puritanism of the nineteenth century found 'vulgar'. This is, of course, precisely one reason why she remains so readable today, unlike many more 'genteel' writers. The 'editor' says that books such as her's and Hall's (he calls him ''All', employing the usual American assertation that no Englishman could pronounce the letter 'h') destroyed 'the sacred compact between stranger and guest'. Similar charges were to be heard from England when, a few years later, the American poet N. P. Willis was to repeat private conversations with English celebrities in his delightful *Pencillings by the Way*. All travel writers face this charge and Mrs Trollope at least tried to praise her hosts and she exempted them from her strictures. Finally, the American 'editor' concluded, 'I have ascertained beyond all reasonable doubt, that the real author is no less a person than Captain Basil Hall or '*All*, as he is called in the literary circles of London . . . is Mrs Trollope in breeches . . . Mrs Trollope is Captain Basil 'All in petticoats'. This actually proves one of Mrs Trollope's assertions that many American men refused to accept that women were capable of any intellectual achievement.

American reviewers were naturally furious with Mrs Trollope. Interest in these reviews was so intense in England that a separate bound volume containing several of them was published.[13] The *American Quarterly Review* took the sensible road of condescension: 'Her mistakes are numerous', which they attributed rather quaintly to her 'education, which appears to have been French and flippant', which shows just how thoroughly Anglo-Saxon were American prejudices. Her complaints were not worthy of much notice as they were 'mostly evils of the tea table and the toilet—subjects, we grant, of infinite importance among the young and budding of her sex.' However, they did praise her for her relentless attacks on the 'noxious indulgence' of spitting. *The New England Magazine* preferred a more personal review: 'There is much in a name . . . the name of Mrs Trollope, therefore, may be, at least, the shadow of a thing.' Perhaps the most interesting review was in the *Western Monthly Review*, by Timothy Flint, a Congregational minister, who had been a close friend of Mrs Trollope in Cincinnati and whose works she had praised to excess in *Domestic Manners*. He naturally resented the attack upon his city and his country. With that peculiar venom reserved for former friends, Flint described Mrs Trollope as 'a short, plump figure, with a ruddy, round, Saxon face of bright complexion . . . singularly unladylike'. Nevertheless, he did praise her for her wide knowledge of literature and her frequent kindness to the poor of Cincinnati. He said that there had been considerable gossip about Hervieu but he defended her from these unwarranted slurs.[14]

Why did Americans react so violently to the book? For some time Americans had been increasingly annoyed at what they saw to be a veritable orchestra of English abuse. There were constant charges that the 'English lords' sent hacks—'scrib-

13 *American Criticisms of Mrs Trollope* (London 1833).
14 Flint's criticisms on Mrs Trollope continued to be used against her as late as 1855. See John Cassell (ed.), *The Popular Educator*, Vol. VI, pp. 778–80.

Introduction

bling hirelings' as the American edition of Mrs Trollope called them—to write down American democracy. A more moderate American view was recorded by Fanny Wright a dozen years before Mrs Trollope's book appeared: 'Cutting words cut deep; and I fear that we are human enough to feel ourselves gradually estranged from a nation that was once our own, and for which we so long cherished an affection . . . had not the *pen* yet more than the sword destroyed it.' Unlike many Americans of that time, Fanny Wright's friend tried to put the problem into some perspective: 'We are young and therefore, perhaps, despised; we are a people fast growing in strength and prosperity, and therefore perhaps envied. We have, doubtless, errors; I never yet saw a nation that had them not; but it is equally certain that we have virtues. An enemy will see only the former; the friend will point to both.'[15]

Americans resented criticisms because they saw themselves as a cause, as well as a country. Even mild censure was an assault not just on the government, but on the people who saw that government as their greatest creation. Of all such criticisms, those from England were the most resented. Partially this was because of the common language and the ready circulation of books and periodicals which were very cheap in America. American newspapers frequently selected hostile comments from English writers and spread their views far and wide. Yet surely the main reason for the outrage was the fact that the criticism was *English*: it came from the mother country and no adolescent likes to be rebuked by his mother about his manners.

How accurate a portrayal was Mrs Trollope's book? Any fair-minded person reading it today will see that she told the truth as she experienced it. Her main fault is that she deals only with part of the United States. She did not go to New England because she had not the funds for extensive travel. Thus she did not see the centre of American literary life that her son, Anthony, was later to enjoy on his many visits. Yet, within the

15 Frances Wright, *Views of Society and Manners in America* (London, 1821), p. 46.

necessary bounds of expense, she tried to experience different aspects of American life from Mississippi steamboats to Maryland farmhouses. Whenever she saw anything she liked, she praised it, often to excess. She liked New York and many other places she saw on her eastern travels, but it was her frontier experiences that influenced her and her readers. Time and again throughout the book she emphasizes she is not writing about 'my friends, nor of my friends' friends'. She was describing not the cultured few but the uncultured many who were peopling the expanding frontier and who were making America different from Europe.

Many of the things she saw and criticized have, thankfully, passed away with the civilizing influences of time. Nevertheless, many of her comments still have a contemporary validity and call for consideration by any current observer of American life. To mention just a few: the prevalence of violence, the dangers of fundamentalist religion, and the emptiness of American cities at night. Whereas so many other travellers wrote about long-dead debates or vanished institutions, Mrs Trollope, like Tocqueville, had the perception to see enduring aspects of American democracy. She had, after all, been in America at a crucial period, when the America of the Founding Fathers was about to be made into the rougher and more democratic America of Andrew Jackson. It is more than symbolic that Jackson himself makes an appearance in *Domestic Manners.* The American Republic—as old as Mrs Trollope herself—was changing into a popular democracy, a change she witnessed and described.

Of the many aspects of American society that fell under her critical gaze, she devoted her most considered attention to the roles of religion and women. She approached religion from the standpoint of a reasonably devout member of the Church of England, the daughter and daughter-in-law of Anglican priests. Throughout all her writings she evinces a deep detestation of Evangelicals, whom she portrayed as hypocrites and philistines. They suppressed the cultivated pleasures she liked, particularly the theatre, because they were incapable of either

Introduction

enjoyment or understanding. Her eldest son, Tom, recalled that her children were taught that Evangelicalism was 'vulgarity . . . [a] type of thing to be met with in tradesmen's back parlours'. To Fanny Trollope, as to her son Anthony, it was absolutely necessary for a clergyman to be a gentleman.

Her views, then, about American fundamentalism developed out of her dislike of English evangelicalism. It was bad enough for an educated English clergyman to try to stifle culture; it was even worse for an illiterate 'cottage apostle' to succeed in doing so. She believed these self-appointed prophets had all the faults of European clericalism, with none of its benefits.

Here is a place where she is still topical, for if she detested the illiterate 'cottage apostles', what would she make of their descendants, the slick semi-literate apostles of the airwaves?

In everything else, her views on American religion are quite tolerant. For example, unlike most other English travellers, she was interested in, and highly praised, the Catholic Church. (She had a sympathy with the Irish: another trait she passed on to her son Anthony.) Mrs Trollope, like Tocqueville again, saw religion as one of the formative influences in American life. If the Frenchman's account is the more profound and analytical, the Englishwoman's is certainly the more colourful and entertaining.

Mrs Trollope devotes a great amount of her book to the position of women in America. Male travellers usually neglected this; Captain Hall, for instance, devoted only part of one chapter of his three-volume work to women. Mrs Trollope believed politics to be an exclusively male province and therefore she made very few, and only passing, references, to political questions. She believed women had a far more important function: to civilize society. She believed that the type of education American women received did not fit them to take the lead in this vital role. Even Fanny Wright, so opposite to Fanny Trollope in almost everything regarding America, agreed with her on that.

Some of Mrs Trollope's criticisms are wrong, or at least over-extended. She is not infrequently guilty of making sweeping generalizations about America, or, indeed, about England, founded upon incomplete information. It is quite amusing to note that several of the attacks she makes against America were also levelled against the mother country by continental travellers. For instance, Mrs Trollope, ever devoted to the theatre, frequently criticizes the behaviour of American audiences. Indeed, Hervieu contributed a drawing of an American showing his 'entire rear' while sitting on the balcony rail (though one American review insisted it was obviously a 'John Bull rear'). A German visitor to England, Prince Pückler-Muskau, has this to say of English audiences at the same time: 'The most striking thing to a foreigner in English theatres is the unheard-of coarseness and brutality of the audiences ... [who] sit in shirt-sleeves.' Mrs Trollope comments that American women 'do not walk well, nor, in fact, do they ever appear to advantage when in movement'. At almost the same time we find the niece of the French Ambassador to England, Prince Talleyrand, writing of Englishwomen, 'lamenting the absence of expression and movement ... They walk badly.' Mrs Trollope echoes a still frequently heard English view that politics in America 'engrosses every conversation; it irritates every temper, it substitutes party spirit for personal esteem ... it vitiates the whole system of society'. At the very time Mrs Trollope was writing this in Maryland, Mrs Arbuthnot, the Duke of Wellington's confidante, was writing in London that politics have 'excited the people into a perfect state of madness ... candidates have been nearly beat to death who were anti-reformers'. Perhaps, again, it is Tocqueville who understands the reason for this similarity of criticisms. 'America', he wrote, 'gives the most perfect picture, for good and for ill, of the special character of the English race.' The French nobleman concluded, 'The American is the Englishman left to himself.'[16]

16 E. M. Butler (ed.), *A Regency Visitor* (London, 1957), p. 83; Philip Ziegler, *The Duchess of Dino* (London, 1962), pp. 217–18; F. Bamford and Duke of Wellington (eds.), *The Journal of Mrs Arbuthnot 1820–32* (London, 2 vols., 1950), II. 419; Alexis de Tocqueville (ed. J. P. Mayer), *Journey to America* (London, 1959), p. 177.

Introduction

The two features of American life that most horrified Mrs Trollope were slavery and spitting. Like almost all British travellers, she went to America already hostile to the institution of slavery. Undoubtedly her friendship with Fanny Wright had already increased her hostility. Mrs Trollope may have gone to America with a liberal's detestation of the idea of slavery; she returned to England with a conservative's fury at American hypocrisy in preaching liberty and practising slavery. This attitude had been a consistent feature of all English criticism of America, from the days of Dr Johnson. It would continue into the 1860s, for example, in innumerable *Punch* cartoons which showed the lanky American with a slave whip in hand.

Mrs Trollope spent little time on Southern plantations. Her acquaintance with slavery was on the smaller farms of Maryland and northern Virginia. Here her book is valuable as showing how the majority of slaves lived and in her comparisons of them with white servants of the time. She also sees much more clearly than other English writers, including Fanny Wright, that racial attitudes were the basis of slavery. In *Domestic Manners*, Mrs Trollope made a powerful attack on slavery but it was not at the centre of the book. In her later writings she was to make even stronger attacks on slavery and to become one of its most influential opponents.

In *Domestic Manners* Mrs Trollope appears to be almost obsessed with the dreadful habit of tobacco spitting. Although she knew of slavery before she left, she had probably never encountered spitting in England. Indeed Prince Pückler-Muskau, who arrived in England only two months before Mrs Trollope left, gave some guidance to Europeans on this point: 'In Austria, don't talk politics; in France, give yourself no airs; and in England, don't spit.' Spitting was common in America, particularly in the West, where the habit of chewing tobacco was widespread. Mrs Trollope's tirades on the habit pleased cultivated Americans; Longfellow, for one, declared he would forgive her all her strictures if she helped to end this noxious practice.

In years to come many perceptive Americans came to accept the validity of many of her other comments. Washington Irving, who had met Mrs Trollope in Paris in 1823, read her book 'not without approbation' in the year in which he returned from his long stay in Europe. A New York newspaper editor who fled to Britain in 1861 to escape from Lincoln's government, recalled the effect of Mrs Trollope's book in his forty years of experience in all parts of America. 'We were dreadfully angry at Mrs Trollope', wrote Dr Nichols, 'but we read her book all the same, or all the more, and profited in no small degree by its lessons.' He could well recall hearing theatre audiences shout 'Trollope! Trollope!' if someone behaved improperly. In spite of this, Dr Nichols concluded, 'I fear that Americans will never be as thankful as they ought to their amusing monitress.'[17]

Yet with an irony that she would have relished, the greatest American praise for Mrs Trollope came from the greatest writer the American frontier produced. About fifty years after Mrs Trollope wrote *Domestic Manners of the Americans*, Mark Twain wrote his classic *Life on the Mississippi*. In it he paid fulsome tribute to the indomitable English lady: 'She knew her subject well, and she set it forth fairly and squarely without any weak ifs and ands and buts. She deserved gratitude but it is an error to suppose she got it.' Twain believed that Mrs Trollope was the best foreign observer of America because 'she lived three years in this civilization of ours; in this body of it—not on the surface of it'.

Indeed, Twain was so impressed with the quality and accuracy of her book that he carried a copy of it with him when he followed her up the Mississippi. That very copy is now in the Arents Collection of the New York Public Library. Twain's marginalia in this book are so interesting that I have included the substantive ones in an appendix to this edition. They have never been considered before in any discussion of Mrs

17 Thomas L. Nichols, *Forty Years of American Life* (London 2 vols., 1864), II. 22.

Introduction

Trollope's accuracy. More than any other comments about her, these undermine those people who still insist she was nothing but—to use the colourful phrase of Professor Alan Nevins—a 'censorious harridan'. Her book does not offer the complete picture of life in early nineteenth-century America, but no one today gives us a larger portion of that picture. Perhaps no other book of the time so conveys the sheer physical beauty of America for, amidst many criticisms of American manners, Mrs Trollope, a true Romantic, revelled in the beauty of America, from the splendour of wild flowers to the grandeur of Niagara. Nor does she neglect to praise man-made beauty such as the rising Capital building in Washington. She also saw the essential greatness of America in her spirit of 'boldness and energy' as when she looked on the Morris Canal, at Paterson, New Jersey. She is still a guide worth following into the vast country, or rather, continent, that was early nineteenth-century America; and no guide has ever been more exasperating or more entertaining.

Having followed this remarkable woman so far, we should finish her story. *Domestic Manners* made her name as an author, and the book was soon translated into French, German, Spanish, and Dutch. Yet, in spite of her earnings from her books, the family had to flee to Belgium so that poor old Mr Trollope could escape arrest for debt. Mrs Trollope wrote several other travel books, on Belgium, Italy, Germany, Austria, and France, where King Louis-Philippe asked her rather mischievously at the Tuileries whether she wished to revisit America. All of these are entertaining, but none survives the changes in politics and life to make it a classic like *Domestic Manners*. She also produced thirty-five novels, most of them in several volumes. In her best novel, *Michael Armstrong*, now unjustly ignored, she became one of the first novelists to depict the sufferings caused by the Industrial Revolution. As her son Anthony put it in his *Autobiography*, 'Her career offers great encouragement to those who have not begun early in life, but are still anxious to do something before they depart hence.' Her achievement is all the more remarkable when we learn that she wrote her early novels while nursing her dying children. All three of the children who accompanied her to America died of consumption. No doubt the tribulations they suffered in America contributed to their early deaths, though Cecilia lived long enough to produce one novel to add to the family total. Several of Mrs Trollope's own novels have American settings: in *The Life and Adventures of Jonathan Jefferson Whitlaw; or, Scenes on the Mississippi*, published five years after her return, she wrote a fierce denunciation of slavery. It was one of the first anti-slavery novels, published fifteen years before *Uncle Tom's Cabin*. It is therefore appropriate that she received a visit at the elegant villa in Florence where she spent the last two decades of her busy life, from another novelist who had lived in Cincinnati, Harriet Beecher Stowe. Mrs Trollope died in 1863, at the very time when the America she had visited was dying in the trenches of Vicksburg and the hills of Gettysburg. In her last moments her thoughts turned towards those children who had accompanied her on her great adventure. Her last words were 'Poor Cecilia'.

Ironically, only a few months before she died there appeared another two-volume work of American travels. Her youngest son Anthony, brought out *North America*. He recalled: 'My mother had thirty years previously written a very popular, but, as I had thought, a somewhat unjust book about our cousins over the water . . . I had entertained for many years an ambition to follow her footsteps there, and to write another book.' When he arrived his wife was rebuked by one porter when he saw the familiar name, 'Mrs Trollope', on the label of her luggage. It was impossible for Rose Trollope to convince the man that she was only a little girl when the infamous *Domestic Manners of the Americans* had appeared. Anthony Trollope at last got to see the Cincinnati bazaar—known to the locals as 'Trollope's Folly'—from which his mother had set out to produce one of the most famous and productive literary families of the century. 'It was under the domination of a quack doctor on one side, and of a college of rights-of-women female medical professors on the other.' 'I believe, sir,' Anthony was told by the proprietor, 'no man or woman ever yet made a dollar in that building.'[18]

18 Anthony Trollope, *An Autobiography*, in The Oxford Trollope (London, 1950), pp. 161–2; Anthony Trollope, *North America* (London, 2 vols., 1862), II. 105.

Note on the Text

IN 1839 Mrs Trollope prepared a fifth English edition of *Domestic Manners*. This edition, for which she received an additional £50, included 'a preface, such notes as the text suggested, and which I think are sufficient to give some interest to a new edition'. (Letter to Richard Bentley, publisher of this edition, 27 August 1839, in the Robert H. Taylor Collection, Princeton, New Jersey.) As this is the final edition supervised by Mrs Trollope, it is the text reprinted here. The numbered footnotes found at the bottom of the pages are those added by Mrs Trollope. Notes by the editor of this Oxford edition are marked by an asterisk and will be found at the back of the book. The sign † refers to comments by Mark Twain in his copy of *Domestic Manners*. These comments are also to be found at the end of the text.

Preface to the First Edition

In offering to the public these volumes on America, their author would rather be considered as endeavouring to excite fresh attention on a very important subject, than as pretending to furnish complete information upon it.

Although much has already been written on the great experiment, as it has been called, now making in government, on the other side of the Atlantic, there appears to be still room for many interesting details on the influence which the political system of the country has produced on the principles, tastes, and manners, of its domestic life.

The author of the following pages has endeavoured, in some degree, to supply this deficiency, by carefully recording the observations she had an opportunity of making during a residence of three years and six months in different parts of the United States.

She leaves to abler pens the more ambitious task of commenting on the democratic form of the American government; while, by describing, faithfully, the daily aspect of ordinary life, she has endeavoured to show how greatly the advantage is on the side of those who are governed by the few, instead of the many. The chief object she has had in view is to encourage her countrymen to hold fast by a constitution that ensures all the blessings which flow from established habits and solid principles. If they forego these, they will incur the fearful risk of breaking up their repose by introducing the jarring tumult and universal degradation which invariably follow in the wild scheme of placing all the power of the State in the hands of the populace.

The United States of America contain a considerable variety

of interesting objects in most branches of natural science, besides much that is new, a good deal that is beautiful, and some things that are wonderful. Nevertheless, as it is the moral and religious condition of the people which, beyond every thing else, demands the attention of the philosophical inquirer, the author would consider her work as completely successful, could she but awaken a more general interest on this subject.

F. T.

HARROW,
   March, 1832

Preface to the Fifth Edition

Six years elapsed since this work first appeared, and very considerable changes have in that time taken place on both sides the Atlantic.

Nevertheless, while re-perusing its pages in order to prepare a new edition for the press, I have found but few points on which I have learned to alter my opinions, and fewer still in which subsequent information has led me to believe that I have misstated facts. Whenever any thing of either kind has struck me, I have acknowledged it freely in the notes subjoined.

There is, in truth, but one point on which, if the book were still to be written, I should be likely to make it greatly different from what it is at present. Had I again to travel through the Union with a view to giving an account of what I saw, I should certainly devote a much larger portion of my attention to the great national feature—negro slavery.

The tremendous exposition of the increasing horrors of this fearful enormity produced by our legislative exertions during 1835 and 1836 for its total abolition throughout all British Colonies, has not only aroused anew every Christian and every human feeling against it, but has shown with terrible clearness, that not all we can do, not all the sacrifices we can make, will avail to relieve our dark-skinned fellow-creatures from the hideous barbarities inflicted on them, so long as other countries, and the wide-spreading southern States of the Union in particular, shall continue to legalise this horrible atrocity. Not surely with any hope that the most flagrant exposure could affect the minds of people so besotted by their avarice as to be insensible to the sure approach of the vengeance which all others so plainly see approaching them—not surely with the slightest hope of this kind would any observations on the subject be offered; but all truth on a theme so tremendously important should be uttered by every voice that can hope to make itself heard.

On other, and less important points, I have had the pleasure of receiving acknowledgements from many who at first raised their voices to contradict me, that my statements were essentially correct, and that in many cases they have been useful; nor have American voices been wanting to confirm this judgment. Were it not, indeed, for the later, and much deeper offence, *partially* given by Jonathan Jefferson Whitlaw, I should have no fear of meeting any thing but a friendly reception from the educated classes were I to revisit America.* But this must not be till slavery be abolished, OR, till that part of the Union which has a right to call itself free, shall separate from that whose fame and whose history rests, and will for ever rest, more on its reputation for slavery, than on its claim to freedom. Till then, indeed, the Union must be a negative one; it is life and death bound up together; and if the courage, enterprise, and industry of the Eastern and free Western States would escape the rottenness that must inevitably spread if they continue thus linked together, they must submit to the mortifying necessity of lessening the map of their Federal territory. But—when the servile vengeance preparing has done its work, the divided States may meet again and shake hands.

LONDON,
April 27, 1839

Domestic Manners of the Americans

Chapter One

Entrance of the Mississippi—Balize

On the 4th of November, 1827, I sailed from London, accompanied by my son and two daughters; and after a favourable, though somewhat tedious voyage, arrived on Christmas-day at the mouth of the Mississippi.

The first indication of our approach to land was the appearance of this mighty river pouring forth its muddy mass of waters, and mingling with the deep blue of the Mexican Gulf. The shores of this river are so utterly flat, that no object upon them is perceptible at sea; and we gazed with pleasure on the muddy ocean that met us; for it told us we were arrived, and seven weeks of sailing had wearied us; yet it was not without a feeling like regret that we passed from the bright blue waves, whose varying aspect had so long furnished our chief amusement, into the murky stream which now received us.

Large flights of pelicans were seen standing upon the long masses of mud which rose above the surface of the waters, and a pilot came to guide us over the bar, long before any other indication of land was visible.

I never beheld a scene so utterly desolate as this entrance of the Mississippi. Had Dante seen it, he might have drawn images of another Bolgia from its horrors. One only object rears itself above the eddying

I

waters: this is the mast of a vessel long since wrecked in attempting to cross the bar; and it still stands, a dismal witness of the destruction that has been, and a boding prophet of that which is to come.

By degrees bulrushes of enormous growth become visible, and a few more miles of mud brought us within sight of a cluster of huts called the Balize, by far the most miserable station that I ever saw made the dwelling of man, but I was told that many families of pilots and fishermen lived there.

For several miles above its mouth, the Mississippi presents no objects more interesting than mud banks, monstrous bulrushes, and now and then a huge crocodile luxuriating in the slime. Another circumstance that gives to this dreary scene an aspect of desolation, is the incessant appearance of vast quantities of drift wood, which is ever finding its way to the different mouths of the Mississippi. Trees of enormous length, often bearing their branches, and still oftener their uptorn roots entire, the victims of the frequent hurricane, come floating down the stream. Sometimes several of these, entangled together, collect among their boughs a quantity of floating rubbish, that gives the mass the appearance of a moving island, bearing a forest, with its roots mocking the heavens; while the dishonoured branches lash the tide in idle vengeance: this, as it approaches the vessel, and glides swiftly past, looks like the fragment of a world in ruins.

As we advanced, however, we were cheered, notwithstanding the season, by the bright tints of southern vegetation. The banks continue invariably flat, but a succession of planters' villas, sometimes merely a residence, and sometimes surrounded by their sugar grounds and negro huts, varied the scene. At no one point was there an inch of what painters call a second distance; and for the length of one hundred and twenty miles, from the Balize to New Orleans, and one

hundred miles above the town, the land is defended
from the encroachments of the river by a high embank-
ment which is called the Levée; without which the
dwellings would speedily disappear, as the river is
evidently higher than the banks would be without it.
When we arrived, there had been constant rains and of
long continuance, and this appearance was, therefore,
unusually striking, giving to " this great natural
feature " the most unnatural appearance imaginable;
and making evident, not only that man had been busy
there, but that even the mightiest works of creation
might be made to bear his impress; it recalled, literally,
Swift's mock-heroic:

> " Nature must give way to art " ;

yet she was looking so mighty, and so unsubdued all the
time, that I could not help fancying she would some day
take the matter into her own hands again; and if so,
farewell to New Orleans.

It is easy to imagine the total want of beauty in such
a landscape; but yet the form and hue of the trees and
plants, so new to us, added to the long privation we had
endured of all sights and sounds of land, made even
these swampy shores seem beautiful. We were, however, impatient to touch as well as see the land; but
the navigation from the Balize to New Orleans is
difficult and tedious, and the two days that it occupied
appeared longer than any we had passed on board.

In truth, to those who have pleasure in contemplating
the phenomena of nature, a sea voyage may endure
many weeks without wearying. Perhaps some may
think that the first glance of ocean and of sky show
all they have to offer; nay, even that that first glance
may suggest more of dreariness than sublimity: but to
me their variety appeared endless, and their beauty
unfailing. The attempt to describe scenery, even
where the objects are prominent and tangible, is very

rarely successful; but where the effect is so subtle and so varying, it must be vain; the impression, nevertheless, is perhaps deeper than any other ; I think it possible I may forget the sensations with which I watched the long course of the gigantic Mississippi; the Ohio and the Potomac may mingle and be confounded with other streams in my memory, I may even recall with difficulty the blue outline of the Alleghany mountains; but never, while I remember any thing, can I forget the first and last hour of light on the Atlantic.

The ocean, however, and all its indescribable charm, no longer surrounded us; we began to feel that our walk on the quarter-deck was very like the exercise of an ass in the mill; that our books had lost half their pages, and that the other half were known by rote; that our beef was very salt, and our biscuits very hard; in short, that having studied the good ship Edward from stem to stern, till we knew the name of every sail, and the use of every pulley, we had had enough of her; and as we lay down, head to head, in our tiny beds for the last time, I exclaimed with no small pleasure,

" To-morrow to fresh fields and pastures new."

Chapter Two

New Orleans—Society—Creoles and Quadroons—Voyage up the Mississippi

ON first touching the soil of a new land, of a new continent, of a new world, it is impossible not to feel considerable excitement and deep interest in almost every object that meets us.   New Orleans presents very little that can gratify the eye of taste, but nevertheless there is much of novelty and interest for a newly-arrived

4

European. The large proportion of blacks seen in the
ſtreets, all labour being performed by them; the grace
and beauty of the elegant Quadroons; the occasional
groups of wild and savage-looking Indians; the unwonted aſpect of the vegetation; the huge and turbid
river, with its low and slimy shore; all help to afford
that species of amusement which proceeds from looking
at what we never saw before.

The town has much the appearance of a French Ville
de Province, and is, in fact, an old Spanish colony
taken by the French. The names of the ſtreets are
French, and the language about equally French and
English. The market is handsome and well supplied,
all produce being conveyed by the river. We were
much pleased by the chant with which the negro
boatmen regulate and beguile their labour on the
river; it consiſts but of very few notes, but they are
sweetly harmonious, and the negro voice is almoſt
always rich and powerful.

By far the moſt agreeable hours I passed at New
Orleans, were those in which I explored with my
children the foreſt near the town. It was our firſt
walk in " the eternal foreſts of the weſtern world ",
and we felt rather sublime and poetical. The trees,
generally speaking, are much too close to be either
large or well-grown; and, moreover, their growth is
often ſtunted by a parasitical plant, for which I could
learn no other name than " Spanish moss "; it droops
gracefully from the boughs, converting the outline
of all the trees it hangs upon into that of weeping
willows. The chief beauty of the foreſt in this region
is from the luxuriant under-growth of palmettoes,
which is decidedly the lovelieſt-coloured and moſt
graceful plant I know. The pawpaw, too, is a
splendid shrub, and in great abundance. We here,
for the firſt time, saw the wild vine, which we afterwards found growing so profusely in every part of

America, as naturally to suggest the idea that the natives ought to add wine to the numerous productions of their plenty-teeming soil.[1] The strong pendant festoons made safe and commodious swings, which some of our party enjoyed, despite the sublime temperament above-mentioned.

Notwithstanding it was mid-winter when we were at New Orleans, the heat was much more than agreeable, and the attacks of the mosquitoes incessant, and most tormenting; yet I suspect that, for a short time, we would rather have endured it, than not have seen oranges, green peas, and red pepper, growing in the open air at Christmas. In one of our rambles we ventured to enter a garden, whose bright orange hedge attracted our attention; here we saw green peas fit for the table, and a fine crop of red pepper ripening in the sun. A young negress was employed on the steps of the house: that she was a slave made her an object of interest to us. She was the first slave we had ever spoken to, and I believe we all felt that we could hardly address her with sufficient gentleness. She little dreamed, poor girl ! what deep sympathy she excited: she answered us civilly and gaily, and seemed amused at our fancying there was something unusual in red-pepper pods; she gave us several of them, and I felt fearful lest a hard mistress might blame her for it. How very childish does ignorance make us! and how very ignorant we are upon almost every subject, where hear-say evidence is all we can get! I left England

[1] The fact, however, is otherwise, and in a very remarkable degree. During my residence in America, I repeatedly tasted native wine from vineyards carefully cultivated, and on the fabrication of which a considerable degree of imported science had been bestowed ; but the very best of it was miserable stuff. It should seem that Nature herself requires some centuries of schooling before she becomes perfectly accomplished in ministering to the luxuries of man, and, perhaps as there is no lack of sunshine, the champagne and Bordeaux of the Union may appear simultaneously with a Shakspeare, a Raphael, and a Mozart.

with feelings so strongly opposed to slavery, that it was not without great pain I witnessed its existence around me. At the sight of every negro man, woman, and child that passed, my fancy wove some little romance of misery, as belonging to each of them. Since I have known more on the subject, and become better acquainted with their real situation, as domestic in-door servants, in America, I have often smiled at recalling what I then felt.

The first symptom of American equality that I perceived, was my being introduced in form to a milliner. It was not at a boarding-house, under the indistinct outline of ' Miss C—— ', nor in the street, through the veil of a fashionable toilette; but in the very penetralia of her temple, standing behind her counter, giving laws to ribbon and to wire, and ushering caps and bonnets into existence. She was an English woman, and I was told that she possessed great intellectual endowments and much information; I really believe this was true. Her manner was easy and graceful, with a good deal of French tournure: and the gentleness with which her fine eyes and sweet voice directed the movements of a young female slave, was really touching: the way, too, in which she blended her French talk of modes with her customers, and her English talk of metaphysics with her friends, had a pretty air of indifference in it, that gave her a superiority with both. I found with her the daughter of a judge, eminent, it was said, both for legal and literary ability; and I heard from many quarters, after I had left New Orleans, that the society of this lady was highly valued by all persons of talent: yet were I, traveller-like, to stop here, and set it down as a national peculiarity, or republican custom, that milliners took the lead in the best society, I should greatly falsify facts.[†] I do not remember the same thing happening to me again; and this is one instance, among a thousand, of the impression every circumſtance makes on entering a new country, and of the propensity, so irresiſtible, to class all things, however accidental, as national and peculiar. On the other hand, however, it is certain that if similar anomalies are unfrequent in America, they are nearly impossible elsewhere.

In the shop of Miss C—— I was introduced to Mr M'Clure, a venerable personage, of gentleman-like appearance, who, in the course of five minutes, propounded as many axioms, as " Ignorance is the only devil;" " Man makes his own exiſtence;" and the like. He was of the New Harmony school, or rather the New Harmony school was of him. He was a man of good fortune, (a Scotchman), I believe, who, after living a tolerably gay life, had "conceived high thoughts, such as Lycurgus loved, who bade flog the little Spartans ", and determined to benefit the species, and immortalise himself, by founding a philosophical school at New Harmony. There was something in the hollow-square legislations of Mr Owen, that ſtruck him as admirable; and he seems, as far as I can under-ſtand, to have intended aiding his views, by a sort of incipient hollow-square drilling; teaching the young ideas of all he could catch to shoot into parallelogramic form and order. This venerable philosopher, like all of his school that I ever heard of, loved better to originate lofty imaginings of faultless syſtems, than to watch their application to praĉtice. With much liberality he purchased and conveyed to the wilderness a very noble colleĉtion of books and scientific in-ſtruments; but not finding among men one whose views were liberal and enlarged as his own, he selected a woman to put into action the machine he had organ-ised. As his acquaintance with this lady had been of long ſtanding, and, as it was said, very intimate, he felt sure that no violation of his rules would have place under her sway; they would aĉt together as one being:

8

he was to perform the functions of the soul, and will everything; she, those of the body, and perform everything.

The principal feature of the scheme was, that (the first liberal outfit of the institution having been furnished by Mr M'Clure), the expense of keeping it up should be defrayed by the profits arising from the labours of the pupils, male and female, which were to be performed at stated intervals of each day, in regular rotation with learned study and scientific research. But unfortunately the soul of the system found the climate of Indiana uncongenial to its peculiar formation; and, therefore, took its flight to Mexico, leaving the body to perform the operations of both, in whatever manner it liked best; and the body, being a French body, found no difficulty in setting actively to work without troubling the soul about it; and soon becoming conscious that the more simple was a machine, the more perfect were its operations, she threw out all that related to the intellectual part of the business, (which, to do poor soul justice, it had laid great stress upon,) and stirred herself as effectually as ever body did, to draw wealth from the thews and sinews of the youths they had collected. When last I heard of this philosophical establishment, she, and a nephew-son, were said to be reaping a golden harvest, as many of the lads had been sent from a distance by indigent parents, for gratuitous education, and possessed no means of leaving it.*

Our stay in New Orleans was not long enough to permit our entering into society; but I was told that it contained two distinct sets of people, both celebrated, in their way, for their social meetings and elegant entertainments. The first of these is composed of Creole families, who are chiefly planters and merchants, with their wives and daughters; these meet together, eat together, and are very grand and aristocratic; each

of their balls is a little Almack's, and every portly dame
of the set is as exclusive in her principles as a lady
patroness.* The other set consists of the excluded but
amiable Quadroons, and such of the gentlemen of the
former class as can by any means escape from the high
places, where pure Creole blood swells the veins at the
bare mention of any being, tainted in the remotest
degree with the negro stain. Of all the prejudices
I have ever witnessed, this appears to me the most
violent, and the most inveterate. Quadroon girls, the
acknowledged daughters of wealthy American or Creole
fathers, educated with all of style and accomplishments
which money can procure at New Orleans, and with all
the decorum that care and affection can give—exquisitely beautiful, graceful, gentle, and amiable, are
not admitted, nay, are not on any terms admissible,
into the society of the Creole families of Louisiana.
They cannot marry; that is to say, no ceremony can
render a union with them legal or binding; yet such is
the powerful effect of their very peculiar grace, beauty,
and sweetness of manner, that unfortunately they
perpetually become the objects of choice and affection.
If the Creole ladies have privilege to exercise the awful
power of repulsion, the gentle Quadroon has the sweet
but dangerous vengeance of possessing that of attraction.
The unions formed with this unfortunate race are said
to be often lasting and happy, as far as any unions can
be so to which a certain degree of disgrace is attached.

There is a French and an English theatre in the
town; but we were too fresh from Europe to care much
for either, or, indeed, for any other of the town delights
of the city; and we soon became eager to commence
our voyage up the Mississippi.

Miss Wright, then less known (though the author of
more than one clever volume) than she has since become,
was the companion of our voyage from Europe; and it
was my purpose to have passed some months with her

and her sister at the estate she had purchased in Tennessee. This lady, since become so celebrated as the advocate of opinions that make millions shudder and some half-score admire, was, at the time of my leaving England with her, dedicated to a pursuit widely different from her subsequent occupations. Instead of becoming a public orator in every town throughout America, she was about, as she said, to seclude herself for life in the deepest forests of the western world, that her fortune, her time, and her talents, might be exclusively devoted to aid the cause of the suffering Africans. Her first object was to show that Nature had made no difference between blacks and whites, excepting in complexion; and this she expected to prove, by giving an education perfectly equal to a class of black and white children. Could this fact be once fully established, she conceived that the negro cause would stand on firmer ground than it had yet done, and the degraded rank which they have ever held amongst civilised nations would be proved to be a gross injustice. This question of the mental equality, or inequality, between us and the negro race, is one of great interest, and has certainly never yet been fairly tried; and I expected for my children and myself both pleasure and information from visiting her establishment, and watching the success of her experiment.

The innumerable steam-boats, which are the stage-coaches and fly-waggons of this land of lakes and rivers, are totally unlike any I had seen in Europe, and greatly superior to them. The fabrics which I think they most resemble in appearance, are the floating baths (*les bains Vigier*) at Paris. The room to which the double line of windows belongs, is a very handsome apartment; before each window a neat little cot is arranged in such a manner as to give its drapery the air of a window-curtain. This room is called the gentlemen's cabin, and their exclusive right to it is somewhat uncourteously insisted upon. The breakfast, dinner, and supper, are laid in this apartment, and the lady passengers are permitted to take their meals there.

On the first of January, 1828, we embarked on board the Belvidere, a large and handsome boat; though not the largest or handsomest of the many which displayed themselves along the wharfs; but she was going to stop at Memphis, the point of the river nearest to Miss Wright's residence, and she was the first that departed after we had got through the custom-house, and finished our sight-seeing.[†]

We found the room destined for the use of the ladies dismal enough, as its only windows were below the stern gallery; but both this and the gentlemen's cabin were handsomely fitted up, and the latter well carpeted; but oh! that carpet! I will not, I may not describe its condition; indeed, it requires the pen of a Swift to do it justice. Let no one who wishes to receive agreeable impressions of American manners, commence his travels in a Mississippi steam-boat; for myself, it is with all sincerity I declare, that I would infinitely prefer sharing the apartment of a party of well-conditioned pigs, to the being confined to its cabin.

I hardly know any annoyance so deeply repugnant to English feelings, as the incessant remorseless spitting of Americans. I feel that I owe my readers an apology for the repeated use of this, and several other odious words; but I cannot avoid them, without suffering the fidelity of description to escape me. It is possible that in this phrase, " Americans," I may be too general. The United States form a continent of almost distinct nations, and I must now, and always, be understood to speak only of that portion of them which I have seen. In conversing with Americans I have constantly found that if I alluded to any thing which they thought I considered as uncouth, they would assure me it was local, and not national; the accidental peculiarity of a very small part, and by no means a specimen of the whole. "That is because you know so little of America," is a phrase I have listened to a thousand times, and in nearly as many different places. *It may be so*—and having made this concession, I protest against the charge of injustice in relating what I have seen.

Chapter Three

Company on Board the Steam-Boat—Scenery of the Mississippi—Crocodiles—Arrival at Memphis—Nashoba

THE weather was warm and bright, and we found the guard of the boat, as they called the gallery that runs round the cabins, a very agreeable station; here we all sat as long as light lasted, and sometimes, wrapped in our shawls, we enjoyed the clear bright beauty of American moonlight long after every passenger but ourselves had retired. We had a full complement of passengers on board. The deck, as is usual, was occupied by the Kentucky flat-boat men, returning from New Orleans, after having disposed of the boat and cargo which they had conveyed thither, with no other labour than that of steering her, the current bringing her down at the rate of four miles an hour. We had about two hundred of these men on board; but the part of the vessel occupied by them is so distinct from the cabins, that we never saw them, except when we stopped to take in wood; and then they ran, or rather sprung and vaulted over each other's heads to the shore, whence they all assisted in carrying wood to supply the steam-engine; the performance of this duty being a stipulated part of the payment of their passage.

From the account given by a man-servant we had on board, who shared their quarters, they are a most disorderly set of persons, constantly gambling and wrangling, very seldom sober, and never suffering a night to pass without giving practical proof of the respect in which they hold the doctrines of equality and community of property. The clerk of the vessel was kind enough to take our man under his protection, and assigned him a berth in his own little nook; but as this was not inaccessible, he told him by no means to detach his watch or money from his person during the night. Whatever their moral characteristics may be, these Kentuckians are a very noble-looking race of men; their average height considerably exceeds that of Europeans, and their countenances, excepting when disfigured by red hair, which is not unfrequent, extremely handsome.

The gentlemen in the cabin (we had no ladies) would certainly, neither from their language, manners, nor appearance, have received that designation in Europe; but we soon found their claim to it rested on more substantial ground; for we heard them nearly all addressed by the titles of general, colonel, and major. On mentioning these military dignities to an English friend some time afterwards, he told me that he too had made the voyage with the same description of company, but remarking that there was not a single captain among them, he made the observation to a fellow-passenger, and asked how he accounted for it. " Oh, sir, the captains are all on deck " was the reply.

Our honours, however, were not all military; for we had a judge among us. I know it is equally easy and invidious to ridicule the peculiarities of appearance and manner in people of a different nation from ourselves; we may, too, at the same moment be undergoing the same ordeal in their estimation; and, moreover, I am by no means disposed to consider whatever is new to

14

me as therefore objectionable; but, nevertheless, it was impossible not to feel repugnance to many of the novelties that now surrounded me.

The total want of all the usual courtesies of the table, the voracious rapidity with which the viands were seized and devoured; the strange uncouth phrases and pronunciation; the loathsome spitting, from the contamination of which it was absolutely impossible to protect our dresses; the frightful manner of feeding with their knives,[†] till the whole blade seemed to enter into the mouth; and the still more frightful manner of cleaning the teeth afterwards with a pocket-knife, soon forced us to feel that we were not surrounded by the generals, colonels, and majors of the old world; and that the dinner-hour was to be anything rather than an hour of enjoyment.

The little conversation that went forward while we remained in the room was entirely political, and the respective claims of Adams and Jackson to the presidency were argued with more oaths and more vehemence than it had ever been my lot to hear.[*] Once a colonel appeared on the verge of assaulting a major, when a huge seven-foot Kentuckian gentleman horse-dealer asked of the heavens to confound them both, and bade them sit still and be d—d. We too thought we should share this sentence; at least, sitting still in the cabin seemed very nearly to include the rest of it, and we never tarried there a moment longer than was absolutely necessary to eat.

The unbroken flatness of the banks of the Mississippi continued unvaried for many miles above New Orleans; but the graceful and luxuriant palmetto, the dark and noble ilex, and the bright orange, were everywhere to be seen, and it was many days before we were weary of looking at them. We occasionally used the opportunity of the boat's stopping to take in wood, for a ten minutes' visit to the shore; we in this manner explored a field of sugar-canes, and loaded ourselves with as much of the sweet spoil as we could carry. Many of the passengers seemed fond of the luscious juice that is easily expressed from the canes, but it was too sweet for my palate. We also visited, in the same rapid manner, a cotton plantation. A handsome spacious building was pointed out to us as a convent, where a considerable number of young ladies were educated by the nuns.

At one or two points the wearisome level line of forest is relieved by *bluffs*, as they call the short intervals of high ground. The town of Natches is beautifully situated on one of these high spots; the climate here, in the warm season, is as fatal as that of New Orleans; were it not for this, Natches would have great attractions to new settlers. The beautiful contrast that its bright green hill forms with the dismal line of black forest that stretches on every side; the abundant growth of pawpaw, palmetto, and orange; the copious variety of sweet-scented flowers that flourish there, all make it appear like an oasis in the desert. Natches is the furthest point to the north at which oranges ripen in the open air, or endure the winter without shelter. With the exception of this sweet spot, I thought all the little towns and villages we passed wretched-looking in the extreme. As the distance from New Orleans increased, the air of wealth and comfort exhibited in its immediate neighbourhood disappeared, and but for one or two clusters of wooden houses, calling themselves towns, and borrowing some pompous name, generally from Greece or Rome, we might have thought ourselves the first of the human race who had ever penetrated into this territory of bears and alligators. But still, from time to time, appeared the hut of the wood-cutter, who supplies the steam-boats with fuel, at the risk, or rather with the assurance of early death, in exchange for dollars and whiskey. These sad dwellings are nearly all of them inundated during the winter, and the best of them are constructed on piles, which permit the water to reach its highest level without drowning the wretched inhabitants. These unhappy beings are invariably the victims of ague, which they meet recklessly, sustained by the incessant use of ardent spirits. The squalid look of the miserable wives and children of these men was dreadful; and often as the spectacle was renewed, I could never look at it with indifference. Their complexion is of a bluish white, that suggests the idea of dropsy; this is invariable, and the poor little ones wear exactly the same ghastly hue. A miserable cow and a few pigs, standing knee-deep in water, distinguish the more prosperous of these dwellings; and on the whole I should say, that I never witnessed human nature reduced so low as it appeared in the wood-cutters' huts on the unwholesome banks of the Mississippi.

It is said that, at some points of this dismal river, crocodiles are so abundant as to add the terror of their attacks to the other sufferings of a dwelling there. We were told a story of a squatter, who having " located " himself close to the river's edge, proceeded to build his cabin. This operation is soon performed, for social feeling and the love of whiskey bring all the scanty neighbourhood round a new-comer, to aid him in cutting down trees, and in rolling up the logs, till the mansion is complete. This was done; the wife and five young children were put in possession of their new home, and slept soundly after a long march. Towards day-break the husband and father was awakened by a faint cry, and looking up, beheld relics of three of his children scattered over the floor, and an enormous crocodile, with several young ones around her, occupied in devouring the remnants of their horrid meal. He looked round for a weapon; but finding none, and aware that unarmed he could do nothing, he raised himself gently on his bed, and contrived to crawl from thence through a window, hoping that his wife, whom he left sleeping, might, with the remaining children, rest undiscovered till his return. He flew to his nearest neighbour and besought his aid; in less than half an hour two men returned with him, all three well armed; but alas! they were too late! the wife and her two babes lay mangled on their bloody bed. The gorged reptiles fell an easy prey to their assailants, who, upon examining the place, found the hut had been constructed close to the mouth of a large hole, almost a cavern, where the monster had hatched her hateful brood.

Among other sights of desolation which mark this region, condemned of Nature, the lurid glare of a burning forest was almost constantly visible after sunset; and when the wind so willed, the smoke arising from it floated in heavy vapour over our heads. Not all the novelty of the scene, not all its vastness, could prevent its heavy horror wearying the spirits. Perhaps the dinners and suppers I have described may help to account for this; but certain it is, that when we had wondered for a week at the ceaseless continuity of forest; had first admired, and then wearied of the festooned drapery of Spanish moss; when we had learned to distinguish the different masses of timber that passed us, or that we passed, as a " snag ", a " log ", or a " sawyer "; when we had finally made up our minds that the gentlemen of the Kentucky and Ohio military establishments were not of the same genus as those of the Tuileries and St James's, we began to wish that we could sleep more hours away. As we advanced to the northward, we were no longer cheered by the beautiful border of palmettoes : and even the amusement of occasionally spying out a sleeping crocodile was over.

Just in this state, when we would have fain believed

that every mile we went carried us two towards Memphis, a sudden and violent shock startled us frightfully.

" It is a sawyer!" said one.

" It is a snag!" cried another.

" We are aground!" exclaimed the captain.

" Aground ? Good heavens ! and how long shall we stay here ?"

" The Lord in His providence can only tell, but long enough to tire my patience, I expect."

And the poor English ladies, how fared they the while ?

Two breakfasts, two dinners, and a supper did they eat, with the Ohio and Kentucky gentlemen, before they moved an inch.   Several steam-boats passed while we were thus enthralled; but some were not strong enough to attempt drawing us off, and some attempted it, but were not strong enough to succeed ; at length a vast and mighty " thing of life " approached, threw out grappling irons, and in three minutes the business was done; again we saw the trees and mud slide swiftly past us; and a hearty shout from every passenger on deck declared their joy.

At length we had the pleasure of being told that we had arrived at Memphis; but this pleasure was considerably abated by the hour of our arrival, which was midnight, and by the rain, which was falling in torrents.

Memphis stands on a high bluff, and at the time of our arrival was nearly inaccessible. The heavy rain which had been falling for many hours would have made any steep ascent difficult; but unfortunately a new road had been recently marked out, which beguiled us into its almost bottomless mud, from the firmer footing of the unbroken cliff. Shoes and gloves were lost in the mire, for we were glad to avail ourselves of all our limbs; and we reached the grand hotel in a most deplorable state.

Miss Wright was well known there; and as soon as her arrival was announced, every one seemed on the alert to receive her, and we soon found ourselves in possession of the best rooms in the hotel. The house was new, and in what appeared to me a very comfortless condition; but I was then new to Western America, and unaccustomed to their mode of " getting along ", as they term it. This phrase is eternally in use among them, and seems to mean existing with as few of the comforts of life as possible.

We slept soundly, however, and rose in the hope of soon changing our mortar-smelling quarters for Miss Wright's Nashoba: but we presently found that the rain which had fallen during the night would make it hazardous to venture through the forests of Tennessee in any sort of carriage; we therefore had to pass the day at our queer comfortless hotel.

The steam-boat had wearied me of social meals, and I should have been thankful to have eaten my dinner of hard venison and peach-sauce in a private room; but this, Miss Wright said, was impossible; the lady of the house would consider the proposal as a personal affront, and, moreover, it would be assuredly refused. This latter argument carried weight with it; and when the great bell was sounded from an upper window of the house, we proceeded to the dining-room. The table was laid for fifty persons, and was already nearly full. Our party had the honour of sitting near " the lady "; but to check the proud feelings to which such distinction might give birth, my servant, William, sat very nearly opposite to me. The company consisted of all the shopkeepers (storekeepers as they are called throughout the United States) of the little town. The mayor also, who was a friend of Miss Wright's, was of the party; he is a pleasing gentleman-like man, and seems strangely misplaced in a little town on the Mississippi. We were told that since the erection of this hotel, it has been the custom for all the male inhabitants of the town to dine and breakfast there. They ate in perfect silence, and with such astonishing rapidity that their dinner was over literally before ours was begun; the instant they ceased to eat, they darted from the table in the same moody silence which they had preserved since they entered the room, and a second set took their places, who performed their silent parts in the same manner. The only sounds heard were those produced by the knives and forks, with the unceasing chorus of coughing, etc. No women were present except ourselves and the hostess; the good women of Memphis being well content to let their lords partake of Mrs Anderson's turkeys and venison, (without their having the trouble of cooking for them,) whilst they regale themselves on mush[1] and milk at home.

The remainder of the day passed pleasantly enough in rambling round the little town, which is situated at the most beautiful point of the Mississippi. The river is here so wide as to give it the appearance of a noble lake; an island covered with lofty forest-trees divides it, and relieves by its broad mass of shadow the uniformity of its waters. The town stretches in a rambling irregular manner along the cliff, from the Wolf River, one of the innumerable tributaries to the Mississippi, to about a mile below it. Half a mile more of the cliff beyond the town is cleared of trees, and produces good pasture for horses, cows, and pigs; sheep they had none. At either end of this space the forest again rears its dark wall, and seems to say to man, "So far shalt thou come, and no farther!" Courage and industry, however, have braved the warning; behind this long street the town straggles back into the forest, and the rude path that leads to the more

---

[1] *Mush* is a preparation of Indian corn, bruised to powder, and which when boiled with milk makes excellent porridge.

diſtant log-dwellings becomes wilder at every ſtep. The ground is broken by frequent water-courses, and the bridges that lead across them are formed by trunks of trees thrown over the ſtream, which support others of smaller growth, that are laid across them. These bridges are not very pleasant to pass; for they totter under the tread of a man, and tremble moſt frightfully beneath a horse or a waggon; they are, however, very piᴄturesque. The great height of the trees, the quantity of pendant vine branches that hang amongſt them, and the variety of gay-plumaged birds, par- ticularly the small green parrot, made us feel we were in a new world; and a repetition of our walk the next morning would have pleased us well : but Miss Wright was anxious to get home, and we were scarcely less so to see her Nashoba. A clumsy sort of caravan drawn by two horses was prepared for us; and we set off in high spirits for an expedition of fifteen miles through the foreſt. To avoid passing one of the bridges above described, which was thought insecure, our negro driver took us through a piece of water, which he assured us was not deep " to matter "; however, we soon loſt sight of our pole, and as we were evidently descending, we gently remonſtrated with him on the danger of proceeding, but he only grinned, and flogged in reply; we soon saw the front wheels disappear, and the horses began to plunge and kick most alarm- ingly, but ſtill without his looking at all diſturbed. At length the splinter-bar gave way, upon which the black philosopher said very composedly, " I expeᴄt you'll beſt be riding out upon the horses, as we've got into an unhandsome fix here." Miss Wright, who sat composedly smiling at the scene, said, " Yes, Jacob, that is what we muſt do "; and with some difficulty we, in this manner, reached the shore, and soon found ourselves again assembled round Mrs Anderson's fire.

It was soon settled that we must delay our departure till the waters had subsided; but Miss Wright was too anxious to reach home to endure this delay, and she set off again on horseback, accompanied by our man-servant, who told me afterwards that they rode through places that might have daunted the boldest hunter, but that " Miss Wright took it quite easy ".

The next day we started again, and the clear air, the bright sun, the novel wildness of the dark forest, and our keenly awakened curiosity, made the excursion delightful, and enabled us to bear, without shrinking, the bumps and bruises we encountered. We soon lost all trace of a road, at least so it appeared to us; for the stumps of the trees, which had been cut away to open a passage, were left standing three feet high. Over these, the high-hung Deerborn, as our carriage was called, passed safely; but it required some miles of experience to convince us that every stump would not be our last. It was amusing to watch the cool and easy skill with which the driver wound his horses and wheels among these stumps;—I thought he might have been imported to Bond Street with great advantage. The forest became thicker and more dreary-looking every mile we advanced; but our ever-grinning negro declared it was a right good road, and that we should be sure to get to Nashoba: and so we did . . . and one glance sufficed to convince me, that every idea I had formed of the place was as far as possible from the truth. Desolation was the only feeling—the only word that presented itself ; but it was not spoken. I think, however, that Miss Wright was aware of the painful impression the sight of her forest-home produced on me; and I doubt not that the conviction reached us both at the same moment, that we had erred in thinking that a few months passed together at this spot could be productive of pleasure to either: but to do her justice, I believe her mind was so exclusively occupied by the object she had then in view, that all things else were worthless, or indifferent to her. I never heard or read of any enthusiasm approaching hers, except in some few instances, in ages past, of religious fanaticism.

It must have been some feeling equally powerful which enabled Miss Wright, accustomed to all the comfort and refinement of Europe, to imagine not only that she herself could exist in this wilderness, but that her European friends could enter there, and not feel dismayed at the savage aspect of the scene. The annexed plate gives a faithful view of the cleared space and buildings which form the settlement.* Each building consisted of two large rooms, furnished in the most simple manner; nor had they as yet collected round them any of those minor comforts which ordinary minds class among the necessaries of life: but in this our philosophical friend seemed to see no evil; nor was there any mixture of affectation in this indifference— it was a circumstance really and truly beneath her notice. Her whole heart and soul were occupied by the hope of raising the African to the level of European intellect; and even now, that I have seen this favourite fabric of her imagination fall to pieces beneath her feet, I cannot recall the self-devotion with which she gave herself to it without admiration.

The only white persons we found at Nashoba, were my amiable friend, Mrs W—— (the sister of Miss Wright) and her husband.* I think they had between thirty and forty slaves, including children; but when I was there no school had been established. Books and other materials for the great experiment had been collected, and one or two professors engaged; but nothing was yet organised. I found my friend Mrs W—— in very bad health, which she confessed she attributed to the climate. This naturally so much alarmed me for my children, that I decided upon leaving the place with as little delay as possible, and did so at the end of ten days.

I do not exactly know what was the immediate cause which induced Miss Wright to abandon a scheme which had taken such possession of her imagination, and on which she had expended so much money; but many months had not elapsed before I learnt, with much pleasure, that she and her sister had also left it. I think it probable that she became aware, upon returning to Nashoba, that the climate was too hostile to their health. All I know farther of Nashoba is, that Miss Wright having found (from some cause or other) that it was impossible to pursue her object, herself accompanied her slaves to Hayti, and left them there, free, and under the protection of the President.

I found no beauty in the scenery round Nashoba, nor can I conceive that it would possess any even in summer. The trees were so close to each other as not to permit the growth of underwood—the great ornament of the forest at New Orleans, and still less of our seeing any openings, where the varying effects of light and shade might atone for the absence of other objects. The clearing round the settlement appeared to me inconsiderable and imperfect; but I was told that they had grown good crops of cotton and Indian corn. The weather was dry and agreeable, and the aspect of the heavens by night surprisingly beautiful; I never saw moonlight so clear, so pure, so powerful.

We returned to Memphis on the 26th of January, 1828, and found ourselves obliged to pass five days there, awaiting a steam-boat for Cincinnati, to which metropolis of the West I was now determined to proceed with my family to await the arrival of Mr Trollope. We were told by every one we spoke to at Memphis, that it was in all respects the finest situation west of the Alleghanies. We found many lovely walks among the broken forest-glades around Memphis, which, together with a morning and evening enjoyment of the effects of a glowing horizon on the river, enabled us to wait patiently for the boat that was to bear us away.

Chapter Four

Departure from Memphis—Ohio River—Louisville—Cincinnati

On the 1st of February, 1828, we embarked on board the Criterion, and once more began to float on the " father of waters ", as the poor banished Indians were wont to call the Mississippi. The company on board was wonderfully like what we had met in coming from New Orleans; I think they must have all been first cousins; and what was singular, they, too, had all arrived at high rank in the army. For many a wearisome mile above the Wolf River the only scenery was still forest—forest—forest; the only variety was produced by the receding of the river at some points, and its encroaching on the opposite shore. These changes are continually going on, but from what cause none could satisfactorily explain to me. Where the river is encroaching, the trees are seen growing in water many feet deep; after some time, the water undermines their roots, and they become the easy victims of the first hurricane that blows. This is one source of the immense quantities of drift wood that float into the Gulf of Mexico. Where the river has receded, a young growth of cane-brake is soon seen starting up with the rapid vegetation of the climate ; these two circumstances in some degree relieve the sameness of the thousand miles of vegetable wall. But we were now approaching the river which is emphatically called " the beautiful ", La Belle Rivière of the New Orleans French; and a few days took us, I trust for ever, out

26

of that murky stream which is as emphatically called
" the deadly ": and well does it seem to merit the title;
the air of its shores is mephitic, and it is said that
nothing that ever sank beneath its muddy surface was
known to rise again.   As truly does " La Belle Rivière "
deserve its name; the Ohio is bright and clear; its
banks are continually varied as it flows through what
is called a rolling country, which seems to mean a
district that cannot show a dozen paces of level ground
at a time.   The primeval forest still occupies a considerable portion of the ground, and hangs in solemn
grandeur from the cliffs; but it is broken by frequent
settlements, where we were cheered by the sight of
herds and flocks.   I imagine that this river presents
almost every variety of river scenery; sometimes its
clear wave waters a meadow of level turf; sometimes it
is bounded by perpendicular rocks; pretty dwellings,
with their gay porticoes are seen, alternately with wild
intervals of forest, where the tangled bear-brake
plainly enough indicates what inhabitants are native
there.   Often a mountain torrent comes pouring its
silver tribute to the stream, and, were there occasionally a ruined abbey, or feudal castle, to mix the romance
of real life with that of nature, the Ohio would be
perfect.

So powerful was the effect of this sweet scenery, that
we ceased to grumble at our dinners and suppers; nay,
we almost learnt to rival our neighbours at table in their
voracious rapidity of swallowing, so eager were we to
place ourselves again on guard, lest we might lose
sight of the beauty that was passing away from us.

Yet these fair shores are still unhealthy.   More than
once we landed, and conversed with the families of the
wood-cutters, and scarcely was there one in which we
did not hear of some member who had " lately died of
the fever ".—They are all subject to ague; and though
their dwellings are infinitely better than those on the

Mississippi, the inhabitants still look like a race that are selling their lives for gold.

Louisville is a considerable town, prettily situated on the Kentucky, or south side of the Ohio; we spent some hours in seeing all it had to show; and had I not been told that a bad fever often rages there during the warm season, I should have liked to pass some months there for the purpose of exploring the beautiful country in its vicinity. Frankfort and Lexington are both towns worth visiting; though from their being *out of the way* places, I never got to either. The first is the seat of the state government of Kentucky, and the last is, I was told, the residence of several independent families, who, with more leisure than is usually enjoyed in America, have its natural accompaniment, more refinement.

The falls of the Ohio are about a mile below Louisville, and produce a rapid too sudden for the boats to pass, except in the rainy season. The passengers are obliged to get out below them, and travel by land to Louisville, where they find other vessels ready to receive them for the remainder of the voyage. We were spared this inconvenience by the water being too high for the rapid to be much felt, and it will soon be altogether removed by the Louisville canal coming into operation, which will permit the steam-boats to continue their progress from below the falls to the town.

The scenery on the Kentucky side is much finer than on that of Indiana, or Ohio. The state of Kentucky was the darling spot of many tribes of Indians, and was reserved among them as a common hunting-ground; it is said, that they cannot yet name it without emotion, and that they have a sad and wild lament that they still chant to its memory. But their exclusion thence is of no recent date; Kentucky has been longer settled than the Illinois, Indiana, or Ohio; and it appears not only more highly cultivated, but more fertile and more picturesque than either. I have rarely seen richer pastures than those of Kentucky. The forest-trees, where not too crowded, are of magnificent growth; and the crops are gloriously abundant, where the thrift-less husbandry has not worn out the soil by an unvary-ing succession of exhausting crops. We were shown ground which had borne abundant crops of wheat for twenty successive years ; but a much shorter period suffices to exhaust the ground, when it is made to produce tobacco without the intermission of some other crop.

We reached Cincinnati on the 10th of February. It is finely situated on the south side of a hill that rises gently from the water's edge: yet it is by no means a city of striking appearance—it wants domes, towers, and steeples; but its landing-place is noble, extending for more than a quarter of a mile. It is well paved, and surrounded by neat, though not handsome, buildings. I have seen fifteen steam-boats lying there at once, and still half the wharf was unoccupied.

On arriving we repaired to the Washington Hotel, and thought ourselves fortunate when we were told that we were just in time for dinner at the table d'hôte; but when the dining-room door was opened, we re-treated with a feeling of dismay at seeing between sixty and seventy men already at table. We took our dinner in another room with the females of the family, and then went forth to seek a house for our permanent accommodation.

We went to the office of an advertising agent, who professed to keep a register of all such information, and described the dwelling we wanted. He made no difficulty, but told us his boy should be our guide through the city, and show us what we sought; we accordingly set out with him, and he led us up one street and down another, but evidently without any determinate object; I therefore stopped, and asked him where-about the houses were which we were going to see.

" I am looking for bills " was his reply.

I thought we could have looked for bills as well without him, and I told him so; upon which he assumed an air of great activity, and began knocking regularly at every door we passed, inquiring if the house was to be let. It was impossible to endure this long, and our guide was dismissed, though I was afterwards obliged to pay him a dollar for his services.

We had the good fortune, however, to find a dwelling before long, and we returned to our hotel, having determined upon taking possession of it as soon as it could be got ready. Not wishing to take our evening meal either with the threescore and ten gentlemen of the dining-room, nor yet with the half-dozen ladies of the bar-room, I ordered tea in my own chamber. A good-humoured Irish woman came forward with a sort of patronising manner, took my hand, and said : " Och, my honey, ye'll be from the old country. I'll see you will have your tay all to yourselves, honey." With this assurance we retired to my room, which was a handsome one as to its size and bed-furniture; but it had no carpet, and was darkened by blinds of paper such as rooms are hung with, which require to be rolled up, and then fastened with strings very awkwardly attached to the window-frames, whenever light or air was wished for. I afterwards met with these same uncomfortable blinds in every part of America.

Our Irish friend soon reappeared, and brought us tea, together with the never-failing accompaniments of American tea-drinking, hung beef, " chipped up " raw, and sundry sweetmeats of brown-sugar hue and flavour. We took our tea, and were enjoying our family talk, relative to our future arrangements, when a loud sharp knocking was heard at our door. My " come in " was answered by the appearance of a portly personage, who proclaimed himself our landlord.

" Are any of you ill ?" he began.

" No, thank you, sir; we are all quite well " was my reply.

" Then, madam, I muſt tell you, that I cannot accommodate you on these terms; we have no family tea-drinkings here, and you muſt live either with me and my wife, or not at all in my house."

This was said with an air of authority that almoſt precluded reply, but I ventured a sort of apologetic hint, that we were ſtrangers, and unaccuſtomed to the manners of the country.

" Our manners are very good manners, and we don't wish any changes from England," rejoined our ſturdy landlord, with an aspeƈt that assuredly did not indicate any very affeƈtionate partiality to the country he named.

I thought of mine hoſt of the Washington afterwards, when reading Scott's *Anne of Geierſtein ;* he, in truth, ſtrongly resembled the innkeeper therein immortalised, who made his gueſts eat, drink, and sleep, juſt where, when, and how he pleased. I made no further remon-ſtrance, but determined to haſten my removal. This we achieved the next day to our great satisfaƈtion.

We were soon settled in our new dwelling, which looked neat and comfortable enough; but we speedily found that it was devoid of nearly all the accommoda-tion that Europeans conceive necessary to decency and comfort. No pump, no ciſtern, no drain of any kind, no duſtman's cart, or any other visible means of getting rid of the rubbish, which vanishes with such celerity in London, that one has no time to think of its exiſtence; but which accumulated so rapidly at Cin-cinnati, that I sent for my landlord to know in what manner refuse of all kinds was to be disposed of.

" Your Help will juſt have to fix them all into the middle of the ſtreet; but you muſt mind, old woman, that it is the middle. I expect you don't know as we have got a law what forbids throwing such things at the sides of the streets; they must just all be cast right into the middle, and the pigs soon takes them off."

In truth the pigs are constantly seen doing Herculean service in this way through every quarter of the city: and though it is not very agreeable to live surrounded by herds of these unsavoury animals, it is well they are so numerous, and so active in their capacity of scavengers; for without them the streets would soon be choked up with all sorts of substances, in every stage of decomposition.

We had heard so much of Cincinnati, its beauty, wealth, and unequalled prosperity, that when we left Memphis, to go thither, we almost felt the delight of Rousseau's novice, " *un voyage à faire, et Paris au bout !*"—As soon, therefore, as our little domestic arrangements were completed, we set forth to view this " wonder of the West", this " prophet's gourd of magic growth "—this " infant Hercules "; and surely no travellers ever paraded a city under circumstances more favourable to their finding it fair to the sight. Three dreary months had elapsed since we had left the glories of London behind us; for nearly the whole of that time we had beheld no other architecture than what our ship and steam-boats had furnished; and, excepting at New Orleans, had seen hardly a trace of human habitations. The sight of bricks and mortar was really refreshing, and a house of three stories looked splendid. Of this splendour we saw repeated specimens, and moreover a brick church, which, from its two little peaked spires, is called the two-horned church. But, alas! the flatness of reality after the imagination has been busy! I hardly know what I expected to find in this city, fresh risen from the bosom of the wilderness, but certainly it was not a little town, about the size of Salisbury, without even an attempt at beauty

in any of its edifices, and with only just enough of
the air of a city to make it noisy and bustling. The
population is greater than the appearance of the town
would lead one to expect. This is partly owing to the
number of free negroes who herd together in an obscure
part of the city, called little Africa; and partly to the
density of the population round the paper-mills and
other manufactories. I believe the number of inhabitants exceeds twenty thousand.

We arrived in Cincinnati in February, 1828, and I
speak of the town as it was then; several small churches
have been built since, whose towers agreeably relieve
its uninteresting mass of buildings. At that time I
think Main Street, which is the principal avenue (and
runs through the whole town, answering to the High
Street of our old cities) was the only one entirely
paved. The *trottoir* is of brick, tolerably well laid,
but it is inundated by every shower, as Cincinnati
has no drains whatever. What makes this omission
the more remarkable is, that the situation of the place
is calculated both to facilitate their construction and to
render them necessary. Cincinnati is built on the side
of a hill that begins to rise at the river's edge; and were
it furnished with drains of the simplest arrangement,
the heavy showers of the climate would keep them
constantly clean: as it is, these showers wash the higher
streets, only to deposit their filth on the first level spot;
and this happens to be in the street second in importance
to Main Street, running at right-angles to it, and
containing most of the large warehouses of the town.
This deposit is a dreadful nuisance, and must be productive of miasma during the hot weather.

The town is built, as I believe most American towns
are, in squares, as they call them; but these squares are
the reverse of ours, being solid instead of hollow.
Each consists, or is intended to consist, when the plan
of the city is completed, of a block of buildings fronting

north, east, west, and south; each house communicating
with an alley, furnishing a back entrance. This plan
would not be a bad one, were the town properly drained;
but as it is, these alleys are horrible abominations, and
must, I conceive, become worse with every passing year.

To the north Cincinnati is bounded by a range of
forest-covered hills, sufficiently steep and rugged to
prevent their being built upon, or easily cultivated, but
not sufficiently high to command from their summits
a view of any considerable extent. Deep and narrow
water-courses, dry in summer, but bringing down heavy
streams in winter, divide these hills into many separate
heights, and this furnishes the only variety the landscape offers for many miles round the town. The
lovely Ohio is a beautiful feature wherever it is visible;
but the only part of the city that has the advantage of
its beauty, is the street nearest to its bank. The hills
of Kentucky, which rise at about the same distance
from the river, on the opposite side, form the southern
boundary to the basin in which Cincinnati is built.

On first arriving, I thought the many tree-covered
hills around very beautiful; but long before my departure, I felt so weary of the confined view, that
Salisbury Plain would have been an agreeable variety.
I doubt if any inhabitant of Cincinnati ever mounted
these hills so often as myself and my children; but it was
rather for the enjoyment of a freer air, than for any
beauty of prospect, that we took our daily climb.
These hills afford neither shrubs nor flowers, but
furnish the finest specimens of millepore in the world;
and the water-courses are full of fossil productions.

The forest-trees are neither large nor well grown, and
so close as to be nearly knotted together at top: even
the wild vine here loses its beauty; for its graceful
festoons bear leaves only when they reach the higher
branches of the tree that supports them, both air and
light being too scantily found below to admit of their

doing more than climbing with a bare stem till they reach a better atmosphere. The herb we call penny-royal was the only one I found in abundance, and that only on the brows, where the ground has been partially cleared; vegetation is impossible elsewhere, and it is this circumstance which makes the " eternal forests " of America so detestable. Near New Orleans the undergrowth of palmetto and pawpaw is highly beautiful; but in Tennessee, Indiana, and Ohio, I never found the slightest beauty in the forest-scenery. Fallen trees in every possible stage of decay, and congeries of leaves that have been rotting since the flood, cover the ground and infect the air. The beautiful variety of foliage afforded by evergreens never occurs; and in Tennessee, and that part of Ohio that surrounds Cincinnati, even the sterile beauty of rocks is wanting. On crossing the water to Kentucky the scene is greatly improved; beech and chestnut, of magnificent growth, border the beautiful river; the ground has been well cleared, and the herbage is excellent: the pawpaw grows abundantly, and is a splendid shrub, though it bears neither fruit nor flowers so far north. The noble tulip-tree flourishes here, and blooms profusely.

The river Licking flows into the Ohio nearly opposite Cincinnati; it is a pretty winding stream, and two or three miles from its mouth has a brisk rapid dancing among white stones, which, in the absence of better rocks, we found very picturesque.

Chapter Five

Cincinnati—Forest Farm—Mr Bullock

THOUGH I do not quite sympathise with those who consider Cincinnati as one of the wonders of the earth, I certainly think it a city of extraordinary size and importance, when it is remembered that thirty years ago the aboriginal forest occupied the ground where it stands; and every month appears to extend its limits and its wealth.

Some of the native political economists assert, that this rapid conversion of a bear-brake into a prosperous city is the result of free political institutions; not being very deep in such matters, a more obvious cause suggested itself to me, in the unceasing goad which necessity applies to industry in this country, and in the absence of all resource for the idle. During nearly two years that I resided in Cincinnati, or its neighbourhood, I neither saw a beggar, nor a man of sufficient fortune to permit his ceasing his efforts to increase it: thus every bee in the hive is actively employed in search of that honey of Hybla, vulgarly called money; neither art, science, learning, nor pleasure, can seduce them from its pursuit. This unity of purpose, backed by the spirit of enterprise, and joined with an acuteness, and absence of probity where interest is concerned, which might set canny Yorkshire at defiance, may well go far towards obtaining its purpose.

The low rate of taxation, too, unquestionably permits a more rapid accumulation of individual wealth than with us; but, till I had travelled through America, I had no idea how much of the money collected in taxes returns among the people, not only in the purchase of what their industry furnishes, but in the actual enjoyment of what is furnished. Were I an English legislator, instead of sending Sedition to the Tower, I would send her to make a tour of the United States. I had a little leaning towards Sedition myself when I set out; but before I had half completed my tour, I was quite cured.

I have read much of the " few and simple wants of rational man ", and I used to give a sort of dreamy acquiescence to the reasoning that went to prove each

36

added want an added woe. Those who reason in a comfortable London drawing-room know little about the matter. Were the aliments which sustain life all that we wanted, the faculties of the hog might suffice us; but if we analyse an hour of enjoyment, we shall find that it is made up of agreeable sensations occasioned by a thousand delicate impressions on almost as many nerves; where these nerves are sluggish from never having been awakened, external objects are less important, for they are less perceived; but where the whole machine of the human frame is in full activity, where every sense brings home to consciousness its touch of pleasure or of pain, then every object that meets the senses is important as a vehicle of happiness or misery. But let no frames so tempered visit the United States; or if they do, let it be with no longer pausing than will store the memory with images which, by the force of contrast, shall sweeten the future.

" Guarda e passa (e poi) ragioniam di lor."

The " simple " manner of living in Western America was more distasteful to me from its levelling effects on the manners of the people, than from the personal privations that it rendered necessary; and yet, till I was without them, I was in no degree aware of the many pleasurable sensations derived from the little elegances and refinements enjoyed by the middle classes in Europe. There were many circumstances, too trifling even for my gossiping pages, which pressed themselves daily and hourly upon us, and which forced us to remember painfully that we were not at home. It requires an abler pen than mine to trace the connection which I am persuaded exists between these deficiencies and the minds and manners of the people. All animal wants are supplied profusely at Cincinnati, and at a very easy rate; but, alas! these go but a little way in the history of a day's enjoyment. The total and universal want of good, or even pleasing, manners, both in males and females, is so remarkable, that I was constantly endeavouring to account for it. It certainly does not proceed from want of intellect: I have listened to much dull and heavy conversation in America, but rarely to any that I could strictly call silly (if I except the everywhere privileged class of very young ladies). They appear to me to have clear heads and active intellects—to be more ignorant on subjects that are only of conventional value, than on such as are of intrinsic importance; but there is no charm, no grace in their conversation. I very seldom, during my whole stay in the country, heard a sentence elegantly turned, and correctly pronounced from the lips of an American. There is always something either in the expression or the accent that jars the feelings and shocks the taste.[1]

[1] In most instances, though perhaps not quite in all, many of these observations are inapplicable to the higher classes of society in the Atlantic cities. There are mansions, for instance, in all of them, wherein little or nothing which can be required by the most refined habits of the educated middle classes, is so conspicuously wanting as to deserve the remarks made in the text ; nay, in many of them, as the reader will find distinctly stated in the description of the best houses at New York, the richness of the decorations exceed what it is usual to find among persons of similar rank in Europe. Nevertheless, the text may stand unchallenged as referring to that portion of the Union which it was intended to describe. As to what follows, relating to the ordinary tone of conversation, it must in truth be allowed to have had in the year 1831 a much more extended application. The intercourse with England, which, happily it is to be hoped for both countries, has increased, and is daily so rapidly increasing between us, must speedily render the remark as obsolete as that of Madame de Staël, who describes English ladies of the highest rank as sitting for hours superintending the boiling of the tea-kettle, while awaiting the termination of the bacchanalian orgies of their husbands. But such lingering tea-drinkings have been in England, and such heavy and ungraceful conversation has been heard to drawl through the drawing-rooms of the republic. On our part we scruple not to acknowledge our obligation to the neighbours who have taught us, during the intimate intercourse of the last twenty years, to amend the above-mentioned abomination indifferently well; nor will our trans-atlantic brothers and sisters, now become our neigh-

I will not pretend to decide whether man is better or worse off for requiring refinement in the manners and customs of the society that surrounds him, and for being incapable of enjoyment without them; but in America, that polish which removes the coarser and rougher parts of our nature, is unknown and undreamed of. There is much substantial comfort, and some display in the larger cities—in many of the more obvious features they are as Paris or as London, being all large assemblies of active and intelligent human beings; but yet they are wonderfully unlike in nearly all their moral features. Now God forbid that any reasonable American (of whom there are so many millions) should ever come to ask me what I mean; I should find it very difficult, nay, perhaps, utterly impossible, to explain myself; but, on the other hand, no European who has visited the Union will find the least difficulty in understanding me. I am in no way competent to judge of the political institutions of America; and if I should occasionally make an observation on their effects, as they meet my superficial glance, they will be made in the spirit and with the feeling of a woman, who is apt to tell what her first impressions may be, but unapt to reason back from effects to their causes. Such observations, if they be unworthy of much attention, are also obnoxious to little reproof; but there are points of national peculiarity of which women may judge as ably as men—all that constitutes the external of society may be fairly trusted to us.

Captain Hall, when asked what appeared to him to constitute the greatest difference between England and America, replied, like a gallant sailor: " The want of loyalty ". Were the same question put to me, I should answer: " The want of refinement ".[†]

bours too, long refuse to confess, that nothing but a personal familiarity with their avowed models could suffice to obliterate all national dissimilarity of manners.

Were Americans, indeed, disposed to assume the plain unpretending deportment of the Switzer, in the days of his picturesque simplicity (when, however, he never chewed tobacco), it would be in bad taste to censure him: but this is not the case; Jonathan will be a fine gentleman, but it must be in his own way—is he not a free-born American ? Jonathan, however, must remember, that if he will challenge competition with the old world, the old world will now and then look out to see how he supports his pretensions.

With their hours of business, whether judicial or mercantile, civil or military, I have nothing to do; I doubt not they are all spent wisely and profitably: but what are the hours of recreation ?—those hours that with us are passed in the enjoyment of all that art can win from nature; when, if the elaborate repast be more deeply relished than sages might approve, it is redeemed from sensuality by the presence of elegance and beauty. What is the American pendant to this ? I will not draw any comparisons between a good dinner-party in the two countries—I have heard American gentlemen say, that they could perceive no difference between them; but in speaking of general manners, I may observe, that it is rarely they dine in society, except in taverns and boarding-houses. Then they eat with the greatest possible rapidity, and in total silence. I have heard it said by American ladies, that the hours of greatest enjoyment to the gentlemen were those in which a glass of mint julap, or egg-nog, receives its highest relish from the absence of all restraint whatever; and when there were no ladies to trouble them.

Notwithstanding all this, the country is a very fine country, well worth visiting for a thousand reasons; nine hundred and ninety-nine of these are reasons founded on admiration and respect; the thousandth is, that we shall feel the more contented with our own. The more unlike a country through which we travel is to all we have left, the more we are likely to be amused; every thing in Cincinnati had this newness; and I should have thought it a place delightful to visit, but to tarry there was not to feel at home.

My home, however, for a time it was to be. We heard on every side, that of all the known places on " the globe called earth ", Cincinnati was the most favourable for a young man to settle in; and I only awaited the arrival of Mr T. to fix our son there, intending to continue with him till he should feel himself sufficiently established. We accordingly determined upon making ourselves as comfortable as possible. I took a larger house, which, however, I did not obtain without considerable difficulty, as, notwithstanding fourteen hundred new dwellings had been erected the preceding year, the demand for houses greatly exceeded the supply. We became acquainted with several amiable people, and we beguiled the anxious interval that preceded Mr T.'s joining us, by frequent excursions in the neighbourhood, which not only afforded us amusement, but gave us an opportunity of observing the mode of life of the country people.

We visited the farm which interested us particularly from its wild and lonely situation, and from the entire dependence of the inhabitants upon their own resources. It was a partial clearing in the very heart of the forest. The house was built on the side of a hill, so steep that a high ladder was necessary to enter the front door, while the back one opened against the hill side: at the foot of this sudden eminence ran a clear stream, whose bed had been deepened into a little reservoir, just opposite the house. A noble field of Indian corn stretched away into the forest on one side, and a few half-cleared acres, with a shed or two upon them, occupied the other, giving accommodation to cows, horses, pigs, and chickens innumerable. Immediately before the house was a small potato-garden, with a few peach and apple trees. The house was built of logs, and consisted of two rooms, besides a little shanty or lean-to, that was used as a kitchen. Both rooms were comfortably furnished with good beds, drawers, etc. The farmer's wife, and a young woman who looked like her sister, were spinning, and three little children were playing about. The woman told me that they spun and wove all the cotton and woollen garments of the family, and knit all the stockings; her husband, though not a shoemaker by trade, made all the shoes. She manufactured all the soap and candles they used, and prepared her sugar from the sugar-trees on their farm. All she wanted with money, she said, was to buy coffee, tea, and whiskey; and she could " get enough any day by sending a batch of butter and chicken to market ". They used no wheat, nor sold any of their corn, which, though it appeared a very large quantity, was not more than they required to make their bread and cakes of various kinds, and to feed all their live stock during the winter. She did not look in health, and said they had all had ague in " the fall "; but she seemed contented and proud of her independence; though it was in somewhat a mournful accent that she said: " 'Tis strange to us to see company. I expect the sun may rise and set a hundred times, before I shall see another *human* that does not belong to the family."

I have been minute in the description of this forest-farm, as I think it the best specimen I saw of the back-woods independence, of which so much is said in America. These people were indeed independent, Robinson Crusoe was hardly more so, and they eat and drink abundantly; but yet it seemed to me that there was something awful and almost unnatural in their loneliness. No village bell ever summoned them to prayer, where they might meet the friendly greeting of their fellow-men. When they die, no spot sacred by ancient reverence will receive their bones—Religion will not breathe her sweet and solemn farewell upon their graves; the husband or the father will dig the pit that is to hold them, beneath the nearest tree; he will himself deposit them within it, and the wind that whispers through the boughs will be their only requiem: but then they pay neither taxes nor tithes, are never expected to pull off a hat or to make a courtesy, and will live and die without hearing or uttering the dreadful words, " God save the king."

* * * * *

About two miles below Cincinnati, on the Kentucky side of the river, Mr Bullock, the well-known proprietor of the Egyptian Hall, has bought a large estate, with a noble house upon it.* He and his amiable wife were devoting themselves to the embellishment of the house and grounds; and certainly there is more taste and art lavished on one of their beautiful saloons, than all Western America can show elsewhere. It is impossible to help feeling that Mr Bullock is rather out of his element in this remote spot; and the gems of art he has brought with him, show as strangely there, as would a bower of roses in Siberia, or a Cincinnati fashionable at Almack's. The exquisite beauty of the spot, commanding one of the finest reaches of the Ohio, the extensive gardens, and the large and handsome mansion, have tempted Mr Bullock to spend a large sum in the purchase of this place; and if any one who has passed his life in London could endure such a change, the active mind and sanguine spirit of Mr Bullock might enable him to do it; but his frank, and truly English hospitality, and his enlightened and inquiring mind, seemed sadly wasted there. I have since heard with pleasure that Mr Bullock has parted with this beautiful but secluded mansion.

Chapter Six

Servants—Society—Evening Parties

THE greatest difficulty in organising a family establishment in Ohio, is getting servants, or, as it is there called, "getting help"; for it is more than petty treason to the republic to call a free citizen a *servant*. The whole class of young women, whose bread depends upon their labour, are taught to believe that the most abject poverty is preferable to domestic service. Hundreds of half-naked girls work in the paper-mills, or in any other manufactory, for less than half the wages they would receive in service; but they think their equality is compromised by the latter, and nothing but the wish to obtain some particular article of finery will ever induce them to submit to it. A kind friend, however, exerted herself so effectually for me, that a tall stately lass soon presented herself, saying "I be come to help you." The intelligence was very agreeable, and I welcomed her in the most gracious manner possible, and asked what I should give her by the year.

"O Gimini!" exclaimed the damsel, with a loud laugh, "you be a downright Englisher, sure enough. I should like to see a young lady engage by the year in America! I hope I shall get a husband before many months, or I expect I shall be an outright old maid, for I be most seventeen already: besides, mayhap I may want to go to school. You must just give me a dollar and a half a week, and mother's slave Phillis must come over once a week, I expect, from t'other side the water, to help me clean."

I agreed to the bargain, of course with all dutiful submission; and seeing she was preparing to set to work in a yellow dress, *parsemé* with red roses, I gently hinted, that I thought it was a pity to spoil so fine a gown, and that she had better change it.

44

" 'Tis just my best and my worst " she answered; " for I've got no other."

And in truth I found that this young lady had left the paternal mansion with no more clothes of any kind than what she had on. I immediately gave her money to purchase what was necessary for cleanliness and decency, and set to work with my daughters to make her a gown. She grinned applause when our labour was completed; but never uttered the slightest expression of gratitude for that, or for any thing else we could do for her. She was constantly asking us to lend her different articles of dress, and when we declined it, she said: " Well, I never seed such grumpy folks as you be; there is several young ladies of my acquaintance what goes to live out now and then with the old women about the town, and they and their gurls always lends them what they asks for; I guess you English thinks we should poison your things, just as bad as if we was negurs." Here I beg to assure the reader, that whenever I give conversations, they were not made *à loisir*, but were written down immediately after they occurred, with all the verbal fidelity my memory permitted.[†]

This young lady left me at the end of two months; because I refused to lend her money enough to buy a silk dress to go to a ball, saying: " Then 'tis not worth my while to stay any longer."

I cannot imagine it possible that such a state of things can be desirable, or beneficial to any of the parties concerned. I might occupy a hundred pages on the subject, and yet fail to give an adequate idea of the sore, angry, ever-wakeful pride that seemed to torment these poor wretches. In many of them it was so excessive, that all feeling of displeasure, or even of ridicule, was lost in pity. One of these was a pretty girl, whose natural disposition must have been gentle and kind; but her good feelings were soured, and her gentleness turned to morbid sensitiveness, by having heard a thousand and a thousand times that she was as good as any other lady; that all men were equal, and women too; and that it was a sin and a shame for a free-born American to be treated like a servant.

When she found she was to dine in the kitchen, she turned up her pretty lip, and said: " I guess that's cause you don't think I'm good enough to eat with you. You'll find that won't do here." I found afterwards that she rarely ate any dinner at all, and generally passed the time in tears. I did everything in my power to conciliate and make her happy, but I am sure she hated me. I gave her very high wages, and she stayed till she had obtained several expensive articles of dress, and then, *un beau matin*, she came to me full dressed, and said: " I must go."—" When shall you return, Charlotte ?"—" I expect you'll see no more of me." And so we parted. Her sister was also living with me; but her wardrobe was not yet completed, and she remained some weeks longer, till it was.

I fear it may be called bad taste to say so much concerning my domestics; but, nevertheless, the circumstances are so characteristic of America, that I must recount another history relating to them. A few days after the departure of my ambitious belle, my cries for " Help " had been so effectual, that another young lady presented herself, with the usual preface " I'm come to help you." I had been cautioned never to ask for a reference for character, as it would not only rob me of that help, but entirely prevent my ever getting another; so, five minutes after she entered, she was installed, bundle and all, as a member of the family. She was by no means handsome, but there was an air of simple frankness in her manner that won us all. For my own part I thought I had got a second Jeanie Deans; for she recounted to me histories of her early youth, wherein her plain good sense and strong mind had enabled her to win her way through a host of cruel step-mothers, faithless lovers, and cheating brothers. Among other things, she told me, with the appearance of much emotion, that she had found, since she came to town, a cure for all her sorrows. "Thanks, and praise for it, I have got religion!" and then she asked if I would spare her to go to meeting every Tuesday and Thursday evening: "You shall not have to want me, Mrs Trollope; for our minister knows that we have all our duties to perform to man, as well as to God, and he makes the meeting late in the evening that they may not cross one another." Who could refuse? Not I; and Nancy had leave to go to meeting two evenings in the week, besides Sundays.

One night that the mosquitoes had found their way under my feet, and prevented my sleeping, I heard some one enter the house very late; I got up, went to the top of the stairs, and, by the help of a bright moon, recognised Nancy's best bonnet. I called to her. "You are very late" said I; "what is the reason of it?"—"O Mrs Trollope", she replied, "I am late, indeed! We have this night had seventeen souls added to our flock. May they live to bless this night! But it has been a long sitting, and very warm; I'll just take a drink of water, and get to bed; you shan't find me later in the morning for it." Nor did I. She was an excellent servant, and performed more than was expected from her; moreover, she always found time to read the Bible several times in the day, and I seldom saw her occupied about any thing without observing that she had placed it near her.

At last she fell sick with the cholera,[1] and her life was despaired of. I nursed her with great care, and sat up the greatest part of two nights with her. She was often delirious, and all her wandering thoughts seemed to ramble to heaven. "I have been a sinner", she

[1] *Not* the Asiatic cholera, which at that time had not visited America.

said, "but I am safe in the Lord Jesus." When she recovered, she asked me to let her go into the country for a few days, to change the air, and begged me to lend her three dollars.

While she was absent, a lady called on me, and inquired, with some agitation, if my servant, Nancy Fletcher, were at home. I replied that she was gone into the country. "Thank God!" she exclaimed; "never let her enter your doors again; she is the most abandoned woman in the town: a gentleman who knows you, has been told that she lives with you, and that she boasts of having the power of entering your house at any hour of the night." She told me many other circumstances, unnecessary to repeat, but all tending to prove that she was a very dangerous inmate.

I expected her home the next evening, and I believe I passed the interval in meditating how to get rid of her without an *éclaircissement*. At length she arrived, and all my study having failed to supply me with any other reason than the real one for dismissing her, I stated it at once. Not the slightest change passed over her countenance, but she looked steadily at me, and said, in a very civil tone: "I should like to know who told you." I replied that it could be of no advantage to her to know, and that I wished her to go immediately. "I am ready to go" she said, in the same quiet tone; "but what will you do for your three dollars?"— "I must do without them, Nancy: good morning to you."—"I must just put up my things" she said, and left the room. About half an hour afterwards, when we were all assembled at dinner, she entered with her usual civil composed air: "Well, I am come to wish you all good b'ye", and with a friendly good-humoured smile she left us.

This adventure frightened me so heartily, that, notwithstanding I had the dread of cooking my own dinner before my eyes, I would not take any more young ladies into my family without receiving some slight sketch of their former history. At length I met with a very worthy Frenchwoman, and soon after with a tidy English girl, to assist her; and I had the good fortune to keep them till a short time before my departure: so, happily, I have no more misfortunes of this nature to relate.

Such being the difficulties respecting domestic arrangements, it is obvious, that the ladies who are brought up amongst them cannot have leisure for any great development of mind; it is, in fact, out of the question: and, remembering this, it is more surprising that some among them should be very pleasing, than that none should be highly instructed.

Had I passed as many evenings in company in any other town that I ever visited as I did in Cincinnati, I should have been able to give some little account of the conversations I had listened to; but, upon reading over my notes, and then taxing my memory to the utmost to supply the deficiency, I can scarcely find a trace of any thing that deserves the name. Such as I have, shall be given in their place. But, whatever may be the talents of the persons who meet together in society, the very shape, form, and arrangement of the meeting is sufficient to paralyse conversation. The women invariably herd together at one part of the room, and the men at the other; but, in justice to Cincinnati, I must acknowledge that this arrangement is by no means peculiar to that city, or to the western side of the Alleghanies. Sometimes a small attempt at music produces a partial re-union; a few of the most daring youths, animated by the consciousness of curled hair and smart waistcoats, approach the pianoforte, and begin to mutter a little to the half-grown pretty things, who are comparing with one another "how many quarters' music they have had." Where the mansion is of sufficient dignity to have two drawing-rooms, the piano, the little ladies, and the slender gentlemen, are left to themselves, and on such occasions the sound of laughter is often heard to issue from among them. But the fate of the more dignified personages, who are left in the other room, is extremely dismal. The gentlemen spit, talk of elections and the price of produce, and spit again. The ladies look at each other's dresses till they know every pin by heart; talk of Parson Somebody's last sermon on the day of judgment, on Dr. T'otherbody's new pills for dyspepsia, till the " tea " is announced, when they all console themselves together for whatever they may have suffered in keeping awake, by taking more tea, coffee, hot cake and custard, hoe cake, johnny cake, waffle cake, and dodger cake, pickled peaches and preserved cucumbers, ham, turkey, hung beef, apple-sauce, and pickled oysters, than ever were prepared in any other country of the known world. After this massive meal is over, they return to the drawing-room, and it always appeared to me that they remained together as long as they could bear it, and then they rise *en masse*, cloak, bonnet, shawl, and exit.

Chapter Seven

Market—Museum—Picture Gallery—Academy of Fine Arts—Drawing School—Phrenological Society—Miss Wright's Lecture

PERHAPS the most advantageous feature in Cincinnati is its market, which, for excellence, abundance, and cheapness, can hardly, I should think, be surpassed in any part of the world, if I except the luxury of fruits, which are very inferior to any I have seen in Europe. There are no butchers, fishmongers, or indeed any shops for eatables, except *bakeries*, as they are called, in the town; everything must be purchased at market; and to

accomplish this, the busy housewife muſt be ſtirring be-
times, or, 'spite of the abundant supply, she will find
her hopes of breakfaſt, dinner, and supper for the day
defeated, the market being pretty well over by eight
o'clock.

The beef is excellent, and the higheſt price when we
were there, four cents (about twopence) the pound.
The mutton was inferior, and so was veal to the eye,
but it ate well, though not very fat; the price was about
the same. The poultry was excellent; fowls or full-
sized chickens, ready for table, twelve cents, but much
less if bought alive, and not quite fat; turkeys about
fifty cents, and geese the same. The Ohio furnishes
several sorts of fish, some of them very good, and always
to be found cheap and abundant in the market. Eggs,
butter, nearly all kinds of vegetables, excellent and at
moderate prices. From June till December, tomatoes
(the great luxury of the American table in the opinion
of moſt Europeans) may be found in the higheſt
perfeƈtion in the market for about sixpence the peck.
They have a great variety of beans unknown in England,
particularly the Lima bean, the seed of which is dressed
like the French haricot; it furnishes a very abundant
crop, and is a moſt delicious vegetable; could it be
naturalised with us, it would be a valuable acquisition.
The Windsor, or broad-bean, will not do well there;
Mr Bullock had them in his garden, where they were
cultivated with much care; they grew about a foot high,
and blossomed, but the pod never ripened. All the
fruit I saw exposed for sale in Cincinnati was moſt
miserable. I passed two summers there, but never
taſted a peach worth eating. Of apricots and neƈtarines
I saw none; ſtrawberries very small, raspberries much
worse; gooseberries very few, and quite uneatable;
currants about half the size of ours, and about double
the price; grapes too sour for tarts; apples abundant,
but very indifferent, none that would be thought good

enough for an English table; pears, cherries, and plums, most miserably bad.[†] The flowers of these regions were at least equally inferior: whether this proceeds from want of cultivation, or from peculiarity of soil, I know not; but after leaving Cincinnati, I was told by a gentleman who appeared to understand the subject, that the state of Ohio had no indigenous flowers or fruits. The water-melons, which in that warm climate furnish a delightful refreshment, were abundant and cheap; but all other melons very inferior to those of France, or even of England when ripened in a common hot-bed.

From the almost total want of pasturage near the city, it is difficult for a stranger to divine how milk is furnished for its supply; but we soon learnt that there are more ways than one of keeping a cow. A large proportion of the families in the town, particularly of the poorer class, have one, though apparently, without any accommodation whatever for it. These animals are fed morning and evening, at the door of the house, with a good mess of Indian corn, boiled with water; while they eat, they are milked, and when the operation is completed, the milk-pail and the meal-tub retreat into the dwelling, leaving the republican cow to walk away, to take her pleasure on the hills, or in the gutters, as may suit her fancy best. They generally return very regularly to give and take the morning and evening meal; though it more than once happened to us, before we were supplied by a regular milk-cart, to have our jug sent home empty, with the sad news that " the cow was not come home, and it was too late to look for her to breakfast now ". Once, I remember, the good woman told us that she had overslept herself and that the cow had come and gone again, " not liking, I expect, to hanker about by herself for nothing, poor thing !"

Cincinnati has not many lions to boast of, but among

them are two museums of natural history; both of these contain many respectable specimens, particularly that of Mr Dorfeuille, who has, moreover, some highly interesting Indian antiquities. He is a man of taste and science, but a collection formed strictly according to their dictates would by no means satisfy the western metropolis. The people have a most extravagant passion for wax figures, and the two museums vie with each other in displaying specimens of this barbarous branch of art. As Mr Dorfeuille cannot trust to his science for attracting the citizens, he has put his ingenuity into requisition, and this has proved to him the surer aid of the two. He has constructed a pandemonium in an upper story of his museum, in which he has congregated all the images of horror that his fertile fancy could devise; dwarfs that by machinery grow into giants before the eyes of the spectator; imps of ebony with eyes of flame; monstrous reptiles devouring youth and beauty; lakes of fire, and mountains of ice; in short, wax, paint, and springs have done wonders. "To give the scheme some more effect", he makes it visible only through a grate of massive iron bars, among which are arranged wires connected with an electrical machine in a neighbouring chamber; should any daring hand or foot obtrude itself within the bars, it receives a smart shock, that often passes through many of the crowd, and the cause being unknown, the effect is exceedingly comic; terror, astonishment, curiosity, all are set in action, and all contribute to make "Dorfeuille's Hell" one of the most amusing exhibitions imaginable.*

There is also a picture gallery at Cincinnati, and this was a circumstance of much interest to us, as our friend Mr H., who had accompanied Miss Wright to America, in the expectation of finding a good opening in the line of historical painting, intended commencing his experiment at Cincinnati. It would be invidious to describe the picture gallery; I have no doubt, that some years hence it will present a very different appearance. Mr H. was very kindly received by many of the gentlemen of the city, and though the state of the fine arts there gave him but little hope that he should meet with much success, he immediately occupied himself in painting a noble historical picture of the landing of General Lafayette at Cincinnati.

Perhaps the clearest proof of the little feeling for art that existed at that time in Cincinnati, may be drawn from the result of an experiment originated by a German, who taught drawing there. He conceived the project of forming a chartered academy of fine arts; and he succeeded in the beginning to his utmost wish, or rather "they fooled him to the top of his bent". Three thousand dollars were subscribed, that is to say, names were written against different sums to that amount; a house was chosen; and finally, application was made to the government, and the charter obtained, rehearsing formally the names of the subscribing members, the professors, and the officers. So far did the steam of their zeal impel them, but at this point it was let off; the affair stood still, and I never heard the academy of fine arts mentioned afterwards.

This same German gentleman, on seeing Mr H.'s sketches, was so well pleased with them, that he immediately proposed his joining him in his drawing school, with an agreement, I believe, that his payment from it should be five hundred dollars a year. Mr H. accepted the proposal: but the union did not last long, and the cause of its dissolution was too American to be omitted. Mr H. prepared his models, and attended the class, which was numerous, consisting both of boys and girls. He soon found that the "sage called Decipline" was not one of the assistants, and he remonstrated against the constant talking, and running from one part of the room to another, but in vain;

finding, however, that he could do nothing till this was discontinued, he wrote some rules, enforcing order, for the purpose of placing them at the door of the academy. When he showed them to his colleague, he shook his head and said: "Very goot, very goot in Europe, but America boys and gals vill not bear it, dey vill do juſt vat dey please; Suur, dey vould all go avay next day." "And you will not enforce these regulations *si nécessaires*, Monsieur?" "O lar! not for de vorld." "*Eh bien*, Monsieur, I muſt leave the young republicans to your management."

I heard another anecdote that will help to show the ſtate of art at this time in the Weſt. Mr Bullock was showing to some gentlemen of the firſt ſtanding, the very *élite* of Cincinnati, his beautiful collection of engravings, when one among them exclaimed: "Have you really done all these since you came here! How hard you muſt have worked!"

I was also told of a gentleman of high Cincinnati *ton*, and critical in his taſte for the fine arts, who, having a drawing put into his hands, representing Hebe and the bird umquhile sacred to Jupiter, demanded in a satirical tone, "What is this?" "Hebe" replied the alarmed collector. "Hebe", sneered the man of taſte; "what the devil has Hebe to do with the American eagle?"

We had not been long at Cincinnati when Dr Caldwell, the Spurzheim of America, arrived there, for the purpose of delivering lectures on phrenology. I attended his lectures, and was introduced to him. He has ſtudied Spurzheim and Combe diligently, and seems to underſtand the science to which he has devoted himself; but neither his lectures nor his conversation had that delightful truth of genuine enthusiasm, which makes liſtening to Dr Spurzheim so great a treat. His lectures, however, produced considerable effect. Between twenty and thirty of the moſt erudite citizens decided upon forming a phrenological society. A meeting was called, and fully attended; a respectable number of subscribers' names was registered, the payment of subscriptions being arranged for a future day. President, vice-president, treasurer, and secretary, were chosen, and the first meeting dissolved with every appearance of energetic perseverance in scientific research.*

The second meeting brought together one half of this learned body, and they enacted rules and laws, and passed resolutions, sufficient, it was said, to have filled three folios.

A third day of meeting arrived, which was an important one, as on this occasion the subscriptions were to be paid. The treasurer came punctually, but found himself alone. With patient hope, he waited two hours for the wise men of the West, but he waited in vain: and so expired the Phrenological Society of Cincinnati.

I had often occasion to remark that the spirit of enterprise or improvement seldom glowed with sufficient ardour to resist the smothering effect of a demand for dollars. The Americans love talking. All great works, however, that promise a profitable result, are sure to meet support from men who have enterprise and capital sufficient to await the return; but where there is nothing but glory, or the gratification of taste to be expected, it is, I believe, very rarely that they give anything beyond " their most sweet voices ".

Perhaps they are right. In Europe we see fortunes crippled by a passion for statues, or for pictures, or for books, or for gems; for all and every of the artificial wants that give grace to life, and tend to make man forget that he is a thing of clay. They are wiser in their generation on the other side of the Atlantic; I rarely saw anything that led to such oblivion there.

Soon after Dr Caldwell's departure, another lecturer appeared upon the scene, whose purpose of publicly addressing the people was no sooner made known than the most violent sensation was excited.

That a lady of fortune, family, and education, whose youth had been passed in the most refined circles of private life, should present herself to the people as a public lecturer, would naturally excite surprise any where, and the *nil admirari* of the old world itself would hardly be sustained before such a spectacle; but in America, where women are guarded by a seven-fold shield of habitual insignificance, it caused an effect that can hardly be described.[†] "Miss Wright, of Nashoba, is going to lecture at the court-house" sounded from street to street, and from house to house. I shared the surprise, but not the wonder; I knew her extraordinary gift of eloquence, her almost unequalled command of words, and the wonderful power of her rich and thrilling voice; and I doubted not that if it was her will to do it, she had the power of commanding the attention, and enchanting the ear of any audience before whom it was her pleasure to appear. I was most anxious to hear her, but was almost deterred from attempting it, by the reports that reached me of the immense crowd that was expected. After many consultations, and hearing that many other ladies intended going, my friend Mrs P——, and myself, decided upon making the attempt, accompanied by a party of gentlemen, and found the difficulty less than we anticipated, though the building was crowded in every part. We congratulated ourselves that we had had the courage to be among the number, for all my expectations fell far short of the splendour, the brilliance, the overwhelming eloquence of this extraordinary orator.

Her lecture was upon the nature of true knowledge, and it contained little that could be objected to by any sect or party; it was intended as an introduction to the strange and startling theories contained in her subsequent lectures, and could alarm only by the hints it contained that the fabric of human wisdom could rest securely on no other base than that of human knowledge.

There was, however, one passage from which common-sense revolted; it was one wherein she quoted that phrase of mischievous sophistry, "all men are born free and equal ".

This false and futile axiom, which has done, is doing, and will do so much harm to this fine country, came from Jefferson; and truly his life was a glorious commentary upon it. I pretend not to criticise his written works, but common-sense enables me to pronounce this, his favourite maxim, false.

Few names are held in higher estimation in America than that of Jefferson; it is the touchstone of the democratic party, and all seem to agree that he was one of the greatest men; yet I have heard his name coupled with deeds which would make the sons of Europe shudder. The facts I allude to are spoken openly by all, not whispered privately by a few; and in a country where religion is the tea-table talk, and its strict observance a fashionable distinction, these facts are recorded, and listened to, without horror, nay, without emotion.

Mr Jefferson is said to have been the father of children by almost all his numerous gang of female slaves. These wretched offspring were also the lawful slaves of their father, and worked in his house and plantations as such; in particular, it is recorded that it was his especial pleasure to be waited upon by them at table, and the hospitable orgies for which his Monticello was so celebrated were incomplete, unless the goblet he quaffed were tendered by the trembling hand of his own slavish offspring.[1][†]

[1] Some years after my return from America, I met at Paris an American gentleman holding a diplomatic situation in that city, who assured me, that the real political principles of Mr Jefferson were exactly the reverse of what he publicly expressed, and that it was impossible any man could be less a democrat at heart than he was.

I once heard it stated by a democratical adorer of this great man, that when, as it sometimes happened, his children by Quadroon slaves were white enough to escape suspicion of their origin, he did not pursue them if they attempted to escape, saying laughingly: " Let the rogues get off, if they can; I will not hinder them." This was stated in a large party, as a proof of his kind and noble nature, and was received by all with approving smiles.

If I know anything of right or wrong—if virtue and vice be indeed something more than words, then was this great American an unprincipled tyrant, and most heartless libertine.

But to return to Miss Wright—it is impossible to imagine anything more striking than her appearance. Her tall and majestic figure, the deep and almost solemn expression of her eyes, the simple contour of her finely formed head, unadorned, excepting by its own natural ringlets; her garment of plain white muslin, which hung around her in folds that recalled the drapery of a Grecian statue, all contributed to produce an effect unlike anything I had ever seen before, or ever expect to see again.

Chapter Eight

Absence of Public and Private Amusement—Churches and Chapels—Influence of the Clergy—A Revival

I NEVER saw any people who appeared to live so much without amusement as the Cincinnatians. Billiards are forbidden by law, so are cards. To sell a pack of cards in Ohio subjects the seller to a penalty of fifty dollars. They have no public balls, excepting, I think, six, during the Christmas holidays. They have no concerts. They have no dinner-parties.

They have a theatre, which is, in fact, the only

public amusement of this triste little town; but they seem to care little about it, and either from economy or distaste, it is very poorly attended. Ladies are rarely seen there, and by far the larger proportion of females deem it an offence against religion to witness the representation of a play. It is in the churches and chapels of the town that the ladies are to be seen in full costume: and I am tempted to believe that a stranger from the continent of Europe would be inclined, on first reconnoitring the city, to suppose that the places of worship were the theatres and cafés of the place. No evening in the week but brings throngs of the young and beautiful to the chapels and meeting-houses, all dressed with care, and sometimes with great pretension; it is there that all display is made, and all fashionable distinction sought. The proportion of gentlemen attending these evening meetings is very small, but often, as might be expected, a sprinkling of smart young clerks makes this sedulous display of ribbons and ringlets intelligible and natural. Were it not for the churches, indeed, I think there might be a general bonfire of best bonnets, for I never could discover any other use for them.

The ladies are too actively employed in the interior of their houses to permit much parading in full dress for morning visits. There are no public gardens or lounging shops of fashionable resort, and were it not for public worship, and private tea-drinkings, all the ladies in Cincinnati would be in danger of becoming perfect recluses.

The influence which the ministers of all the innumerable religious sects throughout America have on the females of their respective congregations, approaches very nearly to what we read of in Spain, or in other strictly Roman Catholic countries. There are many causes for this peculiar influence. Where equality of rank is affectedly acknowledged by the rich, and clamorously claimed by the poor, distinction and preeminence are allowed to the clergy only. This gives them high importance in the eyes of the ladies. I think, also, that it is from the clergy only that the women of America receive that sort of attention which is so dearly valued by every female heart throughout the world. With the priests of America the women hold that degree of influential importance which, in the countries of Europe, is allowed them throughout all orders and ranks of society, except, perhaps, the very lowest; and in return for this they seem to give their hearts and souls into their keeping. I never saw, or read of, any country where religion had so strong a hold upon the women, or a slighter hold upon the men.

I mean not to assert that I met with no men of sincerely religious feelings, or with no women of no religious feelings at all; but I feel perfectly secure of being correct as to the great majority in the statement I have made.

We had not been many months in Cincinnati when our curiosity was excited by hearing the "revival" talked of by every one we met throughout the town. "The revival will be very full", "We shall be constantly engaged during the revival", were the phrases we constantly heard repeated, and for a long time without in the least comprehending what was meant; but at length I learnt that the un-national church of America required to be roused, at regular intervals, to greater energy and exertion. At these seasons the most enthusiastic of the clergy travel the country, and enter the cities and towns by scores, or by hundreds, as the accommodation of the place may admit, and for a week or fortnight, or, if the population be large, for a month, they preach and pray all day, and often for a considerable portion of the night, in the various churches and chapels of the place. This is called a Revival.

I took considerable pains to obtain information on

this subject; but in detailing what I learnt I fear that it is probable I shall be accused of exaggeration; all I can do is cautiously to avoid deserving it. The subject is highly interesting, and it would be a fault of no trifling nature to treat it with levity.

These itinerant clergymen are of all persuasions, I believe, except the Episcopalian, Catholic, Unitarian, and Quaker.[1] I heard of Presbyterians of all varieties; of Baptists of I know not how many divisions; and of Methodists of more denominations than I can remember; whose innumerable shades of varying belief it would require much time to explain and more to comprehend. They enter all the cities, towns, and villages of the Union in succession; I could not learn with sufficient certainty to repeat, what the interval generally is between their visits. These Itinerants are, for the most part, lodged in the houses of their respective followers, and every evening that is not spent in the churches and meeting-houses, is devoted to what would be called parties by others, but which they

[1] The critics who have from time to time reproached me with undue severity in my strictures on the domestic manners of the Americans, have said that a candid examination of matters at home would have shown me that what I reprobated might be found in England, as well as in the United States. In most cases I have felt that this might be rebutted, not by altogether denying the charge, but by showing that what I complained of in the Union as indicative of imperfect civilisation, if existing at all with us, could only be met with among persons in a much lower station of life than any I have quoted as specimens of society in America.

But on the subject treated in the present chapter, justice compels me to avow that no such pleading can avail me.

That such fearful profanation of the holy name of religion has rapidly increased among us since the year 1827, in which I quitted England for America, is most sadly certain, and may account for its exhibition being as new to me, as it was painful. The want of a national church, and of that guardian protection which its episcopal authority seems to promise against its desecration by the ever-varying innovations of sectarian licence, appeared to account for all the profanations I witnessed. But this explanation fails me now.

designate as prayer-meetings. Here they eat, drink, pray, sing, hear confessions, and make converts. To these meetings I never got invited, and therefore I have nothing but hearsay evidence to offer, but my information comes from an eye-witness, and one on whom I believe I may depend. If one half of what I heard may be believed, these social prayer-meetings are by no means the least curious, or the least important part of the business.

It is impossible not to smile at the close resemblance to be traced between the feelings of a first-rate Presbyterian or Methodist lady, fortunate enough to have secured a favourite Itinerant for her meeting, and those of a first-rate London Blue, equally blest in the presence of a fashionable poet. There is a strong family likeness among us all the world over.

The best rooms, the best dresses, the choicest refreshments solemnise the meeting. While the party is assembling, the load-star of the hour is occupied in whispering conversations with the guests as they arrive. They are called brothers and sisters, and the greetings are very affectionate. When the room is full, the company, of whom a vast majority are always women, are invited, entreated, and coaxed to confess before their brothers and sisters, all their thoughts, faults, and follies.

These confessions are strange scenes; the more they confess, the more invariably are they encouraged and caressed. When this is over, they all kneel, and the Itinerant prays extempore. They then eat and drink; and then they sing hymns, pray, exhort, sing, and pray again, till the excitement reaches a very high pitch indeed. These scenes are going on at some house or other every evening during the revival, nay, at many at the same time, for the churches and meeting-houses cannot give occupation to half the Itinerants, though they are all open throughout the day, and till a late hour in the night, and the officiating ministers succeed each other in the occupation of them.

It was at the principal of the Presbyterian churches that I was twice witness to scenes that made me shudder; in describing one, I describe both, and every one; the same thing is constantly repeated.

It was in the middle of summer, but the service we were recommended to attend did not begin till it was dark. The church was well lighted, and crowded almost to suffocation. On entering, we found three priests standing side by side, in a sort of tribune, placed where the altar usually is, handsomely fitted up with crimson curtains, and elevated about as high as our pulpits. We took our places in a pew close to the rail which surrounded it.

The priest who stood in the middle was praying; the prayer was extravagantly vehement, and offensively familiar in expression; when this ended, a hymn was sung, and then another priest took the centre place and preached. The sermon had considerable eloquence, but of a frightful kind. The preacher described, with ghastly minuteness, the last feeble fainting moments of human life, and then the gradual progress of decay after death, which he followed through every process up to the last loathsome stage of decomposition. Suddenly changing his tone, which had been that of sober accurate description, into the shrill voice of horror, he bent forward his head, as if to gaze on some object beneath the pulpit. And as Rebecca made known to Ivanhoe what she saw through the window, so the preacher made known to us what he saw in the pit that seemed to open before him. The device was certainly a happy one for giving effect to his description of hell. No image that fire, flame, brimstone, molten lead, or red hot pincers could supply, with flesh, nerves, and sinews quivering under them, was omitted. The perspiration ran in streams from the face of the preacher; his eyes rolled, his lips were covered with foam, and every feature had the deep expression of horror it would have borne, had he, in truth, been gazing at the scene he described. The acting was excellent. At length he gave a languishing look to his supporters on each side, as if to express his feeble state, and then sat down, and wiped the drops of agony from his brow.

The other two priests arose, and began to sing a hymn. It was some seconds before the congregation could join as usual; every up-turned face looked pale and horror-struck. When the singing ended, another took the centre place, and began in a sort of coaxing affectionate tone, to ask the congregation if what their dear brother had spoken had reached their hearts? Whether they would avoid the hell he had made them see? "Come, then!" he continued, stretching out his arms towards them; "come to us and tell us so, and we will make you see Jesus, the dear gentle Jesus, who shall save you from it. But you must come to him! You must not be ashamed to come to him! This night you shall tell him that you are not ashamed of him; we will make way for you; we will clear the bench for anxious sinners to sit upon. Come, then! come to the anxious bench, and we will show you Jesus! Come! Come! Come!"

Again a hymn was sung, and while it continued, one of the three was employed in clearing one or two long benches that went across the rail, sending the people back to the lower part of the church. The singing ceased, and again the people were invited, and exhorted not to be ashamed of Jesus, but to put themselves upon "the anxious benches", and lay their heads on his bosom. "Once more we will sing", he concluded, "that we may give you time." And again they sung a hymn.

And now in every part of the church a movement was

perceptible, slight at first, but by degrees becoming more decided. Young girls arose, and sat down, and rose again; and then the pews opened, and several came tottering out, their hands clasped, their heads hanging on their bosoms, and every limb trembling, and still the hymn went on; but as the poor creatures approached the rail their sobs and groans became audible. They seated themselves on the "anxious benches"; the hymn ceased, and two of the three priests walked down from the tribune, and going, one to the right, and the other to the left, began whispering to the poor tremblers seated there. These whispers were inaudible to us, but the sobs and groans increased to a frightful excess. Young creatures, with features pale and distorted, fell on their knees on the pavement, and soon sunk forward on their faces; the most violent cries and shrieks followed, while from time to time a voice was heard in convulsive accents, exclaiming "O Lord!", "O Lord Jesus!", "Help me, Jesus!" and the like.

Meanwhile the two priests continued to walk among them; they repeatedly mounted on the benches, and trumpet-mouthed proclaimed to the whole congregation "the tidings of salvation", and then from every corner of the building arose in reply, short sharp cries of "Amen!", "Glory!", "Amen!", while the prostrate penitents continued to receive whispered comfortings, and from time to time a mystic caress. More than once I saw a young neck encircled by a reverend arm. Violent hysterics and convulsions seized many of them, and when the tumult was at the highest, the priest who remained above again gave out a hymn as if to drown it.

It was a frightful sight to behold innocent young creatures, in the gay morning of existence, thus seized upon, horror-struck, and rendered feeble and enervated for ever. One young girl, apparently not more than fourteen, was supported in the arms of another some years older; her face was pale as death; her eyes wide open, and perfectly devoid of meaning; her chin and bosom wet with slaver; she had every appearance of idiotism. I saw a priest approach her, he took her delicate hand. "Jesus is with her! Bless the Lord!" he said, and passed on.

Did the men of America value their women as men ought to value their wives and daughters, would such scenes be permitted among them?

It is hardly necessary to say, that all who obeyed the call to place themselves on the " anxious benches " were women, and by far the greater number, very young women. The congregation was, in general, extremely well-dressed, and the smartest and most fashionable ladies of the town were there; during the whole revival, the churches and meeting-houses were every day crowded with well-dressed people.

It is thus the ladies of Cincinnati amuse themselves: to attend the theatre is forbidden; to play cards is unlawful; but they work hard in their families, and must have some relaxation. For myself, I confess that I think the coarsest comedy ever written would be a less detestable exhibition for the eyes of youth and innocence than such a scene.

Chapter Nine

Schools — Climate — Water-melons — Fourth of July — Storms — Pigs — Moving Houses — Mr Flint — Literature

CINCINNATI contains many schools, but of their rank or merit I had very little opportunity of judging; the only one which I visited was kept by Dr Lock, a gentleman who appears to have liberal and enlarged opinions on the subject of female education. Should his system produce practical results proportionably excellent, the ladies of Cincinnati will probably, some years hence, be much improved in their powers of companionship. I attended the annual public exhibition at this school, and perceived, with some surprise, that the higher branches of science were among the studies of the pretty creatures I saw assembled there. One lovely girl of sixteen *took her degree* in mathematics, and another was examined in moral philosophy. They blushed so sweetly, and looked so beautifully puzzled and confounded, that it might have been difficult for an abler judge than I was, to decide how far they merited the diplomas they received.

This method of letting young ladies graduate, and granting them diplomas on quitting the establishment, was quite new to me; at least, I do not remember to have heard of anything similar elsewhere. I should fear that the time allowed to the fair graduates of Cincinnati for the acquirement of these various branches of education, would seldom be sufficient to permit their reaching the eminence in each which their enlightened instructor anticipates. " A quarter's " mathematics, or " two quarters' " political economy, moral philosophy, algebra and quadratic equations, would seldom, I should think, enable the teacher and the scholar, by their joint efforts, to lay in such a stock of these sciences as would stand the wear and tear of half a score of children, and one help.

*   *   *   *   *

Towards the end of May we began to feel that we were in a climate warmer than any we had been accustomed to, and my son suffered severely from the effects of it. A bilious complaint, attended by a frightful degree of fever, seized him, and for some days we feared for his life. The treatment he received was, I have no doubt, judicious, but the quantity of calomel prescribed was enormous. I asked one day how many grains I should prepare, and was told to give half a tea-spoonful. The difference of climate muſt, I imagine, make a difference in the effect of this drug, or the practice of the old and new world could hardly differ so widely as it does in the use of it. Anſtey, speaking of the Bath physicians, says:

> " No one e'er viewed
> Any one of the medical gentlemen ſtewed."

But I can vouch, upon my own experience, that no similar imputation lies against the gentlemen who prescribe large quantities of calomel in America. To give one inſtance in proof of this, when I was afterwards in Montgomery county, near Washington, a physician attended one of our neighbours, and complained that he was himself unwell. " You muſt take care of yourself, doctor " said the patient: " I do so ", he replied; " I took forty grains of calomel yeſterday, and I feel better than I did ". Repeated and violent bleeding was also had recourse to, in the case of my son, and in a few days he was able to leave his room, but he was dreadfully emaciated, and it was many weeks before he recovered his ſtrength.

As the heat of the weather increased, we heard of much sickness around us. The city is full of physicians, and they were all to be seen driving about in their cabs at a very alarming rate. One of these gentlemen told us, that when a medical man intended settling in a new situation, he always, if he knew his business, walked through the ſtreets at night, before he decided. If he saw the dismal twinkle of the watch-light from many windows, he might be sure that disease was busy, and that the " location " might suit him well. Judging by this criterion, Cincinnati was far from healthy; I began to fear for our health, and determined to leave the city; but for a considerable time I found it impossible to procure a dwelling out of it. . There were many boarding-houses in the vicinity, but they were all overflowing with guests. We were advised to avoid, as much as possible, walking out in the heat of the day; but the mornings and evenings were delightful, particularly the former, if taken sufficiently early. For several weeks I was never in bed after four o'clock, and at this hour I almost daily accompanied my " help " to market, where the busy novelty of the scene afforded me much amusement.

Many waggon-loads of enormous water-melons were brought to market every day, and I was sure to see groups of men, women, and children, seated on the pavement round the spot where they were sold, sucking in prodigious quantities of this watery fruit. Their manner of devouring them is extremely unpleasant; the huge fruit is cut into half-a-dozen sections, of about a foot long, and then, dripping as it is with water, applied to the mouth, from either side of which pour copious streams of the fluid, while, ever and anon, a mouthful of the hard black seeds are shot out in all directions, to the great annoyance of all within reach. When I first tasted this fruit, I thought it very vile stuff indeed; but before the end of the season we all learned to like it. When taken with claret and sugar, it makes delicious wine and water.

It is the custom for the gentlemen to go to market at Cincinnati; the smartest men in the place, and those of the " highest standing " do not scruple to leave their beds with the sun six days in the week, and, prepared with a mighty basket, to sally forth in search of meat, butter, eggs, and vegetables. I have continually seen them returning, with their weighty basket on one arm and an enormous ham depending from the other.

And now arrived the 4th of July, that greatest of all American festivals. On the 4th of July, 1776, the declaration of their independence was signed, at the State-house in Philadelphia.

To me the dreary coldness and want of enthusiasm in American manner is one of their greatest defects, and I therefore hailed the demonstrations of general feeling which this day elicits, with real pleasure. On the 4th of July the hearts of the people seem to awaken from a three hundred and sixty-four days' sleep; they appear high-spirited, gay, animated, social, generous, or at least, liberal in expense; and would they but refrain from spitting on that hallowed day, I should say that, on the 4th of July, at least, they appeared to be an amiable people. It is true that the women have but little to do with the pageantry, the splendour, or the gaiety of the day; but, setting this defect aside, it was indeed a glorious sight to behold a jubilee so heartfelt as this; and had they not the bad taste and bad feeling to utter an annual oration, with unvarying abuse of the mother country, to say nothing of the warlike manifesto called the Declaration of Independence, our gracious king himself might look upon the scene and say that it was good; nay, even rejoice, that twelve millions of bustling bodies, at four thousand miles distance from his throne and his altars, should make their own laws, and drink their own tea, after the fashion that pleased them best.

*   *   *   *   *

One source of deep interest to us, in this new clime, was the frequent recurrence of thunder-storms. Those who have only listened to thunder in England, have but a faint idea of the language which the gods speak when they are angry. Thomson's description, however, will do: it is hardly possible that words can better paint the spectacle, or more truly echo to the sound, than his do. The only point he does not reach is the vast blaze of rose-coloured light that ever and anon sets the landscape on fire.*

In reading this celebrated description in America,

and observing how admirably true it was to nature there, I seemed to get a glimpse at a poet's machinery, and to perceive, that in order to produce effect he must give his images more vast than he finds them in nature; but the proportions must be just, and the colouring true. Every thing seems colossal on this great continent; if it rains, if it blows, if it thunders, it is all done *fortissimo :* but I often felt terror yield to wonder and delight; so grand, so glorious were the scenes a storm exhibited. Accidents are certainly more frequent than with us, but not so much so as reasonably to bring terror home to one's bosom every time a mass of lurid clouds is seen rolling up against the wind.

* * * * *

It seems hardly fair to quarrel with a place because its staple commodity is not pretty, but I am sure I should have liked Cincinnati much better if the people had not dealt so very largely in hogs. The immense quantity of business done in this line would hardly be believed by those who had not witnessed it. I never saw a newspaper without remarking such advertisements as the following:

" Wanted, immediately, 4,000 fat hogs."

" For sale, 2,000 barrels of prime pork."

But the annoyance came nearer than this; if I determined upon a walk up Main Street, the chances were five hundred to one against my reaching the shady side without brushing by a snout fresh dripping from the kennel; when we had screwed our courage to the enterprise of mounting a certain noble-looking sugar-loaf hill, that promised pure air and a fine view, we found the brook we had to cross, at its foot, red with the stream from a pig slaughter-house; while our noses, instead of meeting " the thyme that loves the green hill's breast ", were greeted by odours that I will not describe, and which I heartily hope my readers cannot imagine; our feet, that on leaving the city had expected to press the flowery sod, literally got entangled in pigs' tails and jaw-bones; and thus the prettiest walk in the neighbourhood was interdicted for ever.

* * * * *

One of the sights to stare at in America is that of houses moving from place to place. We were often amused by watching this exhibition of mechanical skill in the streets. They make no difficulty of moving dwellings from one part of the town to another. Those I saw travelling were all of them frame-houses, that is built wholly of wood, except the chimneys; but it is said that brick buildings are sometimes treated in the same manner. The largest dwelling that I saw in motion was one containing two stories of four rooms each; forty oxen were yoked to it. The first few yards brought down the two stacks of chimneys, but it afterwards went on well. The great difficulties were the first getting it in motion and the stopping exactly in the right place. This locomotive power was extremely convenient to Cincinnati, as the constant improvements going on there made it often desirable to change a wooden dwelling for one of brick; and whenever this happened, we were sure to see the ex-No. 100 of Main Street, or the ex-No. 55 of Second Street, creeping quietly out of town, to take possession of an humble suburban station on the common above it.

* * * * *

The most agreeable acquaintance I made in Cincinnati, and indeed one of the most talented men I ever met, was Mr Flint, the author of several extremely clever volumes, and the editor of the *Western Monthly Review*. His conversational powers are of the highest order; he is the only person I remember to have known with first-rate powers of satire, and even of sarcasm,

73

whose kindness of nature and of manner remained perfectly uninjured. In some of his critical notices there is a strength and keenness second to nothing of the kind I have ever read. He is a warm patriot, and so true-hearted an American, that we could not always be of the same opinion on all the subjects we discussed; but whether it were the force and brilliancy of his language, his genuine and manly sincerity of feeling, or his bland and gentleman-like manner that beguiled me, I know not, but certainly he is the only American I ever listened to, whose unqualified praise of his country did not appear to me somewhat overstrained and ridiculous.

On one occasion, but not at the house of Mr Flint, I passed an evening in company with a gentleman, said to be a scholar, and a man of reading; he was also what is called a *serious* gentleman, and he appeared to have pleasure in feeling that his claim to distinction was acknowledged in both capacities. There was a very amiable *serious* lady in the company, to whom he seemed to trust for the development of his celestial pretensions, and to me he did the honour of addressing most of his terrestrial superiority. The difference between us was, that when he spoke to her, he spoke as to a being who, if not his equal, was at least deserving high distinction; and he gave her smiles, such as Michael might have vouchsafed to Eve. To me he spoke as Paul to the offending Jews; he did not, indeed, shake his raiment at me, but he used his pocket-handkerchief so as to answer the purpose; and if every sentence did not end with " I am clean ", pronounced by his lips, his tone, his look, his action, fully supplied the deficiency.

Our poor Lord Byron, as may be supposed, was the bull's-eye against which every dart in his black little quiver was aimed. I had never heard any serious gentleman talk of Lord Byron at full length before, and I listened attentively. It was evident that the noble passages which are graven on the hearts of the genuine lovers of poetry had altogether escaped the serious gentleman's attention; and it was equally evident that he knew by rote all those that they wish the mighty master had never written. I told him so, and I shall not soon forget the look he gave me.

Of other authors his knowledge was very imperfect, but his criticisms very amusing. Of Pope, he said: " He is so entirely gone by, that in *our* country it is considered quite fustian to speak of him."

But I persevered, and named *The Rape of the Lock* as evincing some little talent, and being in a tone that might still hope for admittance in the drawing-room; but, on the mention of this poem, the serious gentleman became almost as strongly agitated as when he talked of *Don Juan;* and I was unfeignedly at a loss to comprehend the nature of his feelings, till he muttered, with an indignant shake of the handkerchief: " The very title!"

At the name of Dryden he smiled, and the smile spoke as plainly as a smile could speak " How the old woman twaddles!"

" We only know Dryden by quotations, madam, and these, indeed, are found only in books that have long since had their day."

" And Shakspeare, sir ?"

" Shakspeare, madam, is obscene, and, thank God, we are sufficiently advanced to have found it out! If we must have the abomination of stage plays, let them at least be marked by the refinement of the age in which we live."

This was certainly being *au courant du jour*.

Of Massinger he knew nothing. Of Ford he had never heard. Gray had had his day. Prior he had never read, but understood he was a very childish writer. Chaucer and Spenser he tied in a couple, and dismissed by saying, that he thought it was neither more nor less than affectation to talk of authors who wrote in a tongue no longer intelligible.

This was the most literary conversation I was ever present at in Cincinnati.[1]

In truth, there are many reasons which render a very general diffusion of literature impossible in America. I can scarcely class the universal reading of newspapers as an exception to this remark; if I could, my statement would be exactly the reverse, and I should say that America beat the world in letters. The fact is, that throughout all ranks of society, from the successful merchant, which is the highest, to the domestic serving man, which is the lowest, they are all too actively employed to read, except at such broken moments as may suffice for a peep at a newspaper. It is for this reason, I presume, that every American newspaper is more or less a magazine, wherein the merchant may scan, while he holds out his hand for an invoice, " Stanzas by Mrs Hemans ",or a garbled extract from Moore's *Life of Byron*; the lawyer may study his brief faithfully, and yet contrive to pick up the valuable dictum of some American critic, that " Bulwer's novels are decidedly superior to Sir Walter Scott's "; nay, even the auctioneer may find time, as he bustles to the tub, or his tribune, to support his pretensions to polite learning, by glancing his quick eye over the columns, and reading that " Miss Mitford's descriptions are indescribable ".* If you buy a yard of ribbon, the shopkeeper lays down his newspaper, perhaps two or three, to measure it. I have seen a brewer's drayman perched on the shaft of his dray and reading one newspaper, while another was tucked under his arm; and I once went into the cottage of a country shoemaker, of the name of Harris, where I saw a newspaper half

[1] The pleasant, easy, unpretending talk on all subjects, which I enjoyed in Mr Flint's family, was an exception to every thing else I met at Cincinnati.

full of "original" poetry, directed to Madison F. Harris. To be sure of the fact, I asked the man if his name were Madison. "Yes, madam, Madison Franklin Harris is my name." The last and the lyre divided his time, I fear too equally, for he looked pale and poor.

This, I presume, is what is meant by the general diffusion of knowledge, so boasted of in the United States; such as it is, the diffusion of it is general enough, certainly; but I greatly doubt its being advantageous to the population.

The only reading men I met with were those who made letters their profession; and of these, there were some who would hold a higher rank in the great republic (not of America, but of letters) did they write for persons less given to the study of magazines and newspapers; and they might hold a higher rank still, did they write for the few and not for the many.[1] I was always drawing a parallel, perhaps a childish one, between the external and internal deficiency of polish and of elegance in the native volumes of the country.[2] Their compositions had not that condensation of thought, or that elaborate finish, the which consciousness of writing for the scholar and the man of taste is calculated to give; nor have their dirty blue paper and slovenly types the polished elegance that fits a volume for the hand or the eye of the fastidious epicure in in literary enjoyment. The first book I bought in America was *The Chronicles of the Canongate*. On asking the price, I was agreeably surprised to hear a

---

[1] That the compositions of Dr Chaning are a brilliant exception to this remark need hardly be stated; except by the occasional (and rare) use of a few words not familiar to us in the sense in which he employs them, his writings may stand a comparison with almost any in the English language.

[2] I must make an exception in favour of the *American Quarterly Review*. To the eye of the body it is in all respects exactly the same thing as the English *Quarterly Review*.

dollar and a half named, being about one sixth of what I used to pay for its fellows in England; but on opening the grim pages, it was long before I could again call them cheap. To be sure, the pleasure of a bright well-printed page ought to be quite lost sight of in the glowing, galloping, bewitching course that the imagination sets out upon with a new Waverley novel; and so it was with me till I felt the want of it; and then I am almost ashamed to confess how often, in turning the thin dusky pages, my poor earth-born spirit paused in its pleasure, to sigh for hot-pressed wire-wove.

Chapter Ten

Removal to the Country—Walk in the Forest—Equality

At length, my wish of obtaining a house in the country was gratified. A very pretty cottage, the residence of a gentleman who was removing into town, for the convenience of his business as a lawyer, was to let, and I immediately secured it. It was situated in a little village about a mile and a half from the town, close to the foot of the hills formerly mentioned as the northern boundary of it. We found ourselves much more comfortable here than in the city. The house was pretty and commodious, our sitting-rooms were cool and airy; we had got rid of the detestable mosquitoes, and we had an ice-house that never failed. Besides all this, we had the pleasure of gathering our tomatoes from our own garden, and receiving our milk from our own cow. Our manner of life was infinitely more to my taste than before; it gave us all the privileges of rusticity, which are fully as incompatible with the residence in a little town of Western America as with a residence in London. We lived on terms of primeval intimacy with our cow; for if we lay down on our lawn,

78

she did not scruple to take a sniff at the book we were reading, but then she gave us her own sweet breath in return. The verge of the cool-looking forest, that rose opposite our windows, was so near, that we often used it as an extra drawing-room, and there was no one to wonder if we went out with no other preparation than our parasols, carrying books and work enough to while away a long summer day in the shade; the meadow that divided us from it was covered with a fine short grass, that continued for a little way under the trees, making a beautiful carpet, while sundry logs and stumps furnished our sofas and tables. But even this was not enough to satisfy us when we first escaped from the city, and we determined upon having a day's enjoyment of the wildest forest scenery we could find. So we packed up books, albums, pencils, and sandwiches; and, despite a burning sun, dragged up a hill so steep, that we sometimes fancied we could rest ourselves against it by only leaning forward a little. In panting and in groaning we reached the top, hoping to be refreshed by the purest breath of heaven; but to have tasted the breath of heaven we must have climbed yet farther, even to the tops of the trees themselves, for we soon found that the air beneath them stirred not, nor ever had stirred, as it seemed to us, since first it settled there, so heavily did it weigh upon our lungs.

Still we were determined to enjoy ourselves, and forward we went, crunching knee-deep through aboriginal leaves, hoping to reach some spot less perfectly airtight than our landing-place. Wearied with the fruitless search, we decided on reposing awhile on the trunk of a fallen tree; being all considerably exhausted, the idea of sitting down on this tempting log was conceived and executed simultaneously by the whole party, and the whole party sunk together through its treacherous surface into a mass of rotten rubbish, that had formed part of the pith and marrow of the eternal forest a hundred years before.

We were by no means the only sufferers by the accident; frogs, lizards, locusts, kattiedids, beetles, and hornets, had the whole of their various tenements disturbed, and testified their displeasure very naturally by annoying us as much as possible in return: we were bit, we were stung, we were scratched; and when, at last, we succeeded in raising ourselves from the venerable ruin, we presented as woful a spectacle as can well be imagined. We shook our (not ambrosial) garments, and panting with heat, stings, and vexation, moved a few paces from the scene of our misfortune, and again sat down; but this time it was upon the solid earth.

We had no sooner begun to " chew the cud " of the bitter fancy that had beguiled us to these mountain solitudes, than a new annoyance assailed us. A cloud of mosquitoes gathered round, and while each sharp proboscis sucked our blood, they teased us with their humming chorus, till we lost all patience, and started again on our feet, pretty firmly resolved never to try the *al fresco* joys of an American forest again. The sun was now in its meridian splendour, but our homeward path was short, and down hill; so again packing up our preparations for felicity, we started homeward, or, more properly speaking, we started; for in looking for an agreeable spot in this dungeon-forest, we had advanced so far from the verge of the hill, that we had lost all trace of the precise spot where we had entered it. Nothing was to be seen but multitudes of tall, slender, melancholy stems, as like as peas, and standing within a foot of each other. The ground, as far as the eye could reach (which certainly was not far), was covered with an unvaried bed of dry leaves; no trace, no track, no trail, as Mr Cooper would call it, gave us a hint which way to turn; and having paused for a moment to meditate, we remembered that chance must decide for us at last, so we set forward, in no very good mood, to encounter new misfortunes. We walked about a quarter of a mile, and coming to a steep descent, we thought ourselves extremely fortunate, and began to scramble down, nothing doubting that it was the same we had scrambled up. In truth, nothing could be more like; but, alas! things that are alike are not the same; when we had slipped and stumbled down to the edge of the wood, and were able to look beyond it, we saw no pretty cottage with the shadow of its beautiful acacias coming forward to meet us: all was different; and, what was worse, all was distant from the spot where we had hoped to be. We had come down the opposite side of the ridge, and had now to win our weary way a distance of three miles round its base. I believe we shall none of us ever forget that walk. The bright, glowing, furnace-like heat of the atmosphere seems to scorch as I recall it. It was painful to tread, it was painful to breathe, it was painful to look round; every object glowed with the reflection of the fierce tyrant that glared upon us from above.

We got home alive, which agreeably surprised us; and when our parched tongues again found power of utterance, we promised each other faithfully never to propose any more parties of pleasure in the grim stove-like forests of Ohio.

We were now in daily expectation of the arrival of Mr T.; but day after day, and week after week passed by, till we began to fear some untoward circumstance might delay his coming till the spring. At last, when we had almost ceased to look out for him, on the road which led from the town, he arrived, late at night, by that which leads across the country from Pittsburgh. The pleasure we felt at seeing him was greatly increased by his bringing with him our eldest son, which was a happiness we had not hoped for. Our walks and our drives now became doubly interesting. The young men, fresh from a public school, found America so totally unlike all the nations with which their reading had made them acquainted, that it was indeed a new world to them. Had they visited Greece or Rome, they would have encountered objects with whose images their minds had been long acquainted; or had they travelled to France or Italy they would have seen only what daily conversation had already rendered familiar; but at our public schools America (except perhaps as to her geographical position) is hardly better known than Fairy Land; and the American character has not been much more deeply studied than that of the Anthropophagi; all, therefore, was new, and everything amusing.

The extraordinary familiarity of our poor neighbours startled us at first, and we hardly knew how to receive their uncouth advances, or what was expected of us in return; however, it sometimes produced very laughable scenes. Upon one occasion, two of my children set off upon an exploring walk up the hills; they were absent rather longer than we expected, and the rest of our party determined upon going out to meet them; we knew the direction they had taken, but thought it would be as well to inquire at a little public-house at the bottom of the hill, if such a pair had been seen to pass. A woman, whose appearance more resembled a Covent Garden market-woman than anything else I can remember, came out and answered my question with the most jovial good humour in the affirmative, and prepared to join us in our search. Her look, her voice, her manner, were so exceedingly coarse and vehement, that she almost frightened me; she passed her arm within mine, and to the inexpressible amusement of my young people, she dragged me on, talking and questioning me without ceasing. She lived but a short distance from us, and I am sure intended to be a very good neighbour; but her violent intimacy made me dread to pass her door; my children, including my sons, she always addressed by their Christian names, excepting when she substituted the word " honey ": this familiarity of address, however, I afterwards found was universal throughout all ranks in the United States.

My general appellation amongst my neighbours was " the English old woman ", but in mentioning each other they constantly employed the term " lady "; and they evidently had a pleasure in using it, for I repeatedly observed, that in speaking of a neighbour, instead of saying Mrs Such-a-one, they described her as " the lady over the way what takes in washing ", or as " that there lady, out by the gully, what is making dip-candles ". Mr Trollope was as constantly called " the old man ", while draymen, butchers' boys, and the labourers on the canal, were invariably denominated " them gentlemen "; nay, we once saw one of the most gentleman-like men in Cincinnati introduce a fellow in dirty shirt-sleeves, and all sorts of detestable et cetera, to one of his friends, with this formula, " D——, let me introduce this gentleman to you!"

Our respective titles certainly were not very important; but the eternal shaking hands with these ladies and gentlemen was really an annoyance, and the more so, as the near approach of the gentlemen was always redolent of whiskey and tobacco.

But the point where this republican equality was the most distressing was in the long and frequent visitations that it produced. No one dreams of fastening a door in Western America; I was told that it would be considered as an affront by the whole neighbourhood. I was thus exposed to perpetual, and most vexatious interruptions from people whom I have often never seen, and whose names still oftener were unknown to me.

Those who are native there, and to the manner born, seem to pass over these annoyances with more skill than

I could ever acquire. More than once I have seen some of my acquaintance beset in the same way, without appearing at all distressed by it; they continued their employment or conversation with me, much as if no such interruption had taken place; when the visitor entered, they would say " How do you do ?" and shake hands.

" Tolerable, I thank ye; how be you ?" was the reply.

If it was a female, she took off her hat; if a male, he kept it on, and then taking possession of the first chair in the way, would retain it for an hour together, without uttering another word; at length, rising abruptly, he would again shake hands, with " Well, now I must be going, I guess", and so take himself off, apparently well contented with their reception.[†]

I could never attain this philosophical composure; I could neither write nor read, and I always fancied I must talk to them. I will give the minutes of a conversation which I once set down after one of these visits, as a specimen of their tone and manner of speaking and thinking. My visitor was a milkman.

" Well now, so you be from the old country ? Ah— you'll see sights here, I guess."

" I hope I shall see many."

" That's a fact. I expect your little place of an island don't grow such dreadful fine corn as you see here ?"

" It grows no corn at all, sir."[1]

" Possible! no wonder, then, that we reads such awful stories of your poor people being starved to death."

" We have wheat, however."

" Ay, for your rich folks, but I calculate the poor seldom gets a belly-full."

" You have certainly much greater abundance here."

" I expect so. Why they do say, that if a poor body

[1] *Corn* always means Indian corn, or maize.

contrives to be smart enough to scrape together a few dollars, that your King George always comes down upon 'em, and takes it all away. Don't he ?"

" I do not remember hearing of such a transaction."

" I guess they be pretty close about it. Your papers ben't like ourn, I reckon ? Now we says and prints iust what we likes."

" You spend a good deal of time reading the news-papers."[1]

" And I'd like you to tell me how we can spend it better. How should freemen spend their time, but looking after their government, and watching that them fellers as we gives offices to, doos their duty, and give themselves no airs ?"

" But I sometimes think, sir, that your fences might be in more thorough repair, and your roads in better order, if less time was spent in politics."

" The Lord! to see how little you knows of a free country! Why, what's the smoothness of a road, put against the freedom of a free-born American ? And what does a broken zigzag signify, comparable to knowing that the men what we have been pleased to send up to Congress, speaks handsome and straight, as we chooses they should ?"[2]

---

[1] Here, again, I fear I must allow that the ten years which have passed over us have been sufficient to destroy the characteristic and national poignancy of this description. If the reading-rooms of the rich throughout the Union have during this period increased their collections of European literature, the beer houses of England have in a tenfold ratio multiplied their half-penny newspapers—nor can the presses of the republic any longer consider themselves as distinguished by the licence boasted of by my friend the milkman, of " printing just what they likes ". Indeed, if recent reports be true, this doubtful blessing has crossed the Atlantic, and abides now solely and wholly in Great Britain.

[2] This too, is now, at least, as much English as American. Having imported so largely before the introduction of steam, what may we not expect after it? Some projectors go so far as to predict that in the course of time, or perhaps, when the hoped-for establishment of balloons is fully organised, we shall have a President sent over by way of an experiment.

" It is from a sense of duty, then, that you all go to the liquor store to read the papers ? "

" To be sure it is, and he'd be no true-born American as didn't. I don't say that the father of a family should always be after liquor, but I do say that I'd rather have my son drunk three times in a week, than not look after the affairs of his country."

*　　　*　　　*　　　*　　　*

Our autumn walks were delightful; the sun ceased to scorch; the want of flowers was no longer peculiar to Ohio; and the trees took a colouring, which in richness, brilliance, and variety, exceeded all description. I think it is the maple, or sugar-tree, that first sprinkles the forest with rich crimson; the beech follows, with all its harmony of golden tints, from pale yellow up to brightest orange. The dog-wood gives almost the purple colour of the mulberry; the chestnut softens all with its frequent mass of delicate brown, and the sturdy oak carries its deep green into the very lap of winter. These tints are too bright for the landscape-painter; the attempt to follow nature in an American autumn scene must be abortive. The colours are in reality extremely brilliant, but the medium through which they are seen increases the effect surprisingly. Of all the points in which America has the advantage of England, the one I felt most sensibly was the clearness and brightness of the atmosphere. By day and by night this exquisite purity of air gives tenfold beauty to every object. I could hardly believe the stars were the same; the Great Bear looked like a constellation of suns; and Jupiter justified all the fine things said of him in those beautiful lines, from I know not what spirited pen, beginning,

> " I look'd on thee, Jove ! till my gaze
> Shrunk, smote by the power of thy blaze." [1]

---

[1] As I have never been able to discover the author of these lines, nor to meet with them any where, except in the Bristol newspaper (the

Autumn Walks

I always remarked that the first silver line of the moon's crescent attracted the eye on the first day, in America, as strongly as it does here on the third. I observed another phenomenon in the crescent moon of that region, the cause of which I less understood. That appearance which Shakspeare describes as " the new moon, with the old moon in her lap ", and which I have heard ingeniously explained as the effect of *earth light*, was less visible there than here.

Cuyp's clearest landscapes have an atmosphere that approaches nearer to that of America than any I remember on canvas; but even Cuyp's *air* cannot reach the lungs, and, therefore, can only give an idea of half the enjoyment; for it makes itself felt as well as seen, and is indeed a constant source of pleasure.

Mercury), from whence I copied them, I think I shall do my readers a benefit if I transcribe them here.

TO THE PLANET JUPITER

I look'd on thee, Jove ! till my gaze
Shrunk, smote by the power of thy blaze,
For in heaven, from the sunset's red throne
To the zenith, thy rival was none.
From thy orb rush'd a torrent of light,
That made the stars dim in thy sight ;
And the half-risen moon seem'd to die,
And leave thee the realm of the sky.
  I look'd on the ocean's broad breast,
The purple was pale in the west ;
But down shot thy long silver spire,
And the waves were like arrows of fire.
I turn'd from the infinite main,
Thy light was the light of the plain ;
'Twas the beacon that blazed on the hill,
Thou wert proud, pure, magnificent, still.

A cloud spread its wing over heaven,
By the light of thy splendour 'twas riven ;
And I saw thy bright front through it shine
Like a god from the depth of his shrine !

Our walks were, however, curtailed in several directions by my old Cincinnati enemies, the pigs; immense droves of them were continually arriving from the country by the road that led to most of our favourite walks; they were often fed and lodged in the prettiest valleys, and worse still, were slaughtered beside the prettiest streams. Another evil threatened us from the same quarter, that was yet heavier. Our cottage had an ample piazza (a luxury almost universal in the country houses of America), which, shaded by a group of acacias, made a delightful sitting-room; from this favourite spot we one day perceived symptoms of building in a field close to it; with much anxiety we hastened to the spot, and asked what building was to be erected there.

" 'Tis to be a slaughter-house for hogs " was the dreadful reply. As there were several gentlemen's houses in the neighbourhood, I asked if such an erection might not be indicted as a nuisance.

" A what ?"

" A nuisance " I repeated, and explained what I meant.

" No, no " was the reply; " that may do very well for your tyrannical country, where a rich man's nose is more thought of than a poor man's mouth; but hogs be profitable produce here, and we be too free for such a law as that, I guess."

During my residence in America little circumstances like the foregoing often recalled to my mind a conversation I once held in France with an old gentleman on the subject of their active police, and its omnipresent gens d'armerie: " *Croyez moi, Madame, il n'y a que ceux, à qui ils ont à faire, qui les trouvent de trop.*" And the old gentleman was right, not only in speaking of France, but of the whole human family, as philosophers call us. The well disposed, those whose own feeling of justice would prevent their annoying others, will never complain of the restraints of the law. All the freedom enjoyed in America, beyond what is enjoyed in England, is enjoyed solely by the disorderly at the expense of the orderly;† and were I a stout knight, either of the sword or of the pen, I would fearlessly throw down my gauntlet, and challenge the whole republic to prove the contrary: but being, as I am, a feeble looker-on, with a needle for my spear, and " I talk " for my device, I must be contented with the power of stating the fact, perfectly certain that I shall be contradicted by one loud shout from Maine to Georgia.

Chapter Eleven

Religion

I HAD often heard it observed, before I visited America, that one of the great blessings of its constitution was the absence of a national religion, the country being thus exonerated from all obligation of supporting the clergy; those only contributing to do so whose principles led them to it. My residence in the country has shown me that a religious tyranny may be exerted very effectually without the aid of the government, in a way much more oppressive than the paying of tithe, and without obtaining any of the salutary decorum, which I presume no one will deny is the result of an established mode of worship.

As it was impossible to remain many weeks in the country without being struck with the strange anomalies produced by its religious system, my early notes contain many observations on the subject; but as nearly the same scenes recurred in every part of the country, I state them here, not as belonging to the West alone, but to the whole Union, the same cause producing the same effect everywhere.

The whole people appear to be divided into an almost

endless variety of religious factions, and I was told, that to be well received in society, it was necessary to declare yourself as belonging to some one of these. Let your acknowledged belief be what it may, you are said to be *not a Christian*, unless you attach yourself to a particular congregation.[†] Besides the broad and well-known distinctions of Episcopalian, Roman Catholic, Presbyterian, Calvinist, Baptist, Quaker, Swedenborgian, Universalist, Dunker, etc., etc., etc., there are innumerable others springing out of these, each of which assumes a church government of its own; of this, the most intriguing and factious individual is invariably the head; and in order, as it should seem, to show a reason for this separation, each congregation invests itself with some queer variety of external observance that has the melancholy effect of exposing *all* religious ceremonies to contempt.

It is impossible, in witnessing all these unseemly vagaries, not to recognise the advantages of an established church as a sort of head-quarters for quiet unpresuming Christians, who are contented to serve faithfully, without insisting upon having each a little separate banner, embroidered with a device of his own imagining.

The Roman Catholics alone appear exempt from the fury of division and sub-division that has seized every other persuasion. Having the Pope for their common head, regulates, I presume, their movements, and prevents the outrageous display of individual whim, which every other sect is permitted.

I had the pleasure of being introduced to the Roman Catholic bishop of Cincinnati, and have never known in any country a priest of a character and bearing more truly apostolic. He was an American, but I should never have discovered it from his pronunciation or manner. He received his education partly in England, and partly in France. His manners were highly polished; his piety active and sincere, and infinitely more mild and tolerant than that of the factious sectarians who form the great majority of the American priesthood.

I believe I am sufficiently tolerant; but this does not prevent my seeing that the object of all religious observances is better obtained, when the government of the church is confided to the wisdom and experience of the most venerated among the people, than when it is placed in the hands of every tinker and tailor who chooses to claim a share in it. Nor is this the only evil attending the want of a national religion, supported by the state. As there is no legal and fixed provision for the clergy, it is hardly surprising that their services are confined to those who can pay them. The vehement expressions of insane or hypocritical zeal, such as were exhibited during " the revival ", can but ill atone for the want of village worship, any more than the eternal talk of the admirable and unequalled government can atone for the continual contempt of social order. Church and state hobble along, side by side, notwithstanding their boasted independence. Almost every man you meet will tell you, that he is occupied in labours most abundant for the good of his country; and almost every woman will tell you, that besides those things that are within (her house), she has coming upon her daily the care of all the churches. Yet spite of this universal attention to the government, its laws are half asleep; and spite of the old women and their Dorcas societies, atheism is awake and thriving.

In the smaller cities and towns, prayer-meetings take the place of almost all other amusements; but as the thinly scattered population of most villages can give no parties, and pay no priests, they contrive to marry, christen, and bury, without them. A stranger taking up his residence in any city of America, must think the natives the most religious people upon earth; but if

chance lead him among her western villages, he
will rarely find either churches or chapels, prayer or
preacher; except, indeed, at that most terrific saturnalia,
" a camp-meeting ". I was much struck with the answer
of a poor woman, whom I saw ironing on a Sunday.
" Do you make no difference in your occupations on a
Sunday ?" I said. " I beant a Christian, ma'am; we
have got no opportunity " was the reply. It occurred
to me, that in a country where " all men are equal ", the
government would be guilty of no great crime, did it
so far interfere as to give them all *an opportunity* of
becoming Christians if they wished it. But should the
federal government dare to propose building a church,
and endowing it, in some village that has never heard
" the bringing home of bell and burial ", it is perfectly
certain that not only the sovereign state where such an
abomination was proposed, would rush into the Congress to resent the odious interference, but that all
the other states would join the clamour, and such an
intermeddling administration would run great risk of
impeachment and degradation.

Where there is a church government so constituted as
to deserve human respect, I believe it will always be
found to receive it, even from those who may not assent
to the dogma of its creed; and where such respect
exists, it produces a decorum in manners and language
often found wanting where it does not. Sectarians
will not venture to rhapsodise, nor infidels to scoff, in
the common intercourse of society. Both are injurious
to the cause of rational religion, and to check both
must be advantageous.

It is certainly possible that some of the fanciful
variations upon the ancient creeds of the Christian
Church, with which transatlantic religionists amuse
themselves, might inspire morbid imaginations in
Europe as well as in America; but before they can disturb the solemn harmony *here*, they must prelude by

a defiance, not only to common-sense, but what is
infinitely more appalling, to common usage. They
must at once rank themselves with the low and the
illiterate, for only such prefer the eloquence of the tub
to that of the pulpit. The aristocracy must ever, as a
body,[1] belong to the established church, and it is but a
small proportion of the influential classes, who would
be willing to allow that they do not belong to the
aristocracy. That such feelings influence the pro-
fessions of men, it were ignorance or hypocrisy to
deny; and that nation is wise who knows how to turn
even such feelings into a wholesome stream of popular
influence.

As a specimen of the tone in which religion is mixed
in the ordinary intercourse of society, I will transcribe
the notes I took of a conversation, at which I was
present, at Cincinnati; I wrote them immediately after
the conversation took place.

Dr A.: " I wish, Mrs M., that you would explain to
me what a revival is. I hear it talked of all over the
city, and I know it means something about Jesus Christ
and religion; but that is all I know; will you instruct me
farther ?"

Mrs M.: " I expect, Dr A., that you want to laugh
at me. But that makes no difference; I am firm in my
principles, and I fear no one's laughter."

Dr A.: " Well, but what is a revival ?"

Mrs M.: " It is difficult, very difficult, to make those
see who have no light; to make those understand whose
souls are darkened. A revival means just an elegant
kindling of the spirit; it is brought about to the Lord's
people by the hands of his saints, and it means salvation
in the highest."

Dr A.: " But what is it the people mean by talking of
feeling the revival ? and waiting in spirit for the revival ?
and the ecstasy of the revival ?"

[1] *Vide* recantation and apology in the note to chapter eight.

Mrs M.: " O Doctor! I am afraid that you are too far gone astray to understand all that. It is a glorious assurance, a whispering of the everlasting covenant, it is the bleating of the lamb, it is the welcome of the shepherd, it is the essence of love, it is the fulness of glory, it is being in Jesus, it is Jesus being in us, it is taking the Holy Ghost into our bosoms, it is sitting ourselves down by God, it is being called to the high places, it is eating and drinking and sleeping in the Lord, it is becoming a lion in the faith, it is being lowly and meek, and kissing the hand that smites, it is being mighty and powerful, and scorning reproof, it is——"

Dr A.: " Thank you, Mrs M., I feel quite satisfied; and I think I understand a revival now almost as well as you do yourself."

Mrs A.: " My! Where can you have learnt all that stuff, Mrs M. ?"

Mrs M.: " How benighted you are! From the Holy Book, from the Word of the Lord, from the Holy Ghost and Jesus Christ themselves."

Mrs A.: " It does seem so droll to me, to hear you talk of ' the Word of the Lord '. Why, I have been brought up to look upon the Bible as nothing better than an old newspaper."

Mrs O.: " Surely, you only say this for the sake of hearing what Mrs M. will say in return—you do not mean it ?"

Mrs A.: " La, yes! to be sure I do."

Dr A.: " I profess that I by no means wish my wife to read all she might find there. What says the Colonel, Mrs M. ?"

Mrs M.: " As to that, I never stop to ask him. I tell him every day that I believe in Father, Son, and Holy Ghost, and that it is his duty to believe in them too; and then my conscience is clear, and I don't care what he believes. Really, I have no notion of one's husband interfering in such matters."

Dr A.: " You are quite right. I am sure I give my wife leave to believe just what she likes: but she is a good woman, and does not abuse the liberty; for she believes nothing."

It was not once, nor twice, nor thrice, but many many times, during my residence in America, that I was present when subjects which custom as well as principle had taught me to consider as fitter for the closet than the tea-table, were thus lightly discussed. I hardly know whether I was more startled at first hearing, in little dainty namby-pamby tones, a profession of atheism over a tea-cup, or at having my attention called from a Johnny cake to a rhapsody on election and the second birth.

But, notwithstanding this revolting licence, persecution exists to a degree unknown, I believe, in our well-ordered land since the days of Cromwell. I had the following anecdote from a gentleman perfectly well acquainted with the circumstances: A tailor sold a suit of clothes to a sailor a few moments before he sailed, which was on a Sunday morning. The corporation of New York prosecuted the tailor, and he was convicted, and sentenced to a fine greatly beyond his means to pay. Mr F., a lawyer of New York, defended him with much eloquence, but in vain. His powerful speech, however, was not without effect; for it raised him such a host of Presbyterian enemies as sufficed to destroy his practice. Nor was this all: his nephew was at the time preparing for the bar, and soon after the above circumstance occurred, his certificates were presented, and refused, with this declaration, that " no man of the name and family of F. should be admitted ". I have met this young man in society; he is a person of very considerable talent; and being thus cruelly robbed of his profession, has become the editor of a newspaper.

Chapter Twelve

Peasantry, compared to that of England—Early Marriages —Charity—Independence and Equality—Cottage Prayer-Meeting

Mohawk, as our little village was called, gave us an excellent opportunity of comparing the peasants of the United States with those of England, and of judging the average degree of comfort enjoyed by each. I believe Ohio gives as fair a specimen as any part of the Union; if they have the roughness and inconveniences of a new state to contend with, they have higher wages and cheaper provisions; if I err in supposing it a mean state in point of comfort, it certainly is not in taking too low a standard.

Mechanics, if good workmen, are certain of employment and good wages, rather higher than with us; the average wages of a labourer throughout the Union is ten dollars a month, with lodging, boarding, washing, and mending; if he lives at his own expense he has a dollar a day. It appears to me that the necessaries of life, that is to say, meat, bread, butter, tea, and coffee (not to mention whiskey), are within the reach of every sober, industrious, and healthy man who chooses to have them; and yet I think that an English peasant, with the same qualifications, would, in coming to the United States, change for the worse. He would find wages somewhat higher, and provisions in Western America considerably lower; but this statement, true as it is, can lead to nothing but delusion if taken apart from other facts, fully as certain, and not less important but which require more detail in describing, and which perhaps cannot be fully comprehended, except by an eye-witness. The American poor are accustomed to eat meat three times a day; I never inquired into the habits of any cottagers in Western America where this was not the case. I found afterwards in Maryland, Pennsylvania, and other parts of the country, where the price of meat was higher, that it was used with more economy; yet still a much larger portion of the weekly income is thus expended than with us. Ardent spirits, though lamentably cheap,[1] still cost something, and the use of them among the men, with more or less of discretion, according to the character, is universal. Tobacco also grows at their doors, and is not taxed; yet this too costs something, and the air of heaven is not in more general use among the men of America than chewing tobacco. I am not now pointing out the evils of dram-drinking; but it is evident that where this practice prevails universally, and often to the most frightful excess, the consequence must be, that the money spent to obtain the dram is less than the money lost by the time consumed in drinking it. Long, disabling, and expensive fits of sickness are incontestably more frequent in every part of America than in England, and the sufferers have no aid to look to, but what they have saved, or what they may be enabled to sell. I have never seen misery exceed what I witnessed in an American cottage where disease has entered.

But if the condition of the labourer be not superior to that of the English peasant, that of his wife and daughters is incomparably worse. It is they who are indeed the slaves of the soil. One has but to look at the wife of an American cottager, and ask her age, to be convinced that the life she leads is one of hardship, privation, and labour. It is rare to see a woman in this station who has reached the age of thirty, without losing every trace of youth and beauty. You continually see women with infants on the knee, that you feel sure are their grand-children, till some convincing proof of

---

[1] About a shilling per gallon is the retail price of good whiskey. If bought wholesale, or of inferior quality, it is much cheaper.

the contrary is displayed. Even the young girls, though often with lovely features, look pale, thin, and haggard. I do not remember to have seen in any single instance among the poor, a specimen of the plump, rosy, laughing physiognomy so common among our cottage girls. The horror of domestic service, which the reality of slavery, and the fable of equality, have generated, excludes the young women from that sure and most comfortable resource of decent English girls; and the consequence is, that with a most irreverent freedom of manner to the parents, the daughters are, to the full extent of the word, domestic slaves. This condition, which no periodical merry-making, no village *fête*, ever occurs to cheer, is only changed for the still sadder burthens of a teeming wife. They marry very young; in fact, in no rank of life do you meet with young women in that delightful period of existence between childhood and marriage, wherein, if only tolerably well spent, so much useful information is gained, and the character takes a sufficient degree of firmness to support with dignity the more important parts of wife and mother. The slender childish thing, without vigour of mind or body, is made to stem a sea of troubles that dims her young eye and makes her cheek grow pale, even before nature has given it the last beautiful finish of the full-grown woman.

" We shall get along " is the answer in full for all that can be said in way of advice to a boy and girl, who take it into their heads to go before a magistrate and " get married ". They do get along, till sickness overtakes them, by means perhaps of borrowing a kettle from one and a teapot from another; but intemperance, idleness, or sickness, will, in one week, plunge those who are even getting along well, into utter destitution; and where this happens, they are completely without resource.

The absence of poor-laws is, without doubt, a

blessing to the country, but they have not that natural and reasonable dependence on the richer classes which, in countries differently constituted, may so well supply their place. I suppose there is less alms-giving in America than in any other Christian country on the face of the globe. It is not in the temper of the people either to give or to receive.*

I extract the following pompous passage from a Washington paper of February, 1829 (a season of uncommon severity and distress), which, I think, justifies my observation: " Among the liberal evidences of sympathy for the suffering poor of this city, two have come to our knowledge which deserve to be especially noticed: the one a donation by the President of the United States to the committee of the ward in which he resides of fifty dollars; the other the donation by a few of the officers of the war department to the Howard and Dorcas Societies, of seventy-two dollars." When such mention is made of a gift of about nine pounds sterling from the sovereign magistrate of the United States, and of thirteen pounds sterling as a contribution from one of the state departments, the inference is pretty obvious, that the sufferings of the destitute in America are not liberally relieved by individual charity.

I had not been three days at Mohawk Cottage, before a pair of ragged children came to ask for medicine for a sick mother; and when it was given to them, the eldest produced a handful of cents, and desired to know what he was to pay. The superfluous milk of our cow was sought after eagerly, but every new-comer always proposed to pay for it. When they found out that " the English old woman " did not sell any thing, I am persuaded they by no means liked her the better for it; but they seemed to think, that if she were a fool it was no reason they should be so too, and accordingly the borrowing, as they called it, became very constant, but always in a form that showed their dignity and freedom. One woman sent to borrow a pound of cheese; another half a pound of coffee; and more than once an intimation accompanied the milk-jug, that the milk must be fresh, and unskimmed: on one occasion the messenger refused milk, and said "Mother only wanted a little cream for her coffee."

I could never teach them to believe, during above a year that I lived at this house, that I would not sell the old clothes of the family; and so pertinacious were they in bargain-making, that often, when I had given them the articles which they wanted to purchase, they would say: " Well, I expect I shall have to do a turn of work for this; you may send for me when you want me." But as I never did ask for the turn of work, and as this formula was constantly repeated, I began to suspect that it was spoken solely to avoid uttering that most un-American phrase, " I thank you."

There was one man whose progress in wealth I watched with much interest and pleasure. When I first became his neighbour, himself, his wife, and four children, were living in one room, with plenty of beef-steaks and onions for breakfast, dinner, and supper; but with very few other comforts. He was one of the finest men I ever saw, full of natural intelligence and activity of mind and body, but he could neither read nor write. He drank but little whiskey, and but rarely chewed tobacco, and was therefore more free from that plague-spot of spitting, which rendered male colloquy so difficult to endure. He worked for us frequently, and often used to walk into the drawing-room and seat himself on the sofa, and tell me all his plans. He made an engagement with the proprietor of the wooded hill before mentioned, by which half the wood he could fell was to be his own. His unwearied industry made this a profitable bargain, and from the proceeds he purchased the materials for building a comfortable frame (or wooden) house; he did the work almoſt entirely himself. He then got a job for cutting rails; and as he could cut twice as many in a day as any other man in the neighbourhood, he made a good thing of it. He then let half his pretty house, which was admirably conſtruĉted, with an ample portico, that kept it always cool. His next ſtep was contraĉting for the building of a wooden bridge; and when I left Mohawk, he had fitted up his half of the building as a hotel and grocery ſtore; and I have no doubt that every sun that sets sees him a richer man than when it rose. He hopes to make his son a lawyer; and I have little doubt that he will live to see him sit in Congress. When this time arrives, the wood-cutter's son will rank with any other member of Congress, not of courtesy, but of right; and the idea that his origin is a dis-advantage, will never occur to the imagination of the moſt exalted of his fellow-citizens.

This is the only feature in American society that I recognise as indicative of the equality they profess. Any man's son may become the equal of any other man's son; and the consciousness of this is certainly a spur to exertion: on the other hand, it is also a spur to that coarse familiarity, untempered by any shadow of respeĉt, which is assumed by the grosseſt and the lowest in their intercourse with the higheſt and moſt refined. This is a positive evil; and, I think, more than balances its advantages.

And here again it may be observed, that the theory of equality may be very daintily discussed by English gentlemen in a London dining-room, when the servant, having placed a fresh bottle of cool wine on the table, respeĉtfully shuts the door, and leaves them to their walnuts and their wisdom; but it will be found less palatable when it presents itself in the shape of a hard greasy paw, and is claimed in accents that breathe less of freedom than of onions and whiskey. Strong, indeed, must be the love of equality in an English breast, if it can survive a tour through the Union.

There was one house in the village which was remarkable from its wretchedness. It had an air of *in*decent poverty about it, which long prevented my attempting an entrance; but at length, upon being told that I could get chickens and eggs there whenever I wanted them, I determined upon venturing. The door being opened to my knock, I very nearly abandoned my almost blunted purpose; I never beheld such a den of filth and misery; a woman, the very image of dirt and disease, held a squalid imp of a baby on her hip-bone, while she kneaded her dough with her right fist only. A great lanky girl, of twelve years old, was sitting on a barrel, knawing a corn-cob. When I made known my business, the woman answered: " No, not I; I got no chickens to sell nor eggs neither, but my son will, plenty, I expect. Here, Nick " (bawling at the bottom of a ladder,) " here's an old woman that wants chickens." Half a moment brought Nick to the bottom of the ladder, and I found my merchant was one of a ragged crew, whom I had been used to observe in my daily walk playing marbles in the dust, and swearing lustily; he looked about ten years old.

" Have you chickens to sell, my boy ?"

" Yes, and eggs too, more nor what you'll buy."

Having inquired price, condition, and so on, I recollected that I had been used to give the same price at market, the feathers plucked, and the chickens prepared for the table; and I told him that he ought not to charge the same.

" Oh, for that, I expect I can fix 'em as well as ever them was what you got in market."

" You fix them!"

" Yes, to be sure; why not ?"

" I thought you were too fond of marbles."

He gave me a keen glance, and said: " You

don't know I.—When will you be wanting the chickens ?"

He brought them at the time directed, extremely well " fixed ", and I often dealt with him afterwards. When I paid him, he always thrust his hand into his breeches pocket, which I presume, as being *the keep*, was fortified more strongly than the dilapidated outworks, and drew from thence rather more dollars, half-dollars, levies, and fips, than his dirty little hand could well hold. My curiosity was excited; and, though I felt an involuntary disgust towards the young Jew, I repeatedly conversed with him.

" You are very rich, Nick " I said to him one day, on his making an ostentatious display of change, as he called it; he sneered with a most unchildish expression of countenance, and replied: " I guess 'twould be a bad job for I if that was all I'd got to show."

I asked him how he managed his business. He told me that he bought eggs by the hundred, and lean chickens by the score, from the waggons that passed their door on the way to market; that he fatted the latter in coops he had made himself, and could easily double their price, and that his eggs answered well too, when he sold them out by the dozen.

" And do you give the money to your mother ?"

" I expect not " was the answer, with another sharp glance of his ugly blue eyes.

" What do you do with it, Nick ?"

His look said plainly, What is that to you ? but he only answered, quaintly enough: " I takes care of it."

How Nick got his first dollar is very doubtful (I was told that when he entered the village store, the person serving always called in another pair of eyes); but having obtained it, the spirit, activity, and industry, with which he caused it to increase and multiply, would have been delightful in one of Miss Edgeworth's dear little, clean, bright-looking boys, who would have carried all he got to his mother; but in Nick it was detestable. No human feeling seemed to warm his young heart, not even the love of self-indulgence; for he was not only ragged and dirty, but looked considerably more than half-starved, and I doubt not his dinners and suppers half fed his fat chickens.

I by no means give this history of Nick, the chicken-merchant, as an anecdote characteristic in all respects of America: the only part of the story which is so is the independence of the little man; and is one instance out of a thousand, of the hard, dry, calculating character that is the result of it. Probably Nick will be very rich; perhaps he will be President. I once got so heartily scolded for saying that I did not think all American citizens were equally eligible to that office, that I shall never again venture to doubt it.

Another of our cottage acquaintance was a market-gardener, from whom we frequently bought vegetables; from the wife of this man we one day received a very civil invitation to " please to come and pass the evening with them in prayer." The novelty of the circumstance, and its great dissimilarity to the ways and manners of our own country, induced me to accept the invitation, and also to record the visit here.

We were received with great attention, and a place was assigned us on one of the benches that surrounded the little parlour. Several persons, looking like mechanics and their wives, were present; every one sat in profound silence, and with that quiet subdued air, that serious people assume on entering a church. At length, a long, black, grim-looking man entered; his dress, the cut of his hair, and his whole appearance, strongly recalled the idea of one of Cromwell's fanatics. He stepped solemnly into the middle of the room, and took a chair that stood there, but not to sit upon it; he turned the back towards him, on which he placed his hands, and stoutly uttering a sound between a hem and

a cough, he deposited freely on either side of him a
considerable portion of masticated tobacco. He then
began to preach. His text was " Live in hope ", and
he continued to expound it for two hours, in a drawling,
nasal tone, with no other respite than what he allowed
himself for expectoration. If I say that he repeated
the words of his text a hundred times, I think I shall
not exceed the truth, for that allows more than a minute
for each repetition, and in fact the whole discourse
was made up of it. The various tones in which he
uttered it might have served as a lesson on emphasis;
as a question—in accents of triumph—in accents of
despair—of pity—of threatening—of authority—of
doubt—of hope—of faith. Having exhausted every
imaginable variety of tone, he abruptly said: " Let us
pray ", and twisting his chair round, knelt before it.
Every one knelt before the seat they had occupied,
and listened for another half-hour to a rant of miserable,
low, familiar jargon, that he presumed to *improviser*
to his Maker as a prayer. In this, however, the
cottage apostle only followed the example set by every
preacher throughout the Union, excepting those of the
Episcopalian and Catholic congregations; *they* only do
not deem themselves privileged to address the Deity in
strains of crude and unweighed importunity. These
ranters may sometimes be very much in earnest, but
surely the least we can say of it is, that they

" Praise their God amiss."

I inquired afterwards of a friend, well acquainted with
such matters, how the grim preacher of " Hope " got
paid for his labours, and he told me that the trade was
an excellent one, for that many a gude wife bestowed
more than a tithe of what her gude man trusted to her
keeping, in rewarding the zeal of these self-chosen
apostles. These sable ministers walk from house to
house, or if the distance be considerable, ride on a com-

fortable ambling nag. They are not only as empty as wind, but resemble it in other particulars; for they blow where they lift, and no man knoweth whence they come, nor whither they go. When they see a house that promises comfortable lodging and entertainment, they enter there, and say to the good woman of the house, " Sifter, shall I pray with you ?" If the answer be favourable, and it is seldom otherwise, he inftals himself and his horse till after breakfaft the next morning. The beft meat, drink, and lodging are his, while he ftays, and he seldom departs without some little contribution in money for the support of the crucified and suffering church. Is it not ftrange that "the moft intelligent people in the world " should prefer such a religion as this, to a form eftablished by the wisdom and piety of the ablest and best among the erring sons of men, solemnly sanctioned by the nation's law, and rendered sacred by the use of their fathers ?

It would be well for all reasoners on the social syftem to observe fteadily, and with an eye obscured by no beam of prejudice, the result of the experiment that is making on the other side of the Atlantic. If I miftake not, they might learn there, better than by any abftract speculation, what are the points on which the magistrates of a great people should dictate to them, and on what points they should be left freely to their own guidance. I sincerely believe that if a fire-worshipper, or an Indian Brahmin, were to come to the United States, prepared to preach and pray in English, he would not be long without a " very respectable congregation ".

The influence of a religion sanctioned by the government, could in no country, in the nineteenth century, interfere with the speculations of a philosopher in his closet, but it might, and muft, fteady the weak and wavering opinions of the multitude. There is something really pitiable in the effect produced by the want of this rudder oar. I knew a family where one was a Methodist, one a Presbyterian, and a third a Baptist: and another, where one was a Quaker, one a declared Atheist, and another an Universalist. These are all females, and all moving in the best society that America affords; but one and all of them as incapable of reasoning on things past, present, and to come, as the infants they nourish, yet one and all of them perfectly fit to move steadily and usefully in a path marked out for them. But I shall be called an itinerant preacher myself if I pursue this theme.[1]

As I have not the magic power of my admirable friend, Miss Mitford, to give grace and interest to the humblest rustic details, I must not venture to linger among the cottages that surrounded us; but before I

---

[1] Since this chapter was written, I have sometimes been led to doubt whether the national and *authorised* indifference in matters of religious belief, which I deprecated in the United States, may not be productive of less moral evil than the *unauthorised* individual secessions from the national worship which I have witnessed in England.

The Methodist, Presbyterian, Baptist, Quaker, Atheist, and Universalist ladies mentioned in the text, acted, one and all of them, upon a universally recognised and received national principle—that each had a right to choose a creed and mode of worship for herself. There was no rebellion in it against paternal, or any other authority; no domestic disunion followed; and the disapprobation with which so loose, unstable, and unscriptural a system may be contemplated, can only be directed against the short-sighted legislation which originated this rope of sand.

No violation of filial respect and duty, no social schism, no renegade turning from the venerable church, which for ages had regulated and cherished the piety of their forefathers, attends this republican indulgence for fancy religions. But widely different is the spectacle presented here, when similar licence is assumed. When every young lady claims a right to be her own bishop, and every parent, who ventures to doubt the lawfulness of her calling, is liable to hear himself doomed to eternal perdition by the voice of his child, the matter assumes a different aspect—as different, indeed, as the act of wantonly pulling down York Minster, and using for the deed the rails of its own altar, from that of thoughtlessly chipping the stones in a quarry, from whence, if skill and will were not wanting, another Minster might be reared.

quit them I must record the pleasing recollection of one or two neighbours of more companionable rank, from whom I received so much friendly attention, and such unfailing kindness, in all my little domestic embarrassments that I shall never recall the memory of Mohawk, without paying an affectionate tribute to these far distant friends. I wish it were within the range of hope, that I might see them again in my own country, and repay, in part, the obligations I owe them.

Chapter Thirteen

Theatre—Fine Arts—Delicacy—Shaking Quakers—Big-Bone Lick—Visit of the President

THE theatre at Cincinnati is small, and not very brilliant in decoration, but in the absence of every other amusement our young men frequently attended it, and in the bright clear nights of autumn and winter, the mile and a half of distance was not enough to prevent the less enterprising members of the family from some-times accompanying them. The great inducement to this was the excellent acting of Mr and Mrs Alexander Drake,[1] the managers. Nothing could be more distinct than their line of acting, but the great versatility of their powers enabled them often to appear together. Her cast was the highest walk of tragedy, and his the broadest comedy; but yet, as Goldsmith says of his sister heroines, I have known them change characters for a whole evening together, and have wept with him and laughed with her, as it was their will and pleasure to ordain. I think in his comedy he was superior to any actor I ever saw in the same parts, except Emery. Alexander Drake's comedy was like that of the French, who never appear to be acting at all; he was himself

[1] Mr Drake was an Englishman.

the comic being the author aimed at depicting. Let him speak whose words he would, from Shakspeare to Colman, it was impossible not to feel that half the fun was his own; he had, too, in a very high degree, the power that Fawcett possessed of drawing tears by a sudden touch of natural feeling. His comic songs might have set the gravity of the judges and bishops together at defiance. Liston is great, but Alexander Drake was greater.

Mrs Drake, formerly Miss Denny, greatly resembles Miss O'Neill; a proof of this is, that Mr Kean, who had heard of the resemblance, arrived at New York late in the evening, and having repaired to the theatre, saw her for the first time across the stage, and immediately exclaimed: "That's Miss Denny." Her voice, too, has the same rich and touching tones, and is superior in power. Her talent is decidedly first-rate. Deep and genuine feeling, correct judgment, and the most perfect good taste, distinguish her play in every character. Her last act of Belvidera is superior in tragic effect to any thing I ever saw on the stage, the one great exception to all comparison, Mrs Siddons, being set aside.

It was painful to see these excellent performers playing to a miserable house, not a third full, and the audience probably not including half a dozen persons who would prefer their playing to that of the vilest strollers. In proof of this, I saw them, as managers, give place to paltry third-rate actors from London, who would immediately draw crowded houses, and be overwhelmed with applause.

Poor Drake died just before we left Ohio, and his wife, who, besides her merit as an actress, is a most estimable and amiable woman, is left with a large family. I have little, or rather no doubt, of her being able to obtain an excellent engagement, in London, but her having property in several of the Western theatres will, I fear, detain her in a neighbourhood where she is neither understood nor appreciated. She told me many very excellent professional anecdotes collected during her residence in the West; one of these particularly amused me as a specimen of Western idiom. A lady who professed a great admiration for Mrs Drake had obtained her permission to be present upon one occasion at her theatrical toilet. She was dressing for some character in which she was to stab herself, and her dagger was lying on the table. The visitor took it up, and examining it with much emotion, exclaimed: "What! do you really jab this into yourself sevagarous?"

We also saw the great American star, Mr Forrest. What he may become I will not pretend to prophesy; but when I saw him play Hamlet at Cincinnati, not even Mrs Drake's sweet Ophelia could keep me beyond the third act. It is true that I have seen Kemble, Macready, Kean, Young, C. Kemble, Cook, and Talma play Hamlet, and I might not, perhaps, be a very fair judge of this young actor's merits; but I was greatly amused when a gentleman, who asked my opinion of him, told me, upon hearing it, that he would not advise me to state it freely in America, "for they would not bear it."

The theatre was really not a bad one, though the very poor receipts rendered it impossible to keep it in high order; but an annoyance infinitely greater than decorations indifferently clean, was the style and manner of the audience. Men came into the lower tier of boxes without their coats; and I have seen shirt sleeves tucked up to the shoulder; the spitting was incessant, and the mixed smell of onions and whiskey was enough to make one feel even the Drakes' acting dearly bought by the obligation of enduring its accompaniments.[1]

[1] I have had the pleasure of being told by a variety of American travellers, whom I have met in England, France, and Germany, that since the publication of this statement, this annoyance at the theatres, not only at Cincinnati, but throughout all the cities of the Union, has been greatly lessened.

The bearing and attitudes of the men are perfectly indescribable; the heels thrown higher than the head, the entire rear of the person presented to the audience, the whole length supported on the benches, are among the varieties that these exquisite posture-masters exhibit. The noises, too, were perpetual, and of the most unpleasant kind; the applause is expressed by cries and thumping with the feet, instead of clapping; and when a patriotic fit seized them, and *Yankee Doodle* was called for, every man seemed to think his reputation as a citizen depended on the noise he made.

Two very indifferent figurantes, probably from the Ambigue Comique, or la Gaieté, made their appearance at Cincinnati while we were there; and had Mercury stepped down, and danced a *pas seul* upon earth, his godship could not have produced a more violent sensation. But wonder and admiration were by no means the only feelings excited; horror and dismay were produced in at least an equal degree. No one, I believe, doubted their being admirable dancers, but every one agreed that the morals of the Western world would never recover the shock. When I was asked if I had ever seen any thing so dreadful before, I was embarrassed how to answer; for the young women had been exceedingly careful, both in their dress and in their dancing, to meet the taste of the people; but had it been Virginie in her most transparent attire, or Taglioni in her most remarkable pirouette, they could not have been more reprobated.* The ladies altogether forsook the theatre; the gentlemen muttered under their breath, and turned their heads aside when the subject was mentioned; the clergy denounced them from the pulpit; and if they were named at the meetings of the saints, it was to show how deep the horror such a theme could produce. I could not but ask myself if virtue were a plant, thriving under one form in one country, and flourishing under a different one in another? If these

Western Americans are right, then how dreadfully wrong are we! It is really a very puzzling subject.

But this was not the only point on which I found my notions of right and wrong utterly confounded; hardly a day passed in which I did not discover that something or other that I had been taught to consider lawful as eating, was held in abhorrence by those around me; many words to which I had never heard an objectionable meaning attached, were totally interdicted, and the strangest paraphrastic sentences substituted. I confess it struck me, that notwithstanding a general stiffness of manner, which I think must exceed that of the Scribes and Pharisees, the Americans have imaginations that kindle with alarming facility. I could give many anecdotes to prove this, but will content myself with a few.

A young German gentleman of perfectly good manners, once came to me greatly chagrined at having offended one of the principal families in the neighbourhood, by having pronounced the word *corset* before the ladies of it. An old female friend had kindly overcome her own feelings so far as to mention to him the cause of the coolness he had remarked, and strongly advised his making an apology. He told me that he was perfectly well disposed to do so, but felt himself greatly at a loss how to word it.

An English lady who had long kept a fashionable boarding-school in one of the Atlantic cities, told me that one of her earliest cares with every new-comer, was the endeavour to substitute real delicacy for this affected precision of manner; among many anecdotes she told me one of a young lady about fourteen, who on entering the receiving room, where she only expected to see a lady who had inquired for her, and finding a young man with her, put her hands before her eyes, and ran out of the room again, screaming " A man! a man! a man!"

On another occasion, one of the young ladies in going

up stairs to the drawing-room, unfortunately met a boy of fourteen coming down, and her feelings were so violently agitated, that she stopped, panting and sobbing, nor would pass on till the boy had swung himself up on the upper banisters, to leave the passage free.

At Cincinnati there is a garden where the people go to eat ices, and to look at roses. For the preservation of the flowers, there is placed at the end of one of the walks a sign-post sort of daub, representing a Swiss peasant girl, holding in her hand a scroll, requesting that the roses might not be gathered. Unhappily for the artist, or for the proprietor, or for both, the petticoat of this figure was so short as to show her ankles. The ladies saw, and shuddered; and it was formally intimated to the proprietor, that if he wished for the patronage of the ladies of Cincinnati, he must have the petticoat of this figure lengthened. The affrighted purveyor of ices sent off an express for the artist and his paint pot. He came, but unluckily not provided with any colour that would match the petticoat; the necessity, however, was too urgent for delay, and a flounce of blue was added to the petticoat of red, giving bright and shining evidence before all men, of the immaculate delicacy of the Cincinnati ladies.

I confess I was sometimes tempted to suspect that this ultra-refinement was not very deep-seated. It often appeared to me like the consciousness of grossness, that wanted a veil; but the veil was never gracefully adjusted. Occasionally, indeed, the very same persons who appeared ready to faint at the idea of a statue would utter some unaccountable sally that was quite startling, and which made me feel that the indelicacy of which we were accused had its limits. The following anecdote is hardly fit to tell, but it explains what I mean too well to be omitted.

A young married lady, of *high standing* and most fastidious delicacy, who had been brought up at one of the Atlantic seminaries of highest reputation, told me that her house, at the distance of half a mile from a populous city, was unfortunately opposite a mansion of worse than doubtful reputation. " It is abominable ", she said, " to see the people that go there; they ought to be exposed. I and another lady, an intimate friend of mine, did make one of them look foolish enough last summer: she was passing the day with me, and while we were sitting at the window, we saw a young man we both knew ride up there; we went into the garden and watched at the gate for him to come back, and when he did, we both stepped out, and I said to him ' Are you not ashamed, Mr William D——, to ride by my house and back again in that manner ?' I never saw a man look so foolish."

In conversing with ladies on the customs and manners of Europe, I remarked a strong propensity to consider every thing as wrong to which they were not accustomed.[1]

I once mentioned to a young lady that I thought a pic-nic party would be very agreeable, and that I would propose it to some of our friends. She agreed that it would be delightful, but she added: " I fear you will not succeed; we are not used to such sort of things here, and I know it is considered very indelicate for ladies and gentlemen to sit down together on the grass."

I could multiply anecdotes of this nature; but I think these sufficient to give an accurate idea of the tone of manners in this particular, and I trust to justify the observations I have made.

One of the spectacles which produced the greatest astonishment on us all was the republican simplicity of the courts of justice. We had heard that the judges indulged themselves on the bench in those extra-

---

[1] Can this be fairly stated as peculiar to the ladies of America? Most assuredly not, and the observation therefore, as applied peculiarly to them, is either invidious or unmeaning.—PECCAVI !

ordinary attitudes which, doubtless, some peculiarity of the American formation leads them to find the most comfortable. Of this we were determined to judge for ourselves, and accordingly entered the court when it was in full business, with three judges on the bench. The annexed sketch will better describe what we saw than anything I can write.

Our winter passed rapidly away, and pleasantly enough, by the help of frosty walks, a little skating, a visit to Big-Bone Lick, and a visit to the shaking Quakers, a good deal of chess, and a good deal of reading, notwithstanding we were almost in the back woods of Western America.

The excursion to Big-Bone Lick, in Kentucky, and that to the Quaker village, were too fatiguing for females at such a season, but our gentlemen brought us home mammoth bones and shaking Quaker stories in abundance.[1]

These singular people, the shaking Quakers of America, give undeniable proof that communities may exist and prosper, for they have continued for many years to adhere strictly to this manner of life, and have been constantly increasing in wealth. They have formed two or three different societies in distant parts of the Union, all governed by the same general laws, and all uniformly prosperous and flourishing.*

There must be some sound and wholesome principle at work in these establishments to cause their success in every undertaking, and this principle must be a powerful one, for it has to combat much that is absurd, and much that is mischievous.

[1] In one of Miss Sedgwick's excellent novels—*Clarence*, if I mistake not—the authoress introduces a description of one of these communities, embracing many particulars on the justice of which our travellers had no means of forming an opinion. If this description be as correct as those of Miss Sedgwick generally are, *absurdity* is certainly the least of the objections to be urged against them.

The societies are generally composed of about an equal proportion of males and females, many of them being men and their wives; but they are all bound by their laws not to cohabit together. Their religious observances are wholly confined to singing and dancing of the most grotesque kind, and this repeated so constantly as to occupy much time; yet these people become rich and powerful wherever they settle themselves. Whatever they manufacture, whatever their farms produce, is always in the highest repute, and brings the highest price in the market. They receive all strangers with great courtesy, and if they bring an introduction they are lodged and fed for any length of time they choose to stay; they are not asked to join in their labours, but are permitted to do so if they wish it.

The Big-Bone Lick was not visited, and even partially examined, without considerable fatigue.

It appeared from the account of our travellers, that the spot which gives the region its elegant name is a deep bed of blue-clay, tenacious and unsound, so much so as to render it both difficult and dangerous to traverse. The digging it has been found so laborious, that no one has yet hazarded the expense of a complete search into its depths for the gigantic relics so certainly hidden there. The clay has never been moved without finding some of them; and I think it can hardly be doubted that money and perseverance would produce a more perfect specimen of an entire mammoth than we have yet seen.[1]

And now the time arrived that our domestic circle was again to be broken up. Our eldest son was to be entered at Oxford, and it was necessary that his father should accompany him: and, after considerable indecision, it was at length determined that I and my

[1] Since the above was written, an immense skeleton, nearly perfect, has been extracted.

daughters should remain another year with our second son. It was early in February, and our travellers prepared themselves to encounter some sharp gales upon the mountains, though the great severity of the cold appeared to be past. We got buffalo robes and double shoes prepared for them, and they were on the eve of departure when we heard that General Jackson, the newly-elected President, was expected to arrive immediately at Cincinnati, from his residence in the West, and to proceed by steam-boat to Pittsburgh on his way to Washington. This determined them not to fix the day of their departure till they heard of his arrival, and then, if possible, to start in the same boat with him; the decent dignity of a private conveyance not being deemed necessary for the President of the United States.

The day of his arrival was, however, quite uncertain, and we could only determine to have every thing very perfectly in readiness, let it come when it would. This resolution was hardly acted upon when the news reached us that the general had arrived at Louisville, and was expected at Cincinnati in a few hours. All was bustle and hurry at Mohawk Cottage; we quickly despatched our packing business, and this being the first opportunity we had had of witnessing such a demonstration of popular feeling, we all determined to be present at the debarkation of the great man. We accordingly walked to Cincinnati, and secured a favourable station at the landing-place, both for the purpose of seing the first magistrate, and of observing his reception by the people. We had waited but for a few moments when the heavy panting of the steam-engines and then a discharge of cannon told that we were just in time; another moment brought his vessel in sight.

Nothing could be better of its kind than his approach to the shore: the noble steam-boat which conveyed him was flanked on each side by one of nearly equal size and splendour: the roofs of all three were covered by a crowd of men; cannon saluted them from the shore as they passed by, to the distance of a quarter of a mile above the town: there they turned about, and came down the river with a rapid but stately motion, the three vessels so close together as to appear one mighty mass upon the water.

When they arrived opposite the principal landing, they swept gracefully round, and the side vessels separating themselves from the centre, fell a few feet back, permitting her to approach before them with her honoured freight. All this manœuvring was extremely well executed, and really beautiful.

The crowd on the shore awaited her arrival in perfect stillness. When she touched the bank the people on board gave a faint huzza, but it was answered by no note of welcome from the land: this cold silence was certainly not produced by any want of friendly feeling towards the new President; during the whole of the canvassing he had been decidedly the popular candidate at Cincinnati, and for months past we had been accustomed to the cry of " Jackson for ever !" from an overwhelming majority; but enthusiasm is not either the virtue or the vice of America.

More than one private carriage was stationed at the water's edge to await the general's orders, but they were dismissed with the information that he would walk to the hotel. Upon receiving this intimation the silent crowd divided itself in a very orderly manner, leaving a space for him to walk through them. He did so, uncovered, though the distance was considerable, and the weather very cold; but he alone (with the exception of a few European gentlemen who were present) was without a hat. He wore his grey hair carelessly, but not ungracefully arranged, and, spite of his harsh gaunt features, he looks like a gentleman and a soldier. He was in deep mourning, having very recently lost his wife; they were said to have been very happy together, and I was pained by hearing a voice near me exclaim, as he approached the spot where I stood: " There goes Jackson; where is his wife ?"   Another sharp voice, at a little distance, cried: "Adams for ever!"   And these sounds were all I heard to break the silence.*

"They manage these matters better " in the East, I have no doubt, but as yet I was still in the West, and still inclined to think that, however meritorious the American character may be, it is not amiable.

Mr T. and his sons joined the group of citizens who waited upon him to the hotel, and were presented to the President in form; that is, they shook hands with him.   Learning that he intended to remain a few hours there, or more properly, that it would be a few hours before the steam-boat would be ready to proceed, Mr T. secured berths on board, and returned, to take a hasty dinner with us.   At the hour appointed by the Captain, Mr T. and his son accompanied the general on board; and by subsequent letters I learnt that they had conversed a good deal with him, and were pleased by his conversation and manners, but deeply disgusted by the brutal familiarity to which they saw him exposed at every place on their progress at which they stopped; I am tempted to quote one passage, as sufficiently descriptive of the manner, which so painfully grated against their European feelings.

" There was not a hulking boy from a keel-boat who was not introduced to the President, unless, indeed, as was the case with some, they introduced themselves; for instance, I was at his elbow when a greasy fellow accosted him thus:

" ' General Jackson, I guess ?'   The general bowed assent.

" ' Why, they told me you was dead.'

" ' No! . Providence has hitherto preserved my life.'
" ' And is your wife alive too ?'

" The general, apparently much hurt, signified the contrary, upon which the courtier concluded his harangue by saying ' Ay, I thought it was the one or the t'other of ye.' "

Chapter Fourteen

American Spring—Controversy between Messrs Owen and Campbell—Public Ball—Separation of the Sexes—American Freedom—Execution

THE American spring is by no means so agreeable as the American autumn; both move with faltering step and slow; but this lingering pace, which is delicious in autumn, is most tormenting in the spring. In the one case you are about to part with a friend, who is becoming more gentle and agreeable at every step, and such steps can hardly be made too slowly; but in the other, you are making your escape from a dreary cavern, where you have been shut up with black frost and biting blasts, and where your best consolation was being smoke-dried.

But, upon second thoughts, I believe it would be more correct, instead of complaining of the slow pace of the American spring, to declare that they have no spring at all. The beautiful autumn often lingers on till Christmas, after which winter can be trifled with no longer, and generally keeps a stubborn hold through the months which we call spring, when he suddenly turns his back, and summer takes his place.

The inconceivable uncertainty of the climate is, however, such, that I will not venture to state about what time this change takes place; for it is certain, that let me name what time I would, it would be easy for any weather journaliser to prove me wrong, by quoting that the thermometer was at 100 at a period which my statement included in the winter; or 50, long after I made the summer commence.

The climate of England is called uncertain; but it can never, I think, be so described by any who have experienced that of the United States. A gentleman, on whose accuracy I could depend, told me he had repeatedly known the thermometer vary above 40 degrees in the space of twelve hours. This most unpleasant caprice of the temperature is, I conceive, one cause of the unhealthiness of the climate.

At length, however, after shivering and shaking till we were tired of it, and having been half ruined in fire-wood, (which, by the way, is nearly as dear as at Paris, and dearer in many parts of the Union), the summer burst upon us full blown, and the ice-house, the piazza, and the jalousies, were again in full requisition.

It was in the early summer of this year (1829) that Cincinnati offered a spectacle unprecedented, I believe, in any age or country. Mr Owen, of Lanark, of New Harmony, of Texas, well known to the world by all or either of these additions, had challenged the whole religious public of the United States to discuss with him publicly the truth or falsehood of all the religions that had ever been propagated on the face of the earth; stating further that he undertook to prove that they were all equally false, and nearly equally mischievous. This most appalling challenge was conveyed to the world through the medium of New Orleans newspapers, and for some time it remained unanswered; at length the Reverend Alexander Campbell, from Bethany (not of Judæa, but of Kentucky), proclaimed, through the same medium, that he was ready to take up the gauntlet. The place fixed for this extraordinary discussion was Cincinnati; the time, the second Monday in May, 1829, being about a year from the time the challenge was accepted; thus giving the disputants time to prepare themselves.*

Mr Owen's preparation, however, could only have been such as those who run may read; for, during the interval, he traversed great part of North America, crossed the Atlantic twice, visited England, Scotland, Mexico, Texas, and I know not how many places besides.

Mr Campbell, I was told, passed this period very differently, being engaged in reading, with great research and perseverance, all the theological works within his reach. But whatever confidence the learning and piety of Mr Campbell might have inspired in his friends, or in the Cincinnati Christians in general, it was not, as it appeared, sufficient to induce Mr Wilson, the Presbyterian minister of the largest church in the town, to permit the display of them within its walls. This refusal was greatly reprobated, and much regretted, as the curiosity to hear the discussion was very general, and no other edifice offered so much accommodation.

A Methodist meeting-house, large enough to contain a thousand persons, was at last chosen; a small stage was arranged round the pulpit, large enough to accommodate the disputants and their stenographers; the pulpit itself was, throughout the whole time, occupied by the aged father of Mr Campbell, whose flowing white hair, and venerable countenance, constantly expressive of the deepest attention, and the most profound interest, made him a very striking figure in the group. Another platform was raised in a conspicuous part of the building, on which were seated seven gentlemen of the city, selected as moderators.

The chapel was equally divided, one half being appropriated to ladies, the other to gentlemen; and the door of entrance reserved for the ladies was carefully guarded by persons appointed to prevent any crowding or difficulty from impeding their approach. I suspect that the ladies were indebted to Mr Owen for this attention; the arrangements respecting them on this occasion were by no means American.

When Mr Owen rose, the building was thronged in every part; the audience, or congregation (I hardly know which to call them), were of the highest rank of citizens, and as large a proportion of best bonnets fluttered there as the " two-horned church " itself could boast.

It was in the profoundest silence, and apparently with the deepest attention, that Mr Owen's opening address was received; and surely it was the most singular one that ever Christian men and women sat to listen to.

When I recollect its object, and the uncompromising manner in which the orator stated his mature conviction that the whole history of the Christian mission was a fraud, and its sacred origin a fable, I cannot but wonder that it was so listened to; yet at the time I felt no such wonder. Never did any one practise the *suaviter in modo* with more powerful effect than Mr Owen. The gentle tone of his voice; his mild, sometimes playful, but never ironical manner; the absence of every vehement or harsh expression; the affectionate interest expressed for " the whole human family "; the air of candour with which he expressed his wish to be convinced he was wrong, if he indeed were so—his kind smile—the mild expression of his eyes—in short, his whole manner, disarmed zeal, and produced a degree of tolerance that those who did not hear him would hardly believe possible.

Half an hour was the time allotted for each haranguer; when this was expired, the moderators were seen to look at their watches. Mr Owen, too, looked at his (without pausing), smiled, shook his head, and said in a parenthesis " a moment's patience ", and continued for nearly another half hour.

Mr Campbell then arose; his person, voice, and manner all greatly in his favour. In his first attack he used the arms which in general have been considered as belonging to the other side of the question. He quizzed Mr Owen most unmercifully; pinched him here for his parallelograms; hit him there for his human perfectibility, and kept the whole audience in a roar of laughter. Mr Owen joined in it most heartily himself, and listened to him throughout with the air of a man who is delighted at the good things he is hearing, and exactly in the cue to enjoy all the other good things that he is sure will follow. Mr Campbell's watch was the only one which reminded us that we had listened to him for half an hour; and having continued speaking for a few minutes after he had looked at it, he sat down with, I should think, the universal admiration of his auditory.

Mr Owen again addressed us; and his first five minutes were occupied in complimenting Mr Campbell with all the strength his exceeding hearty laughter had left him. But then he changed his tone, and said the business was too serious to permit the next half hour to pass so lightly and so pleasantly as the last; and then he read us what he called his twelve fundamental laws of human nature. These twelve laws he has taken so much trouble to circulate to all the nations of the earth, that it must be quite unnecessary to repeat them here. To me they appear twelve truisms, that no man in his senses would ever think of contradicting; but how any one can have conceived that the explanation and defence of these laws could furnish forth occupation for his pen and his voice, through whole years of unwearying declamation, or how he can have dreamed that they could be twisted into a refutation of the Christian religion, is a mystery which I never expect to understand.

From this time Mr Owen intrenched himself behind

his twelve laws, and Mr Campbell, with equal gravity, confined himself to bringing forward the most elaborate theological authorities in evidence of the truth of revealed religion.

Neither appeared to me to answer the other; but to confine themselves to the utterance of what they had uppermost in their own minds when the discussion began. I lamented this on the side of Mr Campbell, as I am persuaded he would have been much more powerful had he trusted more to himself and less to his books. Mr Owen is an extraordinary man, and certainly possessed of talent, but he appears to me so utterly benighted in the mists of his own theories, that he has quite lost the power of looking through them, so as to get a peep at the world as it really exists around him.

At the conclusion of the debate (which lasted for fifteen sittings) Mr Campbell desired the whole assembly to sit down. They obeyed. He then requested all who wished well to Christianity to rise, and a very large majority were in an instant on their legs. He again requested them to be seated, and then desired those who believed not in its doctrines to rise, and a few gentlemen and one lady obeyed. Mr Owen protested against this manœuvre, as he called it, and refused to believe that it afforded any proof of the state of men's minds, or of women's either; declaring, that not only was such a result to be expected, in the present state of things, but that it was the duty of every man who had children to feed, not to hazard the sale of his hogs, or his iron, by a declaration of opinions, which might offend the majority of his customers. It was said, that at the end of the fifteen meetings the numerical amount of the Christians and the infidels of Cincinnati remained exactly what it was when they began.

This was a result that might have been perhaps anticipated; but what was much less to have been expected, neither of the disputants ever appeared to lose their temper. I was told they were much in each other's company, constantly dining together, and on all occasions expressed most cordially their mutual esteem.

All this, I think, could only have happened in America. I am not quite sure that it was very desirable it should have happened anywhere.

In noting the various brilliant events which diversified our residence in the western metropolis, I have omitted to mention the Birthday Ball, as it is called, a festivity which, I believe, has place on the 22nd of February, in every town and city throughout the Union. It is the anniversary of the birth of General Washington, and well deserves to be marked by the Americans as a day of jubilee.

I was really astonished at the *coup d'œil* on entering, for I saw a large room filled with extremely well-dressed company, among whom were many very beautiful girls. The gentlemen also were exceedingly smart; but I had not yet been long enough in Western America not to feel startled at recognising in almost every full-dressed *beau* that passed me, the master or shopman that I had been used to see behind the counter, or lolling at the door of every shop in the city. The fairest and finest *belles* smiled and smirked on them with as much zeal and satisfaction as I ever saw bestowed on an eldest son, and I therefore could feel no doubt of their being considered as of the highest rank. Yet it must not be supposed that there is no distinction of classes; at this same ball I was looking among the many very beautiful girls I saw there for one more beautiful still, with whose lovely face I had been particularly struck at the school examination I have mentioned. I could not find her, and asked a gentleman why the beautiful Miss C—— was not there.

" You do not yet understand our aristocracy " he replied; " the family of Miss C—— are mechanics."

" But the young lady has been educated at the same school as these, whom I see here, and I know her brother has a shop in the town, quite as large, and apparently as prosperous, as those belonging to any of these young men. What is the difference?"

" He is a mechanic: he assists in making the articles he sells; the others call themselves merchants."

The dancing was not quite like, yet not very unlike, what we see at an assize or race ball in a country town. They call their dances cotillions instead of quadrilles, and the figures are called from the orchestra in English, which has a very ludicrous effect on European ears.

The arrangements for the supper were very singular, but eminently characteristic of the country. The gentlemen had a splendid entertainment spread for them in another large room of the hotel, while the poor ladies had each a plate put into their hands, as they pensively promenaded the ball-room during their absence; and shortly afterwards servants appeared bearing trays of sweetmeats, cakes, and creams. The fair creatures then sat down on a row of chairs placed round the walls, and each making a table of her knees, began eating her sweet, but sad and sulky, repast. The effect was extremely comic: their gala-dresses and the decorated room forming a contrast the most unaccountable with their uncomfortable and forlorn condition.

This arrangement was owing neither to economy nor want of a room large enough to accommodate the whole party, but purely because the gentlemen liked it better. This was the answer given me, when my curiosity tempted me to ask why the ladies and gentlemen did not sup together; and this was the answer repeated to me afterwards by a variety of people to whom I put the same question.

I am led to mention this feature of American manners very frequently, not only because it constantly recurs, but because I consider it as being in a great degree the cause of that universal deficiency in good manners and graceful demeanour, both in men and women, which is so remarkable.

Where there is no court, which every where else is the glass wherein the higher orders dress themselves, and which again reflected from them to the classes below, goes far towards polishing, in some degree, a great majority of the population, it is not to be expected that manner should be made so much a study, or should attain an equal degree of elegance; but the deficiency, and the total difference, is greater than this cause alone could account for. The hours of enjoyment are important to human beings every where, and we every where find them preparing to make the most of them. Those who enjoy themselves only in society, whether intellectual or convivial, prepare themselves for it, and such make but a poor figure when forced to be content with the sweets of solitude; while, on the other hand, those to whom retirement affords the greatest pleasure, seldom give or receive much in society. Wherever the highest enjoyment is found by both sexes, in scenes where they meet each other, both will prepare themselves to appear with advantage there. The men will not indulge in the luxury of chewing tobacco, or even of spitting, and the women will contrive to be capable of holding a higher post than that of unwearied tea-makers.

In America, with the exception of dancing, which is almost wholly confined to the unmarried of both sexes, all the enjoyments of the men are found in the absence of the women. They dine, they play cards, they have musical meetings, they have suppers, all in large parties, but all without women. Were it not that such is the custom, it is impossible but that they would have ingenuity enough to find some expedient for sparing the wives and daughters of the opulent the sordid offices of household drudgery, which they almost all perform in their families.   Even in the slave-states, though they may not clear-starch and iron, mix puddings and cakes one half of the day, and watch them baking the other half, still the very highest occupy themselves in their household concerns, in a manner that precludes the possibility of their becoming elegant and enlightened companions.   In Baltimore, Philadelphia, and New York, I met with some exceptions to this; but speaking of the country generally, it is unquestionably true.

Had I not become heartily tired of my prolonged residence in a place I cordially disliked, and which, moreover, I began to fear would not be attended with the favourable results we had anticipated, I should have found an almost inexhaustible source of amusement in the notions and opinions of the people I conversed with; and as it was, I often did enjoy this in a considerable degree.

We received, as I have mentioned, much personal kindness; but this by no means interfered with the national feeling of, I believe, unconquerable dislike, which evidently lives at the bottom of every true American heart against the English.   This shows itself in a thousand little ways, even in the midst of the most kind and friendly intercourse, but often in a manner more comic than offensive.

Sometimes it was thus: " Well, now, I think your government must just be fit to hang themselves for that last war they cooked up; it has been the ruin of you, I expect, for it has just been the making of us."

Then—" Well, I do begin to understand your broken English better than I did; but no wonder I could not make it out very well at first, as you come from London ; for every body knows that London slang is the most dreadful in the world. How queer it is now, that all the people that live in London should put the *h* where it is not, and never will put it where it is."

I was egotistical enough to ask the lady who said this, if she found that I did so.

" No; you do not " was the reply; but she added, with a complacent smile: " It is easy enough to see the pains you take about it; I expect you have heard how we Americans laugh at you all for it, and so you are trying to learn our way of pronouncing."

One lady asked me very gravely, if we had left home in order to get rid of the vermin with which the English of all ranks were afflicted ? " I have heard from un-questionable authority ", she added, " that it is quite impossible to walk through the streets of London with-out having the head filled."

I laughed a little, but spoke not a word. She coloured highly, and said: " There is nothing so easy as to laugh, but truth is truth, laughed at or not."

I must preface the following anecdote by observing, that in America nearly the whole of the insect tribe are classed under the general name of bug; the unfortunate cosmopolite known by that name amongst us is almost the only one not included in this term. A lady abruptly addressed me with " Don't you hate chintzes, Mrs Trollope ?"

" No, indeed " I replied; " I think them very pretty."

" There now! if that is not being English! I reckon you call that loving your country. Well, thank God! we Americans have something better to love our country for than that comes to; we are not obliged to say that we like nasty filthy chintzes to show that we are good patriots."

" Chintzes! what are chintzes ?"

" Possible! do you pretend you don't know what chintzes are ? Why the nasty little stinking blood-suckers that all the beds in London are full of."

I have since been informed that *chinche* is Spanish for bug; but at the time the word suggested only the material of a curtain.

Modesty

Among other instances of that species of modesty so often seen in America, and so unknown to us, I frequently witnessed one, which, while it evinced the delicacy of the ladies, gave opportunity for many lively sallies from the gentlemen. I saw the same sort of thing repeated on different occasions at least a dozen times; *e.g.* a young lady is employed in making a shirt (which it would be a symptom of absolute depravity to name), a gentleman enters, and presently begins the sprightly dialogue with "What are you making, Miss Clarissa?"

"Only a frock for my sister's doll, sir?"

"A frock! not possible. Don't I see that it is not a frock? Come, Miss Clarissa, what is it?"

"'Tis just an apron for one of our negroes, Mr Smith."

"How can you, Miss Clarissa! why is not the two sides joined together? I expect you were better tell me what it is."

"My! why then, Mr Smith, it is just a pillow-case."

"Now that passes, Miss Clarissa! 'Tis a pillow-case for a giant, then. Shall I guess, Miss?"

"Quit, Mr Smith; behave yourself, or I'll certainly be affronted."

Before the conversation arrives at this point, both gentleman and lady are in convulsions of laughter. I once saw a young lady so hard driven by a wit, that to prove she was making a bag, and nothing but a bag, she sewed up the ends before his eyes, showing it triumphantly and exclaiming "There now! what can you say to that?"

One of my friends startled me one day by saying, in an affectionate, but rather compassionate tone, "How will you bear to go back to England to live, and to bring up your children in a country where you know you are considered as no better than the dirt in the streets?"

I begged she would explain.

"Why, you know I would not affront you for any thing; but the fact is, we Americans know rather more than you think for; and certainly, if I was in England, I should not think of associating with any thing but lords. I have always been among the first here, and if I travelled I should like to do the same. I don't mean, I am sure, that I would not come to see you, but you know you are not lords, and therefore I know very well how you are treated in your own country."

I very rarely contradicted statements of this kind, as I found it less trouble, and infinitely more amusing, to let them pass; indeed, had I done otherwise, it would have been of little avail, as among the many conversations I held in America respecting my own country, I do not recollect a single instance in which it was not clear that I knew much less about it than those I conversed with.

On the subject of national glory, I presume I got more than my share of buffeting; for, being a woman, there was no objection to their speaking out. One lady, indeed, who was a great patriot, evinced much delicacy towards me, for upon some one speaking of New Orleans, she interrupted them, saying " I wish you would not talk of New Orleans "; and, turning to me, added with great gentleness, " It must be so painful to your feelings to hear that place mentioned!"*

The immense superiority of the American to the British navy was a constant theme, and to this I always listened, as nearly as possible, in silence. I repeatedly heard it stated (so often, indeed, and from such various quarters, that I think there must be some truth in it) that the American sailors fire with a certainty of slaughter, whereas our shots are sent very nearly at random. "This", said a naval officer of high reputation, " is the blessed effect of your game-laws; your sailors never fire at a mark; whilst our free tars, from their practice in pursuit of game, can any of them split a hair." But the favourite, the constant, the universal sneer that met me every where, was on our old-fashioned attachments to things obsolete. Had they a little wit among them, I am certain they would have given us the cognomen of " My Grandmother, the British ", for that is the tone they take, and it is thus they reconcile themselves to the crude newness of every thing around them.

" I wonder you are not sick of kings, chancellors, and archbishops, and all your fustian of wigs and gowns " said a very clever gentleman to me once, with an affected yawn. " I protest the very sound almost sets me to sleep."

It is amusing to observe how soothing the idea seems, that they are more modern, more advanced than England. Our classic literature, our princely dignities, our noble institutions, are all gone-by relics of the dark ages.

This, and the vastness of their naked territory, make up the flattering unction which is laid upon the soul, as an antidote to the little misgiving which from time to time arises, lest their large country be not of quite so much importance among the nations as a certain paltry old-fashioned little place which they wot of.

I was once sitting with a party of ladies, among whom were one or two young girls, whose curiosity was greater than their patriotism, and they asked me many questions respecting the splendour and extent of London. I was endeavouring to satisfy them by the best description I could give, when we were interrupted by another lady, who exclaimed " Do hold your tongues, girls, about London; if you want to know what a beautiful city is, look at Philadelphia; when Mrs Trollope has been there, I think she will allow that it is better worth talking about than that great overgrown collection of nasty, filthy, dirty streets that they call London."

Once in Ohio, and once in the district of Columbia, I

had an atlas displayed before me, that I might be convinced by the evidence of my own eyes what a very contemptible little country I came from. I shall never forget the gravity with which, on the latter occasion, a gentleman drew out his graduated pencil-case, and showed me, past contradiction, that the whole of the British dominions did not equal in size one of their least important states; nor the air with which, after the demonstration, he placed his feet upon the chimney-piece, considerably higher than his head, and whistled *Yankee Doodle*.

Their glorious institutions, their unequalled freedom, were, of course, not left unsung.

I took some pains to ascertain what they meant by their glorious institutions, and it is with no affectation of ignorance that I profess I never could comprehend the meaning of the phrase, which is, however, on the lip of every American, when he talks of his country. I asked if by their institutions they meant their hospitals and penitentiaries. "Oh no! we mean the glorious institutions which are coeval with the revolution." "Is it ", I asked, "your institution of marriage, which you have made purely a civil and not a religious rite, to be performed by a justice of peace, instead of a clergyman ?"

"Oh no! we speak of our divine political institutions."

Yet still I was in the dark, nor can I guess what they mean, unless they call incessant electioneering, without pause or interval for a single day, for a single hour, of their whole existence, " a glorious institution ".

Their unequalled freedom, I think, I understand better. Their code of common law is built upon ours; and the difference between us is this: in England the laws are acted upon, in America they are not.

I do not speak of the police of the Atlantic cities; I believe it is well arranged: in New York it is celebrated for being so; but out of the range of their influence, the contempt of law is greater than I can venture to state, with any hope of being believed. Trespass, assault, robbery, nay even murder, are often committed without the slightest attempt at legal interference.

During the summer that we passed most delightfully in Maryland, our rambles were often restrained in various directions by the advice of our kind friends, who knew the manners and morals of the country. When we asked the cause, we were told " There is a public-house on that road, and it will not be safe to pass it."

The line of the Chesapeake and Ohio canal passed within a few miles of Mrs S——'s residence. It twice happened during our stay with her, that dead bodies were found partially concealed near it. The circumstance was related as a sort of half-hour's wonder; and when I asked particulars of those who, on one occasion, brought the tale, the reply was " Oh, he was murdered, I expect; or may-be he died of the canal fever; but they say he had marks of being throttled." No inquest was summoned; and certainly no more sensation was produced by the occurrence than if a sheep had been found in the same predicament.

The abundance of food and the scarcity of hanging were also favourite topics, as proving their superiority to England. They are both excellent things, but I do not admit the inference. A wide and most fertile territory, as yet but thinly inhabited, may easily be made to yield abundant food for its population: and where a desperate villain knows that when he has made his town or his village " too hot to hold him ", he has nothing to do but to travel a few miles west, and be sure of finding plenty of beef and whiskey, with no danger that the law shall follow him, it is not extraordinary that executions should be rare.

Once during our residence at Cincinnati, a murderer of uncommon atrocity was taken, tried, convicted, and condemned to death. It had been shown on his trial, that some years before he had murdered a wife and child at New Orleans, but little notice had been taken of it at the time. The crime which had now thrown him into the hands of justice was the recent murder of a second wife, and the chief evidence against him was his own son.

The day of his execution was fixed, and the sensation produced was so great, from the strangeness of the occurrence (no white man having ever been executed at Cincinnati), that persons from sixty miles' distance came to be present at it.

Meanwhile some unco' good people began to start doubts as to the righteousness of hanging a man, and made application to the Governor of the State[1] of Ohio, to commute the sentence into imprisonment. The Governor for some time refused to interfere with the sentence of the tribunal before which he had been tried; but at length, frightened at the unusual situation in which he found himself, he yielded to the importunity of the Presbyterian party who had assailed him, and sent off an order to the sheriff accordingly. But this order was not to reprieve him, but to ask him if he pleased to be reprieved, and sent to the penitentiary instead of being hanged.

The sheriff waited upon the criminal, and made his proposal, and was answered " If any thing could make me agree to it, it would be the hope of living long enough to kill you and my dog of a son: however, I won't agree: you shall have the hanging of me."

The worthy sheriff, to whom the ghastly office of executioner is assigned, said all in his power to persuade him to sign the offered document, but in vain; he obtained nothing but abuse for his efforts.

The day of execution arrived: the place appointed was the side of a hill, the only one cleared of trees near the town; and many hours before the time fixed, we

---

[1] The governors of states have the same power over life and death as is vested, with us, in the Crown.

saw it entirely covered by an immense multitude of men, women, and children. At length the hour arrived, the dismal cart was seen slowly mounting the hill, the noisy throng was hushed into solemn silence: the wretched criminal mounted the scaffold, when again the sheriff asked him to sign his acceptance of the commutation proposed; but he spurned the paper from him, and cried aloud: " Hang me!"

Mid-day was the moment appointed for cutting the rope: the sheriff stood, his watch in one hand, and a knife in the other; the hand was lifted to strike, when the criminal stoutly exclaimed, " I sign " and he was conveyed back to prison, amidst the shouts, laughter, and ribaldry of the mob.

I am not fond of hanging, but there was something in all this that did not look like the decent dignity of wholesome justice.[1]

Chapter Fifteen

Camp-Meeting

IT was in the course of this summer that I found the opportunity I had long wished for, of attending a camp-meeting, and I gladly accepted the invitation of an English lady and gentleman to accompany them in their carriage to the spot where it is held; this was in a wild district on the confines of Indiana.

The prospect of passing a night in the back woods of Indiana was by no means agreeable, but I screwed my

---

[1] It was not till after I had left the United States that the frightful details of Lynch Law reached me. These details are now well known throughout Europe, and must surely be received as a confirmation of the statements made in the foregoing chapter, respecting the insufficiency of the laws, or at least of the manner in which they are enforced, for preventing and punishing crime. Yet these statements are among those which brought upon me the most positive accusations of having falsified facts, and grossly misstated what I saw.

courage to the proper pitch, and set forth determined to see with my own eyes, and hear with my own ears, what a camp-meeting really was. I had heard it said that being at a camp-meeting was like standing at the gate of heaven, and seeing it opened before you; I had heard it said, that being at a camp-meeting was like finding yourself within the gates of hell; in either case there must be something to gratify curiosity, and compensate for the fatigues of a long rumbling ride and a sleepless night.

We reached the ground about an hour before mid-might, and the approach to it was highly picturesque. The spot chosen was the verge of an unbroken forest, where a space of about twenty acres appeared to have been partially cleared for the purpose. Tents of different sizes were pitched very near together in a circle round the cleared space; behind them were ranged an exterior circle of carriages of every description, and at the back of each were fastened the horses which had drawn them thither. Through this triple circle of defence we distinguished numerous fires burning brightly within it; and still more numerous lights flickering from the trees that were left in the enclosure. The moon was in meridian splendour above our heads.

We left the carriage to the care of a servant, who was to prepare a bed in it for Mrs B—— and me, and entered the inner circle. The first glance reminded me of Vauxhall, from the effect of the lights among the trees, and the moving crowd below them; but the second showed a scene totally unlike any thing I had ever witnessed. Four high frames, constructed in the form of altars, were placed at the four corners of the enclosure; on these were supported layers of earth and sod, on which burned immense fires of blazing pine-wood. On one side a rude platform was erected to accommodate the preachers, fifteen of whom attended this meeting, and with very short intervals for necessary refreshment and private devotion, preached in rotation, day and night, from Tuesday to Saturday.

When we arrived the preachers were silent; but we heard issuing from nearly every tent mingled sounds of praying, preaching, singing, and lamentation. The curtains in front of each tent were dropped, and the faint light that gleamed through the white drapery, backed as it was by the dark forest, had a beautiful and mysterious effect, that set the imagination at work; and had the sounds which vibrated around us been less discordant, harsh, and unnatural, I should have enjoyed it; but listening at the corner of a tent, which poured forth more than its proportion of clamour, in a few moments chased every feeling derived from imagination, and furnished realities that could neither be mistaken nor forgotten.

Great numbers of persons were walking about the ground, who appeared like ourselves to be present only as spectators; some of these very unceremoniously contrived to raise the drapery of this tent, at one corner, so as to afford us a perfect view of the interior.

The floor was covered with straw, which round the sides was heaped in masses, that might serve as seats, but which at that moment were used to support the heads and the arms of the close-packed circle of men and women who kneeled on the floor.

Out of about thirty persons thus placed, perhaps half a dozen were men. One of these, a handsome looking youth of eighteen or twenty, kneeled just below the opening through which I looked. His arm was encircling the neck of a young girl who knelt beside him, with her hair hanging dishevelled upon her shoulders, and her features working with the most violent agitation; soon after they both fell forward on the straw, as if unable to endure in any other attitude the burning eloquence of a tall grim figure in black, who, standing erect in the centre, was uttering with incredible vehemence an oration that seemed to hover between praying and preaching; his arms hung stiff and immovable by his side, and he looked like an ill-constructed machine, set in action by a movement so violent, as to threaten its own destruction, so jerkingly, painfully, yet rapidly, did his words tumble out; the kneeling circle ceased not to call, in every variety of tone, on the name of Jesus; accompanied with sobs, groans, and a sort of low howling inexpressibly painful to listen to. But my attention was speedily withdrawn from the preacher, and the circle round him, by a figure which knelt alone at some distance; it was a living image of Scott's Macbriar, as young, as wild, and as terrible. His thin arms, tossed above his head, had forced themselves so far out of the sleeves, that they were bare to the elbow; his large eyes glared frightfully, and he continued to scream without an instant's intermission the word " Glory!" with a violence that seemed to swell every vein to bursting. It was too dreadful to look upon long, and we turned away shuddering.

We made the circuit of the tents, pausing where attention was particularly excited by sounds more vehement than ordinary. We contrived to look into many; all were strewed with straw, and the distorted figures that we saw kneeling, sitting, and lying amongst it, joined to the woful and convulsive cries, gave to each the air of a cell in Bedlam.

One tent was occupied exclusively by negroes. They were all full-dressed, and looked exactly as if they were performing a scene on the stage. One woman wore a dress of pink gauze trimmed with silver lace; another was dressed in pale yellow silk; one or two had splendid turbans; and all wore a profusion of ornaments. The men were in snow white pantaloons, with gay coloured linen jackets. One of these, a youth of coal-black comeliness, was preaching with the most violent gesticulations, frequently springing high from the ground, and clapping his hands over his head. Could our missionary societies have heard the trash he uttered, by way of an address to the Deity, they might perhaps have doubted whether his conversion had much enlightened his mind.

At midnight a horn sounded through the camp, which, we were told, was to call the people from private to public worship; and we presently saw them flocking from all sides to the front of the preachers' stand. Mrs B—— and I contrived to place ourselves with our backs supported against the lower part of this structure, and we were thus enabled to witness the scene which followed, without personal danger. There were about two thousand persons assembled.

One of the preachers began in a low nasal tone, and, like all other Methodist preachers, assured us of the enormous depravity of man as he comes from the hands of his Maker, and of his perfect sanctification after he had wrestled sufficiently with the Lord to get hold of him, *et cetera*. The admiration of the crowd was evinced by almost constant cries of "Amen! Amen!", "Jesus! Jesus!", "Glory! Glory!" and the like. But this comparative tranquillity did not last long; the preacher told them that "this night was the time fixed upon for anxious sinners to wrestle with the Lord"; that he and his brethren "were at hand to help them"; and that such as needed their help were to come forward into "the pen". The phrase forcibly recalled Milton's lines:

> "Blind mouths! that scarce themselves know how to hold
> A sheep-hook, or have learned aught else the least
> That to the faithful herdsman's art belongs!
>
> · · · · · · ·
>
> —But when they list, their lean and flashy songs
> Grate on their scrannel pipes of wretched straw;—
> The hungry sheep look up, and are not fed,
> But swoln with wind, and the rank mist they draw,
> Rot inwardly—and foul contagion spread."

" The pen " was the space immediately below the preacher's stand; we were therefore placed on the edge of it, and were enabled to see and hear all that took place in the very centre of this extraordinary exhibition.

The crowd fell back at the mention of the *pen*, and for some minutes there was a vacant space before us. The preachers came down from their stand, and placed themselves in the midst of it, beginning to sing a hymn, calling upon the penitents to come forth.   As they sang they kept turning themselves round to every part of the crowd, and, by degrees, the voices of the whole multitude joined in chorus.   This was the only moment at which I perceived any thing like the solemn and beautiful effect which I had heard ascribed to this woodland worship.   It is certain that the combined voices of such a multitude heard at dead of night, from the depths of their eternal forests, the many fair young faces turned upward, and looking paler and lovelier as they met the moonbeams, the dark figures of the officials in the middle of the circle, the lurid glare thrown by the altar-fires on the woods beyond, did altogether produce a fine and solemn effect, that I shall not easily forget; but ere I had well enjoyed it, the scene changed, and sublimity gave place to horror and disgust.

The exhortation nearly resembled that which I had heard at " the Revival ", but the result was very different; for, instead of the few hysterical women who had distinguished themselves on that occasion, above a hundred persons, nearly all females, came forward, uttering howlings and groans so terrible that I shall never cease to shudder when I recall them.   They appeared to drag each other forward, and, on the word being given " Let us pray ", they all fell on their knees; but this posture was soon changed for others that permitted greater scope for the convulsive movements of their limbs; and they were soon all lying on the ground in an indescribable confusion of heads and legs. They threw about their limbs with such incessant and violent motion, that I was every instant expecting some serious accident to occur.

But how am I to describe the sounds that proceeded from this strange mass of human beings? I know no words which can convey an idea of it. Hysterical sobbings, convulsive groans, shrieks and screams the most appalling, burst forth on all sides. I felt sick with horror. As if their hoarse and overstrained voices failed to make noise enough, they soon began to clap their hands violently. The scene described by Dante was before me:

> " Quivi sospiri, pianti, ed alti guai
> Risonavan per l' aere
> Orribili favelle
> Parole di dolore, accenti d' ira
> Voci alti e fioche, *e suon di man con elle.*"

Many of these wretched creatures were beautiful young females. The preachers moved about among them, at once exciting and soothing their agonies. I heard the muttered " Sister! dear sister!" I saw the insidious lips approach the cheeks of the unhappy girls; I heard the murmured confessions of the poor victims, and I watched their tormentors, breathing into their ears consolations that tinged the pale cheek with red. Had I been a man, I am sure I should have been guilty of some rash act of interference; nor do I believe that such a scene could have been acted in the presence of Englishmen without instant punishment being inflicted; not to mention the salutary discipline of the treadmill, which, beyond all question, would, in England, have been applied to check so turbulent and so vicious a scene.

After the first wild burst that followed their prostration, the moanings, in many instances, became loudly articulate; and I then experienced a ſtrange vibration between tragic and comic feeling.

A very pretty girl, who was kneeling in the attitude of Canova's Magdalene immediately before us, amongſt an immense quantity of jargon, broke out thus: "Woe! woe to the backsliders! hear it, hear it, Jesus! when I was fifteen my mother died, and I backslided, oh Jesus, I backslided! take me home to my mother, Jesus! take me home to her, for I am weary! Oh John Mitchel! John Mitchel!" and after sobbing piteously behind her raised hands, she lifted her sweet face again, which was as pale as death, and said: "Shall I sit on the sunny bank of salvation with my mother? my own dear mother? oh Jesus, take me home, take me home!"

Who could refuse a tear to this earneſt wish for death in one so young and so lovely? But I saw her, ere I left the ground, with her hand faſt locked, and her head supported by a man who looked very much as Don Juan might, when sent back to earth as too bad for the regions below.

One woman near us continued to "call on the Lord", as it is termed, in the loudeſt possible tone, and without a moment's interval, for the two hours that we kept our dreadful ſtation. She became frightfully hoarse, and her face so red as to make me expeɕt she would burſt a blood-vessel. Among the reſt of her rant, she said: "I will hold faſt to Jesus, I never will let him go; if they take me to hell, I will ſtill hold him faſt, faſt, faſt!"

The ſtunning noise was sometimes varied by the preachers beginning to sing; but the convulsive movements of the poor maniacs only became more violent. At length the atrocious wickedness of this horrible scene increased to a degree of grossness, that drove us from our ſtation: we returned to the carriage at about three o'clock in the morning, and passed the remainder of the night in liſtening to the ever increasing tumult

144

at the pen. To sleep was impossible. At day-break the horn again sounded, to send them to private devotion; and in about an hour afterwards I saw the whole camp as joyously and eagerly employed in preparing and devouring their most substantial breakfasts as if the night had been passed in dancing; and I marked many a fair but pale face, that I recognised as a demoniac of the night, simpering beside a swain, to whom she carefully administered hot coffee and eggs. The preaching saint and the howling sinner seemed alike to relish this mode of recruiting their strength.

After enjoying abundance of strong tea, which proved a delightful restorative after a night so strangely spent, I wandered alone into the forest, and I never remember to have found perfect quiet more delightful.

We soon after left the ground; but before our departure we learnt that a very *satisfactory* collection had been made by the preachers, for Bibles, tracts, and *all other religious purposes*.

Chapter Sixteen

Danger of Rural Excursions—Sickness

It is by no means easy to enjoy the beauties of American scenery in the west, even when you are in a neighbourhood that affords much to admire; at least in doing so, you run considerable risk of injuring your health. Nothing is considered more dangerous than exposure to mid-day heat except exposure to evening damp; and the twilight is so short, that if you set out on an expedition when the fervid heat subsides, you can hardly get half a mile before " sun-down ", as they call it, warns you that you must run or drive home again, as fast as possible, for fear you should get a " chill ".

I believe we braved all this more than any one else in the whole country, and if we had not, we should have left Cincinnati without seeing any thing of the country around it.

Though we kept steadily to our resolution of passing no more sylvan hours in the forests of Ohio, we often spent entire days in Kentucky, tracing the course of a " creek ", or climbing the highest points within our reach, in the hope of catching a glimpse of some distant object. A beautiful reach of the Ohio, or the dark windings of the pretty Licking, were indeed always the most remarkable features in the landscape.

There was one spot, however, so beautiful that we visited it again and again; it was by no means free from mosquitoes; and being on the bank of a stream, with many enormous trees lying on the half-cleared ground around, it was just such a place as we had been told a hundred times was particularly " dangerous "; nevertheless, we dared everything for the sake of dining beside our beautiful rippling stream, and watching the bright sunbeams dancing on the grassy bank, at such a distance from our retreat that they could not heat us. A little below the basin that cooled our wine was a cascade of sufficient dimensions to give us all the music of a waterfall, and all the sparkling brightness of clear water when it is broken again and again by jutting crags.

To sit beside this miniature cascade, and read, or dream away a day, was one of our greatest pleasures.

It was indeed a mortifying fact, that whenever we found out a picturesque nook, where turf, and moss, and deep shade, and a crystal stream, and fallen trees, majestic in their ruin, tempted us to sit down, and be very cool and very happy, we invariably found that that spot lay under the imputation of malaria.

A row upon the Ohio was another of our favourite amusements; but in this, I believe, we were also very singular, for often, when enjoying it, we were shouted at, by the young free-borns on the banks, as if we had been so many monsters.

The only rural amusement in which we ever saw any of the natives engaged was eating strawberries and cream in a pretty garden about three miles from the town: here we actually met three or four carriages; a degree of dissipation that I never witnessed on any other occasion. The strawberries were tolerable strawberries, but the cream was the vilest sky-blue, and the charge half a dollar to each person, which being about the price of half a fat sheep, I thought " pretty considerable much ", if I may be permitted to use an expressive phrase of the country.

We had repeatedly been told, by those who knew the land, that the *second summer* was the great trial to the health of Europeans settled in America; but we had now reached the middle of our second August, and with the exception of the fever one of my sons had suffered from, the summer after our arrival, we had all enjoyed perfect health; but I was now doomed to feel the truth of the above prediction; for before the end of August I fell low before the monster that is for ever stalking through that land of lakes and rivers, breathing fever and death around. It was nine weeks before I left my room, and when I did, I looked more fit to walk into the Potter's Field (as they call the English burying-ground) than any where else.

Long after my general health was pretty well restored, I suffered from the effect of the fever in my limbs, and lay in bed reading, several weeks after I had been pronounced convalescent. Several American novels were brought me. Mr Flint's *Francis Berrian* is excellent; a little wild and romantic, but containing scenes of first-rate interest and pathos. *Hope Leslie*, and *Redwood*, by Miss Sedgwick, an American lady, have both great merit; and I now first read the whole of Mr Cooper's novels. By the time these American studies were completed, I never closed my eyes without seeing myriads of bloody scalps floating round me; long slender figures of Red Indians crept through my dreams with noiseless tread; panthers glared; forests blazed; and whichever way I fled, a light foot, a keen eye, and a long rifle were sure to be on my trail. An additional ounce of calomel hardly sufficed to neutralise the effect of these raw-head and bloody-bones adventures. I was advised to plunge immediately into a course of fashionable novels. It was a great relief to me; but as my head was by no means very clear, I sometimes jumbled strangely together the civilised rogues and assassins of Mr Bulwer, and the wild men, women, and children slayers of Mr Cooper; and, truly, between them, I passed my dreams in very bad company.

Still I could not stand, nor even sit upright. What was I to read next? A happy thought struck me. I determined upon beginning with *Waverley*, and reading through (not for the first time certainly) the whole series. And what a world did I enter upon! The wholesome vigour of every page seemed to communicate itself to my nerves; I ceased to be languid and fretful; and though still a cripple, I certainly enjoyed myself most completely, as long as my treat lasted; but this was a shorter time than any one would believe, who has not found how such volumes melt before the constant reading of a long idle day. When it was over, however, I had the pleasure of finding that I could walk half a dozen yards at a time, and take short airings in an open carriage; and better still, could sleep quietly.

It was no very agreeable conviction which greeted my recovery, that our Cincinnati speculation for my son would in no way answer our expectation; and very soon after, he was again seized with the bilious fever of the country, which terminated in that most distressing of all maladies, an ague. I never witnessed its effects before, and therefore made myself extremely miserable at what those around me considered of no consequence.

I believe this frightful complaint is not immediately

dangerous; but I never can believe that the violent and sudden proſtration of ſtrength, the dreadfully convulsive movements which diſtort the limbs, the livid hue that spreads itself over the complexion, can take place without shaking the seat of health and life. Repeatedly we thought the malady cured, and for a few days the poor sufferer believed himself reſtored to health and ſtrength; but again and again it returned upon him, and he began to give himself up as the victim of ill health. My own health was ſtill very infirm, and it took but little time to decide that we muſt leave Cincinnati. The only impediment to this was, the fear that Mr Trollope, who was to join us in the spring, might have set out, and thus arrive at Cincinnati after we had left it. However, as the time he had talked of leaving England was later in the season, I decided upon running the risk; but the winter had set in with great severity, and the river being frozen, the ſteam-boats could not run; the froſt continued unbroken through the whole of February, and we were almoſt weary of waiting for its departure, which was to be the signal of ours.

The breaking up of the ice on the Licking and Ohio formed a moſt ſtriking spectacle. At night the river presented a solid surface of ice, but in the morning it showed a collection of floating ice-bergs, of every imaginable size and form, whirling againſt each other with frightful violence, and with a noise unlike any sound I remember.

This sight was a very welcome one, as it gave us hopes of immediate departure, but my courage failed, when I heard that one or two ſteam-boats, weary of waiting, meant to ſtart on the morrow. The idea of running againſt these floating islands was really alarming, and I was told by many, that my fears were not without foundation, for that repeated accidents had happened from this cause; and then they talked of the little Miami river, whose mouth we were to pass, sending down masses of ice that might ſtop our progress; in short, we waited patiently and prudently, till the learned in such matters told us that we might ſtart with safety.

Chapter Seventeen

Departure from Cincinnati—Society on Board the Steamboat—Arrival at Wheeling—Bel Esprit

WE quitted Cincinnati the beginning of March, 1830, and I believe there was not one of our party who did not experience a sensation of pleasure in leaving it. We had seen again and again all the queer varieties of its little world; had amused ourselves with its consequence, its taſte, and its ton, till they had ceased to be amusing. Not a hill was left unclimbed, nor a foreſt path unexplored; and, with the exception of two or three individuals, who bore heads and hearts peculiar to no clime, but which are found scattered through the world, as if to keep us every where in good humour with it, we left naught to regret at Cincinnati. The only regret was that we had ever entered it; for we had waſted health, time, and money there.

We got on board the ſteamboat which was to convey us to Wheeling at three o'clock. She was a noble boat, by far the fineſt we had seen. The cabins were above, and the deck passengers, as they are called, were accommodated below. In front of the ladies' cabin was an ample balcony, sheltered by an awning; chairs and sofas were placed there, and even at that early season, nearly all the female passengers passed the whole day there. The name of this splendid vessel was the *Lady Franklin*. By the way, I was often amused by the evident fondness which the Americans show for titles. The wives of their eminent men constantly receive that of "Lady". We heard of Lady Washington, Lady Jackson and many other "ladies". The eternal recurrence of their militia titles is particularly ludicrous, met with, as they are, among the tavern-keepers, market-gardeners, etc. But I think the most remarkable instance which we noticed of this sort of aristocratical longing occurred at Cincinnati. Mr T—— in speaking of a gentleman of the neighbourhood, called him Mr M——. "General M——, sir," observed his companion. "I beg his pardon", rejoined Mr T——, "but I was not aware of his being in the army." "No, sir, not in the army", was the reply, "but he was surveyor-general of the district."

The weather was delightful: all trace of winter had disappeared; and we again found ourselves moving rapidly up the stream, and enjoying all the beauty of the Ohio.

Of the male part of the passengers we saw nothing, excepting at the short silent periods allotted for breakfast, dinner, and supper, at which we were permitted to enter their cabin, and place ourselves at their table.

In the *Lady Franklin* we had decidedly the best of it, for we had our beautiful balcony to sit in. In all respects, indeed, our accommodations were very superior to what we had found in the boat which brought us from New Orleans to Memphis, where we were stowed away in a miserable little chamber close aft, under the cabin, and given to understand by the steward, that it was our duty there to remain "till such time as the bell should ring for meals".

The separation of the sexes, so often mentioned, is no where more remarkable than on board the steamboats. Among the passengers on this occasion we had a gentleman and his wife, who really appeared to suffer from the arrangement. She was an invalid, and he was extremely attentive to her, as far at least as the regulations permitted. When the steward opened the door of communication between the cabins, to permit our approaching the table, her husband was always stationed close to it, to hand her to her place; and when he accompanied her again to the door, he always lingered for a moment or two on the forbidden threshold, nor left his station, till the last female had passed through. Once or twice he ventured, when all but his wife were on the balcony, to sit down beside her for a moment in our cabin, but the instant either of us entered, he started like a guilty thing and vanished.

While mentioning the peculiar arrangements which are thought necessary to the delicacy of the American ladies, or to the comfort of the American gentlemen, I am tempted to allude to a story which I saw in the papers respecting the visits which it was stated Captain Basil Hall persisted in making to his wife and child on board a Mississippi steam-boat, after being informed that doing so was contrary to law. Now I happen to know that neither himself nor Mrs Hall ever entered the ladies' cabin during the whole voyage, as they occupied a state-room which Captain Hall had secured for his party. The veracity of newspaper statements is, perhaps, nowhere quite unimpeachable, but if I am not greatly mistaken, there are more direct falsehoods circulated by the American newspapers than by all the others in the world, and the one great and never-failing source of these voluminous works of imagination is England and the English.

How differently would such a voyage as we were now making be managed on the other side the Atlantic, were such a mode of travelling possible there. Such long calm river excursions would be perfectly delightful, and parties would be perpetually formed to enjoy them. Even were all the parties strangers to each other, the knowledge that they were to eat, drink, and steam away together for a week or fortnight, would induce some thing like a social feeling in any other country.

It is true that the men became sufficiently acquainted to game together, and we were told that the opportunity was considered as so favourable, that no boat left New Orleans without having as cabin passengers one or two gentlemen from that city whose profession it was to drill the fifty-two elements of a pack of cards to profitable duty. This doubtless is an additional reason for the strict exclusion of the ladies from their society. The constant drinking of spirits is another; for though they do not scruple to chew tobacco and to spit incessantly in the presence of women, they generally prefer drinking and gaming in their absence.

I often used to amuse myself with fancying the different scene which such a vessel would display in Europe. The noble length of the gentlemen's cabin would be put into requisition for a dance, while that of the ladies', with their delicious balcony, would be employed for refreshments, instead of sitting down in two long silent melancholy rows, to swallow as much coffee and beef-steak as could be achieved in ten minutes. Then song and music would be heard borne along by the midnight breeze; but on the Ohio, when light failed to show us the bluffs, and the trees, with their images inverted in the stream, we crept into our little cots, listening to the ceaseless churning of the engine, in hopes it would prove a lullaby till morning.

We were three days in reaching Wheeling, where we arrived at last, at two o'clock in the morning, an uncomfortable hour to disembark with a good deal of luggage, as the steam-boat was obliged to go on immediately; but we were instantly supplied with a dray, and in a few moments found ourselves comfortably seated before a good fire, at an hotel near the landing place; our rooms, with fires in them, were immediately ready for us, and refreshments brought, with all that sedulous attention which in this country distinguishes a slave state.[1]   In making this observation, I am very far from intending to advocate the system of slavery; I conceive it to be essentially wrong; but so far as my observation has extended, I think its influence is far less injurious to the manners and morals of the people than the fallacious ideas of equality, which are so fondly cherished by the working classes of the white population in America.   That these ideas are fallacious is obvious, for in point of fact the man possessed of dollars does command the services of the man possessed of no dollars; but these services are given grudgingly, and of necessity, with no appearance of cheerful good-will on the one side, or of kindly interest on the other.   I never failed to mark the difference on entering a slave state. I was immediately comfortable, and at my ease, and felt that the intercourse between me and those who

---

[1] This passage was written during my short stay at Wheeling, and before I had seen any thing of slavery beyond the condition of domestic slaves in one or two well-ordered families.   I permitted the passage, however, to be published as it stood in my MS. because it spoke faithfully the impression received when it was written.   Nay, notwithstanding that the detestation of slavery increased with me, as it must do with all disinterested lookers-on, in proportion to their opportunities of watching its consequences, I still think that when seen as we then saw it its effect will appear less injurious to the country than the false, futile, and preposterous tone assumed by the white population when compelled by necessity to sell their labour in domestic service.

A little reflection, however, will show that this false note itself is in fact generated solely by the existence of slavery.   It is this which renders the idea of domestic service shameful; and had the federal government courage and influence to abolish this iniquitous abuse of power, they would, at the same moment that they righteously did justice to the negro, relieve their country from one of the chief causes of its inferiority in all the graces of civilization ; for it is the struggle of proud but powerless poverty with unprivileged but powerful wealth which stagnates the progress of civilization, as well as of order, in the United States.   Were the sinful and unnatural spectacle of a race degraded by legalized tyranny removed, the gradation of ranks INEVITABLE in the progress of all society would take place naturally, and of necessity, leaving tranquillity and leisure for the progress of refinement.

served me, was profitable to both parties and painful to neither.

It was not till I had leisure for more minute observation that I felt aware of the influence of slavery upon the owners of slaves; when I did, I confess I could not but think that the citizens of the United States had contrived, by their political alchemy, to extract all that was most noxious both in democracy and in slavery, and had poured the strange mixture through every vein of the moral organisation of their country.

Wheeling is in the State of Virginia, and appears to be a flourishing town. It is the point at which most travellers from the West leave the Ohio, to take the stages which travel the mountain road to the Atlantic cities.

It has many manufactories, among others, one for blowing and cutting glass, which we visited. We were told by the workmen that the articles finished there were equal to any in the world; but my eyes refused their assent. The cutting was very good, though by no means equal to what we see in daily use in London; but the chief inferiority is in the material, which is never altogether free from colour. I had observed this also in the glass of the Pittsburgh manufactory, the labour bestowed on it always appearing greater than the glass deserved. They told us also, that they were rapidly improving in the art, and I have no doubt that this was true.

Wheeling has little of beauty to distinguish it, except the ever lovely Ohio, to which we here bade adieu, and a fine bold hill, which rises immediately behind the town. This hill, as well as every other in the neighbourhood, is bored for coal. Their mines are all horizontal. The coal burns well, but with a very black and dirty cinder.

We found the coach, by which we meant to proceed to Little Washington, full, and learnt that we must wait two days before it would again leave the town. Posting was never heard of in the country, and the mail travelled all night, which I did not approve of; we therefore found ourselves compelled to pass two days at the Wheeling hotel.

I know not how this weary interval would have worn away, had it not been for the fortunate circumstance of our meeting with a *bel esprit* among the boarders there. We descended to the common sitting-room (for private parlours there are none) before breakfast the morning after our arrival; several ordinary individuals entered, till the party amounted to eight or nine. Again the door opened, and in swam a female, who had once certainly been handsome, and who, it was equally evident, still thought herself so. She was tall, and well formed, dressed in black, with many gaudy trinkets about her: a scarlet *fichu* relieved the sombre colour of her dress, and a very smart little cap at the back of her head set off an immense quantity of sable hair, which naturally, or artificially, adorned her forehead. A becoming quantity of rouge gave the finishing touch to her figure, which had a degree of pretension about it that immediately attracted our notice. She talked fluently, and without any American restraint, and I began to be greatly puzzled as to who or what she could be; a lady, in the English sense of the word, I was sure she was not, and she was as little like an American female of what they call good standing. A beautiful girl of seventeen entered soon after, and called her " Ma ", and both mother and daughter chattered away, about themselves and their concerns, in a manner that greatly increased my puzzle.

After breakfast, being much in want of amusement, I seated myself by her, and entered into conversation. I found her nothing loath, and in about a minute and a half she put a card into my hand, setting forth that she taught the art of painting upon velvet in all its branches.

She stated to me, with great volubility, that no one but herself and her daughter knew any thing of this invaluable branch of art; but that for twenty-five dollars they were willing to communicate all they knew.

In five minutes more she informed me that she was the author of some of the most cutting satires in the language; and then she presented me a paper, containing a prospectus, as she called it, of a novel, upon an entirely new construction. I was strangely tempted to ask her if it went by steam, but she left me no time to ask any thing, for, continuing the autobiography she had so obligingly begun, she said: " I used to write against all the Adams' faction. I will go up stairs in a moment, and fetch you down my sat-heres against that side. But oh! my dear madam! it is really frightful to think how talent is neglected in this country. Ah! I know what you are going to say, my dear madam, you will tell me that it is not so in yours. I know it! but alas! the Atlantic! However, I really must tell you how I have been treated: not only did I publish the most biting sat-heres against the Adams' faction, but I wrote songs and odes in honour of Jackson; and my daughter, Cordelia, sang a splendid song of my writing, before eight hundred people, entirely and altogether written in his praise; and would you believe it, my dear madam, he has never taken the slightest notice of me, or made me the least remuneration. But you can't suppose I mean to bear it quietly? No! I promise him that is not my way. The novel I have just mentioned to you was begun as a sentimental romance (that perhaps, after all, is my real forte), but after the provocation I received at Washington, I turned it into a sat-hereical novel, and I now call it *Yankee Doodle Court.* By the way, my dear madam, I think if I could make up my mind to cross that terrible Atlantic, I should be pretty well received, after writing *Yankee Doodle Court!*"

I took the opportunity of a slight pause to ask her to

what party she now belonged, since she had forsworn both Adams and Jackson.

" Oh Clay! Clay for ever! he is a real true-hearted republican; the others are neither more nor less than tyrants."*

When next I entered the sitting-room she again addressed me, to deplore the degenerate taste of the age.

" Would you believe it ? I have at this moment a comedy ready for representation; I call it *The Mad Philosopher*. It is really admirable, and its success certain, if I could get it played. I assure you the neglect I meet with amounts perfectly to persecution. But I have found out how to pay them, and to make my own fortune. Sat-here (as she constantly pronounced satire), sat-here is the only weapon that can revenge neglect, and I flatter myself I know how to use it. Do me the favour to look at this."

She then presented me with a tiny pamphlet, whose price, she informed me, was twenty-five cents, which I readily paid to become the possessor of this *chef-d'œuvre*. The composition was pretty nearly such as I antici-pated, excepting that the English language was done to death by her pen still more than by her tongue. The epigraph, which was subscribed " original ", was as follows:

> " Your popularity's on the decline :
>   You had your triumph ! now I'll have mine."

These are rather a favourable specimen of the verses that follow.

In a subsequent conversation she made me acquainted with another talent, informing me that she had played the part of Charlotte, in *Love à la mode*, when General Lafayette honoured the theatre of Cincinnati with his presence.

She now appeared to have run out the catalogue of her accomplishments; and I came to the conclusion that my new acquaintance was a strolling player; but she seemed to guess my thoughts, for she presently added: "It was a Thespian corps that played before the General."

Chapter Eighteen

Departure for the Mountains in the Stage—Scenery of the Alleghany—Haggerstown

THE weather was bleak and disagreeable during the two days we were obliged to remain at Wheeling. I had got heartily tired of my gifted friend; we had walked up every side of the rugged hill, and I set off on my journey towards the mountains with more pleasure than is generally felt in quitting a pillow before daylight, for a cold corner in a rumbling stagecoach.

This was the first time we had got into an American stage, though we had traversed above two thousand miles of the country, and we had all the satisfaction in it, which could be derived from the conviction that we were travelling in a foreign land. This vehicle had no step, and we climbed into it by a ladder; when that was removed I remembered, with some dismay, that the females at least were much in the predicament of sailors, who, "in danger, have no door to creep out": but when a misfortune is absolutely inevitable, we are apt to bear it remarkably well. Who would utter that constant petition of ladies on rough roads, "Let me get out", when compliance would oblige the pleader to make a step of five feet before she could touch the ground?

The coach had three rows of seats, each calculated to hold three persons, and as we were only six, we had, in the phrase of Milton, to "inhabit lax" this exalted abode, and, accordingly, we were for some miles tossed about like a few potatoes in a wheelbarrow. Our knees, elbows, and heads required too much care for their protection to allow us leisure to look out of the windows; but at length the road became smoother, and we became more skilful in the art of balancing ourselves, so as to meet the concussion with less danger of dislocation.

We then found that we were travelling through a very beautiful country, essentially different in its features from what we had been accustomed to round Cincinnati: it is true we had left " *la belle rivière* " behind us, but the many limpid and rapid little streams that danced through the landscape to join it, more than atoned for its loss.

The country already wore an air of more careful husbandry, and the very circumstance of a wide and costly road (though not a very smooth one), which in theory might be supposed to injure picturesque effect, was beautiful to us, who, since we had entered the muddy mouth of the Mississippi, had never seen any thing except a steam-boat and the *levée*, professing to have so noble an object as public accommodation. Through the whole of the vast region we had passed, excepting at New Orleans itself, every trace of the art of man appeared to be confined to the individual effort of " getting along ", which, in Western phrase, means contriving to live with as small a portion of the incumbrances of civilised society as possible.

This road was made at the expense of the government as far as Cumberland, a town situated among the Alleghany mountains; and, from the nature of the ground, must have been a work of great cost. I regretted not having counted the number of bridges between Wheeling and Little Washington, a distance of thirty-four miles; over one stream only there are twenty-five, all passed by the road. They frequently occurred within a hundred yards of each other, so serpentine is its course; they are built of stone, and sometimes very neatly finished.

Little Washington is in Pennsylvania, across a corner of which the road runs. This is a free state, but we were still waited upon by negroes hired from the neighbouring state of Virginia. We arrived at night, and set off again at four in the morning; all, therefore, that we saw of Little Washington was its hotel, which was clean and comfortable. The first part of the next day's journey was through a country much less interesting: its character was unvaried for nearly thirty miles, consisting of an uninterrupted succession of forest-covered hills. As soon as we had wearily dragged to the top of one of these we began to rumble down the other side as rapidly as our four horses could trot; and no sooner arrived at the bottom than we began to crawl up again; the trees constantly so thick and so high as to preclude the possibility of seeing fifty yards in any direction.

The latter part of the day, however, amply repaid us. At four o'clock we began to ascend the Alleghany mountains; the first ridge on the western side is called Laurel Hill, and takes its name from the profuse quantity of evergreens with which it is covered; not any among them, however, being the shrub to which we give the name of laurel.

The whole of this mountain region, through ninety miles of which the road passes, is a garden. The almost incredible variety of plants, and the lavish profusion of their growth, produce an effect perfectly enchanting. I really can hardly conceive a higher enjoyment than a botanical tour among the Alleghany mountains, to any one who had science enough to profit by it.

The magnificent rhododendron first caught our eyes; it fringes every cliff, nestles beneath every rock, and blooms around every tree. The azalea, the shumac, and every variety of that beautiful mischief, the kalmia, are in equal profusion. Cedars of every size and form were above, around, and underneath us; firs more beautiful and more various than I had ever seen, were in equal abundance, but I know not whether they were really such as I had never seen in Europe, or only in infinitely greater splendour and perfection of growth: the species called the hemlock is, I think, second to the cedar only in magnificence. Oak and beech, with innumerable roses and wild vines, hanging in beautiful confusion among their branches, were in many places scattered among the evergreens. The earth was carpeted with various mosses and creeping plants, and though still in the month of March, not a trace of the nakedness of winter could be seen. Such was the scenery that showed us we were indeed among the far-famed Alleghany mountains.

As our noble terrace-road, the Simplon of America,* rose higher and higher, all that is noblest in nature was joined to all that is sweetest. The blue tops of the higher ridges formed the outline; huge masses of rock rose above us on the left, half hid at intervals by the bright green shrubs, while to the right we looked down upon the tops of the pines and cedars which clothed the bottom.

I had no idea of the endless variety of mountain scenery. My notions had been of rocks and precipices, of torrents and of forest trees, but I little expected that the first stop which should recall the garden scenery of our beautiful England would be found among the mountains: yet so it was. From the time I entered America I had never seen the slightest approach to what we call pleasure-grounds: a few very worthless and scentless flowers were all the specimens of gardening I had seen in Ohio; no attempt at garden scenery was ever dreamed of, and it was with the sort of delight with which one meets an old friend, that we looked on the lovely mixture of trees, shrubs, and flowers, that now continually met our eyes. Often on descending into the narrow valleys we found a little spot of cultivation, a garden or a field, hedged round with shumacs, rhododendrons, and azaleas, and a cottage covered with roses. These valleys are spots of great beauty; a clear stream is always found running through them, which is generally converted to the use of the miller at some point not far from the road; and here, as on the heights, great beauty of colouring is given to the landscape, by the bright hue of the vegetation, and the sober grey of the rocks.

The first night we passed among the mountains recalled us painfully from the enjoyment of nature to all the petty miseries of personal discomfort. Arrived at our inn, a forlorn parlour, filled with the blended fumes of tobacco and whiskey, received us; and chilled as we began to feel ourselves with the mountain air, we preferred going to our cold bed-rooms rather than sup in such an atmosphere. We found linen on the beds which they assured us had only been used *a few nights ;* every kind of refreshment we asked for we were answered: " We do not happen to have that article."

We were still in Pennsylvania, and no longer waited upon by slaves; it was, therefore, with great difficulty that we procured a fire in our bed-rooms from the surly-looking *young lady* who condescended to officiate as chamber-maid, and with much more that we extorted clean linen for our beds: that done, we patiently crept into them supperless, while she made her exit, muttering about the difficulty of " fixing English folks ".

The next morning cheered our spirits again; we now enjoyed a new kind of Alpine witchery; the clouds were floating around and below us, and the distant peaks were indistinctly visible as through a white gauze veil, which was gradually lifted up till the sun arose, and again let in upon us the full glory of these interminable heights.

We were told before we began the ascent, that we should find snow four inches deep on the road; but as yet we had seen none, and indeed it was with difficulty we persuaded ourselves that we were not travelling in the midst of summer. As we proceeded, however, we found the northern declivities still covered with it, and at length, towards the summit, the road itself had the promised four inches. The extreme mildness of the air, and the brilliant hue of the evergreens, contrasted strangely with this appearance of winter; it was difficult to understand how the snow could help melting in such an atmosphere.

Again and again we enjoyed all the exhilarating sensations that such scenes must necessarily inspire; but in attempting a continued description of our progress over these beautiful mountains, I could only tell again of rocks, cedars, laurels, and running streams, of blue heights and green valleys, yet the continually varying combinations of these objects afforded us unceasing pleasure. From one point, pre-eminently above any neighbouring ridge, we looked back upon the enormous valley of the West. It is a stupendous view; but having gazed upon it for some moments, we turned to pursue our course, and the certainty that we should see it no more raised no sigh of regret.

We dined, on the second day, at a beautiful spot which we were told was the highest point on the road, being 2,846 feet above the level of the sea. We were regaled luxuriously on wild turkey and mountain venison; which latter is infinitely superior to any furnished by the forests of the Mississippi, or the Ohio. The vegetables also were extremely fine, and we were told by a pretty girl, who superintended the slaves that waited on us (for we were again in Virginia), that the vegetables of the Alleghany were reckoned the finest in America. She told us also, that wild strawberries were profusely abundant, and very fine; that their cows found for themselves, during the summer, plenty of flowery food, which produced a copious supply of milk;

that their spring gave them the purest water, of icy coldness in the warmest seasons; and that the climate was the most delicious in the world, for though the thermometer sometimes stood at ninety, their cool breeze never failed them. What a spot to turn hermit in for a summer! My eloquent mountaineer gave me some specimens of ground plants, far unlike any thing I had ever seen. One particularly, which she called the ground pine, is peculiar, as she told me, to the Alleghany, and in some places runs over whole acres of ground; it is extremely beautiful. The rooms were very prettily decorated with this elegant plant, hung round in festoons.

In many places the clearing has been considerable; the road passes through several fine farms, situated in the sheltered hollows; we were told that the wolves continue to annoy them severely, but that panthers, the terror of the West, are never seen, and bears very rarely. Of snakes, they confessed they had abundance, but very few that were considered dangerous.

In the afternoon we came in sight of the Mononga-hela river; and its banks gave us for several miles a beautiful succession of wild and domestic scenery. In some points, the black rock rises perpendicularly from its margin, like those at Chepstow; at others, a mill, with its owner's cottage, its corn-plat, and its poultry, present a delightful image of industry and comfort.

Brownsville is a busy-looking little town, built upon the banks of this river; it would be pretty, were it not stained by the hue of coal. I do not remember in England to have seen any spot, however near a coal mine, so dyed in black as Wheeling and Brownsville. At this place we crossed the Monongahela in a flat ferry-boat, which very commodiously received our huge coach and four horses.

On leaving the black little town, we were again cheered by abundance of evergreens, reflected in the ſtream, with fantaſtic piles of rock, half visible through the pines and cedars above, giving often the idea of a vaſt gothic caſtle. It was a folly, I confess, but I often lamented they were not such; the travelling for thousands of miles, without meeting any nobler trace of the ages that are passed, than a mass of rotten leaves, or a fragment of fallen rock, produces a heavy, earthly, matter-of-faƈt effeƈt upon the imagination, which can hardly be described, and for which the greateſt beauty of scenery can furnish only an occasional and transitory remedy.[1]

Our second night in the mountains was passed at a solitary house of rather forlorn appearance; but we fared much better than the night before, for they gave us clean sheets, a good fire, and no scolding. We again ſtarted at four o'clock in the morning, and eagerly watched for the firſt gleam of light that should show the same lovely speƈtacle we had seen the day before; nor were we disappointed, though the show was somewhat different. The vapours caught the morning ray, as it firſt darted over the mountain top, and passing it to the scene below, we seemed enveloped in a rainbow.

We had now but one ridge left to pass over, and as we reached the top, and looked down on the new world before us, I hardly knew whether moſt to rejoice that

" All the toil of the long-pass'd way "

was over, or to regret that our mountain journey was drawing to a close.

[1] I have been severely ridiculed by some American friends for my superſtitious clinging to the memory of the little mouldering works of man amid the boundless and eternal majeſty of nature. For a moment the observation seems too pompously powerful to emit an answer. But is it true to our human nature ? If we be pigmies—as in truth we are—it is vain to ſtruggle againſt the faƈt ; and the paſt doings of our father pigmies will (to such as know any thing about their fathers) have an intereſt for the total absence of which neither rocks nor rivers can long atone.

The novelty of my enjoyment had doubtless added much to its keenness. I have never been familiar with mountain scenery. Wales has shown me all I ever saw, and the region of the Alleghany Alps in no way resembles it. It is a world of mountains rising around you in every direction and in every form—savage, vast, and wild; yet almost at every step some lovely spot meets your eye, green, bright, and blooming, as the most cherished nook belonging to some noble Flora in our own beautiful land. It is a ride of ninety miles through kalmias, rhododendrons, azaleas, vines, and roses; sheltered from every blast that blows by vast masses of various coloured rocks, on which

" Tall pines and cedars wave their dark green crests "

while in every direction you have a back ground of blue mountain tops that play at bo-peep with you in the clouds.

After descending the last ridge we reached Haggerstown, a small neat place, between a town and a village; and here, by the piety of the Presbyterian coachmasters, we were doomed to pass an entire day, and two nights, " as the accommodation line must not run on the Sabbath ".

I must, however, mention, that this day of enforced rest was *not* Sunday. Saturday evening we had taken in at Cumberland a portly passenger, whom we soon discovered to be one of the proprietors of the coach. He asked us, with great politeness, if we should wish to travel on the Sabbath, or to delay our journey. We answered that we would rather proceed. " The coach, then, shall go on to-morrow " replied the liberal coachmaster, with the greatest courtesy; and accordingly we travelled all Sunday, and arrived at Haggerstown on Sunday night. At the door of the inn our civil proprietor left us; but when we inquired of the waiter at what hour we were to start on the morrow, he told us that we should be obliged to pass the whole of Monday there, as the coach which was to convey us forward would not arrive from the east till Tuesday morning.

Thus we discovered that the waiving the Sabbath-keeping by the proprietor was for his own convenience, and not for ours, and that we were to be tied by the leg for four and twenty hours notwithstanding. This was quite a Yankee trick.

Luckily for us the inn at Haggerstown was one of the most comfortable I ever entered. It was there that we became fully aware that we had left Western America behind us. Instead of being scolded, as we literally were at Cincinnati, for asking for a private sitting-room, we here had two without asking at all. A waiter, quite *comme il faut*, summoned us to breakfast, dinner, and tea, which we found prepared with abundance, and even elegance. The master of the house met us at the door of the eating-room, and after asking if we wished for any thing not on the table, retired. The charges were in no respect higher than at Cincinnati.

A considerable creek, called Conococheque Creek, runs near the town, and the valley through which it passes is said to be the most fertile in America.

On leaving Haggerstown we found, to our mortification, that we were not to be the sole occupants of the bulky accommodation, two ladies and two gentlemen appearing at the door, ready to share it with us. We again started at four o'clock by the light of a bright moon, and rumbled and nodded through roads considerably worse than those over the mountains.

As the light began to dawn, we discovered our ladies to be an old woman and her pretty daughter.

Soon after daylight we found that our pace became much slower than usual, and that from time to time our driver addressed to his companion on the box many and vehement exclamations. The gentlemen put their heads out to ask what was the matter, but could get no intelligence till the mail overtook us, when both vehicles stopped, and an animated colloquy of imprecations took place between the coachmen. At length we learnt that one of our wheels was broken in such a manner as to render it impossible for us to proceed. Upon this the old lady immediately became a principal actor in the scene. She sprang to the window, and addressing the set of gentlemen who completely filled the mail, exclaimed; " Gentlemen! can't you make room for two ? Only me and my daughter ?" The naïve simplicity of this request set both the coaches into an uproar of laughter. It was impossible to doubt that she acted upon the same principle as the pious Catholic, who, addressing heaven with a prayer for himself alone, added, " *pour ne pas fatiguer ta miséricorde* ". Our laugh, however, never daunted the old woman, or caused her for a moment to cease the reiteration of her request: " Only for two of us, gentlemen!—can't you find room for two ?"

Our situation was really very embarrassing, but not to laugh was impossible. After it was ascertained that our own vehicle could not convey us, and that the mail had not even room for two, we decided upon walking to the next village, a distance, fortunately, of only two miles, and awaiting there the repair of the wheel. We immediately set off, at the brisk pace that six o'clock and a frosty morning in March were likely to inspire, leaving our old lady and her pretty daughter considerably in the rear; our hearts having been rather hardened by the exclusive nature of her prayer for aid.

When we had again started upon our new wheel the driver, to recover the time he had lost, drove rapidly over a very rough road, in consequence of which our self-seeking old lady fell into a perfect agony of terror, and her cries of " We shall be over! oh, Lord! we shall be over! we must be over! we shall be over!" lasted to the end of the stage, which with laughing, walking, and shaking, was a most fatiguing one.

Chapter Nineteen

Baltimore—Catholic Cathedral—St. Mary's College—
Sermons—Infant Schools

As we advanced towards Baltimore the look of cultivation increased, the fences wore an air of greater neatness, the houses began to look like the abodes of competence and comfort, and we were consoled for the loss of the beautiful mountains by knowing that we were approaching the Atlantic.

From the time of quitting the Ohio river, though, unquestionably, it merits its title of " the beautiful ", especially when compared with the dreary Mississippi, I strongly felt the truth of an observation I remembered to have heard in England, that little rivers were more beautiful than great ones. As features in a landscape, this is assuredly the case. Where the stream is so wide that the objects on the opposite shore are indistinct, all the beauty must be derived from the water itself; whereas, when the stream is narrow, it becomes only a part of the composition. The Monongahela, which is in size between the Wye and the Thames, is infinitely more picturesque than the Ohio.

To enjoy the beauty of the vast rivers of this vast country you must be upon the water; and then the power of changing the scenery by now approaching one shore, and now the other, is very pleasing: but travelling as we now did by land, the wild, rocky, narrow, rapid little rivers we encountered, were a thousand times more beautiful. The Potapsco, near which the road runs as you approach Baltimore, is at many points very picturesque. The large blocks of grey rock, now close upon its edge, and now retiring to give room for a few acres of bright green herbage, give great interest and variety to its course.

Baltimore is, I think, one of the handsomest cities to approach in the Union. The noble column erected to the memory of Washington, and the Catholic Cathedral, with its beautiful dome, being built on a commanding eminence, are seen at a great distance. As you draw nearer, many other domes and towers become visible; and as you enter Baltimore Street, you feel that you are arrived in a handsome and populous city.

We took up our quarters at an excellent hotel where the coach stopped, and the next day were fortunate enough to find accommodation in the house of a lady, well known to many of my European friends. With her and her amiable daughter we spent a fortnight very agreeably, and felt quite aware that if we had not arrived in London or Paris, we had, at least, left far behind the " half-horse, half-alligator " tribes of the West, as the Kentuckians call themselves.

Baltimore is in many respects a beautiful city: it has several handsome buildings, and even the private dwelling-houses have a look of magnificence, from the abundance of white marble with which many of them are adorned. The ample flights of steps, and the lofty door frames, are in most of the best houses formed of this beautiful material.

This has been called the city of monuments, from its having the stately column erected to the memory of General Washington, and which bears a colossal statue of him at the top; and another pillar of less dimensions, recording some victory; I forget which. Both these are of brilliant white marble. There are also several pretty marble fountains in different parts of the city, which greatly add to its beauty. These are not, it is true, quite so splendid as that of the Innocents, or many others at Paris, but they are fountains of clear water, and they are built of white marble. There is one which is sheltered from the sun by a roof supported by light columns; it looks like a temple dedicated to the genius of the spring. The water flows into a marble cistern, to which you descend by a flight of steps of delicate whiteness, and return by another. These steps are never without groups of negro girls, some carrying the water on their heads, with that graceful steadiness of step, which requires no aid from the hand; some tripping gaily with their yet unfilled pitchers; many of them singing in the soft rich voice, peculiar to their race; and all dressed with that strict attention to taste and smartness which seems the distinguishing characteristic of the Baltimore females of all ranks.

The Catholic Cathedral is considered by all Americans as a magnificent church, but it can hardly be so classed by any one who has seen the churches of Europe; its interior, however, has an air of neatness that amounts to elegance. The form is a Greek cross, having a dome in the centre; but the proportions are ill preserved; the dome is too low, and the arches which support it are flattened, and too wide for their height. On each side of the high altar are chapels to the Saviour and the Virgin. The altars in these, as well as the high altar, are of native marble of different colours, and some of the specimens are very beautiful. The decorations of the altar are elegant and costly. The prelate is a cardinal, and bears, moreover, the title of " Archbishop of Baltimore ".

There are several paintings in different parts of the church, which we heard were considered as very fine. There are two presented by Louis XVIII; one of these is the Descent from the Cross, by Paulin Guérin; the other a copy from Rubens (as they told us) of a legend of St Louis in the Holy Land; but the composition of the picture is so abominably bad, that I conceive the legend of its being after Rubens muſt be as fabulous as its subjeĉt. The admiration in which these piĉtures are held is an inconteſtable indication of the ſtate of art in the country.

We attended mass in this church the Sunday after our arrival, and I was perfeĉtly aſtonished at the beauty and splendid appearance of the ladies who filled it. Excepting on a very brilliant Sunday at the Tuileries, I never saw so showy a display of morning coſtume, and I think I never saw any where so many beautiful women at one glance. They all appeared to be in full dress, and were really all beautiful.

The sermon (I am very attentive to sermons) was a moſt extraordinary one. The prieſt began by telling us, that he was about to preach upon a vice that he would not "mention or name" from the beginning of the sermon to the end.

Having thus excited the curiosity of his hearers by proposing a riddle to them, he began.

Adam, he said, was moſt assuredly the firſt who had committed this sin, and Cain the next; then following the advice given by the liſtener, in the Plaideurs: "Passons au déluge, je vous prie"; he went on to mention the particular propriety of Noah's family on this point; and then continued: "Now observe, what did God show the greateſt dislike to? What was it that Jesus was never even accused of? What was it Joseph hated the moſt? Who was the disciple that Jesus chose for his friend?"—and thus he went on for nearly an hour, in a ſtrain that was often perfeĉtly unintelligible to me, but which, as far as I could comprehend it, appeared to be a sort of *exposé* and commentary upon private anecdotes which he had found, or fancied he had found, in the Bible. I never saw the attention of a congregation more ſtrongly excited, and I really wished, in Chriſtian charity, that something better had rewarded it.

There are a vast number of churches and chapels in the city, in proportion to its extent, and several that are large and well built; the Unitarian church is the handsomest I have ever seen dedicated to that mode of worship. But the prettiest among them is a little *bijou* of a thing belonging to the Catholic college. The institution is dedicated to St Mary; but this little chapel looks, though in the midst of a city, as if it should have been sacred to St John of the wilderness. There is a sequestered little garden behind it, hardly large enough to plant cabbages in, which yet contains a Mount Calvary, bearing a lofty cross. The tiny path which leads up to this sacred spot, is not much wider than a sheep-track, and its cedars are but shrubs, but all is in proportion; and notwithstanding its fairy dimensions, there is something of holiness and quiet beauty about it, that excites the imagination strangely. The little chapel itself has the same touching and impressive character. A solitary lamp, whose glare is tempered by delicately painted glass, hangs before the altar; the light of day enters dimly, yet richly, through crimson curtains; and the silence with which the well-lined doors opened from time to time, admitting a youth of the establishment who, with noiseless tread, approached the altar, and kneeling, offered a whispering prayer, and retired, had something in it more calculated, perhaps, to generate holy thoughts, than even the swelling anthem heard beneath the resounding dome of St Peter's.

Baltimore has a handsome museum, superintended by one of the Peale family, well known for their devotion to natural science, and to works of art. It is not their fault if the specimens which they are enabled to display in the latter department are very inferior to their splendid exhibitions in the former.

The theatre was closed when we were in Baltimore, but we were told that it was very far from being a popular or fashionable amusement. We were, indeed, told this every where throughout the country, and the information was generally accompanied by the observation, that the opposition of the clergy was the cause of it. But I suspect that this is not the principal cause, especially among the men, who, if they were so implicit in their obedience to the clergy, would certainly be more constant in their attendance at the churches; nor would they, moreover, deem the theatre more righteous because an English actor, or a French dancer performed there; yet on such occasions the theatres overflow. The cause, I think, is in the character of the people. I never saw a population so totally divested of gaiety; there is no trace of this feeling from one end of the Union to the other. They have no fêtes, no fairs, no merry-makings, no music in the streets, no " Punch ", no puppet-shows. If they see a comedy or a farce, they may laugh at it; but they can do very well without it; and the consciousness of the number of cents that must be paid to enter a theatre, I am very sure turns more steps from its doors than any religious feeling. A distinguished publisher of Philadelphia told me that no comic publication had ever yet been found to answer in America.[1]

[1] This is an observation which, though probably quite true at the time it was made, must never be repeated. Major Downing's *Letters* prove, much beyond the power of contradiction, that humour, rich and original, does exist in the United States; and the popularity of the work shows with equal certainty, that when such a treat is given to them, the people know how to enjoy it. Whether a work treating of a subject less vitally near and dear to every bosom than the BANK would have produced an equal sensation, may perhaps be doubted— but this matters little. If an artist can be found skilful enough to dress such a subject in all the whimsical harlequinade of the most exquisite humour, without for a moment losing sight of his commercial object, the glory of the achievement must assuredly be increased by its difficulty : and if American citizens are gay-spirited enough to chuckle at, and enjoy wit, that expends itself on a grave subject, which is both the most familiar and the most important to them, it is easy to predict

We arrived at Baltimore at the season of the " Conference ". I must be excused from giving any very distinct explanation of this term, as I did not receive any. From what I could learn, it much resembles a Revival. We entered many churches, and heard much preaching, and not one of the reverend orators could utter the reproach:

" Peut-on si bien prêcher qu'elle ne dorme au sermon ?"

for I never even dozed at any. There was one preacher whose manner and matter were so peculiar, that I took the liberty of immediately writing down a part of his discourse as a specimen. I confess I began writing in the middle of a sentence, for I waited in vain for a beginning. It was as follows:

" Nevertheless, we must not lose sight of the one important, great, and only object; for the Lord is mighty, his works are great, likewise wonderful, likewise wise, likewise merciful; and, moreover, we must ever keep in mind, and close to our hearts, all his precious blessings, and unspeakable mercies and overflowings; and, moreover, we must never lose sight of, no, never lose sight of, nor ever cease to remember, nor ever let our souls forget, nor ever cease to dwell upon, and to reverence, and to welcome, and to bless, and to give thanks, and to sing hosanna, and give praise "——and here my fragment of paper failed, but this strain continued, without a shadow of meaning that I could trace, and in a voice inconceivably loud, for more than an hour. After he had finished his sermon, a scene exactly

that, in the progress of time, when other topics shall come to divide the public mind with dollars, they will chuckle at, and enjoy wit, otherwise employed.

This, indeed, is already proved by the cordial reception given to the inimitable Slick, which, whether by a native hand or not, is as heartily enjoyed on the other side of the Atlantic as it is by all genuine lovers of true humour on this.

resembling that at the Cincinnati Revival took place. Two other priests assisted in calling forward the people, and in whispering comfort to them. One of these men roared out in the coarsest accents: " Do you want to go to hell to-night ?" The church was almost entirely filled with women, who vied with each other in howlings and contortions of the body; many of them tore their clothes nearly off. I was much amused, spite of the indignation and disgust the scene inspired, by the vehemence of the negro part of the congregation; they seemed determined to bellow louder than all the rest, to show at once their piety and their equality.

At this same chapel, a few nights before, a woman had fallen in a fit of ecstasy from the gallery into the arms of the people below, a height of twelve feet. A young slave who waited upon us at table, when this was mentioned, said that similar accidents had frequently happened, and that once she had seen it herself. Another slave in the house told us, that she " liked religion right well, but that she never took fits in it, 'cause she was always fixed in her best when she went to chapel, and she did not like to have all her best clothes broke up ".

We visited the infant school, instituted in this city by Mr Ibbertson, an amiable and intelligent Englishman. It was the first infant school, properly so called, which I had ever seen, and I was greatly pleased with all the arrangements, and the apparent success of them. The children, of whom we saw about a hundred, boys and girls, were between eighteen months and six years. The apartment was filled with all sorts of instructive and amusing objects; a set of Dutch toys, arranged as a cabinet of natural history, was excellent; a numerous collection of large wooden bricks filled one corner of the room; the walls were hung with gay papers of different patterns, each representing some pretty group of figures; large and excellent coloured engravings of birds and beasts were exhibited in succession as the theme of a little lesson; and the sweet flute of Mr Ibbertson gave tune and time to the prettiest little concert of chirping birds that I ever listened to.

A geographical model, large enough to give clear ideas of continent, island, cape, isthmus, *et cetera*, all set in water, is placed before the children, and the pretty creatures point their little rosy fingers with a look of intense interest, as they are called upon to show where each of them is to be found. The dress, both of boys and girls, was elegantly neat, and their manner, when called upon to speak individually, was well-bred, intelligent, and totally free from the rude indifference, which is so remarkably prevalent in the manners of American children. Mr Ibbertson will be a benefactor to the Union, if he become the means of spreading the admirable method by which he has polished the manner, and awakened the intellect of these beautiful little Republicans. I have conversed with many American ladies on the total want of discipline and subjection which I observed universally among children of all ages, and I never found any who did not both acknowledge and deplore the truth of the remark. In the state of Ohio they have a law (I know not if it exist elsewhere), that if a father strike his son, he shall pay a fine of ten dollars for every such offence. I was told by a gentleman of Cincinnati that he had seen this fine inflicted there, at the requisition of a boy of twelve years of age, whose father, he proved, had struck him for lying. Such a law, they say, generates a spirit of freedom. What else may it generate ?

Mr Ibbertson, who seems perfectly devoted, heart and head to the subject, told me that he was employed in organising successive schools, that should receive the pupils as they advanced in age. If he prove himself as capable of completing education, as he appears to be of beginning it, his institution will be a very valuable one.

It would, indeed, be valuable any where; but in America, where discipline is not, where, from the shell, they are beings "that cannot rule, nor ever will be ruled", it is invaluable.

About two miles from Baltimore is a fort, nobly situated on the Potapsco, and commanding the approach from the Chesapeake bay. As our visit was on a Sunday we were not permitted to enter it. The walk to this fort is along a fine terrace of beautiful verdure, which commands a magnificent view of the city, with its columns, towers, domes, and shipping; and also of the Potapsco river, which is here so wide as to present almost a sea view. This terrace is ornamented with abundance of evergreens, and wild roses innumerable, but the whole region has the reputation of being unhealthy, and the fort itself most lamentably so. Before leaving the city of monuments, I must not omit naming one reared to the growing wealth of the country; Mr Barham's hotel is said to be the most splendid in the Union, and it is certainly splendid enough for a people more luxurious than the citizens of the republic appear yet to be. I heard different, and, indeed, perfectly contradictory accounts of the success of the experiment; but at least every one seemed to agree that the liberal projector was fully entitled to exclaim:

> " 'Tis not in mortals to command success;
> I have done more, Jonathan, I've deserved it."

After enjoying a very pleasant fortnight, the greater part of which was passed in rambling about this pretty city and its environs, we left it, not without regret, and all indulging the hope that we should be able to pay it another visit.

Chapter Twenty

*Voyage to Washington—Capitol—City of Washington
—Congress—Indians—Funeral of a Member of Congress*

By far the shortest route to Washington, both as to distance and time, is by land; but I much wished to see the celebrated Chesapeake bay, and it was therefore decided that we should take our passage in the steamboat. It is indeed a beautiful little voyage, and well worth the time it costs; but as to the beauty of the bay, it must, I think, be felt only by sailors. It is, I doubt not, a fine shelter for ships from the storms of the Atlantic; but its very vastness prevents it striking the eye as beautiful: it is, in fact, only a fine sea view. But the entrance from it into the Potomac river is very noble, and is one of the points at which one feels conscious of the gigantic proportions of the country, without having recourse to a graduated pencil-case.

The passage up this river to Washington is interesting, from many objects that it passes, but beyond all else, by the view it affords of Mount Vernon, the seat of General Washington. It is there that this truly great man passed the last years of his virtuous life, and it is there that he lies buried: it was easy to distinguish, as we passed, the cypress that waves over his grave.

The latter part of the voyage shows some fine river scenery; but I did not discover this till some months afterwards, for we now arrived late at night.

Our first object the next morning was to get a sight of the capitol, and our impatience sent us forth before breakfast. The mists of morning still hung around this magnificent building when first it broke upon our view, and I am not sure that the effect produced was not the greater for this circumstance. At all events, we were struck with admiration and surprise. None of us, I believe, expected to see so imposing a structure on that side the Atlantic. I am ill at describing buildings, but the beauty and majesty of the American capitol might defy an abler pen than mine to do it justice. It stands so finely too, high and alone.

The magnificent western façade is approached from the city by terraces and steps of bolder proportions than I ever before saw. The elegant eastern front, to which many persons give the preference, is on a level with a newly-planted but exceedingly handsome enclosure, which, in a few years, will offer the shade of all the most splendid trees which flourish in the Union, to cool the brows and refresh the spirits of the members. The view from the capitol commands the city and many miles around, and it is itself an object of imposing beauty to the whole country adjoining.

We were again fortunate enough to find a very agreeable family to board with; and soon after breakfast left our comfortless hotel near the water, for very pleasant apartments in F—— Street.[1]

I was delighted with the whole aspect of Washington; light, cheerful, and airy, it reminded me of our fashionable watering-places. It has been laughed at by foreigners, and even by natives, because the original plan of the city was upon an enormous scale, and but a very small part of it has been as yet executed. But I confess I see nothing in the least degree ridiculous about it; the original design, which was as beautiful as it was extensive, has been in no way departed from, and all that has been done has been done well. From the base of the hill on which the capitol stands extends a street of most magnificent width, planted on each side with trees, and ornamented by many splendid shops. This street, which is called Pennsylvania Avenue, is above a mile in length, and at the end of it is the handsome mansion of the President; conveniently near to

[1] The streets that intersect the great avenues in Washington are distinguished by the letters of the alphabet.

his residence are the various public offices, all handsome, simple, and commodious; ample areas are left round each, where grass and shrubs refresh the eye. In another of the principal ſtreets is the general poſt-office, and not far from it a very noble town-hall. Towards the quarter of the President's house are several handsome dwellings, which are chiefly occupied by the foreign miniſters. The houses in the other parts of the city are scattered, but without ever losing sight of the regularity of the original plan; and to a person who has been travelling much through the country, and marked the immense quantity of new manufactories, new canals, new rail-roads, new towns, and new cities, which are springing, as it were, from the earth in every part of it, the appearance of the metropolis rising gradually into life and splendour, is a spectacle of high hiſtoric intereſt.

Commerce had already produced large and handsome cities in America before she had attained to an individual political exiſtence, and Washington may be scorned as a metropolis, where such cities as Philadelphia and New York exiſt; but I considered it as the growing metropolis of the growing population of the Union, and it already possesses features noble enough to suſtain its dignity as such.

The residence of the foreign legations and their families gives a tone to the society of this city which diſtinguishes it greatly from all others. It is also, for a great part of the year, the residence of the senators and representatives, who muſt be presumed to be the *élite* of the entire body of citizens, both in respect to talent and education. This cannot fail to make Washington a more agreeable abode than any other city in the Union.

The total absence of all sights, sounds, or smells of commerce, adds greatly to the charm. Inſtead of drays you see handsome carriages; and inſtead of the busy buſtling huſtle of men, shuffling on to a sale of " dry goods " or " prime bread ſtuffs ", you see very well-dressed personages lounging leisurely up and down Pennsylvania Avenue.

Mr Pishey Thompson, the English bookseller, with his pretty collection of all sorts of pretty literature fresh from London, and Mr Somebody, the jeweller, with his brilliant shop full of trinkets, are the principal points of attraction and business. What a contraſt to all other American cities! The members, who pass several months every year in this lounging easy way, with no labour but a little talking, and with the *douceur* of eight dollars a day to pay them for it, muſt feel the change sadly when their term of public service is over.

There is another circumſtance which renders the evening parties at Washington extremely unlike those of other places in the Union; this is the great majority of gentlemen. The expense, the trouble, or the necessity of a ruling eye at home, one or all of these reasons, prevents the members' ladies from accompanying them to Washington; at leaſt, I heard of very few who had their wives with them. The female society is chiefly to be found among the families of the foreign miniſters, those of the officers of ſtate, and of the few members, the wealthieſt and moſt ariſtocratic of the land, who bring their families with them. Some few independent persons reside in or near the city, but this is a class so thinly scattered that they can hardly be accounted a part of the population.

But, ſtrange to say, even here a theatre cannot be supported for more than a few weeks at a time. I was told that gambling is the favourite recreation of the gentlemen, and that it is carried to a very considerable extent; but here, as elsewhere within the country, it is kept extremely well out of sight. I do not think I was present with a pack of cards a dozen times during more than three years that I remained in the country. Billiards are much played, though in moſt places the amusement is illegal. It often appeared to me that the old women of a State made the laws, and the young men broke them.

Notwithstanding the diminutive size of the city, we found much to see and to amuse us.

The patent office is a curious record of the fertility of the mind of man when left to its own resources; but it gives ample proof also that it is not under such circumstances it is most usefully employed. This patent office contains models of all the mechanical inventions that have been produced in the Union, and the number is enormous. I asked the man who showed these, what proportion of them had been brought into use; he said about one in a thousand; he told me also, that they chiefly proceeded from mechanics and agriculturists settled in remote parts of the country, who had begun by endeavouring to hit upon some contrivance to enable them to *get along* without sending some thousand and odd miles for the thing they wanted. If the contrivance succeeded, they generally became so fond of this offspring of their ingenuity, that they brought it to Washington for a patent.

At the secretary of state's office we were shown autographs of all the potentates with whom the Union were in alliance; which, I believe, pretty well includes all. To the parchments bearing these royal signs manual were appended, of course, the official seals of each, enclosed in gold or silver boxes of handsome workmanship: I was amused by the manner in which one of their own, just prepared for the court of Russia, was displayed to us, and the superiority of their decorations pointed out. They were superior, and in much better taste than the rest; and I only wish that the feeling that induced this display would spread to every corner of the Union, and mix itself with every act and with every sentiment. Let America give a fair portion of her attention to the arts and the graces that embellish life, and I will make

184

her another visit, and write another book as unlike this as possible.[1]

Among the royal signatures, the only ones which much interested me were two from the hand of Napoleon. The earliest of these, when he was first consul, was a most illegible scrawl, and, as the tradition went, was written on horseback; but his writing improved greatly after he became an emperor, the subsequent signature being firmly and clearly written—I longed to steal both.

The purity of the American character, formed and founded on the purity of the American government, was made evident to our senses by the display of all the offerings of esteem and regard which had been presented by various sovereigns to the different American ministers who had been sent to their courts. The object of the law which exacted this deposit from every individual so honoured, was, they told us, to prevent the possibility of bribery being used to corrupt any envoy of the Republic. I should think it would be a better way to select for the office such men as they felt could not be seduced by a sword or a snuff-box. But they, doubtless, know their own business best.

The bureau for Indian affairs contains a room of great interest; the walls are entirely covered with original portraits[2] of all the chiefs who, from time to time, have come to negotiate with their great father, as they call the President. These portraits are by Mr King, and, it cannot be doubted, are excellent likenesses, as are all the portraits I have ever seen from the

[1] This must not be done, as I have been recently informed, till Jonathan Jefferson Whitlow is forgotten—or the system of slavery abolished.

[2] The beautiful engravings of these portraits, which have recently reached us, would be *perfect*, were they not quite so *good*. They convey the peculiar expression of this fast perishing and most interesting race admirably, but give much too favourable an idea of the pictorial excellence of the originals.

hands of that gentleman. The countenances are full of expression, but the expression in most of them is extremely similar; or rather, I should say that they have but two sorts of expression; the one is that of very noble and warlike daring, the other of a gentle and naïve simplicity, that has no mixture of folly in it, but which is inexpressibly engaging, and the more touching, perhaps, because at the moment we were looking at them, those very hearts which lent the eyes such meek and friendly softness, were wrung by a base, cruel, and most oppressive act of their *great father*.

We were at Washington at the time that the measure for chasing the last of several tribes of Indians from their forest homes, was canvassed in Congress, and finally decided upon the *fiat* of the President. If the American character may be judged by their conduct in this matter, they are most lamentably deficient in every feeling of honour and integrity. It is among themselves, and from themselves, that I have heard the statements which represent them as treacherous and false almost beyond belief in their intercourse with the unhappy Indians. Had I, during my residence in the United States, observed any single feature in their national character that could justify their eternal boast of liberality and the love of freedom, I might have respected them, however much my taste might have been offended by what was peculiar in their manners and customs. But it is impossible for any mind of common honesty not to be revolted by the contradictions in their principles and practice. They inveigh against the governments of Europe, because, as they say, they favour the powerful and oppress the weak. You may hear this declaimed upon in Congress, roared out in taverns, discussed in every drawing-room, satirised upon the stage, nay, even anathematised from the pulpit: listen to it, and then look at them at home;

you will see them with one hand hoisting the cap of liberty, and with the other flogging their slaves. You will see them one hour lecturing their mob on the indefeasible rights of man, and the next driving from their homes the children of the soil, whom they have bound themselves to protect by the most solemn treaties.

In justice to those who approve not this treacherous policy, I will quote a paragraph from a New York paper, which shows that there are some among them who look with detestation on the bold bad measure decided upon at Washington in the year 1830.

" We know of no subject, at the present moment, of more importance to the character of our country for justice and integrity than that which relates to the Indian tribes in Georgia and Alabama, and particularly the Cherokees in the former state. The act passed by Congress, just at the end of the session, co-operating with the tyrannical and iniquitous statute of Georgia, strikes a formidable blow at the reputation of the United States, in respect to their faith, pledged in almost innumerable instances, in the most solemn treaties and compacts."

There were many objects of much interest shown us at this Indian bureau; but, from the peculiar circumstances of this most unhappy and ill-used people, it was a very painful interest.

The dresses worn by the chiefs when their portraits were taken, are many of them splendid, from the embroidery of beads and other ornaments; and the room contains many specimens of their ingenuity, and even of their taste. There is a glass case in the room, wherein are arranged specimens of worked muslin, and other needle-work, some very excellent handwriting, and many other little productions of male and female Indians, all proving clearly that they are perfectly capable of civilisation. Indeed, the circumstance which renders their expulsion from their own, their native lands, so peculiarly lamentable is, that they were yielding rapidly to the force of example; their lives were no longer those of wandering hunters, but they were becoming agriculturists, and the tyrannical arm of brutal power has not now driven them, as formerly, only from their hunting grounds, their favourite springs, and the sacred bones of their fathers, but it has chased them from the dwellings their advancing knowledge had taught them to make comfortable; from the newly-ploughed fields of their pride; and from the crops their sweat had watered. And for what ? To add some thousand acres of territory to the half peopled wilderness which borders them.

The Potomac, on arriving at Washington, makes a beautiful sweep, which forms a sort of bay, round which the city is built. Just where it makes the turn, a wooden bridge is thrown across, connecting the shores of Maryland and Virginia. This bridge is a mile and a quarter in length, and is ugly enough.[1] The navy-yard and arsenal are just above it, on the Maryland side, and make a handsome appearance on the edge of the river, following the sweep above-mentioned. Near the arsenal (much too near) is the penitentiary, which, as it was just finished, and not inhabited, we examined in every part. It is built for the purpose of solitary confinement for life. A gallows is a much less nerve-shaking spectacle than one of these awful cells, and assuredly, when imprisonment therein for life is substituted for death, it is no mercy to the criminal; but if it be a greater terror to the citizen, it may answer the purpose better. I do not conceive, that out of a hundred human beings who had been thus confined for a year, one would be found at the end of it who would continue to linger on there, *certain it was for ever*, if the

[1] It has since been washed away by the breaking up of the frost of February, 1831.

alternative of being hanged were offered to them. I had written a description of these horrible cells, but Captain Hall's picture of a similar building is so accurate and so clear, that it is needless to insert it.

Still following the sweep of the river, at the distance of two miles from Washington, is George Town, formerly a place of considerable commercial importance, and likely, I think, to become so again, when the Ohio and Chesapeake canal, which there mouths into the Potomac, shall be in full action. It is a very pretty town, commanding a lovely view, of which the noble Potomac and the almost nobler capitol, are the great features. The country rises into a beautiful line of hills behind Washington, which form a sort of undulating terrace on to George Town; this terace is almost entirely occupied by a succession of gentlemen's seats. At George Town the Potomac suddenly contracts itself, and begins to assume that rapid, rocky, and irregular character which marks it afterwards, and renders its course, till it meets the Shenandoah at Harper's Ferry, a series of the most wild and romantic views that are to be found in America.

Attending the debates in Congress was, of course, one of our great objects; and, as an English woman, I was perhaps the more eager to avail myself of the privilege allowed. It was repeatedly observed to me that, at least in this instance, I must acknowledge the superior gallantry of the Americans, and that they herein give a decided proof of surpassing the English in a wish to honour the ladies, as they have a gallery in the House of Representatives erected expressly for them, while in England they are rigorously excluded from every part of the House of Commons.

But the inference I draw from this is precisely the reverse of that suggested. It is well known that the reason why the House of Commons was closed against ladies was, that their presence was found too attractive, and that so many members were tempted to neglect the business before the House, that they might enjoy the pleasure of conversing with the fair critics in the galleries, that it became a matter of national importance to banish them—and they were banished. It will be long ere the American legislature will find it necessary to pass the same law for the same reason. A lady of Washington, however, told me an anecdote which went far to show that a more intellectual turn in the women would produce a change in the manners of the men. She told me, that when the Miss Wrights were in Washington, with General Lafayette, they very frequently attended the debates, and that the most distinguished members were always crowding round them. For this unwonted gallantry they apologized to their beautiful country-women by saying, that if they took equal interest in the debates, the galleries would be always thronged by the members.

The privilege of attending these debates would be more valuable could the speakers be better heard from the gallery; but, with the most earnest attention, I could only follow one or two of the orators, whose voices were peculiarly loud and clear. This made it really a labour to listen; but the extreme beauty of the chamber was of itself a reason for going again and again. It was, however, really mortifying to see this splendid hall, fitted up in so stately and sumptuous a manner, filled with men sitting in the most unseemly attitudes, a large majority with their hats on, and nearly all spitting to an excess that decency forbids me to describe.

Among the crowd, who must be included in this description, a few were distinguished by not wearing their hats, and by sitting on their chairs like other human beings, without throwing their legs above their heads. Whenever I inquired the name of one of these exceptions, I was told that it was Mr This or Mr That, of *Virginia*.

Congress

One day we were fortunate enough to get placed on the sofas between the pillars, on the floor of the house; the galleries being shut up, for the purpose of making some alterations, which it was hoped might improve the hearing in that part of the house occupied by the members, and which is universally complained of, as being very defective.[1]   But in our places on the sofas we found we heard very much better than up stairs, and well enough to be extremely amused by the rude eloquence of a thorough horse and alligator orator from Kentucky, who entreated the house repeatedly to " go the whole hog ".

If I mistake not, every debate I listened to in the American Congress was upon one and the same subject, namely, the entire independence of each individual state, with regard to the federal government.   The jealousy on this point appeared to me to be the very strangest political feeling that ever got possession of the mind of man.   I do not pretend to judge the merits of this question.   I speak solely of the very singular effect of seeing man after man start eagerly to his feet, to declare that the greatest injury, the basest injustice, the most obnoxious tyranny that could be practised against the state of which he was a member, would be a vote of a few million dollars for the purpose of making their roads or canals; or for drainage; or, in short, for any purposes of improvement whatsoever.[2]

[1] As a proof of this defective hearing in the Hall of Congress, I may quote a passage from a newspaper report of a debate on improvements.   It was proposed to suspend a ceiling of glass fifteen feet above the heads of the members.   A member speaking in favour of this proposal, said, " Members would then, at least, be able to understand what was the question before the House, an advantage which most of them did not now possess, respecting more than half the propositions upon which they voted."

[2] This strange jealousy is an illustration, *en grand*, of the democratic principle, and if pushed to its utmost perfection, would speedily dislocate every social compact, and leave each individual man as gloriously free as a bear on the unsophisticated shores of Bering's Straits.

During the month we were at Washington, I heard a great deal of conversation respecting a recent exclusion from Congress of a gentleman, who, by every account, was one of the most esteemed men in the house, and, I think, the father of it. The crime for which this gentleman was out-voted by his own particular friends and admirers was, that he had given his vote for a grant of public money for the purpose of draining a most lamentable and unhealthy district, called "the *dismal swamp*"!

One great boast of the country is, that they have no national debt, or that they shall have none in two years. This seems not very wonderful considering their productive tariff, and that the income paid to their president is 6000*l*. per annum; other government salaries being in proportion, and all internal improvements, at the expense of the government treasury, being voted unconstitutional.

The senate-chamber is, like the Hall of Congress, a semicircle, but of very much smaller dimensions. It is most elegantly fitted up, and what is better still, the senators, generally speaking, look like gentlemen. They do not wear their hats, and the activity of youth being happily past, they do not toss their heels above their heads. I would I could add they do not spit; but, alas! "I have an oath in heaven", and may not write an untruth.

A very handsome room, opening on a noble stone balcony, is fitted up as a library for the members. The collection, as far as a very cursory view could enable me to judge, was very like that of a private English gentleman, but with less Latin, Greek, and Italian. This room also is elegantly furnished; rich Brussels carpet; library tables, with portfolios of engravings; abundance of sofas, and so on. The view from it is glorious, and it looks like the abode of luxury and taste.

I can by no means attempt to describe all the apartments of this immense building, but the magnificent rotunda in the centre must not be left unnoticed. It is, indeed, a noble hall, a hundred feet in diameter, and of an imposing loftiness, lighted by an ample dome.

Almost any pictures (excepting the cartoons) would look paltry in this room, from the immense height of the walls; but the subjects of the four pictures which are placed there are of such high historic interest, that they should certainly have a place somewhere, as national records.   One represents the signing of the declaration of independence; another the resignation of the presidency by the great Washington; another the celebrated victory of General Gates at Saratoga; and the fourth . . . I do not well remember, but I think it is some other martial scene, commemorating a victory; I rather think that of York Town.

One other object in the capitol must be mentioned, though it occurs in so obscure a part of the building, that one or two members to whom I mentioned it, were not aware of its existence.   The lower part of the edifice, a story below the rotunda, etc., has a variety of committee rooms, courts, and other places of business. In a hall leading to some of these rooms, the ceiling is supported by pillars, the capitals of which struck me as peculiarly beautiful.   They are composed of the ears and leaves of the Indian corn, beautifully arranged, and forming as graceful an outline as the acanthus itself. This was the only instance I saw, in which America has ventured to attempt national originality; the success is perfect.   A sense of fitness always enhances the effect of beauty.   I will not attempt a long essay on the subject, but if America, in her vastness, her immense natural resources, and her remote grandeur, would be less imitative, she would be infinitely more picturesque and interesting.

The President has regular evening parties, every

other Wednesday, which are called his *levées*; the laſt syllable is pronounced by every one as long as possible, being exaƈtly the reverse of the French and English manner of pronouncing the same word. The effeƈt of this, from the very frequent repetition of the word in all companies, is very droll, and for a long time I thought people were quizzing these public days. The reception rooms are handsome, particularly the grand saloon, which is elegantly, nay, splendidly furnished; this has been done since the visit of Captain Hall, whose remarks upon the former ſtate of this room may have haſtened its decoration; but there are a few anomalies in some parts of the entertainment, which are not very courtly. The company are about as seleƈt as that of an Eaſter-day ball at the Mansion-house.

The churches at Washington are not superb; but the Episcopalian and Catholic were filled with elegantly dressed women. I observed a greater proportion of gentlemen at church at Washington than any where else.

The Presbyterian ladies go to church three times in the day, but the general appearance of Washington on a Sunday is much less puritanical than that of moſt other American towns: the people walk about, and there are no chains in the ſtreets, as at Philadelphia, to prevent their riding or driving, if they like it.

The ladies dress well, but not so splendidly as at Baltimore. I remarked that it was not very unusual at Washington for a lady to take the arm of a gentleman who was neither her husband, her father, nor her brother. This remarkable relaxation of American decorum has been probably introduced by the foreign legations. But though, as the seat of government, Washington muſt be considered as the mirror of fashion, and the model for national etiquette, there appeared to be even in the higheſt quarters so little attention to ceremony, that it is possible many things might be permitted there, which would be objected to elsewhere.

At about a mile from the town, on the high terrace-ground above described, is a very pretty place, to which the proprietor has given the name of Kaleirama.   It is not large, or in any way magnificent, but the view from it is charming; and it has a little wood behind, covering about two hundred acres of broken ground, that slopes down to a dark cold little river, so closely shut in by rocks and ever-greens, that it might serve as a noon-day bath for Diana and her nymphs.   The whole of this wood is filled with wild flowers, but such as we cherish fondly in our gardens.

A ferry at George Town crosses the Potomac, and about two miles from it, on the Virginian side, is Arlington, the seat of Mr Custis, who is the grandson of General Washington's wife.   It is a noble-looking place, having a portico of stately white columns, which, as the mansion stands high, with a back ground of dark woods, forms a beautiful object in the landscape. At George Town is a nunnery, where many young ladies are educated, and a little distance from it, a college of Jesuits for the education of young men, where, as their advertisements state, " the humanities are taught ".

We attended mass at the chapel of the nunnery, where the female voices that performed the chant were very pleasing.   The shadowy form of the veiled abbess in her little sacred parlour, seen through a grating and a black curtain, but rendered clearly visible by the light of a Gothic window behind her, drew a good deal of our attention; every act of genuflexion, even the telling her beads was discernible, but so mistily, that it gave her indeed the appearance of a being who had already quitted this life, and was hovering on the confines of the world of shadows.

The convent has a considerable inclosure attached to

it, where I frequently saw, from the heights above it, dark figures in awfully thick black veils walking solemnly up and down.

The American lady, who was the subject of one of Prince Hohenlohe's celebrated miracles, was pointed out to us at Washington. All the world declare that her recovery was marvellous.

*　　*　　*　　*　　*

There appeared to be a great many foreigners at Washington, particularly French. In Paris I have often observed that it was a sort of fashion to speak of America as a new Utopia, especially among the young liberals, who, before the happy accession of Philip, fancied that a country without a king was the land of promise; but I sometimes thought that, like many other fine things, it lost part of its brilliance when examined too nearly; I overhead the following question and answer pass between two young Frenchmen, who appeared to have met for the first time.

" *Eh bien, Monsieur, comment trouvez-vous la liberté et l'égalité mises en action ?*"

" *Mais, Monsieur, je vous avoue que le beau idéal que nous autres, nous avons conçu de tout cela à Paris, avait quelque chose de plus poétique que ce que nous trouvons ici !*"

On another occasion I was excessively amused by the tone in which one of these young men replied to a question put to him by another Frenchman. A pretty-looking woman, but exceedingly deficient in *tournure*, was standing alone at a little distance from them, and close at their elbows stood a very awkward-looking gentleman. " *Qui est cette dame ?*" said the inquirer. "*Monsieur*", said my young *fat*, with an indescribable grimace, " *c'est la femelle de ce male* ", indicating his neighbour by an expressive curl of his upper lip.

The theatre was not open while we were in Washington, but we afterwards took advantage of our vicinity to the city to visit it. The house is very small, and most astonishingly dirty and void of decoration, considering that it is the only place of public amusement that the city affords. I have before mentioned the want of decorum at the Cincinnati theatre, but certainly that of the capital at least rivalled it in the freedom of action and attitude; a freedom which seems to disdain the restraints of civilised manners. One man in the pit was seized with a violent fit of vomiting, which appeared not in the least to annoy or surprise his neighbours; and the happy coincidence of a physician being at that moment personated on the stage, was hailed by many of the audience as an excellent joke, of which the actor took advantage, and elicited shouts of applause by saying " I expect my services are wanted elsewhere ".

The spitting was incessant; and not one in ten of the male part of the illustrious legislative audience sat according to the usual custom of human beings; the legs were thrown sometimes over the front of the box, sometimes over the side of it; here and there a senator stretched his entire length along a bench; and in many instances the front rail was preferred as a seat.

I remarked one young man, whose handsome person, and most elaborate toilet, led me to conclude he was a first-rate personage, and so I doubt not he was; nevertheless, I saw him take from the pocket of his silk waistcoat a lump of tobacco, and daintily deposit it within his cheek.

I am inclined to think this most vile and universal habit of chewing tobacco is the cause of a remarkable peculiarity in the male physiognomy of Americans; their lips are almost uniformly thin and compressed. At first I accounted for this upon Lavater's theory, and attributed it to the arid temperament of the people; but it is too universal to be so explained; whereas the habit above mentioned, which pervades all classes (excepting the literary), well accounts for it, as the act of expressing the juices of this loathsome herb enforces exactly that position of the lips, which gives this remarkable peculiarity to the American countenance.

A member of Congress died while we were at Washington, and I was surprised by the ceremony and dignity of his funeral. It seems that whenever a senator or member of Congress dies during the session, he is buried at the expense of the government (this ceremony not coming under the head of internal improvement), and the arrangements for the funeral are not interfered with by his friends, but become matters of state. I transcribed the order of the procession as being rather grand and stately.

Chaplains of both Houses
Physicians who attended the deceased
Committee of arrangement

THE BODY

(Pall borne by six members)

The Relations of the deceased, with the Senators and Representatives
of the State to which he belonged, as
Mourners
Sergeant at arms of the House of Representatives
The House of Representatives
Their Speaker and Clerk preceding
The Senate of the United States
The Vice-President and Secretary preceding

THE PRESIDENT

The procession was of considerable extent, but not on foot, and the majority of the carriages were hired for the occasion. The body was interred in an open " graveyard " near the city. I did not see the monument erected on this occasion, but I presume it was in the same style as several others I have remarked in the same burying-ground, inscribed to the memory of members who had died at Washington. These were square blocks of masonry without any pretension to splendour.

Chapter Twenty-One

Stonington—Great Falls of the Potomac

THE greatest pleasure I had promised myself in visiting Washington was the seeing of a very old friend, who had left England many years ago, and married in America; she was now a widow, and, as I believed, settled in Washington. I soon had the mortification of finding that she was not in the city; but ere long I learnt that her residence was not more than ten miles from it. We speedily met, and it was settled that we should pass the summer with her in Maryland, and after a month devoted to Washington, we left it for Stonington.*

We arrived there the beginning of May, and the kindness of our reception, the interest we felt in becoming acquainted with the family of my friend, the extreme beauty of the surrounding country, and the lovely season, altogether, made our stay there a period of great enjoyment.

I wonder not that the first settlers in Virginia, with the bold Captain Smith of chivalrous memory at their head, should have fought so stoutly to dispossess the valiant father of Pocohontas of his fair domain, for I certainly never saw a more tempting territory. Stonington is about two miles from the most romantic point of the Potomac River, and Virginia spreads her wild, but beautiful, and most fertile Paradise, on the opposite shore. The Maryland side partakes of the same character, and perfectly astonished us by the profusion of her wild fruits and flowers.

We had not been long within reach of the great falls of the Potomac before a party was made for us to visit them; the walk from Stonington to these falls is through scenery that can hardly be called forest, park, or garden; but which partakes of all three. A little English girl accompanied us, who had but lately left her home; she exclaimed, " Oh! how many English ladies would glory in such a garden as this!"—and in truth they might; cedars, tulip-trees, planes, shumacs, junipers, and oaks of various kinds, moſt of them new to us, shaded our path.   Wild vines, with their rich expansive leaves, and their sweet blossom, rivalling the mignonette in fragance, cluſtered round their branches.   Strawberries in full bloom, violets, anemones, heart's-ease, and wild pinks, with many other, and ſtill lovelier flowers, which my ignorance forbids me to name, literally covered the ground.   The arbor judæ, the dog-wood, in its fulleſt glory of ſtar-like flowers, azaleas, and wild roses, dazzled our eyes whichever way we turned them.   It was the moſt flowery two miles I ever walked.

The sound of the falls is heard at Stonington, and the gradual increase of this sound is one of the agreeable features of this delicious walk.   I know not why the rush of waters is so delightful to the ear; all other monotonous sounds are wearying, and harass the spirits, but I never met any one who did not love to liſten to a waterfall.   A rapid ſtream, called the " Branch Creek ", was to be crossed ere we reached the spot where the falls are firſt visible.   This rumbling, turbid, angry little rivulet, flows through evergreens and flowering underwood, and is crossed *à plusieurs reprises*, by logs thrown from rock to rock.   The thundering noise of the ſtill unseen falls suggeſts an idea of danger while crossing these rude bridges, which hardly belongs to them; having reached the other side of the creek, we continued under the shelter of the evergreens for another quarter of a mile, and then emerged upon a sight that drew a shout of wonder and delight from us all.   The rocky depths of an enormous river were opened before our eyes, and so huge are the black crags that inclose it, that the thundering torrents of water rushing through, over, and among the rocks of this awful chasm, appear lost and swallowed up in it.

The river, or rather the bed of it, is here of great width, and most frightful depth, lined on all sides with huge masses of black rock of every imaginable form. The flood that roars through them is seen only at intervals; here in a full heavy sheet of green transparent water, falling straight and unbroken; there dashing along a narrow channel, with a violence that makes one dizzy to see and hear. In one place an unfathomed pool shows a mirror of inky blackness, and as still as night; in another the tortured, twisted cataract tumbles headlong in a dozen different torrents, half hid by the cloud of spray they send high into the air. Despite this uproar, the slenderest, loveliest shrubs peep forth from among these hideous rocks, like children smiling in the midst of danger. As we stood looking at this tremendous scene, one of our friends made us remark, that the poison alder, and the poison vine, threw their graceful, but perfidious branches, over every rock, and assured us also that innumerable tribes of snakes found their dark dwellings among them.

To call this scene beautiful would be a strange abuse of terms, for it is altogether composed of sights and sounds of terror. The falls of the Potomac are awfully sublime: the dark deep gulf which yawns before you, the foaming, roaring cataract, the eddying whirlpool, and the giddy precipice, all seem to threaten life, and to appal the senses. Yet it was a great delight to sit upon a high and jutting crag, and look and listen.

I heard with pleasure that it was to the Virginian side of the Potomac that the "felicity hunters" of Washington resorted to see this fearful wonder, for I never saw a spot where I should less have liked the annoying "how d'ye" of a casual rencontre. One could not even give or receive the exciting " is it not charming ?" which Rousseau talks of, for if it were uttered, it could not be heard, or, if heard, would fall most earthly dull on the spirit, when wrapt by the magic of such a scene. A look, or the silent pressure of the arm, is all the interchange of feeling that such a scene allows, and in the midst of my terror and my pleasure, I wished for the arm and the eye of some few from the other side of the Atlantic.

The return from such a scene is more soberly silent than the approach to it; but the cool and quiet hour, the mellowed tints of some gay blossoms, and the closed bells of others, the drowsy hum of the insects that survive the day, and the moist freshness that forbids the foot to weary in its homeward path, have all enjoyment in them, and seem to harmonise with the half-wearied, half-excited state of spirits, that such an excursion is sure to produce: and then the entering the cool and moonlit portico, the well-iced sangaree, or still more refreshing coffee, that awaits you, is all delightful; and if to this be added the happiness of an easy sofa, and a friend like my charming Mrs S——, to soothe you with an hour of Mozart, the most fastidious European might allow that such a day was worth waking for.

Chapter Twenty-Two

Small Landed Proprietors—Slavery

I now, for the first time since I crossed the mountains, found myself sufficiently at leisure to look deliberately round, and mark the different aspects of men and things in a region which, though bearing the same name, and calling itself the same land, was, in many respects, as different from the one I had left, as Amsterdam from St Petersburg. There every man was straining and struggling, and striving for himself (heaven knows!). Here every white man was waited upon, more or less, by a slave. There, the newly-cleared lands, rich with the vegetable manure accumulated for ages, demanded the slightest labour to return the richest produce; where the plough entered, crops the most abundant followed; but where it came not, no spot of native verdure, no native fruits, no native flowers cheered the eye; all was close, dark, stifling forest. Here the soil had long ago yielded its first fruits; much that had been cleared and cultivated for tobacco (the most exhausting of crops) by the English, required careful and laborious husbandry to produce any return; and much was left as sheep-walks. It was in these spots that the natural bounty of the soil and climate was displayed by the innumerable wild fruits and flowers which made every dingle and bushy dell seem a garden.

On entering the cottages I found also a great difference in the manner of living. Here, indeed, there were few cottages without a slave, but there were fewer still that had their beef-steak and onions for breakfast, dinner, and supper. The herrings of the bountiful Potomac supply their place. These are excellent "relish", as they call it, when salted, and, if I mistake not, are sold at a dollar-and-a-half per thousand. Whiskey, however, flows everywhere at the same fatally cheap rate of twenty cents (about one shilling) the gallon, and its hideous effects are visible on the countenance of every man you meet.

The class of people the most completely unlike any existing in England are those who, farming their own freehold estates, and often possessing several slaves, yet live with as few of the refinements, and, I think I may say, with as few of the comforts of life, as the very poorest English peasant. When in Maryland, I went into the houses of several of these small proprietors, and remained long enough, and looked and listened sufficiently, to obtain a tolerably correct idea of their manner of living.

One of these families consisted of a young man, his wife, two children, a female slave, and two young lads, slaves also. The farm belonged to the wife, and I was told, consisted of about three hundred acres of indifferent land, but all cleared. The house was built of wood, and looked as if the three slaves might have overturned it, had they pushed hard against the gable end. It contained one room, of about twelve feet square, and another adjoining it, hardly larger than a closet: this second chamber was the lodging-room of the white part of the family. Above these rooms was a loft, without windows, where I was told the " staying company " who visited them, were lodged. Near this mansion was a " shanty ", a black hole, without any window, which served as a kitchen and all other offices, and also as the lodging of the blacks.

We were invited to take tea with this family, and readily consented to do so. The furniture of the room was one heavy huge table, and about six wooden chairs. When we arrived the lady was in rather a dusky dishabille, but she vehemently urged us to be seated, and then retired into the closet-chamber above mentioned, whence she continued to address to us from behind the door all kinds of " genteel country visiting talk ", and at length emerged upon us in a smart new dress.

Her female slave set out the great table, and placed upon it cups of the very coarsest blue ware, a little brown sugar in one, and a tiny drop of milk in another; no butter, though the lady assured us she had a " *deary* " and two cows. Instead of butter, she " hoped we would fix a little relish with our crackers ", in ancient English, eat salt meat and dry biscuits. Such was the fare, and for guests that certainly were intended to be honoured. I could not help recalling the delicious repasts which I remembered to have enjoyed at little dairy farms in

England, not *possessed*, but rented, and at high rents too; where the clean, fresh coloured, bustling mistress herself skimmed the delicious cream, herself spread the yellow butter on the delightful brown loaf, and placed her curds, and her junket, and all the delicate treasures of her dairy before us, and then, with hospitable pride, placed herself at her board, and added the more delicate "relish" of good tea and good cream. I remembered all this, and did not think the difference atoned for, by the dignity of having my cup handed to me by a slave. The lady I now visited, however, greatly surpassed my quondam friends in the refinement of her conversation. She ambled through the whole time the visit lasted, in a sort of elegantly mincing familiar style of gossip, which, I think, she was imitating from some novel; for I was told she was a great novel reader, and left all household occupations to be performed by her slaves. To say she addressed us in a tone of equality, will give no adequate idea of her manner; I am persuaded that no misgiving on the subject ever entered her head. She told us that their estate was her divi-*dend* of her father's property. She had married a first cousin, who was as fine a gentleman as she was a lady, and as idle, preferring hunting (as they call shooting) to any other occupation. The consequence was, that but a very small portion of the divi-*dend* was cultivated, and their poverty was extreme. The slaves, particularly the lads, were considerably more than half naked; but the air of dignity with which, in the midst of all this misery, the lanky lady said to one of the young negroes "Attend to your young master, Lycurgus" must have been heard to be conceived in the full extent of its mock heroic.

Another dwelling of one of these landed proprietors was a hovel as wretched as the one above described, but there was more industry within it. The gentleman, indeed, was himself one of the numerous tribes of regular whiskey drinkers, and was rarely capable of any work; but he had a family of twelve children, who, with their skeleton mother, worked much harder than I ever saw negroes do. They were, accordingly, much less elegant and much less poor than the heiress; yet they lived with no appearance of comfort, and with, I believe, nothing beyond the necessaries of life. One proof of this was, that the worthless father would not suffer them to raise, even by their own labour, any garden vegetables, and they lived upon their fat pork, salt fish, and corn bread, summer and winter, without variation. This I found was frequently the case among the farmers. The luxury of whiskey is more appreciated by the men than all the green delicacies from the garden, and if all the ready money goes for that and their darling chewing tobacco, none can be spent by the wife for garden seeds; and as far as my observation extended, I never saw any American *ménage* where the toast and no toast question would have been decided in favour of the lady.

There are some small farmers who hold their lands as tenants, but these are by no means numerous: they do not pay their rent in money, but by making over a third of the produce to the owner; a mode of paying rent considerably more advantageous to the tenant than the landlord; but the difficulty of obtaining *money* in payment, excepting for mere retail articles, is very great in all American transactions. " I can pay in pro-*duce* " is the offer which I was assured is constantly made on all occasions, and, if rejected: " Then I guess we can't deal " is the usual rejoinder. This statement does not, of course, include the great merchants of great cities, but refers to the mass of the people scattered over the country; it has, indeed, been my object in speaking of the customs of the people, to give an idea of what they are *generally*.

The effect produced upon English people by the sight of slavery in every direction is very new, and not very agreeable, and it is not the less painfully felt from hearing upon every breeze the mocking words " All men are born free and equal ". One muſt be in the heart of American slavery, fully to appreciate that wonderfully fine passage in Moore's Epiſtle to Lord Viscount Forbes, which describes perhaps more faithfully, as well as more powerfully, the political ſtate of America, than anything that has ever been written upon it:

> Oh ! Freedom, Freedom, how I hate thy cant !
> Not eaſtern bombaſt, nor the savage rant
> Of purpled madmen, were they numbered all
> From Roman Nero, down to Russian Paul,
> Could grate upon my ear so mean, so base,
> As the rank jargon of that faƈious race,
> Who, poor of heart, and prodigal of words,
> Born to be slaves, and ſtruggling to be lords,
> But pant for licence, while they spurn controul,
> And shout for rights, with rapine in their soul !
> Who can, with patience, for a moment see
> The medley mass of pride and misery,
> Of whips and charters, manacles and rights,
> Of slaving blacks and democratic whites,
> Of all the pyebald polity that reigns
> In free confusion o'er Columbia's plains ?
> To think that man, thou juſt and gentle God !
> Should ſtand before thee with a tyrant's rod,
> O'er creatures like himself, with soul from thee,
> Yet dare to boaſt of perfeƈ liberty ;
> Away, away, I'd rather hold my neck
> By doubtful tenure from a Sultan's beck,
> In climes where liberty has scarce been named,
> Nor any right but that of ruling claimed,
> Than thus to live, where baſtard freedom waves
> Her fuſtian flag in mockery o'er slaves ;
> Where (motley laws admitting no degree
> Betwixt the vilely slaved, and madly free)
> Alike the bondage and the licence suit,
> The brute made ruler, and the man made brute !

The condition of domeſtic slaves, however, does not generally appear to be bad; but the ugly feature is, that should it be so, they have no power to change it.   I have seen much kind attention bestowed upon the health of slaves; but it is on these occasions impossible to forget, that did this attention fail, a valuable piece of property would be endangered. Unhappily the slaves, too, know this; and the consequence is, that real kindly feeling very rarely can exist between the parties. It is said that slaves born in a family are attached to the children of it, who have grown up with them. This may be the case where the petty acts of infant tyranny[1] have not been sufficient to conquer the kindly feeling naturally produced by long and early association; and this sort of attachment may last as long as the slave can be kept in that state of profound ignorance which precludes reflection. The law of Virginia has taken care of this. The State legislators may truly be said to be " wiser in their generation than the children of light ", and they ensure their safety by forbidding light to enter among them. By the law of Virginia it is penal to teach any slave to read, and it is penal to be aiding and abetting in the act of instructing them. This law speaks volumes. Domestic slaves are, generally speaking, tolerably well fed, and decently clothed; and the mode in which they are lodged seems a matter of great indifference to them. They are rarely exposed to the lash, and they are carefully nursed in sickness. These are the favourable features of their situation. The sad one is, that they *may* be sent to *the south*, and sold. This is the dread of all the slaves north of Louisiana. The sugar plantations, and more than

---

[1] Perhaps the most disgusting part of the spectacle (except the often recurring infliction of personal punishment) is that in which all that is most hateful in our nature is displayed in the infant tyranny of white children towards their slaves. I cannot even at this distance of time recall the puny bullying and well-taught ingenious insult of almost baby children towards stalwart slaves, who raised their heads towards heaven like men, but seemed to have lost the right of being so classed, without a feeling of indignation that makes my heart beat painfully.

all, the rice grounds of Georgia and the Carolinas, are the terror of American negroes; and well they may be, for they open an early grave to thousands; and to *avoid loss*, it is needful to make their previous labour pay their value.

There is something in the system of breeding and rearing negroes in the Northern States, for the express purpose of sending them to be sold in the South, that strikes painfully against every feeling of justice, mercy, or common humanity. During my residence in America I became perfectly persuaded that the state of a domestic slave in a gentleman's family was preferable to that of a hired American " help ", both because they are more cared for and valued, and because their condition being born with them, their spirits do not struggle against it with that pining discontent which seems the lot of all free servants in America. But the case is widely different with such as, in their own persons or those of their children " loved in vain ", are exposed to the dreadful traffic above-mentioned. In what is their condition better than that of the kidnapped negroes on the coast of Africa ? Of the horror in which this enforced migration is held, I had a strong proof during our stay in Virginia. The father of a young slave, who belonged to the lady with whom we boarded, was destined to this fate, and within an hour after it was made known to him, he sharpened the hatchet with which he had been felling timber, and with his right hand severed his left from the wrist.

But this is a subject on which I do not mean to dilate; it has been lately treated most judiciously by a far abler hand.[1] Its effects on the moral feelings and external manners of the people are all I wish to observe upon, and these are unquestionably most injurious. The same man who beards his wealthier and more educated neighbour with the bullying boast " I'm as good as you,"

[1] See Captain Hall's *Travels in America*.

turns to his slave, and knocks him down, if the furrow
he has ploughed or the log he has felled, please not this
stickler for equality. This is a glaring falsehood on
the very surface of such a man's principles that is
revolting. It is not among the higher classes that the
possession of slaves produces the worst effects. Among
the poorer class of landholders, who are often as
profoundly ignorant as the negroes they own, the
effect of this plenary power over males and females is
most demoralising; and the kind of coarse, not to say
brutal, authority which is exercised, furnishes the most
disgusting moral spectacle I ever witnessed. In all
ranks, however, it appeared to me that the greatest and
best feelings of the human heart were paralysed by the
relative positions of slave and owner. The characters,
the hearts of children, are irretrievably injured by it.
In Virginia we boarded for some time in a family
consisting of a widow and her four daughters, and I
there witnessed a scene strongly indicative of the effect
I have mentioned. A young female slave, about
eight years of age, had found on the shelf of a cupboard
a biscuit, temptingly buttered, of which she had eaten
a considerable portion before she was observed. The
butter had been copiously sprinkled with arsenic for
the destruction of rats, and had been thus most in-
cautiously placed by one of the young ladies of the
family. As soon as the circumstance was known, the
lady of the house came to consult me as to what had
best be done for the poor child; I immediately mixed a
large cup of mustard and water (the most rapid of all
emetics), and got the little girl to swallow it. The
desired effect was instantly produced, but the poor
child, partly from nausea and partly from the terror
of hearing her death proclaimed by half-a-dozen
voices round her, trembled so violently that I thought
she would fall. I sat down in the court where we were
standing, and, as a matter of course, took the little

sufferer in my lap. I observed a general titter among the white members of the family, while the black stood aloof and looked stupefied. The youngest of the family, a little girl about the age of the young slave, after gazing at me for a few moments in utter astonishment, exclaimed: "My! if Mrs Trollope has not taken her in her lap, and wiped her nasty mouth! Why, I would not have touched her mouth for two hundred dollars!"

The little slave was laid on a bed, and I returned to my own apartments; some time afterwards I sent to inquire for her, and learnt that she was in great pain. I immediately went myself to inquire farther, when another young lady of the family, the one by whose imprudence the accident had occurred, met my anxious inquiries with ill-suppressed mirth—told me they had sent for the doctor—and then burst into uncontrollable laughter. The idea of really sympathizing in the sufferings of a slave appeared to them as absurd as weeping over a calf that had been slaughtered by the butcher. The daughters of my hostess were as lovely as features and complexion could make them; but the neutralizing effect of this total want of feeling upon youth and beauty must be witnessed to be conceived.

There seems in general a strong feeling throughout America that none of the negro race can be trusted; and as fear, according to their notions, is the only principle by which a slave can be actuated, it is not wonderful if the imputation be just. But I am persuaded that, were a different mode of moral treatment pursued, most important and beneficial consequences would result from it. Negroes are very sensible to kindness, and might, I think, be rendered more profitably obedient by the practice of it towards them, than by any other mode of discipline whatever. To emancipate them entirely throughout the Union cannot, I conceive, be thought of, consistently with the safety of the country; but, were the possibility of amelioration taken into the consideration of the legislature, with all the wisdom, justice, and mercy that could be brought to bear upon it, the negro population of the Union might cease to be a terror, and their situation no longer be a subject either of indignation or of pity.

I observed every where throughout the slave states that all articles which can be taken and consumed are constantly locked up, and in large families, where the extent of the establishment multiplies the number of keys, these are deposited in a basket, and consigned to the care of a little negress, who is constantly seen following her mistress's steps with this basket on her arm, and this, not only that the keys may be always at hand, but because, should they be out of sight one moment, that moment would infallibly be employed for purposes of plunder. It seemed to me in this instance, as in many others, that the close personal attendance of these sable shadows must be very annoying; but whenever I mentioned it, I was assured that no such feeling existed, and that use rendered them almost unconscious of their presence.

I had, indeed, frequent opportunities of observing this habitual indifference to the presence of their slaves. They talk of them, of their condition, of their faculties, of their conduct, exactly as if they were incapable of hearing. I once saw a young lady who, when seated at table between a male and a female, was induced by her modesty to intrude on the chair of her female neighbour to avoid the indelicacy of touching the elbow of *a man*. I once saw this very young lady lacing her stays with the most perfect composure before a negro footman. A Virginian gentleman told me that, ever since he had married, he had been accustomed to have a negro girl sleep in the same chamber with himself and his wife. I asked for what purpose this nocturnal attendance was necessary ? "Good heaven!" was the reply. "If I wanted a glass of water during the night, what would become of me ?"

Chapter Twenty-Three

Fruits and Flowers of Maryland and Virginia—Copper-Head Snake—Insects—Elections

OUR summer in Maryland (1830) was delightful. The thermometer stood at 94, but the heat was by no means so oppressive as what we had felt in the West. In no part of North America are the natural productions of the soil more various, or more beautiful. Strawberries of the richest flavour sprung beneath our feet; and when these passed away, every grove, every lane, every field looked like a cherry orchard, offering an inexhaustible profusion of fruit to all who would take the trouble to gather it. Then followed the peaches; every hedge-row was planted with them, and though the fruit did not equal in size or flavour those ripened on our garden walls, we often found them good enough to afford a delicious refreshment on our long rambles. But it was the flowers, and the flowering shrubs that, beyond all else, rendered this region the most beautiful I had ever seen (the Alleghany always excepted). No description can give an idea of the variety, the profusion, the luxuriance of them. If I talk of wild roses, the English reader will fancy I mean the pale ephemeral blossoms of our bramble hedges; but the wild roses of Maryland and Virginia might be the choicest favourites of the flower-garden. They are rarely very double, but the brilliant eye atones for this. They are of all shades, from the deepest crimson to the tenderest pink. The scent is rich and delicate; in size they exceed any single roses I ever saw, often measuring above four inches in diameter. The leaf greatly resembles that of the china rose; it is large, dark, firm, and brilliant. The sweet-brier grows wild, and blossoms abundantly; both leaves and flowers are considerably larger than with us. The acacia, or as it is there called the locust, blooms with great richness and profusion; I have gathered a branch less than a foot long, and counted twelve full bunches of flowers on it. The scent is equal to the orange-flower. The dogwood is another of the splendid white blossoms that adorn the woods. Its lateral branches are flat, like a fan, and dotted all over with star-like blossoms, as large as those of the gum-cistus. Another pretty shrub, of smaller size, is the poison alder. It is well that its noxious qualities are very generally known, for it is most tempting to the eye by its delicate fringe-like bunches of white flowers. Even the touch of this shrub is poisonous, and produces violent swelling. The arbor judæ is abundant in every wood, and its bright and delicate pink is the earliest harbinger of the American spring. Azaleas, white, yellow, and pink; kalmias of every variety, the too sweet magnolia, and the stately rhododendron, all grow in wild abundance there. The plant known in England as the Virginia creeper, is often seen climbing to the top of the highest forest trees, and bearing a large trumpet-shaped blossom of a rich scarlet. The sassafras is a beautiful shrub, and I cannot imagine why it has not been naturalised in England, for it has every appearance of being extremely hardy. The leaves grow in tufts, and every tuft contains leaves of five or six different forms. The fruit is singularly beautiful; it resembles in form a small acorn, and is jet black; the cup and stem looking as if they were made of red coral. The graceful and fantastic grapevine is a feature of great beauty, and its wandering festoons bear no more resemblance to our well-trained vines, than our stunted azaleas, and tiny magnolias, to their thriving American kindred.

There is another charm that haunts the summer wanderer in America, and it is perhaps the only one found in greatest perfection in the West: but it is beautiful every where. In a bright day, during any of the summer months, your walk is through an atmosphere of butterflies, so gaudy in hue, and so varied in form, that I often thought they looked like flowers on the wing. Some of them are very large, measuring three or four inches across the wings; but many, and I think the most beautiful, are smaller than ours. Some have wings of the most dainty lavender colour, and bodies of black; others are fawn and rose colour; and others again are orange and bright blue. But pretty as they are, it is their number, even more than their beauty, that delights the eye. Their gay and noiseless movement as they glance through the air, crossing each other in chequered maze, is very beautiful. The humming-bird is another pretty summer toy; but they are not sufficiently numerous, nor do they live enough on the wing to render them so important a feature in the transatlantic show, as the rainbow-tinted butterflies. The fire-fly was a far more brilliant novelty. In moist situations, or before a storm, they are very numerous, and in the dark sultry evening of a burning day, when all employment was impossible, I have often found it a pastime to watch their glancing light, now here, now there; now seen, now gone: shooting past with the rapidity of lightning, and looking like a shower of falling stars, blown about in the breeze of evening.

*   *   *   *   *

In one of our excursions we encountered and slew a copper-head snake. I escaped treading on it by about three inches. While we were contemplating our conquered foe, and doubting in our ignorance if he were indeed the deadly copper-head we had so often heard described, a farmer joined us, who, as soon as he cast his eyes on our victim, exclaimed: " My! if you have not got a copper. That's right down well done, they be darnation beasts." He told us that he had once seen a copper-head bite himself to death, from being teased by a stick, while confined in a cage where he could find no other victim. We often heard terrible accounts of the number of these desperate reptiles to be found on the rocks near the great falls of the Potomac; but not even the terror these stories inspired could prevent our repeated visits to that sublime scene; luckily our temerity was never punished by seeing any there. Lizards, long, large, and most hideously like a miniature crocodile, I frequently saw, gliding from the fissures of the rocks, and darting again under shelter, perhaps beneath the very stone I was seated upon; but every one assured us they were harmless. Animal life is so infinitely abundant, and in forms so various, and so novel to European eyes, that it is absolutely necessary to divest oneself of all the petty terrors which the crawling, creeping, hopping, and buzzing tribes can inspire, before taking an American summer ramble. It is, I conceive, quite impossible for any description to convey an idea of the sounds which assail the ears from the time the short twilight begins, until the rising sun scatters the rear of darkness, and sends the winking choristers to rest.

Be where you will (excepting in the large cities) the appalling note of the bull-frog will reach you, loud, deep, and hoarse, issuing from a thousand throats in ceaseless continuity of croak. The tree-frog adds her chirping and almost human voice; the kattiedid repeats her own name through the livelong night; the whole tribe of locusts chirp, chirrup, squeak, whiz, and whistle, without allowing one instant of interval to the weary ear; and when to this the mosquito adds her threatening hum, it is wonderful that any degree of fatigue can obtain for the listener the relief of sleep. In fact, it is only in ceasing to listen that this blessing can be found. I passed many feverish nights during my first summer, literally in listening to this most astounding mixture of noises, and it was only when they became too familiar to excite attention, that I recovered my rest.

I know not by what whimsical link of association the recapitulation of this insect din suggests the recollection of other discords, at least as harsh, and much more troublesome.

Even in the retirement in which we passed this summer, we were not beyond reach of the election fever, which is constantly raging through the land. Had America every attraction under heaven that nature and social enjoyment can offer, this electioneering madness would make me fly it in disgust. It engrosses every conversation, it irritates every temper, it substitutes party spirit for personal esteem, and, in fact, vitiates the whole system of society.

When a candidate for any office starts, his party endow him with every virtue, and with all the talents. They are all ready to peck out the eyes of those who oppose him, and in the warm and mettlesome south-western states, do literally often perform this operation; but as soon as he succeeds, his virtues and his talents vanish, and, excepting those holding office under his appointment, every man Jonathan of them sets off again full gallop to elect his successor. When I first arrived in America Mr John Quincy Adams was President, and it was impossible to doubt, even from the statement of his enemies, that he was every way calculated to do honour to the office. All I ever heard against him was, that " he was too much of a gentleman "; but a new candidate must be set up, and Mr

Adams was out-voted for no other reason, that I could learn, but because it was " beſt to change ".—" Jackson for ever!" was, therefore, screamed from the majority of mouths, both drunk and sober, till he was elected; but no sooner in his place, than the same ceaseless operation went on again, with " Clay for ever " for its war-whoop.

I was one morning paying a visit, when a party of gentlemen arrived at the same house, on horse-back. The one whose air proclaimed him the chief of his party, left us not long in doubt as to his business, for he said, almoſt in entering:

" Mr P——, I come to ask for your vote."

" Who are you for, sir ?" was the reply.

" Clay for ever!" the rejoinder; and the vote was promised.

This gentleman was candidate for a place in the State representation, whose members have a vote in the presidential election.

I was introduced to him as an English woman: he addressed me with: " Well, madam, you see we do these things openly and above-board here; you mince such matterʀ more, I expect."

After his departure his hiſtory and ſtanding were discussed. " Mr M. is highly respectable, and of very good ſtanding; there can be no doubt of his election if he is a thorough-going Clay-man " said my hoſt.

I asked what his ſtation was.

The lady of the house told me that his father had been a merchant, and when this future legislator was a young man, he had been sent by him to some port in the Mediterranean as his supercargo. The youth, being a free-born high-spirited youth, appropriated the proceeds to his own uses, traded with great success upon the fund thus obtained, and returned, after an absence of twelve years, a gentleman of fortune and excellent ſtanding. I expressed some little disapprobation of this proceeding, but was assured that Mr M. was considered by every one as a very " honourable man ".

Were I to relate one-tenth part of the dishonest transactions recounted to me by Americans, of their fellow-citizens and friends, I am confident that no English reader would give me credit for veracity; it would, therefore, be very unwise to repeat them, but I cannot refrain from expressing the opinion that nearly four years of attentive observation impressed on me, namely, that the moral sense is on every point blunter than with us. Make an American believe that his next door neighbour is a very worthless fellow, and I dare say (if he were quite sure he could make nothing by him) he would drop the acquaintance; but as to what constitutes a worthless fellow, people differ on the opposite sides of the Atlantic, almost by the whole decalogue. There is, as it appeared to me, an obtusity on all points of honourable feeling.[1]

" Cervantes laughed Spain's chivalry away ", but he did not laugh away that better part of chivalry, so beautifully described by Burke as " the unbought grace of life, the cheap defence of nations, that chastity of honour, which feels a stain as a wound, which ennobles whatever it touches, and by which vice itself loses half its evil, by losing all its grossness."* The better part of chivalry still mixes with gentle blood in every part of Europe, nor is it less fondly guarded than when sword and buckler aided its defence. Perhaps this unbought grace of life is not to be looked for where chivalry has never been. I certainly do not lament the decadence of knight errantry, nor wish to exchange the protection of the laws for that of the doughtiest champion who

[1] It is remarkable how often in re-perusing these pages, it strikes me that since they were written, the old country has in many points assimilated itself to the new. If my memory does not entirely fail me, there was more attention shown to moral character formerly, and a greater necessity for those who sought advancement to stand well in public opinion as to their worth and honour than at present.

ever set lance in rest; but I do, in truth, believe that this knightly sensitiveness of honourable feeling is the best antidote to the petty soul-degrading transactions of every-day life, and that the total want of it is one reason why this free-born race care so very little for the vulgar virtue called probity.

Chapter Twenty-Four

Journey to Philadelphia—Chesapeake and Delaware Canal—City of Philadelphia—Miss Wright's Lecture

In the latter part of August, 1830, we paid a visit to Philadelphia, and, notwithstanding the season, we were so fortunate as to have both bright and temperate weather for the expedition. The road from Washington to Baltimore, which was our first day's journey, is interesting in summer from the variety and luxuriance of the foliage which borders a great part of it.

We passed the night at Baltimore, and embarked next morning on board a steam-boat for Philadelphia. The scenery of the Elk river, upon which you enter soon after leaving the port of Baltimore, is not beautiful. We embarked at six in the morning, and at twelve reached the Chesapeake and Delaware canal; we then quitted the steam-boat, and walked two or three hundred yards to the canal, where we got on board a pretty little decked boat, sheltered by a neat awning, and drawn by four horses. This canal cuts across the state of Delaware, and connects the Chesapeake and Delaware rivers: it has been a work of great expense, though the distance is not more than thirteen miles; for a considerable part of this distance the cutting has been very deep, and the banks are in many parts thatched, to prevent their crumbling. At the point where the cutting is deepest, a light bridge is thrown across, which, from its great height, forms a striking object to the travellers passing below it. Every boat that passes this canal pays a toll of twenty dollars.

Nothing can be less interesting than that part of the state of Delaware through which this cut passes, the Mississippi hardly excepted. At one, we reached the Delaware river, at a point nearly opposite Delaware Fort, which looks recently built, and is very handsome.[1] Here we again changed our vessel, and got on board another of their noble steam-boats; both these changes were made with the greatest regularity and dispatch.

There is nothing remarkable in the scenery of the Delaware. The stream is wide and the banks are flat; a short distance before you reach Philadelphia two large buildings of singular appearance strike the eye. On inquiry I learnt that they were erected for the purpose of sheltering two ships of war. They are handsomely finished, with very neat roofs, and are ventilated by many windows. The expense of these buildings must have been considerable, but as the construction of the vast machines they shelter was more so, it may be good economy.

We reached Philadelphia at four o'clock in the afternoon. The approach to this city is not so striking as that to Baltimore; though much larger, it does not now show itself so well; it wants domes and columns: it is, nevertheless, a beautiful city. Nothing can exceed its neatness; the streets are well paved, the foot-way, as in all the old American cities, is of brick, like the old pantile walk at Tunbridge Wells. This is almost entirely sheltered from the sun by the awnings, which, in all the principal streets, are spread from the shop windows to the edge of the pavement.

The city is built with extreme and almost wearisome regularity; the streets, which run north and south, are distinguished by numbers, from one to—I know not

[1] This fort was destroyed by fire a few months afterwards.

how many, but I paid a visit in Twelfth Street; these are intersected at right angles by others, which are known by the names of various trees; Mulberry (more commonly called Arch Street), Chesnut, and Walnut, appear the most fashionable: in each of these there is a theatre. This mode of distinguishing the streets is commodious to strangers, from the facility it gives of finding out whereabouts you are; if you ask for the United States Bank, you are told it is in Chesnut, between Third and Fourth, and as the streets are all divided from each other by equal distances, of about three hundred feet, you are sure of not missing your mark. There are many handsome houses, but none that are very splendid; they are generally of brick, and those of the better order have white marble steps, and some few, door-frames of the same beautiful material; but, on the whole, there is less display of it in the private dwellings than at Baltimore.

The Americans all seem greatly to admire this city, and to give it the preference in point of beauty to all others in the Union, but I do not agree with them. There are some very handsome buildings, but none of them so placed as to produce a striking effect, as is the case both with the Capitol and the President's house, at Washington. Notwithstanding these fine buildings, one or more of which are to be found in all the principal streets, the *coup d'œil* is every where the same. There is no Place de Louis Quinze or Carrousel, no Regent Street or Green Park, to make one exclaim "How beautiful!" all is even, straight, uniform, and un-interesting.

There is one spot, however, about a mile from the town, which presents a lovely scene. The water-works of Philadelphia have not yet perhaps as wide-extended fame as those of Marly, but they are not less deserving it. At a most beautiful point of the Schuylkill River, the water has been forced up into a magnificent reservoir, ample and elevated enough to send it through the

whole city. The vast yet simple machinery by which
this is achieved is open to the public, who resort in such
numbers to see it, that several evening stages run from
Philadelphia to Fair Mount for their accommodation.
But interesting and curious as this machinery is, Fair
Mount would not be so attractive had it not something
else to offer. It is, in truth, one of the very prettiest
spots the eye can look upon. A broad wear is thrown
across the Schuylkill, which produces the sound and
look of a cascade. On the farther side of the river is a
gentleman's seat, the beautiful lawns of which slope to
the water's edge, and groups of weeping willows and
other trees throw their shadows on the stream. The
works themselves are enclosed in a simple but very
handsome building of freestone, which has an extended
front opening upon a terrace, which overhangs the
river: behind the building, and divided from it only by
a lawn, rises a lofty wall of solid lime-stone rock, which
has, at one or two points, been cut into, for the passage
of the water into the noble reservoir above. From the
crevices of this rock the catalpa was every where
pushing forth, covered with its beautiful blossom.
Beneath one of these trees an artificial opening in the
rock gives passage to a stream of water, clear and bright
as crystal, which is received in a stone basin of simple
workmanship, having a cup for the service of the thirsty
traveller. At another point, a portion of the water,
in its upward way to the reservoir, is permitted to
spring forth in a perpetual *jet d'eau*, that returns in a
silver shower upon the head of a marble *naiad* of snowy
whiteness. The statue is not the work of Phidias; but
its dark, rocky background, the flowery catalpas which
shadow it, and the bright shadow through which it
shows itself, altogether make the scene one of singular
beauty; add to which, the evening on which I saw
it was very sultry, and the contrast of this cool spot
to all besides certainly enhanced its attractions; it

was impossible not to envy the nymph her eternal shower-bath.

On returning from this excursion we saw hand-bills in all parts of the city, announcing that Miss Wright was on that evening to deliver her parting address to the citizens of Philadelphia, at the Arch Street theatre, previous to her departure for Europe. I immediately determined to hear her, and did so, though not without some difficulty, from the crowds who went thither with the same intention. The house, which is a very pretty one, was filled in every part, including the stage, with a well-dressed and most attentive audience. There was a larger proportion of ladies present than I ever saw on any other occasion in an American theatre. One reason for this might be, perhaps, that they were admitted gratis.

Miss Wright came on the stage surrounded by a bodyguard of Quaker ladies, in the full costume of their sect. She was, as she always is, startling in her theories, but powerfully eloquent, and, on the whole, was much applauded, though one passage produced great emotion, and some hissing. She stated broadly, on the authority of Jefferson, furnished by his posthumous works, that " Washington was not a Christian ". One voice from the crowded pit exclaimed, in an accent of indignation, " Washington was a Christian "; but it was evident that the majority of the audience considered Mr Jefferson's assertion as a compliment to the country's idol, for the hissing was soon triumphantly clapped down. General Washington himself, however, gives a somewhat different account of his own principles; for, in his admirable farewell address on declining a re-election to the Presidency, I find the following passage:

" Of all the dispositions and habits which lead to political prosperity' religion and morality are indispensable supports. In vain would that man claim the tribute of patriotism who would labour to subvert these great pillars of human happiness, these firmest props of the destinies of men and citizens. A volume could not trace all their connections with private and public felicity. And let us with caution indulge the supposition that morality can be maintained without religion; reason and experience both forbid us to expect that national morality can prevail in exclusion of religious principle."

Whether Mr Jefferson or himself knew best what his principles were, I will not decide; but, at least, it appears fair, when repeating one statement, to add the other also.

Chapter Twenty-Five

Washington Square—American Beauty—Gallery of Fine Arts—Antiques—Theatres—Museum

OUR mornings were spent, as all travellers' mornings must be, in asking questions, and in seeing all that the answers told us it was necessary to see. Perhaps this can be done in no city with more facility than in Philadelphia; you have nothing to do but to walk up one straight street, and down another, till all the parallelograms have been threaded. In doing this you will see many things worth looking at. The United States and Pennsylvania banks are the most striking buildings, and are both extremely handsome, being of white marble, and built after Grecian models. The State House has nothing externally to recommend it, but the room shown as that in which the declaration of independence was signed, and in which the estimable Lafayette was received, half a century after he had shed his noble blood in aiding to obtain it, is an interesting spot. At one end of this room is a statue in wood of General Washington; on its base is the following inscription:

First in Peace,
First in War,
and
First in the hearts of his Countrymen.

There is a very pretty enclosure before the Walnut Street entrance to the State House, with good well-kept gravel walks, and many of their beautiful flowering trees. It is laid down in grass, not in turf; that, indeed, is a luxury I never saw in America. Near this enclosure is another of much the same description, called Washington Square. Here there was an excellent crop of clover; but as the trees are numerous, and highly beautiful, and several commodious seats are placed beneath their shade, it is, spite of the long grass, a very agreeable retreat from heat and dust. It was rarely, however, that I saw any of these seats occupied; the Americans have either no leisure, or no inclination for those moments of *délassement* that all other people, I believe, indulge in. Even their drams, so universally taken by rich and poor, are swallowed standing, and, excepting at church, they never have the air of leisure or repose. This pretty Washington Square is surrounded by houses on three sides, but (lasso!) has a prison on the fourth; it is, nevertheless, the nearest approach to a London Square that is to be found in Philadelphia.

One evening, while the rest of my party went to visit some objects which I had before seen, I agreed to await their return in this square, and sat down under a magnificent catalapa, which threw its fragrant blossoms in all directions; the other end of the bench was occupied by a young lady, who was employed in watching the gambols of a little boy. There was something in her manner of looking at me, and exchanging a smile when her young charge performed some extraordinary feat of activity on the grass, that persuaded me she was not an American. I do not remember who spoke first, but we were presently in a full flow of conversation. She spoke English with elegant correctness, but she was a German, and with an ardour of feeling which gave her a decidedly foreign air in Philadelphia, she talked to me of her country, of all she had left, and of all she had found, or rather of all she had not found, for thus ran her lament:

"They do not love music, oh no! and they never amuse themselves—no; and their hearts are not warm, at least they seem not so to strangers; and they have no ease, no forgetfulness of business and of care—no, not for a moment. But I will not stay long, I think, for I should not live."

She told me that she had a brother settled there as a merchant, and that she had passed a year with him; but she was hoping soon to return to her father-land.

I never so strongly felt the truth of the remark, that expression is the soul of beauty, as in looking at, and listening to this young German. She was any thing but handsome; it is true she had large eyes, full of gentle expression, but every feature was irregular; but, oh! the charm of that smile, of that look of deep feeling which animated every feature when she spoke of her own Germany! The tone of her voice, the slight and graceful action which accompanied her words, all struck me as so attractive, that the half hour I passed with her was continually recurring to my memory. I had often taxed myself with feeling something like prejudice against the beautiful American women; but this half hour set my conscience at rest; it is not prejudice which causes one to feel that regularity of features is insufficient to interest, or even to please, beyond the first glance. I certainly believe the women of America to be the handsomest in the world, but as surely do I believe that they are the least attractive.

*　　*　　*　　*　　*

We visited the nineteenth annual exhibition of the Pennsylvania academy of the fine arts; 431 was the number of objects exhibited, which were so arranged

227

as to fill three tolerably large rooms, and one smaller, called the directors' room. There were among the number about thirty engravings, and a much larger proportion of water-colour drawings: about seventy had the P.A. (Pennsylvanian Academician) annexed to the name of the artist.

The principal historical composition was a large scripture piece by Mr Washington Alston. This gentleman is spoken of as an artist of great merit, and I was told that his manner was much improved since this picture was painted (it bears date, 1813). I believe it was for this picture Mr Alston received a prize at the British Gallery.

There was a portrait of a lady, which in the catalogue is designated as " the White Plume ", which had the reputation of being the most admired in the collection, and the artist, Mr Ingham, is said to rank highest among the portrait-painters of America. This picture is of very high finish, particularly the drapery, which is most elaborately worked, even to the pile of the velvet; the management of the light is much in the manner of Good; but the drawing is very defective, and the contour, though the face is a lovely one, hard and unfleshy. From all the conversations on painting which I listened to in America, I found that the finish of drapery was considered as the highest excellence, and next to this, the resemblance in a portrait; I do not remember ever to have heard the words *drawing* or *composition* used in any conversation on the subject.

One of the rooms of this academy has inscribed over its door

ANTIQUE STATUE GALLERY

The door was open, but just within it was a screen, which prevented any objects in the room being seen from without. Upon my pausing to read this inscription, an old woman who appeared to officiate as guardian of the gallery, bustled up, and addressing me with an air of much mystery, said: " Now, ma'am, now: this is just the time for you—nobody can see you— make haste."

I stared at her with unfeigned surprise, and disengaging my arm, which she had taken apparently to hasten my movements, I very gravely asked her meaning.

" Only, ma'am, that the ladies like to go into that room by themselves, when there be no gentlemen watching them."

On entering this mysterious apartment, the first thing I remarked, was a written paper, deprecating the disgusting depravity which had led some of the visitors to mark and deface the casts in a most indecent and shameless manner. This abomination has unquestionably been occasioned by the coarse-minded custom which sends alternate groups of males and females into the room. Were the antique gallery thrown open to mixed parties of ladies and gentlemen, it would soon cease. Till America has reached the degree of refinement which permits of this, the antique casts should not be exhibited to ladies at all. I never felt my delicacy shocked at the Louvre, but I was strongly tempted to resent as an affront the hint I received, that I might steal a glance at what was deemed indecent Perhaps the arrangements for the exhibition of this room, the feelings which have led to them, and the result they have produced, furnish as good a specimen of the kind of delicacy on which the Americans pride themselves, and of the peculiarities arising from it, as can be found. The room contains about fifty casts, chiefly from the antique.

In the directors' room I was amused at the means which a poet had hit upon for advertising his works, or rather HIS WORK, and not less at the elaborate notice of it. His portrait was suspended there, and attached to the frame was a paper inscribed thus:

PORTRAIT OF THE AUTHOR

of

The Fredoniad, or Independence Preserved; a political, naval, and military poem, on the late war of 1812, in forty cantos; the whole compressed in four volumes; each volume averaging more then 305 pages,

By RICHARD EMMONS, M.D.

*   *   *   *   *

I went to the Chesnut Street Theatre to see Mr Booth, formerly of Drury Lane, in the character of Lear, and a Mrs Duff in Cordelia; but I have seen too many Lears and Cordelias to be easily pleased; I thought the whole performance very bad. The theatre is of excellently moderate dimensions, and prettily decorated. It was not the fashionable season for the theatres, which I presume must account for the appearance of the company in the boxes, which was any thing but elegant; nor was there more decorum of demeanour than I had observed elsewhere; I saw one man in the lower tier of boxes deliberately take off his coat that he might enjoy the refreshing coolness of shirt sleeves; all the gentlemen wore their hats, and the spitting was unceasing.

On another evening we went to the Walnut Street Theatre; the chief attraction of the night was furnished by the performance of a young man who had been previously exhibited as " a living skeleton ". He played the part of Jeremiah Thin, and certainly looked the part well; and here I think must end my praise of the evening's performances.

The great and most striking contrast between this city and those of Europe, is perceived after sun-set; scarcely a sound is heard; hardly a voice or a wheel breaks the stillness. The streets are entirely dark, except where a stray lamp marks an hotel or the like; no shops are open, but those of the apothecary, and here and there a cook's shop; scarcely a step is heard, and for a note of music, or the sound of mirth, I listened in vain. In leaving the theatre, which I always did before the after-piece, I saw not a single carriage; the night of Miss Wright's lecture, when I stayed to the end, I saw one. This darkness, this stillness, is so great, that I almost felt it awful. As we walked home one fine moonlight evening from the Chesnut Street house, we stopped a moment before the United States Bank, to look at its white marble columns by the subdued light, said to be so advantageous to them; the building did, indeed, look beautiful; the incongruous objects around were hardly visible, while the brilliant white of the building, which by daylight is dazzling, was mellowed into fainter light and softer shadow.

While passing before this modern temple of Theseus, we remarked that we alone seemed alive in this great city; it was ten o'clock, and a most lovely cool evening, after a burning day, yet all was silence. Regent Street, Bond Street, with their blaze of gas-light *bijouterie*, and still more the Italian Boulevard of Paris, rose in strong contrast on the memory; the light, which outshines that of day — the gay, graceful, laughing throng — the elegant saloons of Tortoni, with all their varieties of cooling nectar — were all remembered.* Is it an European prejudice to deem that the solitary dram swallowed by the gentlemen on quitting an American theatre indicates a lower and more vicious state of manners, than do the ices so sedulously offered to the ladies on leaving a French one?

* * * * *

The museum contains a good collection of objects illustrative of natural history, and some very interesting specimens of Indian antiquities; both here and at Cincinnati I saw so many things resembling Egyptian relics, that I should like to see the origin of the Indian nations inquired into more accurately than has yet been done.

The shops, of which there appeared to me to be an unusually large proportion, are very handsome; many of them in a style of European elegance. Lottery offices abound, and that species of gambling is carried to a great extent. I saw fewer carriages in Philadelphia than either at Baltimore or Washington, but in the winter, I was told, they were more numerous.

Many of the best families had left the city for different watering-places, and others were daily following. Long Branch is a fashionable bathing place on the Jersey shore, to which many resort, both from this place and from New York; the description given of the manner of bathing appeared to me rather extraordinary, but the account was confirmed by so many different people, that I could not doubt its correctness. The shore, it seems, is too bold to admit of bathing machines, and the ladies have, therefore, recourse to another mode for ensuring the enjoyment of a sea-bath with safety. The accommodation at Long Branch is almost entirely at large boarding-houses, where all the company live at a *table d'hôte*. It is customary for ladies on arriving to look round among the married gentlemen, the first time they meet at table, and to select the one her fancy leads her to prefer as a protector in her purposed visits to the realms of Neptune; she makes her request, which is always graciously received, that he would lead her to taste the briny wave; but another fair one must select the same protector, else the arrangement cannot be complete, as custom does not authorise *tête à tête* immersion.

Quakers

Chapter Twenty-Six

*Quakers—Presbyterians—Itinerant Methodist Preacher—
Market—Influence of Females on Society*

I HAD never chanced, among all my wanderings, to
enter a Quaker Meeting-house; and as I thought I
could nowhere make my first visit better than at
Philadelphia, I went under the protection of a Quaker
lady to the principal *orthodox* meeting of the city. The
building is large but perfectly without ornament; the
men and women are separated by a rail which divides
it into two equal parts; the meeting was very full on
both sides, and the atmosphere almost intolerably hot.
As they glided in at their different doors, I spied many
pretty faces peeping from the prim head-gear of the
females, and as the broad-brimmed males sat down, the
welcome which Parney supposes prepared for them in
heaven, recurred to me:

"Entre donc, et garde ton chapeau."

The little bonnets and the large hats were ranged in
long rows, and their stillness was for a long time so unbroken, that I could hardly persuade myself the figures
they surmounted were alive. At length a grave square
man arose, laid aside his ample beaver, and after
another solemn interval of silence, he gave a deep groan,
and as it were by the same effort uttered "Keep thy
foot". Again he was silent for many minutes, and
then he continued for more than an hour to put forth
one word at a time, but at such an interval from each
other that I found it quite impossible to follow his
meaning, if, indeed, he had any. My Quaker friend
told me she knew not who he was, and that she much
regretted I had heard so poor a preacher. After he
had concluded, a gentleman-like old man (a physician
by profession) arose, and delivered a few moral

233

sentences in an agreeable manner; soon after he had sat down, the whole congregation rose, I know not at what signal, and made their exit. It is a singular kind of worship, if worship it may be called, where all prayer is forbidden; yet it appeared to me, in its decent quietness, infinitely preferable to what I had witnessed at the Presbyterian and Methodist Meeting-houses. A great schism had lately taken place among the Quakers of Philadelphia; many objecting to the over-strict discipline of the orthodox. Among the seceders there are again various shades of difference; I met many who called themselves Unitarian Quakers, others were Hicksites, and others again, though still wearing the Quaker habit, were said to be Deists.

We visited many churches and chapels in the city, but none that would elsewhere be called handsome, either internally or externally.

I went one evening, not a Sunday, with a party of ladies to see a Presbyterian minister inducted. The ceremony was wofully long, and the charge to the young man awfully impossible to obey, at least if he were a man, like unto other men. It was matter of astonishment to me to observe the deep attention, and the unwearied patience with which some hundreds of beautiful young girls who were assembled there (not to mention the old ladies) listened to the whole of this tedious ceremony; surely there is no country in the world where religion makes so large a part of the amusement and occupation of the ladies. Spain, in its most catholic days, could not exceed it; besides, in spite of the gloomy horrors of the Inquisition, gaiety and amusement were not there offered as a sacrifice by the young and lovely.

The religious severity of Philadelphian manners is in nothing more conspicuous than in the number of chains thrown across the streets on a Sunday to prevent horses and carriages from passing. Surely the Jews could not exceed this country in their external observances. What the gentlemen of Philadelphia do with themselves on a Sunday, I will not pretend to guess, but the prodigious majority of females in the churches is very remarkable. Although a large proportion of the population of this city are Quakers, the same extra-ordinary variety of faith exists here, as every where else in the Union, and the priests have, in some circles, the same unbounded influence which has been mentioned elsewhere.

One history reached me, which gave a terrible picture of the effect this power may produce; it was related to me by my mantua-maker; a young woman highly estimable as a wife and mother, and on whose veracity I perfectly rely. She told me that her father was a widower, and lived with his family of three daughters at Philadelphia. A short time before she married, an itinerant preacher came to the city, who contrived to obtain an intimate footing in many respectable families. Her father's was one of these, and his influence and authority were great with all the sisters, but particu-larly with the youngest. The young girl's feelings for him seem to have been a curious mixture of spiritual awe and earthly affection. When she received a hint from her sisters that she ought not to give him too much en-couragement till he spoke out, she showed as much holy resentment as if they had told her not to say her prayers too devoutly. At length the father remarked the sort of covert passion that gleamed through the eyes of his godly visitor, and he saw too the pallid anxious look which had settled on the young brow of his daughter; either this, or some rumours he had heard abroad, or both together, led him to forbid this man his house. The three girls were present when he did so, and all uttered a deprecating " Oh father!" but the old man added stoutly : " If you show yourself here again, reverend sir, I will not only teach you the way out of

my house, but out of the city also." The preacher
withdrew, and was never heard of in Philadelphia
afterwards; but when a few months had passed, strange
whispers began to creep through the circle which had
received and honoured him, and, in due course of
time, no less than seven unfortunate girls produced
living proofs of the wisdom of my informant's worthy
father. In defence of this dreadful story I can only
make the often repeated quotation, "I tell the tale as
'twas told to me"; but, in all sincerity I must add, that
I have no doubt of its truth.

*   *   *   *   *

I was particularly requested to visit the market of
Philadelphia, at the hour when it presented the busiest
scene; I did so, and thought few cities had any thing
to show better worth looking at; it is, indeed, the very
perfection of a market, the *beau idéal* of a notable housewife, who would confide to no deputy the important
office of caterer. The neatness, freshness, and entire
absence of every thing disagreeable to sight or smell,
must be witnessed to be believed. The stalls were
spread with snow-white napkins; flowers and fruit,
if not quite of Paris or London perfection, yet bright,
fresh, and fragrant; with excellent vegetables in the
greatest variety and abundance, were all so delightfully
exhibited, that objects less pleasing were overlooked
and forgotten. The dairy, the poultry-yard, the forest,
the river, and the ocean, all contributed their spoil;
in short, for the first time in my life, I thought a market
a beautiful object. The prices of most articles were, as
nearly as I could calculate between dollars and francs,
about the same as at Paris; certainly much cheaper
than in London, but much dearer than at Exeter.

My letters of introduction brought me acquainted
with several amiable and interesting people. There is
something in the tone of manners at Philadelphia that

I liked; it appeared to me that there was less affectation of ton there than elsewhere. There is a quietness, a composure in a Philadelphian drawing-room, that is quite characteristic of a city founded by William Penn. The dress of the ladies, even those who are not Quakers, partakes of this; they are most elegantly neat, and there was a delicacy and good taste in the dress of the young ladies that might serve as a model to the whole Union. There can hardly be a stronger contrast in the style of dress between any two cities than may be remarked between Baltimore and Philadelphia; both are costly, but the former is distinguished by gaudy splendour, the latter by elegant simplicity.

It is said that this city has many gentlemen distinguished by their scientific pursuits; I conversed with several well-informed and intelligent men, but there is a cold dryness of manner and an apparent want of interest in the subjects they discuss, that, to my mind, robs conversation of all its charm. On one occasion I heard the character and situation of an illustrious officer discussed, who had served with renown under Napoleon, and whose high character might have obtained him favour under the Bourbons, could he have abandoned the principles which led him to dislike their government. This distinguished man had retreated to America after the death of his master, and was endeavouring to establish a sort of Polytechnic academy at New York: in speaking of him, I observed, that his devotion to the cause of freedom must prove a strong recommendation in the United States. " Not the least in the world, madam " answered a gentleman who ranked deservedly high among the *literati* of the city; " it might avail him much in England, perhaps, but here we are perfectly indifferent as to what people's principles may be."

This I believe to be exactly true, though I never before heard it avowed as a national feature.

The want of warmth, of interest, of feeling, upon all subjects which do not immediately touch their own concerns, is universal, and has a most paralysing effect upon conversation. All the enthusiasm of America is concentrated to the one point of her own emancipation and independence; on this point nothing can exceed the warmth of her feelings. She may, I think, be compared to a young bride, a sort of Mrs Major Waddle; her independence is to her as a newly-won bridegroom; for him alone she has eyes, ears, or heart— the honeymoon is not over yet—when it is, America will, perhaps, learn more coquetry, and know better how to *faire l'aimable* to other nations.

I conceive that no place in the known world can furnish so striking a proof of the immense value of literary habits as the United States, not only in enlarging the mind, but what is of infinitely more importance, in purifying the manners. During my abode in the country I not only never met a literary man who was a tobacco chewer or a whiskey-drinker, but I never met any who were not, that had escaped these degrading habits. On the women, the influence is, if possible, still more important; unfortunately, the instances are rare, but they are to be found. One admirable example occurs in the person of a young lady of Cincinnati; surrounded by a society totally incapable of appreciating, or even of comprehending her, she holds a place among it, as simply and unaffectedly as if of the same species; young, beautiful and gifted by nature with a mind singularly acute and discriminating, she has happily found such opportunities of cultivation as might distinguish her in any country; it is, indeed, that best of all cultivation which is only to be found in domestic habits of literature, and in that hourly education which the daughter of a man of letters receives when she is made the companion and friend of her father. This young lady is the more admirable as she contrives to unite all the multifarious duties which usually devolve upon American ladies, with her intellectual pursuits. The companion and efficient assistant of her father's literary labours, the active aid in all the household cares of her mother, the tender nurse of a delicate infant sister, the skilful artificer of her own always elegant wardrobe, ever at leisure, and ever prepared to receive with the sweetest cheerfulness her numerous acquaintance, the most animated in conversation, the most indefatigable in occupation, it was impossible to know her, and study her character, without feeling that such women were " the glory of all lands," and, could the race be multiplied, would speedily become the reformers of all the grossness and ignorance that now degrade her own. Is it to be imagined that, if fifty modifications of this charming young woman were to be met at a party, the men would dare to enter it reeking with whiskey, their lips blackened with tobacco, and convinced, to the very centre of their hearts and souls, that women were made for no other purpose than to fabricate sweetmeats and gingerbread, construct shirts, dark stockings, and become mothers of possible presidents ? Assuredly not. Should the women of America ever discover what their power might be, and compare it with what it is, much improvement might be hoped for. While, at Philadelphia, among the handsomest, the wealthiest, and the most distinguished of the land, their comparative influence in society, with that possessed in Europe by females holding the same station, occurred forcibly to my mind.

Let me be permitted to describe the day of a Philadelphian lady of the first class, and the inference I would draw from it will be better understood.

It may be said that the most important feature in a woman's history is her maternity. It is so; but the object of the present observation is the social, and not the domestic influence of woman.

This lady shall be the wife of a senator and a lawyer in the highest repute and practice. She has a very handsome house, with white marble steps and door-posts, and a delicate silver knocker and door-handle; she has very handsome drawing rooms (very handsomely furnished, there is a sideboard in one of them, but it is very handsome, and has very handsome decanters and cut glass water-jugs upon it); she has a very handsome carriage, and a very handsome free black coachman; she is always very handsomely dressed; and, moreover, she is very handsome herself.

She rises, and her first hour is spent in the scrupulously nice arrangement of her dress; she descends to her parlour neat, stiff, and silent; her breakfast is brought in by her free black footman; she eats her fried ham and her salt fish, and drinks her coffee in silence, while her husband reads one newspaper, and puts another under his elbow; and then, perhaps, she washes the cups and saucers. Her carriage is ordered at eleven; till that hour she is employed in the pastry-room, her snow-white apron protecting her mouse-coloured silk. Twenty minutes before her carriage should appear, she retires to her chamber, as she calls it, shakes, and folds up her still snow-white apron, smooths her rich dress, and with nice care, sets on her elegant bonnet, and all her handsome *et cætera;* then walks down stairs, just at the moment that her free black coachman announces to her free black footman that the carriage waits. She steps into it, and gives the word: "Drive to the Dorcas society." Her footman stays at home to clean the knives, but her coachman can trust his horses while he opens the carriage door, and his lady not being accustomed to a hand or an arm, gets out very safely without, though one of her own is occupied by a work-basket, and the other by a large roll of all those indescribable matters which ladies take as offerings to Dorcas societies. She enters the parlour appropriated for the meeting, and finds seven other ladies, very like herself, and takes her place among them; she presents her contribution, which is accepted with a gentle circular smile, and her parings of broad cloth, her ends of ribbon, her gilt paper, and her minikin pins, are added to the parings of broad cloth, the ends of ribbon, the gilt paper, and the minikin pins with which the table is already covered; she also produces from her basket three ready-made pincushions, four ink-wipers, seven paper matches, and a paste-board watch-case; these are welcomed with acclamations, and the youngest lady present deposits them carefully on shelves, amid a prodigious quantity of similar articles. She then produces her thimble, and asks for work; it is presented to her, and the eight ladies all stitch together for some hours. Their talk is of priests and of missions; of the profits of their last sale, of their hopes from the next; of the doubt whether young Mr This, or young Mr That should receive the fruits of it to fit him out for Liberia; of the very ugly bonnet seen at church on Sabbath morning, of the very handsome preacher who performed on Sabbath afternoon, and of the very large collection made on Sabbath evening. This lasts till three, when the carriage again appears, and the lady and her basket return home; she mounts to her chamber, carefully sets aside her bonnet and its appurtenances, puts on her scolloped black silk apron, walks into the kitchen to see that all is right, then into the parlour, where, having cast a careful glance over the table prepared for dinner, she sits down, work in hand, to await her spouse. He comes, shakes hands with her, spits, and dines. The conversation is not much, and ten minutes suffice for the dinner; fruit and toddy, the newspaper and the work-bag succeed. In the evening the gentleman, being a savant, goes to the Wister society, and afterwards plays a snug rubber at a neighbour's. The lady receives at tea a young

missionary and three members of the Dorcas society.—
And so ends her day.

For some reason or other, which English people are
not very likely to underſtand, a great number of young
married persons board by the year, inſtead of " going to
houskeeping ", as they call having an eſtablishment of
their own.   Of course this ſtatement does not include
persons of large fortune, but it does include very many
whose rank in society would make such a mode of life
quite impossible with us.   I can hardly imagine a contrivance more effeċtual for ensuring the insignificance of
a woman, than marrying her at seventeen and placing
her in a boarding-house.   Nor can I easily imagine a
life of more uniform dulness for the lady herself; but
this certainly is a matter of taſte.   I have heard many
ladies declare, that it is " juſt quite the perfeċtion of
comfort to have nothing to fix for oneself ".   Yet
despite these assurances, I always experienced a feeling
which hovered between pity and contempt, when I
contemplated their mode of exiſtence.

How would a newly-married Englishwoman endure
it, her head and her heart full of the one dear scheme:

" Well-ordered home, *his* dear delight to make " ?

She muſt rise exaċtly in time to reach tne boarding-
table at the hour appointed for breakfaſt, or she will get
a ſtiff bow from the lady president, cold coffee, and no
egg.   I have been sometimes greatly amused upon
these occasions by watching a little scene in which the
bye-play had much more meaning than the words
uttered.   The faſting, but tardy lady, looks round the
table, and having ascertained that there is no egg
left, says diſtinċtly: " I will take an egg, if you please."
But as this is addressed to no one in particular, no one
in particular answers it, unless it happen that her
husband is at table before her, and then he says,
" There are no eggs, my dear."   Whereupon the lady

president evidently cannot hear, and the greedy culprit who has swallowed two eggs (for there are always as many eggs as noses) looks pretty considerably afraid of being found out. The breakfast proceeds in sombre silence, save that sometimes a parrot, and sometimes a canary bird, ventures to utter a timid note. When it is finished, the gentlemen hurry to their occupations, and the quiet ladies mount the stairs, some to the first, some to the second, and some to the third stories, in an inverse proportion to the number of dollars paid, and ensconce themselves in their respective chambers. As to what they do there it is not very easy to say; but I believe they clear-starch a little, and iron a little, and sit in a rocking-chair, and sew a great deal. I always observed that the ladies who boarded wore more elaborately worked collars and petticoats than any one else. The plough is hardly a more blessed instrument in America than the needle. How could they live without it ? But time and the needle wear through the longest morning, and happily the American morning is not very long, even though they breakfast at eight.

It is generally about two o'clock that the boarding gentlemen meet the boarding ladies at dinner. Little is spoken, except a whisper between the married pairs. Sometimes a sulky bottle of wine flanks the plate of one or two individuals, but it adds nothing to the mirth of the meeting, and seldom more than one glass to the good cheer of the owners. It is not then, and it is not there, that the gentlemen of the Union drink. Soon, very soon, the silent meal is done, and then, if you mount the stairs after them, you will find from the doors of the more affectionate and indulgent wives, a smell of cigars steam forth, which plainly indicates the felicity of the couple within. If the gentleman be a very polite husband, he will, as soon as he has done smoking and drinking his toddy, offer his arm to his wife, as far as the corner of the street where his store, or his office is situated, and there he will leave her to turn which way she likes. As this is the hour for being full dressed, of course she turns the way she can be most seen. Perhaps she pays a few visits; perhaps she goes to chapel; or, perhaps, she enters some store where her husband deals, and ventures to order a few notions; and then she goes home again—no, not home—I will not give that name to a boarding-house, but she re-enters the cold heartless atmosphere in which she dwells, where hospitality can never enter, and where interest takes the management instead of affection. At tea they all meet again, and a little trickery is perceptible to a nice observer in the manner of partaking the pound-cake, etc. After this, those who are happy enough to have engagements, hasten to keep them; those who have not, either mount again to the solitude of their chamber, or, what appeared to me much worse, remain in the common sitting room, in a society cemented by no tie, endeared by no connexion, which choice did not bring together, and which the slightest motive would break asunder. I remarked that the gentlemen were generally obliged to go out every evening on business, and, I confess, the arrangement did not surprise me.

It is not thus that the women can obtain that influence in society which is allowed to them in Europe, and to which both sages and men of the world have agreed in ascribing such salutary effects. It is in vain that " collegiate institutes " are formed for young ladies, or that " academic degrees " are conferred upon them. It is after marriage, and when these young attempts upon all the sciences are forgotten, that the lamentable insignificance of the American woman appears; and till this be remedied, I venture to prophesy that the tone of their drawing-rooms will not improve.

Whilst I was at Philadelphia a great deal of attention was excited by the situation of two criminals, who had been convicted of robbing the Baltimore mail, and were lying under sentence of death. The rare occurrence of capital punishment in America makes it always an event of great interest; and the approaching execution was repeatedly the subject of conversation at the boarding-table. One day a gentleman told us he had that morning been assured that one of the criminals had declared to the visiting clergyman that he was certain of being reprieved, and that nothing the clergyman could say to the contrary made any impression upon him. Day after day this same story was repeated, and commented upon at table, and it appeared that the report had been heard in so many quarters, that not only was the statement received as true but it began to be conjectured that the criminal had some ground for his hope. I learnt from these daily conversations that one of the prisoners was an American and the other an Irishman, and it was the former who was so strongly persuaded that he should not be hanged. Several of the gentlemen at table, in canvassing the subject, declared that, if the one were hanged and the other spared, this hanging would be a murder and not a legal execution. In discussing this point, it was stated that very nearly all the white men who had suffered death since the declaration of Independence had been Irishmen. What truth there may be in this general statement I have no means of ascertaining; all I know is that I heard it made. On this occasion, however, the Irishman was hanged, and the American was not.

Chapter Twenty-Seven

Return to Stonington—Thunder-Storm—Emigrants—Illness—Alexandria

A FORTNIGHT passed rapidly away in this great city, and, doubtless, there was still much left unseen when we quitted it, according to previous arrangement, to return to our friends in Maryland. We came back by a different route, going by land from Newcastle to French Town, instead of passing by the canal. We reached Baltimore in the middle of the night, but finished our repose on board the steam-boat, and started for Washington at five o'clock the next morning.

Our short abode amid the heat and closeness of a city made us enjoy more than ever the beautiful scenery around Stonington. The autumn, which soon advanced upon us, again clothed the woods in colours too varied and gaudy to be conceived by those who have never quitted Europe; and the stately maize, waving its flowing tassels, as the long drooping blossoms are called, made every field look like a little forest. A rainy spring had been followed by a summer of unusual heat; and towards the autumn frequent thunder-storms of terrific violence cleared the air, but at the same time frightened us almost out of our wits. On one occasion I was exposed, with my children, to the full fury of one of these awful visitations. We suffered considerable terror during this storm, but when we were all again safe, and comfortably sheltered, we rejoiced that the accident had occurred, as it gave us the best possible opportunity of witnessing, in all its glory, a transatlantic thunder-storm. It was, however, great imprudence that exposed us to it, for we quitted the house, and mounted a hill at a considerable distance from it, for the express purpose of watching to advantage the extraordinary aspect of the clouds. When we reached the top of the hill half the heavens appeared hung with a heavy curtain; a sort of deep blue black seemed to colour the very air; the buzzards screamed, as with heavy wing they sought the earth. We ought, in common prudence, to have immediately retreated to the house, but the scene was too beautiful to be left. For several minutes after we reached our station, the air appeared perfectly without movement, no flash broke through the seven-fold cloud, but a flickering light was visible, darting to and fro behind it. By degrees the thunder rolled onward, nearer and nearer, till the inky cloud burst asunder, and cataracts of light came pouring from behind it. From that moment there was no interval, no pause, the lightning did not flash, there were no claps of thunder, but the heavens blazed and bellowed above and round us, till stupor took the place of terror, and we stood utterly confounded. But we were speedily aroused, for suddenly, as if from beneath our feet, a gust arose which threatened to mix all the elements in one. Torrents of water seemed to bruise the earth by their violence; eddies of thick dust rose up to meet them; the fierce fires of heaven only blazed the brighter for the falling flood; while the blast almost out-roared the thunder. But the wind was left at last the lord of all, for after striking with wild force, now here, now there, and bringing worlds of clouds together in most hostile contact, it finished by clearing the wide heavens of all but a few soft straggling masses, whence sprung a glorious rainbow, and then retired, leaving the earth to raise her half-crushed forests; and we, poor pigmies, to call back our frighted senses, and recover breath as we might.

During this gust, it would have been impossible for us to have kept our feet; we crouched down under the shelter of a heap of stones, and, as we informed each other, looked most dismally pale.

Many trees were brought to the earth before our eyes; some torn up by the roots, and some mighty stems snapt off several feet from the ground. If the West Indian hurricanes exceed this, they must be terrible indeed.

The situation of Mrs S——'s house was considered as remarkably healthy, and I believe justly so, for on more than one occasion, persons who were suffering from fever and ague at the distance of a mile or two, were perfectly restored by passing a week or fortnight at Stonington; but the neighbourhood of it, particularly on the side bordering the Potomac, was much otherwise, and the mortality among the labourers on the canal was frightful.

I have elsewhere stated my doubts if the labouring poor of our country mend their condition by emigrating to the United States, but it was not till the opportunity which a vicinity to the Chesapeake and Ohio canal gave me, of knowing what their situation was after making the change, that I became fully aware how little it was to be desired for them.

Of the white labourers on this canal, the great majority are Irishmen; their wages are from ten to fifteen dollars a month, with a miserable lodging, and a large allowance of whiskey. It is by means of this hateful poison that they are tempted, and indeed enabled for a time, to stand the broiling heat of the sun in a most noxious climate: for through such, close to the romantic but unwholesome Potomac, the line of the canal has hitherto run. The situation of these poor strangers, when they sink at last in "*the fever*", which sooner or later is sure to overtake them, is dreadful. There is a strong feeling against the Irish in every part of the Union, but they will do twice as much work as a negro, and therefore they are employed. When they fall sick, they may and must look with envy on the slaves around them; for they are cared for; they are watched and physicked, as a valuable horse is watched and physicked: not so the Irishman, he is literally thrown on one side, and a new comer takes his place. Details of their sufferings, and unheeded death, too painful to dwell upon, often reached us; on one occasion, a farmer calling at the house, told the family that a poor man, apparently in a dying condition, was lying beside a little brook at the distance of a quarter of a mile. The spot was immediately visited by some of the family, and there in truth lay a poor creature, who was already past the power of speaking; he was conveyed to the house, and expired during the night. By inquiring at the canal, it was found that he was an Irish labourer, who having fallen sick, and spent his last cent, had left the stifling shanty where he lay, in the desperate attempt of finding his way to Washington, with what hope I know not. He did not appear above twenty, and as I looked on his pale young face, which even in death expressed suffering, I thought that perhaps he had left a mother and a home to seek wealth in America. I saw him buried under a group of locust trees, his very name unknown to those who laid him there, but the attendance of the whole family at the grave gave a sort of decency to his funeral which rarely, in that country, honours the poor relics of British dust; but no clergyman attended, no prayer was said, no bell was tolled; these, indeed, are ceremonies unthought of, and in fact unattainable without much expense, at such a distance from a town; had the poor youth been an American, he would have been laid in the earth in the same unceremonious manner. But had this poor Irish lad fallen sick in equal poverty and destitution among his own people, he would have found a blanket to wrap his shivering limbs. and a kindred hand to close his eyes.

The poor of Great Britain, whom distress, or a spirit of enterprise tempt to try another land, ought, for many reasons, to repair to Canada;[1] there they would meet co-operation and sympathy, instead of malice, hatred, and all uncharitableness.

I frequently heard vehement complaints, and constantly met the same in the newspapers, of a practice stated to be very generally adopted in Britain, of sending out cargoes of parish paupers to the United

[1] On this point also a considerable change has taken place. The advantages of emigration to Canada have become very doubtful.

States. A Baltimore paper heads some such remarks with the words

"INFAMOUS CONDUCT !"

and then tells us of a cargo of aged paupers just arrived from England, adding: " John Bull has squeezed the orange, and now insolently casts the skin in our faces." Such being the feeling, it will be readily believed that these unfortunates are not likely to meet much kindness or sympathy in sickness, or in suffering of any kind. If the American statements be correct, and that different parishes are induced, from an excessive population, to pay the voyage and outfit of some of their paupers across the Atlantic, why not send them to Canada ?

It is certain, however, that all the inquiries I could make failed to substantiate these American statements. All I could ascertain was, that many English and Irish poor arrived yearly in the United States, with no other resources than what their labour furnished. This, though very different from the newspaper stories, is quite enough to direct attention to the subject. It is generally acknowledged that the suffering among our labouring classes arises from the excess of our population; and it is impossible to see such a country as Canada, its extent, its fertility, its fine climate, and know that it is British ground, without feeling equal sorrow and astonishment that it is not made the means of relief. How earnestly it is to be wished that some part of that excellent feeling which is for ever at work in England to help the distressed, could be directed systematically to the object of emigration to the Canadas. Large sums are annually raised for charitable purposes by weekly subscriptions of one penny; were only a part of the money so obtained to be devoted to this object, hundreds of families might yearly be sent to people our own land. The religious feeling which so naturally mixes with every charitable purpose, would there find the best field for its exertions. Where could a missionary, whether Protestant or Catholic, find a holier mission than that which sent him to comfort and instruct his countrymen in the wilderness ? or where could he reap a higher reward in this world, than seeing that wilderness growing into fertile fields under the hands of his flock ?

*   *   *   *   *

I never saw so many autumn flowers as grow in the woods and sheep-walks of Maryland; a second spring seemed to clothe the fields; but with grief and shame I confess, that of these precious blossoms I scarcely knew a single name. I think the Michaelmas daisy, in wonderful variety of form and colour, and the prickly pear were almost my only acquaintance: let no one visit America without having first studied botany; it is an amusement, as a clever friend of mine once told me, that helps one wonderfully up and down hill, and must be superlatively valuable in America, both from the plentiful lack of other amusements, and the plentiful material for enjoyment in this; besides if one is dying to know the name of any of these lovely strangers, it is a thousand to one against his finding any one who can tell it.

The prettiest eclipse of the moon I ever saw was that of September of this year (1830). We had been passing some hours amid the solemn scenery of the Potomac falls, and just as we were preparing to quit it, the full moon arose above the black pines, with half our shadow thrown across her. The effect of her rising thus eclipsed was more strange, more striking by far, than watching the gradual obscuration; and as I turned to look at the black chasm behind me, and saw the deadly alder, and the poison-vine waving darkly on the rocks around, I thought the scene wanted nothing but the figure of a palsied crone, plucking the fatal branches to concoct some charm of mischief.

Whether some such maga dogged my steps, I know not, but many hours had not elapsed ere I again felt the noxious influence of an American autumn. This fever, " built in th' elipse ", speedily brought me very low, and though it lasted not so long as that of the preceding year, I felt persuaded I should never recover from it. Though my forebodings were not verified by the event, it was declared that change of air was necessary, and it was arranged for me (for I was perfectly incapable of settling any thing for myself), that I should go to Alexandria, a pretty town at the distance of about fifteen miles, which had the reputation of possessing a skilful physician.

It was not without regret that we quitted our friends at Stonington; but the prescription proved in a great degree efficacious; a few weeks' residence in Alexandria restored my strength sufficiently to enable me to walk to a beautiful little grassy terrace, perfectly out of the town, but very near it, from whence we could watch the various craft that peopled the Potomac between Alexandria and Washington. But though gradually regaining strength, I was still far from well; all plans for winter gaiety were abandoned, and finding ourselves very well accommodated, we decided upon passing the winter where we were. It proved unusually severe; the Potomac was so completely frozen as to permit considerable traffic to be carried on by carts, crossing on the ice from Maryland. This had not occurred before for thirty years. The distance was a mile and a quarter, and we ventured to brave the cold, and walk across the bright and slippery mirror, to make a visit on the opposite shore; the fatigue of keeping our feet was by no means inconsiderable, but we were rewarded by seeing as noble a winter landscape around us as the eye could look upon.

When at length the frost gave way, the melting snow produced freshes so violent as to carry away the long bridge at Washington; large fragments of it, with the railing still erect, came floating down amidst vast blocks of ice, during many successive days, and it was curious to see the intrepidity with which the young sailors of Alexandria perilled their lives to make spoil of the timber.

The solar eclipse on the 12th of February, 1831, was nearer total than any I ever saw, or ever shall see. It was completely annular at Alexandria, and the bright ring which surrounded the moon's shadow, though only 81° in breadth, gave light sufficient to read the smallest print; the darkness was considerably lessened by the snow, which, as the day was perfectly unclouded, reflected brightly all the light that was left us.

Notwithstanding the extreme cold, we passed the whole time in the open air, on a rising ground near the river; in this position many beautiful effects were perceptible; the rapid approach and change of shadows, the dusky hue of the broad Potomac, that seemed to drink in the feeble light, which its snow-coloured banks gave back to the air, the gradual change of every object from the colouring of bright sunshine to one sad universal tint of dingy purple, the melancholy lowing of the cattle, and the short, but remarkable suspension of all labour, gave something of mystery and awe to the scene that we shall long remember.

During the following months, I occupied myself partly in revising my notes, and arranging these pages; and partly in making myself acquainted, as much as possible, with the literature of the country.

While reading and transcribing my notes, I underwent a strict self-examination. I passed in review all I had seen, all I had felt, and scrupulously challenged every expression of disapprobation; the result was, that I omitted in transcription much that I had written, as containing unnecessary details of things which had displeased me; yet as I did so, I felt strongly that there was no exaggeration in them; but such details, though true, might be ill-natured, and I retained no more than were necessary to convey the general impressions I received. While thus reviewing my notes, I discovered that many points, which all scribbling travellers are expected to notice, had been omitted; but a few pages of miscellaneous observations will, I think, supply all that can be expected from so idle a pen.

Chapter Twenty-Eight

American Cooking—Evening Parties—Dress—Sleighing —Money-Getting Habits—Tax-Gatherer's Notice— Indian Summer—Anecdote of the Duke of Saxe- Weimar

In relating all I know of America, I surely must not omit so important a feature as the cooking. There are sundry anomalies in the mode of serving even a first-rate table; but as these are altogether matters of custom, they by no means indicate either indifference or neglect in this important business; and whether castors are placed on the table, or on the side-board; whether soup, fish, patties, and salad, be eaten in orthodox order or not, signifies but little. I am hardly capable, I fear, of giving a very erudite critique on the subject; general observations, therefore, must suffice. The ordinary mode of living is abundant, but not delicate. They consume an extraordinary quantity of bacon. Ham and beef-steaks appear morning, noon, and night. In eating, they mix things together with the strangest incongruity imaginable. I have seen eggs and oysters eaten together; the sempiternal ham with apple-sauce; beef-steak with stewed peaches; and salt fish with

254

onions. The bread is every where excellent, but they rarely enjoy it themselves, as they insist upon eating horrible half-baked hot rolls both morning and evening. The butter is tolerable, but they have seldom such cream as every little dairy produces in England; in fact, the cows are very roughly kept, compared with ours. Common vegetables are abundant and very fine. I never saw secale or cauliflowers, and either from the want of summer rain, or the want of care, the harvest of green vegetables is much sooner over than with us. They eat the Indian corn in a great variety of forms; sometimes it is dressed green, and eaten like peas; sometimes it is broken to pieces when dry, boiled plain, and brought to table like rice; this dish is called hominy. The flour of Indian corn is made into at least a dozen different sorts of cakes; but in my opinion all bad. This flour mixed in the proportion of one third with fine wheat, makes by far the best bread I ever tasted.

I never saw turbot, salmon, or fresh cod; but the rock and shad are excellent. There is a great want of skill in the composition of sauces; not only with fish, but with every thing. They use very few made dishes, and I never saw any that would be approved by our savants. They have an excellent wild duck, called the Canvas Back, which, if delicately served, would surpass the black cock; but the game is very inferior to ours; they have no hares, and I never saw a pheasant. They seldom indulge in second courses, with all their ingenious temptations to the eating a second dinner; but almost every table has its dessert (invariably pronounced *desart*), which is placed on the table before the cloth is removed, and consists of pastry, preserved fruits, and creams. They are " extravagantly fond ", to use their own phrase, of puddings, pies, and all kinds of "sweets", particularly the ladies; but are by no means such connoisseurs in soups and ragoûts as the gastronomes of Europe. Almost every one drinks water at table;

and by a strange contradiction, in the country where hard drinking is more prevalent than in any other, there is less wine taken at dinner; ladies rarely exceed one glass, and the great majority of females never take any. In fact, the hard drinking so universally acknowledged, does not take place at jovial dinners, but, to speak plain English, in solitary dram-drinking. Coffee is not served immediately after dinner, but makes part of the serious matter of tea-drinking, which comes some hours later. Mixed dinner parties of ladies and gentlemen are very rare, and unless several foreigners are present, but little conversation passes at table. It certainly does not, in my opinion, add to the well ordering a dinner table, to set the gentlemen at one end of it, and the ladies at the other; but it is very rarely that you find it otherwise.

Their large evening parties are supremely dull; the men sometimes play cards by themselves, but if a lady plays, it must not be for money; no écarté, no chess; very little music, and that little lamentably bad. Among the blacks I heard some good voices, singing in tune; but I scarcely ever heard a white American, male or female, go through an air without being out of tune before the end of it; nor did I ever meet any trace of science in the singing I heard in society. To eat inconceivable quantities of cake, ice, and pickled oysters —and to show half their revenue in silks and satins, seem to be the chief object they have in these parties.

The most agreeable meetings, I was assured by all the young people, were those to which no married women are admitted; of the truth of this statement I have not the least doubt. These exclusive meetings occur frequently, and often last to a late hour; on these occasions, I believe, they generally dance. At regular balls married ladies are admitted, but seldom take much part in the amusement. The refreshments are always profuse and costly, but taken in a most uncomfortable manner. I have known many private balls, where every thing was on the most liberal scale of expense, where the gentlemen sat down to supper in one room, while the ladies took theirs, standing in another.

What we call picnics are very rare, and when attempted, do not often succeed well. The two sexes can hardly mix for the greater part of a day without great restraint and ennui ; it is quite contrary to their general habits; the favourite indulgences of the gentlemen (smoking cigars and drinking spirits) can neither be indulged in with decency nor resigned with complacency.

The ladies have strange ways of adding to their charms. They powder themselves immoderately, face, neck, and arms, with pulverised starch; the effect is indescribably disagreeable by day-light, and not very favourable at any time. They are also most unhappily partial to false hair, which they wear in surprising quantities; this is the more to be lamented, as they generally have very fine hair of their own. I suspect this fashion to arise from an indolent mode of making their toilet, and from accomplished ladies' maids not being very abundant; it is less trouble to append a bunch of waving curls here, there, and every where, than to keep their native tresses in perfect order.

Though the expense of the ladies' dress greatly exceeds, in proportion to their general style of living, that of the ladies of Europe, it is very far (excepting in Philadelphia) from being in good taste. They do not consult the seasons in the colours or in the style of their costume; I have often shivered at seeing a young beauty picking her way through the snow with a pale rose-coloured bonnet, set on the very top of her head; I knew one young lady whose pretty little ear was actually frost-bitten from being thus exposed. They never wear muffs or boots, and appear extremely shocked at the sight of comfortable walking shoes and cotton stockings, even when they have to step to their sleighs over ice and snow. They walk in the middle of winter with their poor little toes pinched into a miniature slipper, incapable of excluding as much moisture as might bedew a primrose. I must say in their excuse, however, that they have, almost universally, extremely pretty feet. They do not walk well, nor, in fact, do they ever appear to advantage when in movement. I know not why this should be, for they have abundance of French dancing-masters among them, but somehow or other it is the fact. I fancied I could often trace a mixture of affectation and of shyness in their little mincing unsteady step, and the ever-changing position of the hands. They do not dance well: perhaps I should rather say they do not look well when dancing; lovely as their faces are, they cannot, in a position that exhibits the whole person, atone for the want of *tournure*, and for the universal defect in the formation of the bust, which is rarely full or gracefully formed.

I never saw an American man walk or stand well; notwithstanding their frequent militia drillings, they are nearly all hollow chested and round shouldered: perhaps this is occasioned by no officer daring to say to a brother free-born " Hold up your head "; whatever the cause, the effect is very remarkable to a stranger. In stature, and in physiognomy, a great majority of the population, both male and female, are strikingly handsome, but they know not how to do their own honours; half as much comeliness elsewhere would produce ten times as much effect.

Nothing can exceed their activity and perseverance in all kinds of speculation, handicraft, and enterprise, which promises a profitable pecuniary result. I heard an Englishman, who had been long resident in America, declare that in following, in meeting, or in overtaking, in the street, on the road, or in the field, at the theatre, the coffee-house, or at home, he had never overheard Americans conversing without the word DOLLAR being pronounced between them. Such unity of purpose, such sympathy of feeling, can, I believe, be found nowhere else, except, perhaps, in an ants' nest. The result is exactly what might be anticipated. This sordid object, for ever before their eyes, must inevitably produce a sordid tone of mind, and worse still, it produces a seared and blunted conscience on all questions of probity. I know not a more striking evidence of the low tone of morality which is generated by this universal pursuit of money, than the manner in which the New England States are described by Americans. All agree in saying that they present a spectacle of industry and prosperity delightful to behold, and this is the district and the population most constantly quoted as the finest specimen of their admirable country; yet I never met a single individual in any part of the Union who did not paint these New Englanders as sly, grinding, selfish, and tricking. The Yankees (as the New Englanders are called) will avow these qualities themselves with a complacent smile, and boast that no people on the earth can match them at overreaching in a bargain.[1] I have heard them unblushingly relate stories of their cronies and friends, which, if believed among us, would banish the heroes from the fellowship of honest men for ever; and all this is uttered with a simplicity which sometimes led me to doubt if the speakers knew what honour and honesty meant. Yet the Americans declare that "they are the most moral people upon earth". Again and again I have heard this asserted, not only in conversation, and by their writings, but even from the pulpit. Such broad assumption of superior virtue demands examination, and after four years of attentive

---

[1] *Vide* the exquisite personifications of *Sam Slick, the Watchmaker.* His "soft soder" and his "human nater" furnish an abstract and brief chronicle of the whole race.

and earnest observation and inquiry, my honest conviction is, that the standard of moral character in the United States is very greatly lower than in Europe. Of their religion, as it appears outwardly, I have had occasion to speak frequently; I pretend not to judge the heart, but, without any uncharitable presumption, I must take permission to say, that both Protestant England and Catholic France[1] show an infinitely superior religious and moral aspect to mortal observation, both as to reverend decency of external observance, and as to the inward fruit of honest dealing between man and man.

In other respects I think no one will be disappointed who visits the country expecting to find no more than common sense might teach him to look for, namely[2], a vast continent, by far the greater part of which is still in the state in which nature left it, and a busy, bustling, industrious population, hacking and hewing their way

[1] As well as both Catholic and Protestant Germany.

[2] It is perhaps impossible (the absolutely savage life being put out of the question) for human nature to appear under aspects more strongly contrasted than the traveller may see it in the United States and in Austria.

All that is useful and desirable in the one, is exactly what is found wanting in the other; while nothing that is objectionable in either can find a parallel in its moral and political antipodes.

The bustling, struggling, crafty, enterprising, industrious, swaggering, drinking, boasting, money-getting Yankee, who cares not who was his grandfather, and meditates on nothing, past, present, or to come, but his dollars, his produce, and his slaves, is as unlike the longsome, speculative, frank, contented, sober, tranquil, yet gay-spirited Austrian, who glories in the glories of his race, and who sings and dances through to-day, without disturbing himself about the morrow, as the square blocks of brick and mortar which constitute a transatlantic city, are to the venerable, fantastic, beautiful remains of a dozen centuries, scattered up and down the time-honoured region of Germany.

A contrast as striking might be found, too, in the comparative value and reprobation accorded to each, by those who examine and pass judgment on them; and so violent would the discrepancy of opinion be found that an unprejudiced listener to both might be apt to doubt the value of human judgment on any subject.

through it. What greatly increases the interest of this spectacle, is the wonderful facility for internal commerce, furnished by the rivers, lakes, and canals, which thread the country in every direction, producing a rapidity of progress in all commercial and agricultural speculation altogether unequalled. This remarkable feature is perceptible in every part of the Union into which the fast spreading population has hitherto found its way, and forms, I think, the most remarkable and interesting peculiarity of the country. I hardly remember a single town where vessels of some description or other may not constantly be seen in full activity.

Their carriages of every kind are very unlike ours; those belonging to private individuals seem all constructed with a view to summer use, for which they are extremely well calculated, but they are by no means comfortable in winter. The waggons and carts are built with great strength, which is indeed necessary, from the roads they often have to encounter. The stage-coaches are heavier and much less comfortable than those of France; to those of England they can bear no comparison. I never saw any harness that I could call handsome, nor any equipage which, as to horses, carriage, harness, and servants, could be considered as complete. The sleighs are delightful, and constructed at so little expense that I wonder we have not all got them in England, lying by in waiting for the snow, which often remains with us long enough to permit their use. Sleighing is much more generally enjoyed by night than by day, for what reason I could never discover, unless it be, that no gentlemen are to be found disengaged from business in the mornings. Nothing, certainly, can be more agreeable than the gliding smoothly and rapidly along, deep sunk in soft furs, the moon shining with almost mid-day splendour, the air of crystal brightness, and the snow sparkling on every side, as if it were sprinkled with diamonds. And then the noiseless movement of the horses, so mysterious and unwonted, and the gentle tinkling of the bells you meet and carry, all help at once to soothe and excite the spirits; in short, I had not the least objection to sleighing by night, I only wished to sleigh by day also.

Almost every resident in the country has a carriage they call a carryall, which name I suspect to be a corruption of the cariole so often mentioned in the pretty Canadian story of Emily Montagu.* It is clumsy enough, certainly, but extremely convenient, and admirably calculated, with its thick roof and movable draperies, for every kind of summer excursion.

Their steam-boats, were the social arrangements somewhat improved, would be delightful, as a mode of travelling; but they are very seldom employed for excursions of mere amusement: nor do I remember seeing pleasure-boats, properly so called, at any of the numerous places where they might be used with so much safety and enjoyment.

How often did our homely adage recur to me: "All work, and no play, would make Jack a dull boy": Jonathan is a very dull boy. We are by no means so gay as our lively neighbours on the other side the Channel; but, compared with Americans, we are whirligigs and teetotums; every day is a holiday, and every night a festival.

Perhaps if the ladies had quite their own way, a little more relaxation would be permitted; but there is one remarkable peculiarity in their manners, which precludes the possibility of any dangerous outbreaking of the kind: few ladies have any command of ready money entrusted to them. I have been a hundred times present when bills for a few dollars, perhaps for one, have been brought for payment to ladies living in perfectly easy circumstances, who have declared themselves without money, and referred the claimant to their husbands for payment. On every occasion where

262

immediate disbursement is required it is the same; even in shopping for ready cash, they say: " Send a bill home with the things, and my husband will give you a draft."

I think that it was during my stay at Washington, that I was informed of a government regulation, which appeared to me curious; I therefore record it here.

Every Deputy Post-master is required to insert in his return the title of every newspaper received at his office for distribution.* This return is laid before the Secretary of State, who, perfectly knowing the political character of each newspaper, is thus enabled to feel the pulse of every limb of the monster mob. This is a well-imagined device for getting a peep at the politics of a country where newspapers make part of the daily food; but is it quite consistent with their entire freedom? I do not believe we have any such tricks to regulate the disposal of offices and appointments.

I believe it was in Indiana that Mr T—— met with a printed notice relative to the payment of taxes, which I preserved as a curious sample of the manner in which the free citizens are coaxed and reasoned into obeying the laws.

"LOOK OUT, DELINQUENTS

" Those indebted to me for taxes, fees, notes, and accounts, are specially requested to call and pay the same on or before the 1st day of December, 1828, as no longer indulgence will be given. I have called time and again, by advertisement and otherwise, to little effect; but now the time has come when my situation requires immediate payment from all indebted to me. It is impossible for me to pay off the amount of the duplicates of taxes and my other debts without recovering the same of those from whom it is due. I am at a loss to know the reason why those charged with taxes neglect to pay; from the negligence of many, it would seem that they think the money is mine, or that I have funds to discharge the taxes due to the State, and that I can wait with them until it suits their convenience to pay. The money is not mine; neither have I the funds to settle amount of the duplicate. My only resort is to collect; in doing so I should be sorry to have to resort to the authority given me by law for the recovery of the same. It should be the first object of every good citizen to pay his taxes, for it is in that way government is supported. Why are taxes assessed, unless they are collected? Depend upon it, I shall proceed to collect agreeably to law; so govern yourselves accordingly.

> JOHN SPENCER,
> Sh'ff and Collector, D.C.

Nov. 20, 1828.

N.B. On Thursday, the 27th inst. A. St. Clair and Geo. H. Dunn, Esqrs., depart for Indianapolis; I wish as many as can pay to do so, to enable me to forward as much as possible, to save the twenty-one per cent. that will be charged against me after the 8th of December next.

> J. S."

The first autumn I passed in America, I was surprised to find a great and very oppressive return of heat, accompanied with a heavy mistiness in the air, long after the summer heats were over; when this state of the atmosphere comes on, they say "We have got to the Indian summer." On desiring to have this phrase explained, I was told that the phenomenon described as the *Indian summer* was occasioned by the Indians setting fire to the woods, which spread heat and smoke to a great distance; but I afterwards met with the following explanation, which appears to me much more reasonable. "The Indian summer is so called because, at the particular period of the year in which it obtains, the Indians break up their village communities, and go to the interior to prepare for their winter hunting. This season seems to mark a dividing line, between the heat of summer, and the cold of winter, and is, from its mildness, suited to these migrations. The cause of this heat is the slow combustion of the leaves and other vegetable matter of the boundless and interminable forests. Those who at this season of the year have penetrated these forests, know all about it. To the feet the heat is quite sensible, whilst the ascending vapour warms every thing it embraces, and spreading out into the wide atmosphere, fills the circuit of the heavens with its peculiar heat and smokiness."

This unnatural heat sufficiently accounts for the sickliness of the American autumn. The effect of it is extremely distressing to the nerves, even when the general health continues good; to me, it was infinitely more disagreeable than the glowing heat of the dog-days.

A short time before we arrived in America, the Duke of Saxe-Weimar made a tour of the United States.* I heard many persons speak of his unaffected and amiable manners, yet he could not escape the dislike which every trace of gentlemanly feeling is sure to create among the ordinary class of Americans. As an amusing instance of this, I made the following extract from a newspaper:

" A correspondent of the *Charlestown Gazette* tells an anecdote connected with the Duke of Saxe-Weimar's recent journey through our country, which we do not recollect to have heard before, although some such story is told of the veritable Capt. Basil Hall. The scene occurred on the route between Augusta and Milledgeville. It seems that the sagacious Duke engaged three or four, or more seats, in the regular stage, for the accommodation of himself and suite, and thought by this that he had secured the monopoly of the vehicle. Not so, however; a traveller came along, and entered his name upon the book, and secured his seat by payment of the customary charges. To the Duke's great surprise on entering the stage, he found our traveller comfortably housed in one of the most eligible seats, wrapt up in his fearnought, and snoring like a buffalo. The Duke, greatly irritated, called for the question of consideration. He demanded, in broken English, the cause of the gross intrusion, and insisted in a very princely manner, though not, it seems, in very princely language, upon the incumbent vacating the seat in which he had made himself so impudently at home. But the Duke had yet to learn his first lesson of republicanism. The driver was one of those sturdy southrons, who can always, and at a moment's warning, whip his weight in wild cats: and he as resolutely told the Duke, that the traveller was as good, if not a better man, than himself; and that no alteration of the existing arrangement could be permitted. Saxe-Weimar became violent at this opposition, so unlike any to which his education hitherto had ever subjected him, and threatened John with the application of the bamboo. This was one of those threats which in Georgia dialect would subject a man to ‘a rowing up salt river’; and, accordingly, down leaped our driver from his box, and peeling himself for the combat, he leaped about the vehicle in the most wild-boar style, calling upon the prince of a five acre patch to put his threat in execution. But he of the star refused to make up issue in the way suggested, contenting himself with assuring the enraged southron of a complaint to his excellency the Governor, on arriving at the seat of government. This threat was almost as unlucky as the former, for it wrought the individual for whom it was intended into that species of fury, which, though discriminating in its madness, is nevertheless without much limit in its violence, and he swore that the Governor might go to——, and for his part he would just as lief lick the Governor as the Duke; he'd like no better fun than to give both Duke and Governor a dressing in the same breath; could do it, he had little doubt, etc. etc.; and instigating one fist to diverge into the face of the marvelling and panic-stricken nobleman, with the other he thrust him down into a seat alongside the traveller, whose presence had been originally of such sore discomfort to his excellency, and bidding the attendants jump in with their discomfited master, he mounted his box in triumph, and went on his journey."

I fully believe that this brutal history would be as distasteful to the travelled and polished few who are to be found scattered through the Union, as it is to me; but if they do not deem the *possibility* of such a scene to be a national degradation, I differ from them. The American people (speaking of the great mass) have no more idea of what constitutes the difference between this " Prince of a five acre patch ", and themselves, than a dray-horse has of estimating the points of the elegant victor of the race-course. Could the dray-horse speak, when expected to yield the daintiest stall to his graceful rival, he would say, " A horse is a horse "; and is it not with the same logic that the transatlantic Houyhnhnm puts down all superiority with " a man is a man " ?

This story justifies the reply of Talleyrand, when asked by Napoleon what he thought of the Americans: " Sire, ce sont des fiers cochons, et des cochons fiers."

Chapter Twenty-Nine

Literature—Extracts—Fine Arts—Education

The character of the American literature is, generally speaking, pretty justly appreciated in Europe. The immense exhalation of periodical trash, which penetrates into every cot and corner of the country, and which is greedily sucked in by all ranks, is unquestionably one great cause of its inferiority. Where newspapers are the principal vehicles of the wit and wisdom of a people, the higher graces of composition can hardly be looked for.

That there are many among them who can write well, is most certain; but it is at least equally so, that they have little encouragement to exercise the power in any manner more dignified than becomes the editor of a newspaper or a magazine. As far as I could judge, their best writers are far from being the most popular. The general taste is decidedly bad; this is obvious, not only from the mass of slip-slop poured forth by the daily and weekly press, but from the inflated tone of eulogy in which their insect authors are lauded.

To an American writer I should think it must be a flattering distinction to escape the admiration of the newspapers. Few persons of taste, I imagine, would like such notice as the following, which I copied from a New York paper, where it followed the advertisement of a partnership volume of poems by a Mr and Mrs Brooks; but of such are their literary notices chiefly composed:

"The lovers of impassioned and classical numbers may promise themselves much gratification from the muse of Brooks, while the many-stringed harp of his lady, the Norna of the Courier Harp, which none but she can touch, has a chord for every heart."

Another obvious cause of inferiority in the national literature, is the very slight acquaintance with the best models of composition, which is thought necessary for persons called well educated. There may be reason for deprecating the lavish expense of time bestowed in England on the acquirement of Latin and Greek, and it may be doubtful whether the power of composing in these languages, with correctness and facility, be worth all the labour it costs; but as long as letters shall be left on the earth, the utility of a perfect familiarity with the exquisite models of antiquity cannot be doubted. I think I run no risk of contradiction, when I say that an extremely small proportion of the higher classes in America possess this familiar acquaintance with the classics. It is in vain to suppose that translations may suffice. Noble as are the thoughts the ancients have left us, their power of expression is infinitely more important as a study to modern writers: and this no translation can furnish. Nor did it appear to me that their intimacy with modern literature was such as to assist them much in the formation of style. What they class as modern literature seems to include little beyond the English publications of the day.

To speak of Chaucer, or even Spenser, as a modern, appears to them inexpressibly ridiculous: and all the rich and varied eloquence of Italy, from Dante to Monti, is about as much known to them, as the Welsh effusions of Urien and Modred to us.

Rousseau, Voltaire, Diderot, etc., were read by the old federalists; but now they seem known more as naughty words than as great names. I am much mistaken if a hundred untravelled Americans could be found, who have read Boileau or La Fontaine. Still fewer are acquainted with that delightful host of French female writers, whose memoirs and letters sparkle in every page with unequalled felicity of style. The literature of Spain and Portugal is no better known; and as for " the wits of Queen Anne's day ", they are laid *en masse* upon a shelf, in some score of very old-fashioned houses, together with Sherlock and Taylor, as much too antiquated to suit the immensely rapid progress of mind which distinguishes America.

The most perfect examples of English writing, either of our own, or of any former day, have assuredly not been produced by the imitation of any particular style; but the *Fairy Queen* would hardly have been written, if the *Orlando* had not; nor would Milton have been the perfect poet he was, had Virgil and Tasso been unknown to him. It is not that the scholar mimics in writing the phrases he has read, but that he can neither think, feel, nor express himself as he might have done, had his mental companionship been of a lower order.

They are great novel readers, but the market is chiefly furnished by England. They have, however, a few very good native novels. Mr Flint's *Francis Berrian* is delightful. There is a vigour and freshness in his writing that is exactly in accordance with what one looks for in the literature of a new country; and yet, strange to say, it is exactly what is most wanting in that of America. It appeared to me that the style of their imaginative compositions was almost always affected and inflated. Even in treating their great national subject of romance, the Indians, they are seldom either powerful or original. A few well-known general features, moral and physical, are presented over and over again in all their Indian stories, till in reading them you lose all sense of individual character. Mr Flint's *History of the Mississippi Valley* is a work of great interest and information, and will, I hope, in time find its way to England, where I think it is much more likely to be appreciated than in America.

Dr Channing is a writer too well-known in England to require my testimony to his great ability. As a preacher he has, perhaps, hardly a rival any where. This gentleman is an Unitarian; and I was informed by several persons well acquainted with the literary characters of the country, that nearly all their distinguished men were of this persuasion.[1]

---

[1] That this statement was perfectly correct, I have every reason to believe; nor is an obvious reason for the fact wanting. The mind of a man devoted to letters undergoes a process which renders the endurance of the crude ignorant ranting of the great majority among the various sects of American preachers intolerable; and accordingly they have taken refuge in the cold comfortless stillness of Unitarianism.

Mr Pierpoint is a very eloquent preacher, and a sweet poet. His works are not so well known among us as they ought to be. Mr Everett has written some beautiful lines; and if I may judge from the specimens of his speeches, as preserved in the volume entitled *Eloquence of the United States*, I should say that he shone more as a poet than an orator. But American fame has decided otherwise.

Mr M. Flint, of Louisiana, has published a volume of poems which ought to be naturalized here.* Mr Hallock, of New York, has much facility of versification, and is greatly in fashion as a drawing-room poet; but I think he has somewhat too much respect for himself, and too little for his readers.

It is, I think, Mr Bryant, who ranks highest as the poet of the Union. This is too lofty an eminence for me to attack; besides, " I am of another parish ", and therefore, perhaps, no very fair judge.

From miscellaneous poetry I made a great many extracts; but upon returning to them for transcription, I thought that ill-nature and dulness (" Oh ill-matched pair!") would be more served by their insertion, than wholesome criticism.

The massive *Fredoniad* of Dr Emmons, in forty cantos, I never read; but as I did not meet a single native who had, I hope this want of poetical enterprise will be excused.

They have very few native tragedies: not more than half a dozen, I believe, and those of very recent date. It would be ungenerous to fall heavily upon these; the attempt alone, nearly the most arduous a poet can make, is of itself honourable; and the success at least equal to that in any other department of literature.

Mr Paulding is a popular writer of novels; some of his productions have been recently republished in England. Miss Sedgwick is also well known among us; her *Hope Leslie* is a beautiful story. Mr Washington Irving and Mr Cooper have so decidedly chosen another field, whereon to reap their laurels, that it is hardly necessary to name them here.

I am not, of course, competent to form any opinion of their scientific works; but some papers which I read almost accidentally, appeared to me to be written with great clearness, and neatness of definition.

It appears extraordinary that a people who loudly declare their respect for science, should be entirely without observatories. Neither at their seats of learning, nor in their cities, does any thing of the kind exist; nor did I in any direction hear of individuals given to the study of astronomy.

I had not the pleasure of making any acquaintance with Mr Bowditch of Boston; but I know that this gentleman ranks very high as a mathematician in the estimation of the scientific world of Europe.

Jefferson's posthumous works were very generally circulated whilst I was in America. They are a mighty mass of mischief. He wrote with more perspicuity than he thought, and his hot-headed democracy has done a fearful injury to his country. Hollow and unsound as his doctrines are, they are but too palatable to a people, each individual of whom would rather derive his importance from believing that none are above him, than from the consciousness that in his station he makes part of a noble whole. The social system of Mr Jefferson, if carried into effect, would make of mankind an unamalgamated mass of grating atoms, where the darling " I'm as good as you," would soon take the place of the law and the Gospel.[1] As it is, his principles, though happily

[1] If the information which, as stated in a former note, I have re ceived since my return to Europe, from a distinguished citizen of the United States, be correct, namely, that the private sentiments of Mr Jefferson were exactly the reverse of all he published, and that he declared his conviction during his hours of social confidence, that the existence of a practical democracy was a prodigious fable, what is the judgment that must be passed upon him ? The United States have paid,

not fully put in action, have yet produced most lamentable results. The assumption of equality, however empty, is sufficient to tincture the manners of the poor with brutal insolence, and subjects the rich to the paltry expediency of sanctioning the falsehood, however deep their conviction that it is such. It cannot, I think, be denied that the great men of America attain to power and to fame, by eternally uttering what they know to be untrue. American citizens are not equal. Did Washington feel them to be so, when his word out-weighed (so happily for them) the votes of thousands? Did Franklin think that all were equal when he shouldered his way from the printing press to the cabinet? True, he looked back in high good humour, and with his kindest smile told the poor devils whom he left behind, that they were all his equals; but Franklin did not speak the truth, and he knew it. The great, the immortal Jefferson, himself, he who, when past the threescore years and ten, still taught young females to obey his nod, and so became the father of unnumbered generations of groaning slaves, what was his matin and his vesper hymn—*All men are born free and equal?* Did the venerable father of the gang believe it? Or did he too purchase his immortality by a lie?

*　　*　　*　　*　　*

From the five heavy volumes of the *Eloquence of the United States*, I made a few extracts, which I give more for the sake of their political interest, than for any purpose of literary criticism.

Mr Hancock (one of those venerated men who signed the act of Independence), in speaking of England, thus expresses himself: "But if I was possessed of the gift of prophecy, I dare not (except by Divine

---

and will long continue to pay, a grievously heavy penalty for this " great man's popularity ". They are not, as a people, what they would have been had Jefferson never lived, and Washington remained their unrivalled authority.

command) unfold the leaves on which the destiny of that once powerful kingdom is inscribed." It is impossible not to regret that Mr Hancock should thus have let " I dare not, wait upon I would." It would have been exceedingly edifying to have known before-hand all the terrible things the republic was about to do for us.

This prophetic orator spoke the modest, yet awful words, above quoted, nearly sixty years ago; in these latter days men are become bolder, for in a modern 4th of July oration, Mr Rush, without waiting, I think, for Divine command, gives the following amiable portrait of the British character:

" In looking at Britain, we see a harshness of in-dividual character in the general view of it, which is perceived and acknowledged by all Europe; a spirit of unbecoming censure as regards all customs and institutions not their own: a ferocity in some of the characteristics of national manners, pervading their very pastimes, which no other modern people are endued with the blunted sensibility to bear;[1] an uni-versal self-assumed superiority, not innocently mani-festing itself in speculative sentiments among them-selves, but unamiably indulged when with foreigners, of whatever description, in their own country, or when they themselves are the temporary sojourners in a foreign country; a code of criminal law that forgets to feel for human frailty, that sports with human mis-fortune, that has shed more blood in deliberate judicial severity for two centuries past, constantly increasing, too, in its sanguinary hue, than has ever been sanctioned by the jurisprudence of any ancient or modern nation, civilised and refined like herself; the merciless whippings in her army, peculiar to herself alone, the conspicuous commission and freest acknowledgment of vice in the upper classes; the overweening distinctions shown to

[1] Negro-flogging is not classed as a pastime.

opulence and birth, so destructive of a sound moral sentiment in the nation, so baffling to virtue. These are some of the traits that rise up to a contemplation of the inhabitants of this isle."

Where is the alchemy that can extract from Captain Hall's work one thousandth part of the ill-will contained in this one passage ? Yet America has resounded from shore to shore with execrations against his barbarous calumnies. But now we will listen to another tone Let us see how Americans can praise. Mr Everett, in a recent 4th of July oration, speaks thus:

" We are authorized to assert that the era of our in dependence dates the establishment of the only perfect organisation of government." Again: " Our government is in its theory perfect, and in its operation it is perfect also. Thus we have solved the great problem in human affairs." And again: " A frame of government, perfect in its principles, has been brought down from the airy regions of Utopia, and has found a local habitation and a name in our country."

Among my miscellaneous reading, I got hold of an American publication giving a detailed and, indeed, an official, account of the capture of Washington by the British in 1814. An event so long past, and of so little ultimate importance, is, perhaps, hardly worth alluding to; but there are some passages in the official documents which I thought very amusing.

At the very moment of receiving the attack of the British on the heights of Bladensburgh, there seems to have been a most curious puzzle among the American generals, as to where they were to be stationed, and what they were to do. It is stated that the British threw themselves forward in open order, advancing singly. The American general (Winden) goes on in his narrative to describe what followed, thus:

" Our advanced riflemen now began to fire, and continued it for half a dozen rounds, when I observed them to run back to an orchard. They halted there, and seemed for a moment about returning to their original position, but in a few moments entirely broke, and retired to the left of Stanburg's line. The advanced artillery immediately followed the riflemen.

" The first three or four rockets fired by the enemy were much above the heads of Stanburg's line; but the rockets having taken a more horizontal direction, an universal flight of the centre and left of this brigade was the consequence. The 5th regiment and the artillery still remained, and I hoped would prevent the enemy's approach, but they advanced singly, their fire annoyed the 5th considerably, when I ordered it to retire, to put it out of the reach of the enemy. This order was, however, immediately countermanded, from an aversion to retire before the necessity became stronger, and from a hope that the enemy would issue in a body, and enable us to act upon him on terms of equality. But the enemy's fire beginning to annoy the 5th still more, by wounding several of them, and a strong column passing up the road, and deploying on its left, I ordered them to retire; their retreat became a flight of absolute and total disorder."

Of Beall's regiment, the general gives the following succinct account: " It gave one or two ineffectual fires and fled."

In another place he says piteously: "The cavalry would do any thing but charge."

General Armstrong's gentle and metaphysical account of the business was, that " Without all doubt the determining cause of our disasters is to be found in the love of life."

This affair at Washington, which in its results was certainly advantageous to America, inasmuch as it caused the present beautiful capitol to be built in the place of the one we burnt, was, nevertheless, considered as a national calamity at the time. In a volume of miscellaneous poems I met with one, written with the patriotic purpose of cheering the country under it; one triplet struck me as rather alarming for us, however soothing to America:

> " Supposing George's house at Kew
> Were burnt, as we intend to do,
> Would that be burning England too ?"

I think I have before mentioned that no work of mere pleasantry has hitherto been found to answer; but a recent attempt of the kind has been made, with what success cannot as yet be decided. The editors are comedians belonging to the Boston company, and it is entitled *The American Comic Annual*. It is accompanied by etchings, somewhat in the manner but by no means with the spirit, of Cruikshank's. Among the pleasantries of this lively volume are some biting attacks upon us, particularly upon our utter incapacity of speaking English. We really must engage a few American professors, or we shall lose all trace of classic purity in our language. As a specimen, and rather a favourable one, of the work, I transcribed an extract from a little piece, entitled *Sayings and Doings: a Fragment of a Farce*. One of the personages of this farce is an English gentleman, a Captain Mandaville, and among many speeches of the same kind, I selected the following. Collins's *Ode* is the subject of conversation.

"A——r, A—a—a it stroiks me that that you manetion his the hode about hangger and ope and orror and revenge you know. I've eard Mrs Sitdowns hencored in it at Common Garden and Doory Lane in the ight of her poplarity you know. By the boye, hall the hactin in Amareka is werry orrid. You're honely in the hinfancy of the istoryonic hart you know; your performers never haspirate the haitch in sich vords for instance as hink and hoats, and leave out the *w* in wice wanity you know; and make nothink of homittin the *k* in somethink."[1]

There is much more in the same style, but, perhaps, this may suffice. I have given this passage chiefly because it affords an example of the manner in which the generality of Americans are accustomed to speak of the English pronunciation and phraseology.

It must be remembered, however, here and every where, that this phrase, " the Americans ", does not include the instructed and travelled portion of the community.

It would be absurd to swell my little volumes with extracts in proof of the veracity of their contents, but having spoken of the taste of their lighter works, and also of the general tone of manners, I cannot forbear inserting a page from an American annual (*The Token*), which purports to give a scene from fashionable life. It is part of a dialogue between a young lady of the " highest standing " and her " tutor ", who is moreover her lover, though not yet acknowledged.

" ' And so you won't tell me', said she, ' what has come over you, and why you look as grave and sensible as a Dictionary, when, by general consent, even mine, " motley's the only wear " ?'

" ' Am I so grave, Miss Blair ?'

" ' Are you so grave, Miss Blair ? One would think I had not got my lesson to day. Pray, sir, has the black ox trod upon your toe since we parted ?'

[1] Of the correctness of this imitation of the colloquial style of English gentlemen, I will give no opinion; on this point every person must judge for himself . . . but on reperusing it I am tempted to insert a few extracts from a MS. which we brought home with us, which was the result of my having desired every member of my family to note down whatever words or phrases struck them as new to English ears—and from the collection thus made, I composed several dialogues, some portions of which may serve fairly enough as a *pendant* to the *Fragment of a Farce*. This *pendant* will be found at the end of the chapter.

"Philip tried to laugh, but he did not succeed; he bit his lip and was silent.

" ' I am under orders to entertain you, Mr Blondel, and if my poor brain can be made to gird this fairy isle, I shall certainly be obedient. So I begin with playing the leech. What ails you, sir ?'

" ' Miss Blair!' he was going to remonstrate.

" ' Miss Blair! Now, pity I'm a quack! for whip me, if I know whether Miss Blair is a fever or an ague. How did you catch it, sir ?'

" Really, Miss Blair——'

" ' Nay, I see you don't like doctoring; I give over, and now I'll be sensible. It's a fine day, Mr Blondel.'

" ' Very.'

" ' A pleasant lane, this, to walk in, if one's company were agreeable.'

" ' Does Mr Skefton stay long ?' asked Philip, abruptly.

" ' No one knows.'

" ' Indeed! are you so ignorant ?'

" ' And why does your wisdom ask that question ?' "

In no society in the world can the advantage of travel be so conspicuous as in America. In other countries a tone of unpretending simplicity can more than compensate for the absence of enlarged views or accurate observation; but this tone is not to be found in America, or if it be, it is only among those who, having looked at that insignificant portion of the world not included in the Union, have learnt to know how much is still unknown within the mighty part which is. For the rest, they all declare, and do in truth believe, that they only, among the sons of men, have wit and wisdom, and that one of their exclusive privileges is that of speaking English *elegantly*. There are two reasons for this latter persuasion; the one is, that the great majority have never heard any English but their own, except from the very lowest of the Irish; and the other, that those who have chanced to find themselves in the society of the few educated English who have visited America, have discovered that there is a marked difference between their phrases and accents and those to which they have been accustomed, whereupon they have, of course, decided that no Englishman can speak English.

The reviews of America contain some good clear-headed articles; but I sought in vain for the playful vivacity and the keenly-cutting satire, whose sharp edge, however painful to the patient, is of such high utility in lopping off the excrescences of bad taste, and levelling to its native clay the heavy growth of dulness. Still less could I find any trace of that graceful familiarity of learned allusion and general knowledge which mark the best European reviews, and which make one feel in such perfectly good company while perusing them. But this is a tone not to be found either in the writings or conversation of Americans; as distant from pedantry as from ignorance, it is not learning itself, but the effect of it; and so pervading and subtle is its influence, that it may be traced in the festive halls and gay drawing-rooms of Europe as certainly as in the cloistered library or student's closet; it is, perhaps, the last finish of highly-finished society.

A late American Quarterly has an article on a work of Dr Von Schmidt Phiseldek, from which I made an extract, as a curious sample of the dreams they love to batten on.

Dr Von Phiseldek (not Fiddlestick), who is not only a doctor of philosophy but a knight of Dannebrog to boot, has never been in America, but he has written a prophecy, showing that the United States must and will govern the whole world, because they are so very big, and have so much uncultivated territory: he prophesies that an union will take place between North and South America, which will give a death-blow to Europe, at no distant period; though he modestly adds that he does not pretend to designate the precise period at which this will take place. This Danish prophecy, as may be imagined, enchants the reviewer. He exhorts all people to read Dr Phiseldek's book, because " nothing but good can come of such contemplations of the future, and because it is eminently calculated to awaken the most lofty anticipations of the destiny which awaits them, and will serve to impress upon the nation the necessity of being prepared for such high destiny." In another place the reviewer bursts out: " America, young as she is, has become already the beacon, the patriarch of the struggling nations of the world "; and afterwards adds: " It would be departing from the natural order of things, and the ordinary operations of the great scheme of Providence, it would be shutting our ears to the voice of experience, and our eyes to the inevitable connection of causes and their effects, were we to reject the extreme probability, not to say *moral certainty*, that the old world is destined to receive its influences in future from the new." There are twenty pages of this article, but I will only give one passage more; it is an instance of the sort of reasoning by which American citizens persuade themselves that the glory of Europe is, in reality, her reproach. " Wrapped up in a sense of his superiority, the European reclines at home, shining in his borrowed plumes, derived from the product of every corner of the earth, and the industry of every portion of its inhabitants, with which his own natural resources would never have invested him, he continues revelling in enjoyments which nature has denied him."

The *American Quarterly* deservedly holds the highest place in their periodical literature, and, therefore, may be fairly quoted as striking the key-note for the chorus of public opinion. Surely it is nationality rather than patriotism which leads it thus to speak in scorn of the successful efforts of enlightened nations to win from every corner of the earth the riches which nature has scattered over it.

*   *   *   *   *

The incorrectness of the press is very great; they make strange work in the reprints of French and Italian; and the Latin, I suspect, does not fare much better: I believe they do not often meddle with Greek.

With regard to the fine arts, their paintings, I think, are quite as good, or rather better, than might be expected from the patronage they receive; the wonder is that any man can be found with courage enough to devote himself to a profession in which he has so little chance of finding a maintenance. The trade of a carpenter opens an infinitely better prospect; and this is so well known, that nothing but a genuine passion for the art could beguile any one to pursue it. The entire absence of every means of improvement, and effectual study, is unquestionably the cause why those who manifest this devotion cannnot advance farther. I heard of one young artist, whose circumstances did not permit his going to Europe, but who being nevertheless determined that his studies should, as nearly as possible, resemble those of the European academies, was about to commence drawing the human figure, for which purpose he had provided himself with a thin silk dress, in which to clothe his models, as no one of any station, he said, could be found who would submit to sit as a model without clothing.

It was at Alexandria that I saw what I consider as the best picture by an American artist that I met with. The subject was Hagar and Ishmael. It had recently arrived from Rome, where the painter, a young man of the name of Chapman, had been studying for three years. His mother told me that he was twenty-two years of age, and passionately devoted to the art; should he, on returning to his country, receive sufficient encouragement to keep his ardour and his industry alive, I think I shall hear of him again.

*   *   *   *   *

Much is said about the universal diffusion of education in America, and a vast deal of genuine admiration is felt and expressed at the progress of mind throughout the Union. They believe themselves in all sincerity to have surpassed, to be surpassing, and to be about to surpass, the whole earth in the intellectual race. I am aware that not a single word can be said, hinting a different opinion, which will not bring down a transatlantic anathema on my head; yet the subject is too interesting to be omitted. Before I left England I remember listening with much admiration to an eloquent friend, who deprecated our system of public education, as confining the various and excursive faculties of our children to one beaten path, paying little or no attention to the peculiar powers of the individual.

This objection is extremely plausible, but doubts of its intrinsic value must, I think, occur to every one who has marked the result of a different system throughout the United States.

From every inquiry I could make, and I took much pains to obtain accurate information, it appeared that much is attempted, but very little beyond reading, writing, and book-keeping, is thoroughly acquired. Were we to read a prospectus of the system pursued in any of our public schools, and that of a first-rate seminary in America, we should be struck by the confined scholastic routine of the former, when compared to the varied and expansive scope of the latter; but let the examination go a little farther, and I believe it will be found that the old-fashioned school discipline of England has produced something higher, and deeper too, than that which roars so loud, and thunders in the index.

They will not afford to let their young men study till two or three and twenty, and it is therefore declared, *ex cathedra Americana*, to be unnecessary. At sixteen, often much earlier, education ends, and money-making begins; the idea that more learning is necessary than can be acquired by that time, is generally ridiculed as obsolete monkish bigotry; added to which, if the seniors willed a more prolonged discipline, the juniors would refuse submission. When the money-getting begins, leisure ceases, and all of lore which can be acquired afterwards, is picked up from novels, magazines, and newspapers.

At what time can the taste be formed? How can a correct and polished style, even of speaking, be acquired? or when can the fruit of the two thousand years of past thinking be added to the native growth of American intellect? These are the tools, if I may so express myself, which our elaborate system of school discipline puts into the hands of our scholars; possessed of these, they may use them in whatever direction they please afterwards, they can never be an incumbrance.

No people appear more anxious to excite admiration and receive applause than the Americans, yet none take so little trouble, or make so few sacrifices to obtain it. This may answer among themselves, but it will not with the rest of the world; individual sacrifices must be made and national economy enlarged, before America can compete with the old world in taste, learning, and liberality.

The reception of General Lafayette is the one single instance in which the national pride has overcome the national thrift; and this was clearly referable to the one single feeling of enthusiasm of which they appear capable, namely, the triumph of their successful struggle for national independence. But though this feeling will be universally acknowledged as a worthy and lawful source of triumph and of pride, it will not serve to trade upon for ever, as a fund of glory and high station among the nations. Their fathers were colonists; they fought stoutly, and became an independent people. Success and admiration, even the admiration of those whose yoke they had broken, cheered the successful heroes while living, still sheds a glory round their remote and untitled sepulchres, and will illumine the page of their history for ever.

Their children inherit the independence; they inherit too the honour of being the sons of brave fathers; but this will not give them the reputation at which they aim, of being scholars and gentlemen, nor will it enable them to sit down for evermore to talk of their glory, while they drink mint julap and chew tobacco, swearing by the beard of Jupiter (or some other oath) that they are very graceful, and agreeable, and, moreover, abusing every body who does not cry out Amen!

To doubt that talent and mental power of every kind exist in America would be absurd; why should it not ? But in taste and learning they are wofully deficient; and it is this which renders them incapable of graduating a scale by which to measure themselves. Hence arises that overweening complacency and self-esteem, both national and individual, which at once renders them so extremely obnoxious to ridicule, and so peculiarly restive under it.

If they will scorn the process by which other nations have become what they avowedly intend to be, they must rest satisfied with the praise and admiration they receive from each other; and turning a deaf ear to the criticisms of the old world, consent to be their " own prodigious great reward."

* * * * *

Alexandria has its churches, chapels, and conventicles as abundantly, in proportion to its size, as any city in the Union. I visited most of them, and in the Episcopal and Catholic heard the services performed quietly and reverently.

The best sermon, however, that I listened to was in a Methodist church, from the mouth of a Piquot Indian. It was impossible not to be touched by the simple sincerity of this poor man. He gave a picture frightfully eloquent of the decay of his people under the united influence of the avarice and intemperance of the white men. He described the effect of the religious feeling which had recently found its way among them as most salutary. The purity of his moral feeling, and the sincerity of his sympathy with his forest brethren, made it unquestionable that he must be the most valuable priest who could officiate for them. His English was very correct, and his pronunciation slightly tinctured by native accent.

*　　*　　*　　*　　*

While we were still in the neighbourhood of Washington, a most violent and unprecedented schism occurred in the cabinet. The four secretaries of State all resigned, leaving General Jackson to manage the queer little State barge alone.

Innumerable contradictory statements appeared upon this occasion in the papers, and many a cigar was thrown aside, ere half consumed, that the disinterested politician might give breath to his cogitations on this extraordinary event; but not all the eloquence of all the smokers, nor even the ultra-diplomatic expositions which appeared from the seceding secretaries themselves, could throw any light on the mysterious business. It produced, however, the only tolerable caricature I ever saw in the country. It represents the President seated alone in his cabinet, wearing a look of much discomfiture, and making great exertions to detain one of four rats, who are running off, by placing his foot on the tail. The rats' heads bear a very sufficient

A Fragment

resemblance to the four ex-ministers. General Jackson, it seems, had requested Mr Van Buren, the Secretary of State, to remain in office till his place was supplied; this gave occasion to a *bon mot* from his son, who, being asked when his father would be in New York, replied: "When the President takes off his foot."

A FRAGMENT

[Scene a bed-room. Morning. Mrs Rapp has just got out of bed, and is shaking some part of the dress in which she has passed the night. Mr Rapp remains in bed, and addresses two lads who are sleeping together on a low couch, which during the day is pushed under the bed occupied by their parents]

MR RAPP: Come boys! up with ye! I wish I may be scorched if I don't send ye both east of sunrise if you don't jump slick.

MRS RAPP: Benjamin Franklin! Jefferson Monro! D'ye hear dad, both of ye? You've all got to mind the market, I calculate, this day. 'Tis our quilting frolic,[1] and I must have every thing jam.

MR RAPP: Keep cool, wife. Benjamin Franklin, my son, be a fine fellow, and bring me a stiff tumbler. Three quarters and one, may be. Quick, my hero, and you will be president, I calculate.

BENJAMIN FRANKLIN *[crawling slowly out of bed]*: Don't be in a lather, father, before you are shaved. I'll do your job, I expect, if you won't be in such a tarnation fuss. *[After quitting the bed, Ben. Franklin turns, and gives his brother Jefferson Monro a kick in the*

---

[1] The ladies of the Union are great workers, and, among other enterprises of ingenious industry, they frequently fabricate patchwork quilts. When the external composition of one of these is completed, it is usual to call together their neighbours and friends to witness, and assist at the *quilting*, which is the completion of this elaborate work. These assemblings are called "quilting frolics", and they are always solemnised with much good cheer and festivity.

ribs, and says] We are free and equal, I reckon, from Maine to Georgia, so you shan't be down while I am up, squire.

JEFFERSON MONRO [*starting up*] : What d'ye want with me, all of ye?

MRS RAPP: Well! if that don't beat creation! Why, 'tis quilting frolic, my man, and lying a-bed won't convene, I calculate.

BENJAMIN FRANKLIN [*goes to a table on which whiskey, water, and glasses, stand ready, and, having mixed a tumbler according to order, he takes a pretty considerable sip, and exclaims in a whisper*]: That's jam!

MR RAPP: Look at him now! If he don't suck like an Ingin?[1] Fill it up, my hero, but mind which 'canter 'tis from. Come slick, boy—don't spill it. I'm as dry as a cob.

[*Benjamin Franklin presents the tumbler, and Mr. Rapp tastes it*]

MR RAPP: That's first rate. Now go the whole hog, and we will send you to Congress in no time; light a cigar for me, and you shall see if I don't smoke it.

MRS RAPP [*opening a door that leads to another room*]: Angelina, my daughter, stir! will you? Dad will be off to market in no time, and who's to fix the breakfast? I must be thinking of the quilting, and Clementina, I guess, must have her sleep out. So jump up slick, there's a fine gal.

ANGELINA [*from her bed*]: How you do pother, mother. There's no reason in creation why your fine help here, that's snorting like a 'possum shouldn't be stirring as well as me.

MRS RAPP: My! How you do talk, Angelina! As if you did not know she'd be off, frolic or no frolic, if we did but affront her the least bit in the world.

ANGELINA: Well, I guess I shall set to, and start her, any how. She'll behave herself if I promise to loan

---

[1] In old English, Indian.

her my poppy flowers for her hair to-night, for she is sick with longing to wear them. So here goes [*screaming*], Clementina!

Mr Rapp [*rising, and slowly commencing the business of the toilet*]: Well, wife, you'd best be after telling me what's to be got from market, for I shall be off like a gun. I have got no time to lose, for I must see what the slang-mongers[1] say of this new bank job.

* * * * *

[*Mrs Rapp explains her wishes, and the whole family by degrees descend to the kitchen, when Mr Rapp sets off for market, taking Benjamin Franklin and two large baskets with him*]

Mrs Rapp: There they go, that's jam! and now we must set to slick. I wonder that black beast Lily isn't come yet. Her missis promised to loan her to me for the day for fifty cents, and my pink waist-ribbon, and a pretty bargain I shall make it if she don't come till doomsday. We shall be right down magged without her.

Angelina: That's a fact, for it won't convene for me to be mixing dough cakes and Johnny cakes all day. I've got to fix my dress, I promise you, and as to Clementina she'll do just as much as she likes I expect, and no more.

Clementina: You may say that, Angelina; and where's the lady what a white help as would do more? But if Mrs Rapp will loan me five dollars to make up the price of my silk frock what I'm going to have, may be I'll be chirk at it, and get her through. What d'ye say, Mrs Rapp? I guess you'd best be doing what I ask you, for you'll look streaked, I calculate, if the folks come before you're right fixed.

Mrs Rapp: Well, now, if that don't make me crawl all over to think of it! Say no more, that's a jam gal; I'll have to loan the dollars, I expect, so be spry now,

---

[1] Newspaper writers.

and get all the rations out ready for fixing the cakes, slick away. Don't sneak it, Clementina, but go the whole hog for me.

CLEMENTINA: Let me alone, Mrs Rapp. Once and awhile I don't mind a spell of work, if I get what I want for it; so mind your business, and I'll mind mine: and see if I don't swiggle my way through, afore quilting time. But mind, old woman, you must not be spying after me, and sneaking about what don't concern you. If you'll be after frying the steaks and inyons for breakfast, and then fix the keeping room, I'll look after the cakes; but I won't carry 'em, mind.

MRS RAPP: Go to the bakery, Jefferson Monro, and ask one of the young gentlemen, if he'll be so genteel as to step over about noon for the cakes for my quilting frolic.

ANGELINA: Well now, mother, I expect that you calculate upon loaning me your ringlets for to-night?

MRS RAPP: If that don't beat all creation. How d'ye think I am to fix myself, then?

ANGELINA: Loan me the two corkscrews then, mother, just to hang behind my spit curls, and keep the short bunches for yourself.

MRS RAPP: Well, I expect it will make muddy water between us if I say no, my daughter. But thanks be to the praise, here comes black Lily. What makes you so late, you nasty nigger varment?

LILY: Oh my missus! There was such a swod of market ladies and gentlemen, comed over in the first boat, that I was 'most mashed to a slab in pushing to get in among 'em, they was all scrouging so thick one upon t'other; and after I had swiggled and swiggled, they made no bones of tossing me 'most into the water; and 'twas all I could do to streak it to dry footing.

MRS RAPP: I calculate, Miss Lily, you gave 'em some nigger impendence, 'cause you was upon crossing to a free state.

LILY: No, my missus, I told 'em I wasn't sneaking it, but was coming to help a grand lady; and then one of 'em fetched me a clip over my shoulders, and said it was best show me my place afore I crossed.

MRS RAPP: My! what a long jabber! 'Twas lucky you comed when you did, I tell you, for I was getting homely, that's a fact; and now set to, Miss Lily, or you'll hear of the cow-hide when you cross back again.

Enter JEFFERSON MONRO

JEFFERSON MONRO: The gentleman at the bakery says as you must fetch over the cakes yourself, if you wants 'em fixed, for he's got no mind that such trotting would be good for him.

MRS RAPP: Cross crither! I should like 'peshily to see him soused in Big Muddy Creek, that's a fact. But here comes father.

Enter MR RAPP *and* BENJAMIN FRANKLIN, *from Market*

MRS RAPP: Back already, Squire? And how have you got along?

MR RAPP: Well now, I don't know exactly, but you must be clever, wife, and not be after putting my dander up, by faulting me if all is not slick right.

MRS RAPP: Let's look it, husband. I'm all of a crawl till I see how my tea's to be.

BENJAMIN FRANKLIN [*taking off his hat, which is filled with peaches*]: Well mother, here's my part of the job—that's for your dulcits—and they bean't smashed nothing to speak of, for sauce.

MRS RAPP: Now then, father.

MR RAPP: Well; there's your turkey—and a first rater—half-a-dollar for that; and here be your right chickens for frying. Bean't they little beauties? hardly bigger than humming birds; a dollar seventy-five for they. Three fips for the hominy, a levy for the squash, and a quarter for the limes; inyons a fip, carolines a levy, green cobs ditto. And now comes the tarnation plague of the whole. I know you'll be homely, wife; but you may allot upon it if you be, you'll eventuate by getting the worst of it, for I shall be tarnation wrathy on my side.

Mrs Rapp: Well, don't sneak it. What is it, man? say.

Mr Rapp: Well, then, I've got no pickled oysters.

Mrs Rapp: Possible! But you needn't be looking fierce, Thomas Rapp. I'm not going to fault you, but I expect you'll convene you'd have conducted better if you hadn't obliviated what looks so 'peshily elegant on a tea-table.

Mr Rapp: Woman, I did not obliviate. There was none to be had for money, so don't look streaked about what can't be helped; but be spry, and give me my breakfast slick.

[*The family sit down to breakfast in the kitchen. Clementina eats with them, and Lily waits upon them all. Mr Rapp then departs for his store, saying as he goes out*] You need not allot upon seeing me till sundown; your dinner won't be over jam to-day, I calculate, so I shall contrive it to the hotel.

*   *   *   *   *

[*Mrs Rapp, her daughter Angelina, her white help Clementina, and her borrowed slave Lily, labour unremittingly throughout the day to prepare for the tea in the best style of quilting frolic liberality. Benjamin Franklin and Jefferson Monro are employed during the whole time in running errands. By about 5 o'clock all is completed; Mrs Rapp and her daughter are full dressed in the keeping room; whiskey, water, sugar, and tumblers, are ranged upon the sideboard; and the two boys, washed, combed, and properly adorned in all respects, receive their mother's instructions for their behaviour*]

Mrs Rapp: Well now, be sure to behave yourselves both of you, and remember, above all things, to shake all the gentlemen as they come in, and to take the ladies' bonnets and their shoes if any of 'em change. We shall have a swod of company, and you must not sneak it in no way, but keep looking about you chirk and lively; and when any gentleman squints towards the sideboard, run slick and mix him some whiskey.

BENJAMIN FRANKLIN: Keep cool, mother, I know a thing or two.

MRS RAPP [*turning to Angelina*]: Well, my daughter, I must say you look pretty considerable jam, and them corkscrews do convene, that's a fact. You are dreadful handsome, Angelina. I expect nobody can dubiate that. But you must be 'peshily spry to-night, or you may allot upon it we shall have father's dander up. I tell you he is talking from July to eternity about the quarters you have had; and you may realise that after the quilting is over, he'll be looking to you to happify the company with your accomplishments. Well! there they come across the clover lot, lock and lock together. My! what a swod of them, all in a slush! Why, here's every body about creation, that's a fact.

[*Enter a great many American ladies and gentlemen*]

Chapter Thirty

Journey to New York—Delaware River—Stage-Coach —City of New York—Collegiate Institute for Young Ladies — Theatres — Public Garden — Churches— Morris Canal—Fashions—Carriages

AT length, spite of the lingering pace necessarily attending consultations, and arrangements across the Atlantic, our plans were finally settled; the coming spring was to show us New York and Niagara, and the early summer was to convey us home.

No sooner did the letter arrive which decided this,

than we began our preparations for departure. We took our laſt voyage on the Potomac, we bade a laſt farewell to Virginia and gave a laſt day to some of our kind friends near Washington.

The spring, though slow and backward, was sufficiently advanced to render the journey pleasant; and though the road from Washington to Baltimore was less brilliant in foliage than when I had seen it before, it ſtill had much of beauty. The azaleas were in full bloom, and the delicate yellow blossom of the sassafras almoſt rivalled its fruit in beauty.

At Baltimore we again embarked on a gigantic ſteam-boat, and reached Philadelphia in the middle of the night. Here we changed our boat, and found time, before ſtarting in the morning, to take a laſt look at the Doric and Corinthian porticoes of the two celebrated temples dedicated to Mammon.

The Delaware River, above Philadelphia, ſtill flows through a landscape too level for beauty, but it is rendered intereſting by a succession of gentlemen's seats, which, if less elaborately finished in architecture and garden grounds, than the lovely villas on the Thames, are ſtill beautiful objeCts to gaze upon as you float rapidly paſt on the broad silvery ſtream that washes their lawns. They present a piCture of wealth and enjoyment that accords well with that noble city to which they are an appendage. One mansion arreſted our attention, not only from its being more than usually large and splendid, but from its having the monument which marked the family reſting-place, rearing itself in all the gloomy grandeur of black and white marble, exaCtly opposite the door of entrance.

In Virginia and Maryland we had remarked that almoſt every family mansion had its little grave yard, sheltered by locuſt and cypress trees; but this decorated dwelling of the dead seemed rather a melancholy ornament in the grounds.

We had, for a considerable distance, a view of the dwelling of Joseph Bonaparte, which is situated on the New Jersey shore, in the midst of an extensive tract of land, of which he is the proprietor.*

Here the ex-monarch has built several houses, which are occupied by French tenants. The country is very flat, but a terrace of two sides has been raised, commanding a fine reach of the Delaware River; at the point where this terrace forms a right angle, a lofty chapel has been erected, which looks very much like an observatory; I admired the ingenuity with which the Catholic prince has united his religion and his love of a fine terrestrial prospect. The highest part of the building presents, in every direction, the appearance of an immense cross; the transept, if I may so express it, being formed by the projection of an ample balcony, which surrounds a tower.

A Quaker gentleman, from Philadelphia, exclaimed, as he gazed on the mansion: "There we see a monument of fallen royalty! Strange, that dethroned kings should seek and find their best strong-hold in a Republic!"

There was more of philosophy than of scorn in his accent, and his countenance was the symbol of gentleness and benevolence; but I overheard many unquaker-like jokes from others, as to the comfortable assurance a would-be king must feel of a faithful alliance between his head and shoulders.

At Trenton, the capital of New Jersey, we left our smoothly-gliding comfortable boat for the most detestable stage-coach that ever Christian built to dislocate the joints of his fellow-men. Ten of these torturing machines were crammed full of the passengers who left the boat with us. The change in our movement was not more remarkable than that which took place in the tempers and countenances of our fellow-travellers. Gentlemen who had lounged on sofas, and balanced themselves in chairs, all the way from Philadelphia, with all the conscious fascinations of stiff stays and neck-cloths, which, while doing to death the rash beauties who ventured to gaze, seemed but a whalebone panoply to guard the wearer, these pretty youths so guarded from without, so sweetly at peace within, now crushed beneath their armour, looked more like victims on the wheel, than dandies armed for conquest; their whalebones seemed to enter into their souls, and every face grew grim and scowling. The pretty ladies too, with their expansive bonnets, any one of which might handsomely have filled the space allotted to three—how sad the change! I almost fancied they must have been of the race of Undine, and that it was only when they heard the splashing of water that they could smile. As I looked into the altered eyes of my companions, I was tempted to ask, "Look I as cross as you?" Indeed, I believe that, if possible, I looked crosser still, for the roads and the vehicle together were quite too much for my philosophy.

At length, however, we found ourselves alive on board the boat which was to convey us down the Raraton River to New York.

We fully intended to have gone to bed, to heal our bones, on entering the steam-boat, but the sight of a table neatly spread determined us to go to dinner instead. Sin and shame would it have been, indeed, to have closed our eyes upon the scene which soon opened before us. I have never seen the bay of Naples, I can therefore make no comparison, but my imagination is incapable of conceiving any thing of the kind more beautiful than the harbour of New York. Various and lovely are the objects which meet the eye on every side, but the naming them would only be to give a list of words, without conveying the faintest idea of the scene. I doubt if ever the pencil of Turner could do it justice, bright and glorious as it rose upon us. We seemed to enter the harbour of New York upon waves of liquid gold, and as we darted past the green isles which rise from its bosom, like guardian sentinels of the fair city, the setting sun stretched his horizontal beams farther and farther at each moment, as if to point out to us some new glory in the landscape.

New York, indeed, appeared to us, even when we saw it by a soberer light, a lovely and a noble city. To us who had been so long travelling through half-cleared forests, and sojourning among an "I'm-as-good-as-you" population, it seemed, perhaps, more beautiful, more splendid, and more refined than it might have done, had we arrived there directly from London; but making every allowance for this, I must still declare that I think New York one of the finest cities I ever saw, and as much superior to every other in the Union (Philadelphia not excepted), as London to Liverpool, or Paris to Rouen. Its advantages of position are, perhaps, unequalled any where. Situated on an island, which I think it will one day cover, it rises like Venice, from the sea, and like that fairest of cities in the days of her glory, receives into its lap tribute of all the riches of the earth.

The southern point of Manhattan Island divides the waters of the harbour into the North and East rivers; on this point stands the city of New York, extending from river to river, and running northward to the extent of three or four miles. I think it covers nearly as much ground as Paris, but is much less thickly peopled. The extreme point is fortified towards the sea by a battery, and forms an admirable point of defence; but in these piping days of peace, it is converted into a public promenade, and one more beautiful, I should suppose, no city could boast. From hence commences the splendid Broadway, as the fine avenue is called, which runs through the whole city. This noble street may vie with any I ever saw, for its length and breadth, its handsome shops, neat awnings, excellent *trottoir*, and well-dressed pedestrians. It has not the crowded glitter of Bond Street equipages, nor the gorgeous fronted palaces of Regent Street; but it is magnificent in its extent, and ornamented by several handsome buildings, some of them surrounded by grass and trees. The Park, in which stands the noble city-hall, is a very fine area. I never found that the most graphic description of a city could give me any feeling of being there; and even if others have the power, I am very sure I have not, of setting churches and squares, and long drawn streets, before the mind's eye. I will not, therefore, attempt a detailed description of this great metropolis of the new world; but will only say that during the seven weeks we stayed there, we always found something new to see and to admire; and were it not so very far from all the old-world things which cling about the heart of an European, I should say that I never saw a city more desirable as a residence.

The dwelling houses of the higher classes are extremely handsome, and very richly furnished. Silk or satin furniture is as often, or oftener, seen than chintz; the mirrors are as handsome as in London; the cheffoniers, slabs, and marble tables as elegant; and in addition, they have all the pretty tasteful decoration of French porcelain, and ormolu in much greater abundance, because at a much cheaper rate. Every part of their houses is well carpeted, and the exterior finishings, such as steps, railings, and door frames, are very superior. Almost every house has handsome green blinds on the outside; balconies are not very general, nor do the houses display, externally, so many flowers as those of Paris and London; but I saw many rooms decorated within, exactly like those of an European *petite maîtresse*. Little tables, looking and smelling like flower beds, portfolios, nicknacks, bronzes, busts, cameos, and alabaster vases, illustrated copies of lady-like rhymes bound in silk, and, in short, all the cox-comalities of the drawing-room scattered about with the same profuse and studied negligence as with us.

Hudson Square and its neighbourhood is, I believe, the most fashionable part of the town; the square is beautiful, excellently well planted with a great variety of trees, and only wanting our frequent and careful mowing to make it equal to any square in London. The iron railing which surrounds this enclosure is as high and as handsome as that of the Tuileries, and it will give some idea of the care bestowed on its decoration, to know that the gravel for the walks was conveyed by barges from Boston, not as ballast, but as freight.

The great defect in the houses is their extreme uniformity—when you have seen one you have seen all. Neither do I quite like the arrangement of the rooms. In nearly all the houses the dining and drawing-rooms are on the same floor, with ample folding doors between them; when thrown together they certainly make a very noble apartment; but no doors can be barrier sufficient between dining and drawing-rooms. Mixed dinner parties of ladies and gentlemen, however, are very rare, which is a great defect in the society, not only as depriving them of the most sociable and hospitable manner of meeting, but as leading to frequent dinner parties of gentlemen without ladies, which certainly does not conduce to refinement.

The evening parties, excepting such as are expressly for young people, are chiefly conversational; we were too late in the season for large parties, but we saw enough to convince us that there is society to be met with in New York, which would be deemed delightful any where. Cards are very seldom used; and music, from their having very little professional aid at their parties, is seldom, I believe, as good as what is heard at private concerts in London.

The Americans have certainly not the same *besoin* of

being amused as other people; they may be the wiser for this, perhaps, but it makes them less agreeable to a looker-on.

There are three theatres at New York, all of which we visited. The Park Theatre is the only one licensed by fashion, but the Bowery is infinitely superior in beauty; it is indeed as pretty a theatre as I ever entered, perfect as to size and proportion, elegantly decorated, and the scenery and machinery equal to any in London, but it is not the fashion. The Chatham is so utterly condemned by *bon ton*, that it requires some courage to decide upon going there; nor do I think my curiosity would have penetrated so far, had I had not seen Miss Mitford's *Rienzi* advertised there. It was the first opportunity I had had of seeing it played, and, spite of very indifferent acting, I was delighted. The interest must have been great, for till the curtain fell, I saw not one quarter of the queer things around me: then I observed in the front row of a dress-box a lady performing the most maternal office possible; several gentlemen without their coats, and a general air of contempt for the decencies of life, certainly more than usually revolting.

At the Park Theatre I again saw the American Roscius, Mr Forrest. He played the part of Damon, and roared, I thought, very unlike a nightingale. I cannot admire this celebrated performer.

Another night we saw Cinderella there; Mrs Austin was the prima donna, and much admired. The piece was extremely well got up, and on this occasion we saw the Park Theatre to advantage, for it was filled with well-dressed company; but still we saw many " yet un-razored lips " polluted with the grim tinge of the hateful tobacco, and heard, without ceasing, the spitting, which of course is its consequence. If their theatres had the orchestra of the Feydeau, and a choir of angels to boot, I could find but little pleasure, so long as they were followed by this running accompaniment of *thorough base*.

Institute for Young Ladies

Whilst at New York, the prospectus of a fashionable boarding-school was presented to me. I made some extracts from it, as a specimen of the enlarged scale of instruction proposed for young females:

"Brooklyn Collegiate Institute
for Young Ladies,
Brooklyn Heights, opposite the City of
New York

JUNIOR DEPARTMENT
Sixth Class

Latin Grammar, Liber Primus; Jacob's Latin Reader (first part); Modern Geography; Intellectual and Practical Arithmetic finished; Dr Barber's Grammar of Elocution; Writing, Spelling, Composition, and Vocal Music.

Fifth Class

Jacob's Latin Reader (second part); Roman Antiquities, Sallust; Clark's Introduction to the Making of Latin; Ancient and Sacred Geography; Studies of Poetry; Short Treatise on Rhetoric; Map Drawing, Composition, Spelling, and Vocal Music.

Fourth Class

Cæsar's Commentaries; first five books of Virgil's Æneid; Mythology; Watts on the Mind; Political Geography (Woodbridge's large work); Natural History; Treatise on the Globes; Ancient History; Studies of Poetry concluded; English Grammar, Composition, Spelling, and Vocal Music.

SENIOR DEPARTMENT
Third Class

Virgil (finished); Cicero's Select Orations; Modern History; Plane Geometry; Moral Philosophy; Critical Reading of Young's Poems; Perspective Drawing; Rhetoric; Logic, Composition, and Vocal Music.

Second Class

Livy; Horace (Odes); Natural Theology; small Compend of Ecclesiastical History; Female Biography; Algebra; Natural Philosophy (Mechanics, Hydrostatics, Pneumatics, and Acoustics); Intellectual Philosophy; Evidences of Christianity; Composition, and Vocal Music.

First Class

Horace (finished); Tacitus; Natural Philosophy (Electricity, Optics, Magnetism, Galvanism); Astronomy, Chemistry, Mineralogy, and Geology; Compend of Political Economy; Composition, and Vocal Music.

The French, Spanish, Italian, or Greek languages may be attended to, if required, at any time."

The Exchange is very handsome, and ranks about midway between the heavy gloom that hangs over our London merchants, and the light and lofty elegance which decorates the Bourse at Paris. The churches are plain, but very neat, and kept in perfect repair within and without; but I saw none which had the least pretension to splendour; the Catholic Cathedral at Baltimore is the only church in America which has.

At New York, as every where else, they show within, during the time of service, like beds of tulips, so gay, so bright, so beautiful, are the long rows of French bonnets and pretty faces; rows but rarely broken by the unribboned heads of the male population; the proportion is about the same as I have remarked elsewhere. Excepting at New York, I never saw the other side of the picture, but there I did. On the opposite side of the North River, about three miles higher up, is a place called Hoboken. A gentleman who possessed a handsome mansion and grounds there, also possessed the right of ferry, and to render this productive, he has restricted his pleasure grounds to a few beautiful acres, laying out the remainder simply and tastefully as a public walk. It is hardly possible to imagine one of greater attraction; a broad belt of light underwood and flowering shrubs, studded at intervals with lofty forest trees, runs for two miles along a cliff which overhangs the matchless Hudson; sometimes it feathers the rocks down to its very margin, and at others leaves a pebbly shore, just rude enough to break the gentle waves, and make a music which mimics softly the loud chorus of the ocean.—Through this beautiful little wood a broad well-gravelled terrace is led by every point which can exhibit the scenery to advantage; narrower and wider paths diverge at intervals, some into the deeper shadow of the woods, and some shelving gradually to the pretty coves below.

The price of entrance to this little Eden is the six cents you pay at the ferry. We went there on a bright Sunday afternoon, expressly to see the humours of the place. Many thousand persons were scattered through the grounds; of these we ascertained, by repeatedly counting, that nineteen-twentieths were men. The ladies were at church. Often as the subject has pressed upon my mind, I think I never so strongly felt the conviction that the Sabbath-day, the holy day, the day on which alone the great majority of the Christian world can spend their hours as they please, is ill passed (if passed entirely) within brick walls, listening to an earth-born preacher, charm he never so wisely.[1]

> " Oh! how can they renounce the boundless store
> Of charms, which Nature to her vot'ries yields!
> The warbling woodland, the resounding shore,
> The pomp of groves, and garniture of fields,
> All that the genial ray of morning gilds,

---

[1] Compare a Sunday, the greater part of which is passed in church, and the rest in rigid abstinence from every occupation which nature seems to have made congenial to the mind of man, with the simple, holy, patriarchal Sunday of Sir Walter Scott, as described in that most perfect of all existing biographies, Lockhart's Life of him.

> And all that echoes to the song of even,
> All that the mountain's sheltering bosom yields,
> And all the dread magnificence of heaven;
> Oh! how can they renounce, and hope to be forgiven!"

How is it that the men of America, who are reckoned good husbands and good fathers, while they themselves enjoy sufficient freedom of spirit to permit their walking forth into the temple of the living God, can leave those they love best on earth bound in the iron chains of a most tyrannical fanaticism? How can they breathe the balmy air, and not think of the tainted atmosphere so heavily weighing upon breasts still dearer than their own? How can they gaze upon the blossoms of the spring, and not remember the fairer cheeks of their young daughters, waxing pale, as they sit for long sultry hours, immured with hundreds of fellow victims, listening to the roaring vanities of a preacher, canonised by a college of old women? They cannot think it needful to salvation, or they would not withdraw themselves. Wherefore is it? Do they fear these self-elected, self-ordained priests, and offer up their wives and daughters to propitiate them? Or do they deem their hebdomadal freedom more complete, because their wives and daughters are shut up four or five times in the day at church or chapel? It is true, that at Hoboken, as everywhere else, there are *reposoirs*, which, as you pass them, blast the sense for a moment, by reeking forth the fumes of whiskey and tobacco, and it may be that these cannot be entered with a wife or daughter. The proprietor of the grounds, however, has contrived with great taste to render these abominations not unpleasing to the eye; there is one in particular, which has quite the air of a Grecian temple, and did they drink wine instead of whiskey, it might be inscribed to Bacchus; but in this particular, as in many others, the ancient and modern republics differ.

It is impossible not to feel, after passing one Sunday

in the churches and chapels of New York, and the next in the gardens of Hoboken, that the thousands of well-dressed men you see enjoying themselves at the latter, have made over the thousands of well-dressed women you saw exhibited at the former, into the hands of the priests, at least, for a day. The American people arrogate to themselves a character of superior morality and religion, but this division of their hours of leisure does not give me a favourable idea of either.

I visited all the exhibitions in New York. The Medici of the Republic must exert themselves a little more before these can become even respectable. The worst of the business is, that with the exception of about half a dozen individuals, the good citizens are more than contented, they are delighted.

The newspaper lungs of the Republic breathe forth praise and triumph, nay, almost pant with ecstasy in speaking of their native *chef d' œuvres*. I should be hardly believed were I to relate the instances which fell in my way, of the utter ignorance respecting pictures to be found among persons of the *first standing* in society. Often where a liberal spirit exists, and a wish to patronise the fine arts is expressed, it is joined to a profundity of ignorance on the subject almost inconceivable. A doubt as to the excellence of their artists is very nervously received, and one gentleman, with much civility, told me, that at the present era, all the world were aware that competition was pretty well at an end between our two nations, and that a little envy might naturally be expected to mix with the surprise with which the mother country beheld the distance at which her colonies were leaving her behind them.

I must, however, do the few artists with whom I became acquainted, the justice to say, that their own pretensions are much more modest than those of their patrons for them. I have heard several confess and deplore their ignorance of drawing, and have repeatedly remarked a sensibility to the merit of European artists, though perhaps only known by engravings, and a deference to their authority, which showed a genuine feeling for the art.   In fact, I think that there is a very considerable degree of natural talent for painting in America, but it has to make its way through darkness and thick night.   When an academy is founded, their first care is to hang the walls of its exhibition room with all the unutterable trash that is offered to them.   No living models are sought for; no discipline as to the manner of study is enforced.   Boys who know no more of human form, than they do of the eyes, nose, and mouth in the moon, begin painting portraits.   If some of them would only throw away their palettes for a year, and learn to draw; if they would attend anatomical lectures, and take notes, not in words, but in forms, of joints and muscles, their exhibitions would soon cease to be so utterly below criticism.

The most interesting exhibition open when I was there was, decidedly, Colonel Trumbull's; and how the patriots of America can permit this truly national collection to remain a profitless burden on the hands of the artist, it is difficult to understand.   Many of the sketches are masterly; but, like his illustrious countryman, West, his sketches are his *chef d'œuvres*.

I can imagine nothing more perfect than the interior of the public institutions of New York.   There is a practical good sense in all their arrangements, that must strike foreigners very forcibly.   The Asylum for the Destitute offers a hint worth taking.   It is dedicated to the reformation of youthful offenders of both sexes, and it is as admirable in the details of its management as in its object.   Every part of the institution is deeply interesting; but there is a difference very remarkable between the boys and the girls.   The boys are, I think, the finest set of lads I ever saw brought together;

bright-looking, gay, active, and full of intelligence.
The girls are exactly the reverse; heavy, listless, indifferent, and melancholy. In conversing with the
gentleman who is the general superintendent of the
establishment, I made the remark to him, and he told
me that the reality corresponded with the appearance.
All of them had been detected in some act of dis-
honesty; but the boys, when removed from the evil
influence which had led them so to use their ingenuity,
rose like a spring when a pressure is withdrawn; and
feeling themselves once more safe from danger and
from shame, hope and cheerfulness animated every
countenance. But the poor girls, on the contrary,
can hardly look up again. They are as different
as an oak and a lily after a storm. The one, when the
fresh breeze blows over, shakes the raindrops from its
crest, and only looks the brighter; the other, its silken
leaves once soiled, shrinks from the eye, and is levelled
to the earth for ever.

*   *   *   *   *

We spent a delightful day in New Jersey, in visiting,
with a most agreeable party, the inclined planes, which
are used instead of locks on the Morris canal.

This is a very interesting work; it is one among a
thousand which prove the people of America to be the
most enterprising in the world. I was informed that
this important canal, which connects the waters of the
Hudson and the Delaware, is a hundred miles long, and
in this distance overcomes a variation of level amounting
to sixteen hundred feet. Of this, fourteen hundred are
achieved by inclined planes. The planes average about
sixty feet of perpendicular lift each, and are to support
about forty tons. The time consumed in passing
them is twelve minutes for one hundred feet of perpendicular rise. The expense is less than a third of
what locks would be for surmounting the same rise.

If we set about any more canals, this may be worth attending to.

The Morris canal is certainly an extraordinary work; it not only varies its level sixteen hundred feet, but at one point runs along the side of a mountain at thirty feet above the tops of the highest buildings in the town of Paterson, below; at another, it crosses the falls of the Passaic, in a stone aqueduct, sixty feet above the water in the river.* This noble work in a great degree owes its existence to the patriotic and scientific energy of Mr. Cadwallader Colden.

There is no point in the national character of the Americans which commands so much respect as the boldness and energy with which public works are undertaken and carried through. Nothing stops them if a profitable result can be fairly hoped for. It is this which has made cities spring up amidst the forests with such inconceivable rapidity; and could they once be thoroughly persuaded that any point of the ocean had a hoard of dollars beneath it, I have not the slightest doubt that in about eighteen months we should see a snug covered rail-road leading direct to the spot.

*   *   *   *   *

I was told at New York, that in many parts of the state it was usual to pay the service of the Presbyterian ministers in the following manner. Once a year a day is fixed, on which some member of every family in a congregation meet at their minister's house in the afternoon. They each bring an offering (according to their means) of articles necessary for housekeeping. The poorer members leave their contributions in a large basket, placed for the purpose close to the door of entrance. Those of more importance, and more calculated to do honour to the piety of the donors, are carried into the room where the company is assembled. Sugar, coffee, tea, cheese, barrels of flour, pieces of

Irish linen, sets of china and of glass, were among the articles mentioned to me as usually making parts of these offerings. After the party is assembled, and the business of giving and receiving is dispatched, tea, coffee, and cakes are handed round; but these are not furnished at any expense either of trouble or money to the minister, for selected ladies of the congregation take the whole arrangement upon themselves. These meetings are called spinning visits.

Another New York custom, which does not seem to have so reasonable a cause, is the changing house once a year. On the 1st of May the city of New York has the appearance of sending off a population flying from the plague, or of a town which had surrendered on condition of carrying away all their goods and chattels. Rich furniture and ragged furniture, carts, waggons, and drays, ropes, canvas, and straw, packers, porters, and draymen, white, yellow, and black, occupy the streets from east to west, from north to south, on this day. Every one I spoke to on the subject complained of this custom as most annoying, but all assured me it was un-avoidable, if you inhabit a rented house. More than one of my New York friends have built or bought houses solely to avoid this annual inconvenience.

There are a great number of negroes in New York, all free; their emancipation having been completed in 1827. Not even in Philadelphia, where the anti-slavery opinions have been the most active and violent, do the blacks appear to wear an air of so much consequence as they do at New York. They have several chapels, in which negro ministers officiate; and a theatre, in which none but negroes perform. At this theatre a gallery is appropriated to such whites as choose to visit it; and here only are they permitted to sit; following in this, with nice etiquette, and equal justice, the arrangement of the white theatres, in all of which is a gallery appro-priated solely to the use of the blacks. I have often, particularly on a Sunday, met groups of negroes elegantly dressed; and have been sometimes amused by observing the very superior air of gallantry assumed by the men, when in attendance on their *belles*, to that of the whites in similar circumſtances. On one occasion we met in Broadway a young negress in the extreme of the fashion, and accompanied by a black *beau*, whose toilet was equally ſtudied; eye-glass, guard-chain, nothing was omitted; he walked beside his sable goddess uncovered, and with an air of the moſt tender devotion.

At the window of a handsome house which they were passing, ſtood a very pretty white girl, with two gentle-men beside her; but, alas! both of them had their hats on, and one was smoking!

If it were not for the peculiar manner of walking, which diſtinguishes all American women, Broadway might be taken for a French ſtreet, where it was the fashion for very smart ladies to promenade. The dress is entirely French; not an article (except perhaps the cotton ſtockings) muſt be English, on pain of being ſtigmatised as out of the fashion. Every thing English is decidedly *mauvais ton ;* English materials, English fashions, English accent, English manner, are all terms of reproach; and to say that an unfortunate looks like an English woman, is the cruelleſt satire which can be uttered.

I remember visiting France almoſt immediately after we had made the moſt offensive invasion of her territory that can well be imagined; yet, despite the feelings which lengthened years of war muſt have engendered, it was the fashion to admire every thing English. I suppose family quarrels are more difficult to adjuſt; for fifteen years of peace have not been enough to calm the angry feelings of brother Jonathan towards the land of his fathers:

" The which he hateth passing well."

It is hardly needful to say that the most courteous amenity of manner distinguishes the reception given to foreigners by the patrician class of Americans.

Gentlemen, in the old-world sense of the term, are the same every where; and an American gentleman and his family know how to do the honours of their country to strangers of every nation, as well as any people on earth. But this class, though it decidedly exists, is a very small one, and cannot in justice be represented as affording a specimen of the whole.

*　　*　　*　　*　　*

Most of the houses in New York are painted on the outside, but in a manner carefully to avoid disfiguring the material which it preserves: on the contrary, nothing can be neater. They are now using a great deal of a beautiful stone called Jersey freestone; it is of a warm rich brown, and extremely ornamental to the city wherever it has been employed. They have also a grey granite of great beauty. The trottoir paving, in most of the streets, is extremely good, being of large flag stones, very superior to the bricks of Philadelphia.

At night the shops, which are open till very late, are brilliantly illuminated with gas, and all the population seem as much alive as in London or Paris. This makes the solemn stillness of the evening hours in Philadelphia more remarkable.

There are a few trees in different parts of the city, and I observed many young ones planted, and guarded with much care; were they more abundant it would be extremely agreeable, for the reflected light of their fierce summer sheds intolerable day.

Ice is in profuse abundance; I do not imagine that there is a house in the city without the luxury of a piece of ice to cool the water, and harden the butter.

The hackney coaches are the best in the world,[1] but

---

[1] Excepting those of Vienna.

abominably dear, and it is necessary to be on the *qui vive* in making your bargain with the driver; if you do not, he has the power of charging immoderately. On my first experiment I neglected this, and was asked two dollars and a half for an excursion of twenty minutes. When I referred to the waiter of the hotel, he asked if I had made a bargain. " No." " Then I expect " (with the usual look of triumph) " that the Yankee has been too smart for you."

The private carriages of New York are infinitely handsomer and better appointed than any I saw elsewhere; the want of smart liveries destroys much of the gay effect; but, on the whole, a New York summer equipage, with the pretty women and beautiful children it contains, looks extremely well in Broadway, and would not be much amiss any where.

The luxury of the New York aristocracy is not confined to the city; hardly an acre of Manhattan Island but shows some pretty villa or stately mansion. The most chosen of these are on the north and east rivers, to whose margins their lawns descend. Among these, perhaps, the loveliest is one situated in the beautiful village of Bloomingdale: here, within the space of sixteen acres, almost every variety of garden scenery may be found. To describe all its diversity of hill and dale, of wood and lawn, of rock and river, would be in vain; nor can I convey an idea of it by comparison, for I never saw any thing like it. How far the elegant hospitality which reigns there may influence my impressions, I know not; but, assuredly, no spot I have ever seen dwells more freshly on my memory, nor did I ever find myself in a circle more calculated to give delight in meeting and regret at parting, than that of Woodlawn.

Chapter Thirty-One

Reception of Captain Basil Hall's Book in the United States

HAVING now arrived nearly at the end of our travels, I am induced, ere I conclude, again to mention what I consider as one of the most remarkable traits in the national character of the Americans; namely, their exquisite sensitiveness and soreness respecting every thing said or written concerning them. Of this, perhaps, the most remarkable example I can give, is the effect produced on nearly every class of readers by the appearance of Captain Basil Hall's *Travels in North America*. In fact it was a sort of moral earthquake, and the vibration it occasioned through the nerves of the Republic, from one corner of the Union to the other, was by no means over when I left the country in July, 1831, a couple of years after the shock.

I was in Cincinnati when these volumes came out, but it was not till July, 1830, that I procured a copy of them. One bookseller to whom I applied told me that he had had a few copies before he understood the nature of the work, but that after becoming acquainted with it, nothing should induce him to sell another. Other persons of his profession must, however, have been less scrupulous, for the book was read in city, town, village, and hamlet, steam-boat, and stage-coach, and a sort of war-whoop was sent forth perfectly unprecedented in my recollection upon any occasion whatever.

It was fortunate for me that I did not procure these volumes till I had heard them very generally spoken of, for the curiosity I felt to know the contents of a work so violently anathematised, led me to make inquiries which elicited a great deal of curious feeling.

An ardent desire for approbation, and a delicate sensitiveness under censure, have always, I believe, been considered as amiable traits of character; but the condition into which the appearance of Capt. Hall's work threw the Republic, shows plainly that these feelings, if carried to excess, produce a weakness which amounts to imbecility.

It was perfectly astonishing to hear men, who, on other subjects, were of sane judgment, utter their opinions upon this. I never heard of any instance in which the common sense generally found in national criticism was so overthrown by passion. I do not speak of the want of justice, and of fair and liberal interpretation; these, perhaps, were hardly to be expected. Other nations have been called thin-skinned, but the citizens of the Union have, apparently, no skins at all; they wince if a breeze blows over them, unless it be tempered with adulation. It was not, therefore, very surprising that the acute and forcible observations of a traveller they knew would be listened to, should be received testily. The extraordinary features of the business were, first, the excess of the rage into which they lashed themselves; and, secondly, the puerility of the inventions by which they attempted to account for the severity with which they fancied they had been treated.

Not content with declaring that the volumes contained no word of truth from beginning to end (which is an assertion I heard made very nearly as often as they were mentioned), the whole country set to work to discover the causes why Capt. Hall had visited the United States, and why he had published his book.

I have heard it said, with as much precision and gravity as if the statement had been conveyed by an official report, that Capt. Hall had been sent out by the British government expressly for the purpose of checking the growing admiration of England for the government of the United States—that it was by a commission from the Treasury he had come, and that it was only in obedience to orders that he had found any thing to object to.

I do not give this as the gossip of a coterie; I am persuaded that it is the belief of a very considerable portion of the country. So deep is the conviction of this singular people that they cannot be seen without being admired, that they will not admit the possibility that any one should honestly and sincerely find aught to disapprove in them, or their country.

At Philadelphia I met with a little anonymous book, written to show that Capt. Basil Hall was in no way to be depended on, for that he not only slandered the Americans, but was himself, in other respects, a person of very equivocal morals. One proof of this is given by a quotation of the following playful account of the distress occasioned by the want of a bell. The commentator calls it an instance of "shocking coarseness".

" One day I was rather late for breakfast, and, as there was no water in my jug, I set off, post haste, half shaved, half dressed, and more than half vexed, in quest of water, like a seaman on short allowance, hunting for rivulets on some unknown coast. I went up stairs, and down stairs, and in the course of my researches into half a dozen different apartments, might have stumbled on some lady's chamber, as the song says, which, considering the plight I was in, would have been awkward enough."

Another indication of this moral coarseness is pointed out in the passage where Capt. Hall says he never saw a flirtation all the time he was in the Union.

The charge of ingratitude also was echoed from mouth to mouth. That he should himself bear testimony to the unvarying kindness of the reception he met with, and yet find fault with the country, was declared on all hands to be a proof of the most abominable ingratitude that it ever entered into the heart of man to conceive. I once ventured before about a dozen people to ask whether more blame would not attach to an author, if he suffered himself to be bribed by individual kindness to falsify facts, than if, despite all personal considerations, he stated them truly?

" Facts!" cried the whole circle at once, " facts! I tell you there is not a word of fact in it from beginning to end."

The American Reviews are, many of them, I believe, well-known in England; I need not, therefore, quote them here, but I sometimes wondered that they, none of them, ever thought of translating Obadiah's curse into classic American ; if they had done so, only placing (he, Basil Hall) between brackets, instead of (he, Obadiah), it would have saved them a world of trouble.

I can hardly describe the curiosity with which I sat down at length to peruse these tremendous volumes; still less can I do justice to my surprise at their contents. To say that I found not one exaggerated statement throughout the work, is by no means saying enough. It is impossible for any one who knows the country not to see that Capt. Hall earnestly sought out things to admire and commend.   When he praises, it is with evident pleasure; and when he finds fault, it is with evident reluctance and restraint, excepting where motives purely patriotic urge him to state roundly what it is for the benefit of his country should be known.

In fact, Capt. Hall saw the country to the greatest possible advantage.   Furnished, of course, with letters of introduction to the most distinguished individuals, and with the still more influential recommendation of his own reputation, he was received in full drawing-room style and state from one end of the Union to the other.   He saw the country in full dress, and had little or no opportunity of judging of it unhoused, un-anointed, unannealed, with all its imperfections on its head, as I and my family too often had.

Capt. Hall had certainly excellent opportunities of making himself acquainted with the form of the government and the laws; and of receiving, moreover, the best oral commentary upon them, in conversation with the most distinguished citizens. Of these opportunities he made excellent use; nothing important met his eye which did not receive that sort of analytical attention which an experienced and philosophical traveller alone can give. This has made his volumes highly interesting and valuable; but I am deeply persuaded, that were a man of equal penetration to visit the United States with no other means of becoming acquainted with the national character than the ordinary working-day intercourse of life, he would conceive an infinitely lower idea of the moral atmosphere of the country than Capt. Hall appears to have done; and the internal conviction on my mind is strong, that if Capt. Hall had not placed a firm restraint on himself, he must have given expression to far deeper indignation than any he has uttered against many points in the American character, with which he shows, from other circumstances, that he was well acquainted. His rule appears to have been to state just so much of the truth as would leave on the minds of his readers a correct impression, at the least cost of pain to the sensitive folks he was writing about. He states his own opinions and feelings, and leaves it to be inferred that he has good grounds for adopting them; but he spares the Americans the bitterness which a detail of the circumstances would have produced.

If any one chooses to say that some wicked antipathy to twelve millions of strangers is the origin of my opinion, I must bear it; and were the question one of mere idle speculation, I certainly would not court the abuse I must meet for stating it. But it is not so. I know that among the best, the most pious, the most benevolent of my countrymen, there are hundreds, nay,

I fear thousands, who conscientiously believe that a greater degree of political and religious liberty (such as is possessed in America) would be beneficial for us. How often have I wished, during my abode in the United States, that one of these conscientious, but mistaken reasoners, fully possessed of his country's confidence, could pass a few years in the United States, sufficiently among the mass of the citizens to know them, and sufficiently at leisure to trace effects to their causes. Then might we look for a statement which would teach these mistaken philanthropists to tremble at every symptom of democratic power among us; a statement which would make even our sectarians shudder at the thought of hewing down the Established Church; for they would be taught, by fearful example, to know that it was the bulwark which protects us from the gloomy horrors of fanatic superstition on one side, and the still more dreadful inroads of infidelity on the other. And more than all, such a man would see as clear as light, that where every class is occupied in getting money and no class in spending it, there will neither be leisure for worshipping the theory of honesty, nor motive strong enough to put its restrictive doctrines in practice. Where every man is engaged in driving hard bargains with his fellows, where is the honoured class to be found, into which gentleman-like feelings, principles, and practice, are necessary as an introduction?

That there are men of powerful intellect, benevolent hearts, and high moral feeling in America, I know: and I could, if challenged to do so, name individuals surpassed by none of any country in these qualities; but they are excellent, despite their institutions, not in consequence of them. It is not by such that Capt. Hall's statements are called slanders, nor is it from such that I shall meet the abuse which I well know these pages will inevitably draw upon me; and I only trust I may be able to muster as much self-denial as my predecessor, who asserts, in his recently published *Fragments*, that he has read none of the American criticisms on his book. He did wisely, if he wished to retain an atom of his kindly feeling toward America; and he has, assuredly, lost but little on the score of information; for these criticisms, generally speaking, consist of mere downright personal abuse, or querulous complaints of his ingratitude and ill usage of them; complaints which it is quite astonishing that any persons of spirit could indulge in.

The following good-humoured paragraphs from the *Fragments*, must, I think, rather puzzle the Americans. Possibly they may think that Capt. Hall is quizzing them, when he says he has read none of their criticisms; but I think there is in these passages internal evidence that he has not seen them. For if he had read one-fiftieth part of the vituperation of his *Travels*, which it has been my misfortune to peruse, he could hardly have brought himself to write what follows.

If the Americans still refuse to shake the hand proffered to them in the true old John Bull spirit, they are worse folks than even I take them for.

Capt. Hall, after describing the hospitable reception he formerly met with at a boarding-house in New York, goes on thus: " If our hostess be still alive, I hope she will not repent of having bestowed her obliging attentions on one, who so many years afterwards made himself, he fears, less popular in her land, than he could wish to be amongst a people to whom he owes so much, and for whom he really feels so much kindness. He still anxiously hopes, however, they will believe him when he declares, that, having said in his recent publication no more than what he conceived was due to strict truth, and to the integrity of history, as far as his observations and opinions went, he still feels, as he always has, and ever must continue to feel towards America, the heartiest good-will.

" The Americans are perpetually repeating that the foundation-stone of their liberty is fixed on the doctrine, that every man is free to form his own opinions, and to promulgate them in candour and in moderation. Is it meant that a foreigner is excluded from these privileges ? If not, may I ask, in what respect have I passed these limitations ? The Americans have surely no fair right to be offended because my views differ from theirs; and yet I am told I have been rudely handled by the press of that country. If my motives are distrusted, I can only say, I am sorely belied. If I am mistaken, regret at my political blindness were surely more dignified than anger on the part of those with whom I differ; and if it shall chance that I am in the right, the best confirmation of the correctness of my views, in the opinion of indifferent persons, will perhaps be found in the soreness of those who wince when the truth is spoken.

" Yet, after all, few things would give me more real pleasure than to know that my friends across the water would consent to take me at my word; and, considering what I have said about them as so much public matter, which it truly is, agree to reckon me, in my absence, as they always did, when I was amongst them, and, I am sure, they would count me, if I went back again, as a private friend. I differed with them in politics, and I differ with them now as much as ever; but I sincerely wish them happiness individually; and, as a nation, I shall rejoice if they prosper. As the Persians write: ' What can I say more ?' And I only hope these few words may help to make my peace with people who justly pride themselves on bearing no malice. As for myself, I have no peace to make; for I have studiously avoided reading any of the American criticisms on my book, in order that the kindly feelings I have ever entertained towards that country should not be ruffled. By this abstinence I may have lost some information, and perhaps missed many opportunities of correcting erroneous impressions. But I set so much store by the pleasing recollection of the journey itself, and of the hospitality with which my family were every where received, that whether it be right, or whether it be wrong, I cannot bring myself to read any thing which might disturb these agreeable associations. So let us part in peace; or, rather, let us meet again in cordial communication; and if this little work shall find its way across the Atlantic, I hope it will be read there without reference to any thing that has passed between us; or, at all events, with reference only to those parts of our former intercourse which are satisfactory to all parties."—Hall's *Fragments*, vol. i, p. 200.

I really think it is impossible to read, not only this passage, but many others in these delightful little volumes, without feeling that their author is as little likely to deserve the imputation of harshness and ill-will, as any man that ever lived.

In reading Capt. Hall's volumes on America, the observation which, I think, struck me the most forcibly, and which certainly came the most completely home to my own feelings, was the following:

" In all my travels, both amongst Heathens and amongst Christians, I have never encountered any people by whom I found it nearly so difficult to make myself understood as by the Americans."

I have conversed in London and in Paris with foreigners of many nations, and often through the misty medium of an idiom imperfectly understood; but I remember no instance in which I found the same difficulty in conveying my sentiments, my impressions, and my opinions to those around me, as I did in America. Whatever faith may be given to my assertion, no one who has not visited the country can possibly conceive to what extent it is true. It is less necessary, I imagine, for the mutual understanding of persons conversing together, that the language should be the same, than that their ordinary mode of thinking, and habits of life, should, in some degree, assimilate; whereas, in point of fact, there is hardly a single point of sympathy between the Americans and us; but whatever the cause, the fact is certainly as I have stated it; and herein, I think, rests the only apology for the preposterous and un-dignified anger felt and expressed against Capt. Hall's work. They really cannot, even if they wished it, enter into any of his views, or comprehend his most ordinary feelings; and, therefore, they cannot believe in the sincerity of the impressions he describes. The candour which he expresses, and evidently feels, they mistake for irony, or totally distrust; his unwillingness to give pain to persons from whom he has received kindness, they scornfully reject as affectation; and, although they must know right well, in their own secret hearts, how infinitely more they lay at his mercy than he has chosen to betray, they pretend, even to themselves, that he has exaggerated the bad points of their character and in-stitutions; whereas, the truth is, that he has let them off with a degree of tenderness which may be quite suitable for him to exercise, however little merited; while, at the same time, he has most industriously magnified their merits, whenever he could possibly find any thing favourable. One can perfectly well understand why Capt. Hall's avowed Tory principles should be dis-approved of in the United States, especially as (with a questionable policy from a bookselling point of view, in these reforming times,) he volunteers a profession of political faith, in which, to use Kentucky phrase, " he goes the whole hog ", and bluntly avows, in his con-cluding chapter, that he not only holds stoutly to Church and State, but that he conceives the English House of Commons to be, if not quite perfect, at least as much so for all the required purposes of representation as it can by possibility be made in practice. Such a downright thorough-going Tory and Anti-reformer, pretending to judge of the workings of the American democratical system, was naturally held to be a monstrous abomination, and it has been visited accordingly, both in America, and, as I understand, with us also. The experience which Capt. Hall has acquired in visits to every part of the world, during twenty or thirty years, goes for nothing with the Radicals on either side the Atlantic; on the contrary, precisely in proportion to the value of that authority which is the result of actual observation, are they irritated to find its weight cast into the opposite scale. Had not Capt. Hall been converted by what he saw in North America, from the Whig faith he exhibited in his description of South America, his book would have been far more popular in England during the last two years of public excitement: it may, perhaps, be long before any justice is done to Capt. Hall's book in the United States, but a less time will probably suffice to establish its claim to attention at home.

Chapter Thirty-Two

*Journey to Niagara—Hudson—West Point—Hyde Park
—Albany—Yankees—Trenton Falls—Rochester—
Genesee Falls—Lockport*

How quickly weeks glide away in such a city as New York, especially when you reckon among your friends some of the most agreeable people in either hemisphere. But we had still a long journey before us, and one of the wonders of the world was to be seen.

On the 30th of May we set off for Niagara. I had heard so much of the surpassing beauty of the North River, that I expected to be disappointed, and to find reality flat after description. But it is not in the power of man to paint with a strength exceeding that of nature, in such scenes as the Hudson presents. Every mile shows some new and startling effect of the combination of rocks, trees, and water; there is no interval of flat or insipid scenery, from the moment you enter upon the river at New York, to that of quitting it at Albany, a distance of 180 miles.

For the first twenty miles the shore of New Jersey, on the left, offers almost a continued wall of trap rock, which from its perpendicular form, and lineal fissures, is called the Palisados. This wall sometimes rises to the height of a hundred and fifty feet, and sometimes sinks down to twenty. Here and there a watercourse breaks its uniformity; and every where the brightest foliage, in all the splendour of the climate and the season fringed and chequered the dark barrier. On the opposite shore, Manhattan Island, with its leafy coronet gemmed with villas, forms a lovely contrast to these rocky heights.

After passing Manhattan Island, the eastern shore gradually assumes a wild and rocky character, but ever varying; woods, lawns, pastures, and towering cliffs all meet the eye in quick succession, as the giant steam-boat cleaves its swift passage up the stream.

For several miles the voyage is one of great interest, independent of its beauty, for it passes many points where important events of the revolutionary war took place.

It was not without a pang that I looked on the spot where poor André was taken, and another where he was executed.

Several forts, generally placed in most commanding situations, still show, by their battered ruins, where the struggle was strongest; and I felt no lack of that moral interest so entirely wanting in the New States, and without which no journey can, I think, continue long without wearying the spirits.

About forty miles from New York you enter upon the Highlands, as a series of mountains which then flank the river on both sides, are called. The beauty of this scenery can only be conceived when it is seen. One might fancy that these capricious masses, with all their countless varieties of light and shade, were thrown together to show how passing lovely rocks and woods and water could be. Sometimes a lofty peak shoots suddenly up into the heavens, showing in bold relief against the sky; and then a deep ravine sinks in solemn shadow, and draws the imagination into its leafy recesses. For several miles the river appears to form a succession of lakes; you are often enclosed on all sides by rocks rising directly from the very edge of the stream, and then you turn a point, the river widens, and again woods, lawns, and villages are reflected on its bosom.

The state prison of Sing Sing is upon the edge of the water, and has no picturesque effect to atone for the painful images it suggests; the " Sleepy Hollow " of Washington Irving, just above it, restores the imagination to a better tone.

West Point, the military academy of the United States, is fifty miles from New York. The scenery around it is magnificent, and though the buildings of the establishment are constructed with the handsome and unpicturesque regularity which marks the work of governments, they are so nobly placed, and so embosomed in woods, that they look beautiful. The lengthened notes of a French horn, which I presume was attending some of their military manœuvres, sounded with deep and solemn sweetness as we passed.

About thirty miles further is Hyde Park, the magnificent seat of Dr Hosack; here the misty summit of the distant Catskill begins to form the outline of the landscape; it is hardly possible to imagine any thing more beautiful than this place. We passed a day there with great enjoyment; and the following morning set forward again in one of those grand floating hotels called steam-boats. Either on this day, or the one before, we had two hundred cabin passengers on board, and they all sat down together to a table spread abundantly, and with considerable elegance. A continual succession of gentlemen's seats, many of them extremely handsome, borders the river to Albany. We arrived there late in the evening, but had no difficulty in finding excellent accommodation.

Albany is the state capital of New York, and has some very handsome public buildings; there are also some curious relics of the old Dutch inhabitants.

The first sixteen miles from Albany we travelled in a stage, to avoid a multitude of locks at the entrance of the Erie canal; but at Schenectady we got on board one of the canal packet-boats for Utica.

With a very delightful party of one's own choosing, fine temperate weather, and a strong breeze to chase the mosquitoes, this mode of travelling might be very agreeable, but I can hardly imagine any motive of convenience powerful enough to induce me again to imprison myself in a canal boat under ordinary circumstances. The accommodation being greatly restricted, every body, from the moment of entering the boat, acts upon a system of unshrinking egotism. The library of a dozen books, the backgammon board, the tiny berths, the shady side of the cabin, are all jostled for in a manner to make one greatly envy the power of the snail; at the moment I would willingly have given up some of my human dignity for the privilege of creeping into a shell of my own. To any one who has been accustomed, in travelling, to be addressed with, "Do sit here, you will find it more comfortable", the "You must go there, I made for this place first," sounds very unmusical.

There is a great quietness about the women of America (I speak of the exterior manner of persons casually met), but somehow or other, I should never call it gentleness. In such trying moments as that of *fixing* themselves on board a packet-boat, the men are prompt, determined, and will compromise any body's convenience, except their own. The women are doggedly steadfast in their will, and, till matters are settled, look like hedgehogs, with every quill raised, and firmly set, as if to forbid the approach of any one who might wish to rub them down. In circumstances where an English woman would look proud, and a French woman *nonchalante*, an American lady looks grim: even the youngest and the prettiest can set their lips, and knit their brows, and look as hard and unsocial as their grandmothers.

Though not in the Yankee or New England country, we were bordering upon it sufficiently to meet in the stages and boats many delightful specimens of this most peculiar race. I like them extremely well, but I would not wish to have any business transactions with them, if I could avoid it, lest, to use their own phrase, " they should be too smart for me ".

It is by no means rare to meet elsewhere, in this working-day world of ours, people who push acuteness to the verge of honesty, and sometimes, perhaps, a little bit beyond; but, I believe, the Yankee is the only one who will be found to boast of doing so. It is by no means easy to give a clear and just idea of a Yankee; if you hear his character from a Virginian, you will believe him a devil; if you listen to it from himself, you might fancy him a god—though a tricky one: Mercury turned righteous and notable. Matthews did very well, as far as " I expect ", " I calculate ", and " I guess "; but this is only the shell; there is an immense deal within, both of sweet and bitter.* In acuteness, cautiousness, industry, and perseverance, he resembles the Scotch; in habits of frugal neatness, he resembles the Dutch; in love of lucre he doth greatly resemble the sons of Abraham; but in frank admission, and superlative admiration of all his own peculiarities, he is like nothing on earth but himself.

The Quakers have been celebrated for the pertinacity with which they avoid giving a direct answer; but what Quaker could ever vie with a Yankee in this sort of fencing? Nothing, in fact, can equal their skill in evading a question, excepting that with which they set about asking one. I am afraid that in repeating a conversation which I overheard on board the Erie canal boat, I shall spoil it, by forgetting some of the little delicate doublings which delighted me, yet I wrote it down immediately. Both parties were Yankees, but strangers to each other: one of them having, by gentle degrees, made himself pretty well acquainted with the point from which every one on board had started, and that for which he was bound, at last attacked his brother Reynard thus:

" Well, now, which way may you be travelling ?"

" I expect this canal runs pretty nearly west."

" Are you going far with it ?"

" Well, now, I don't rightly know how many miles it may be."

" I expect you'll be from New York ?"

" Sure enough I have been at New York, often and often."

" I calculate, then, 'tis not there as you stop ?"

" Business must be minded, in stopping and in stirring."

" You may say that. Well, I look then you'll be making for the Springs ?"

" Folks say as all the world is making for the Springs, and I expect a good sight of them is."

" Do you calculate upon stopping long when you get to your journey's end ?"

" 'Tis my business must settle that, I expect."

" I guess that's true, too; but you'll be for making pleasure a business for once, I calculate ?"

" My business don't often lie in that line."

" Then, may be, it is not the Springs as takes you this line ?"

" The Springs is a right elegant place, I reckon."

" It is your health, I calculate, as makes you break your good rules ?"

" My health don't trouble me much, I guess."

" No ? Why, that's well. How is the markets, sir? Are bread stuffs up ?"

" I an't just capable to say."

" A deal of money's made by just looking after the article at the fountain's head."

" You may say that."

" Do you look to be making great dealings in produce up the country ?"

" Why that, I expect, is difficult to know."

" I calculate you'll find the markets changeable these times ?"

" No markets ben't very often without changing."

" Why, that's right down true. What may be your biggest article of produce ?"

" I calculate, generally, that's the biggest as I makes most by."

" You may say that. But what do you chiefly call your most particular branch ?"

" Why, that's what I can't justly say."

And so they went on, without advancing or giving an inch, till I was weary of listening; but I left them still at it when I stepped out to resume my station on a trunk at the bow of the boat, where I scribbled in my notebook this specimen of Yankee conversation.

* * * * *

The Erie canal has cut through much solid rock, and we often passed between magnificent cliffs. The little falls of the Mohawk form a lovely scene; the rocks over which the river runs are most fantastic in form. The fall continues nearly a mile; and a beautiful village, called the Little Falls, overhangs it. As many locks occur at this point, we quitted the boat, that we might the better enjoy the scenery, which is of the wildest description. Several other passengers did so likewise; and I was much amused by one of our Yankees, who very civilly accompanied our party, pointing out to me the wild state of the country, and apologising for it, by saying that the property all round thereabouts had been owned by an Englishman. " And you'll excuse me, ma'am, but when the English gets a spot of wild ground like this here, they have no notions about it like us; but the Englishman have sold it, and if you was to see it five years hence, you would not know it again; I'll engage there will be by that half a score elegant factories—'tis a true shame to let such a privi-lege of water lie idle."

We reached Utica at twelve o'clock the following day, pretty well fagged by the sun by day, and a crowded cabin by night; lemon-juice and iced-water (without sugar) kept us alive. But for this delightful recipe, feather fans, and eau de Cologne, I think we should have failed altogether; the thermometer stood at 90°.

At two, we set off in a very pleasant airy carriage for Trenton Falls, a delightful drive of fourteen miles. These falls have become within the last few years only second in fame to Niagara. The West Canada Creek, which in the map shows but as a paltry stream, has found its way through three miles of rock, which, at many points, is 150 feet high. A forest of enormous cedars is on their summit; and many of that beautiful species of white cedar which droops its branches like the weeping-willow, grow in the clefts of the rock, and in some places almost dip their dark foliage in the torrent. The rock is of a dark-grey limestone, and often presents a wall of unbroken surface. Near the hotel a flight of very alarming steps leads down to the bed of the stream,

330

and on reaching it you find yourself enclosed in a deep
abyss of solid rock, with no visible opening but that
above your head. The torrent dashes by with inconceivable rapidity; its colour is black as night; and
the dark ledge of rock on which you stand, is so
treacherously level with it, that nothing warns you of
danger. Within the last three years two young people,
though surrounded by their friends, have stepped an
inch too far, and disappeared from among them, as if
by magic, never to revisit earth again. This broad flat
ledge reaches but a short distance, and then the perpendicular wall appears to stop your farther progress;
but there is a spirit of defiance in the mind of man:
he will not be stayed either by rocks or waves. By the
aid of gunpowder a sufficient quantity of the rock has
been removed to afford a fearful footing round a point,
which, when doubled, discloses a world of cataracts, all
leaping forward together in most magnificent confusion.
I suffered considerably before I reached the spot where
this grand scene is visible: a chain firmly fastened to the
rock serves to hang by, as you creep along the giddy
verge, and this enabled me to proceed so far; but here
the chain failed, and my courage with it, though the
rest of the party continued for some way farther, and
reported largely of still increasing sublimity. But my
knees tottered, and my head swam; so while the rest
crept onward, I sat down to wait their return on the
floor of rock which had received us on quitting the
steps.

A hundred and fifty feet of bare black rock on one
side, an equal height covered with solemn cedars on the
other, an unfathomed torrent roaring between them, the
fresh remembrance of the ghastly legend belonging to
the spot, and the idea of my children clinging to the
dizzy path I had left, was altogether sombre enough;
but I had not sat long before a tremendous burst of
thunder shook the air; the deep chasm answered from

either side, again, again, and again; I thought the rock I sat upon trembled: but the whole effect was so exceedingly grand, that I had no longer leisure to think of fear; my children immediately returned, and we enjoyed together the darkening shadows cast over the abyss, the rival clamour of the torrent and the storm, and that delightful exaltation of the spirits which sets danger at defiance. A few heavy rain drops alarmed us more than all the terrors of the spot, or rather they recalled our senses, and we retreated by the fearful steps, reaching our hotel unwetted and unharmed. The next morning we were again early afoot; the last night's storm had refreshed the air, and renewed our strength. We now took a different route; and instead of descending, as before, walked through the dark forest along the cliff, sufficiently near its edge to catch fearful glimpses of the scene below. After some time the path began to descend, and at length brought us to the shanty, commemorated in Miss Sedgwick's *Clarence*. This is by far the finest point of the falls. There is a little balcony in front of the shanty, literally hanging over the tremendous whirlpool; though frail, it makes one fancy oneself in safety, and reminded me of the feeling with which I have stood on one side a high gate, watching a roaring bull on the other. The walls of this shanty are literally covered with autographs, and I was inclined to join the laugh against the egotistical trifling, when one of the party discovered "Trollope, England" amidst the innumerable scrawls. The well-known characters were hailed with such delight, that I think I shall never again laugh at any one for leaving their name where it is possible a friend may find it.

We returned to Utica to dinner, and found that we must either wait till the next day for the Rochester coach, or again submit to the packet-boat. Our impatience induced us to prefer the latter; not very wisely, I think, for every annoyance seemed to increase upon us. The Oneida and the Genesee country are both extremely beautiful, but had we not returned by another route we should have known but little about it. From the canal nothing is seen to advantage, and very little is seen at all. My chief amusement, I think, was derived from names. One town consisting of a whiskey-store and a warehouse, is called Port Byron. At Rome the first name I saw over a store was Remus, doing infinite honour, I thought, to the classic lore of his godfathers and godmothers; but it would be endless to record all the drolleries of this kind which we met with. We arrived at Rochester, a distance of a hundred and forty miles, on the second morning after leaving Utica, fully determined never to enter a canal boat again, at least not in America.

Rochester is one of the most famous of the cities built on the Jack and Bean-stalk principle. There are many splendid edifices in wood; and certainly more houses, warehouses, factories, and steam-engines than ever were collected together in the same space of time; but I was told by a fellow-traveller that the stumps of the forest are still to be found firmly rooted in the cellars.

The fall of the Genesee is close to the town, and in the course of a few months will, perhaps, be in the middle of it. It is a noble sheet of water, of a hundred and sixty feet perpendicular fall; but I looked at it through the window of a factory, and as I did not like that, I was obligingly handed to the door-way of a sawing-mill; in short, " the great water privilege " has been so ingeniously taken advantage of, that no point can be found where its voice and its movement are not mixed and confounded with those of the " admirable machinery of this flourishing city ".

The Genesee fall is renowned as being the last and fatal leap of the adventurous madman Sam Patch; he had leaped it once before, and rose to the surface of the river in perfect safety; but the last time he was seen to falter as he took the leap, and was never heard of more. It seems that he had some misgivings of his fate; for a pet bear, which he had always taken with him on his former break - neck adventures, and which had constantly leaped after him without injury, he on this occasion left behind, in the care of a friend, to whom he bequeathed him " in case of his not returning ". We saw the bear, which is kept at the principal hotel; he is a noble creature, and more completely tame than I ever saw any animal of the species.

Our journey now became wilder every step; the un-broken forest often skirted the road for miles, and the sight of a log-hut was an event. Yet the road was, for the greater part of the day, good, running along a natural ridge, just wide enough for it. This ridge is a very singular elevation; and by all the inquiry I could make, the favourite theory concerning it is, that it was formerly the boundary of Lake Ontario, near which it passes. When this ridge ceased, the road ceased too; and for the rest of the way to Lockport, we were most painfully jumbled and jolted over logs and through bogs, till every joint was nearly dislocated.

Lockport is, beyond all comparison, the strangest-looking place I ever beheld. As fast as half a dozen trees were cut down, a *factory* was raised up; stumps still contest the ground with pillars, and porticoes are seen to struggle with rocks. It looks as if the demon of machinery, having invaded the peaceful realms of nature, had fixed on Lockport as the battle ground on which they should strive for mastery. The fiend insists that the streams should go one way, though the gentle mother had ever led their dancing steps another; nay, the very rocks must fall before him, and take what form he wills. The battle is lost and won. Nature is fairly routed, and driven from the field, and the rattling, crackling, hissing, splitting demon has taken possession of Lockport for ever.

We slept there, dismally enough. I never felt more out of humour at what the Americans call improvement; it is, in truth, as it now stands, a most hideous place, and gladly did I leave it behind me.

Our next stage was to Lewiston: for some miles before we reached it we were within sight of the British frontier; and we made our salaams.

The monument of the brave General Brock stands on an elevated point near Queenstown, and is visible at a great distance.*

We breakfasted at Lewiston, but felt every cup of coffee as a sin, so impatient were we, as we approached the end of our long pilgrimage, to reach the shrine, which nature seems to have placed at such a distance from her worshippers, on purpose to try the strength of their devotion.

A few miles more would bring us to the high altar; but first we had to cross the ferry, for we were determined upon taking our first view from British ground. The Niagara river is very lovely here; the banks are bold, rugged, and richly coloured, both by rocks and woods; and the stream itself is bright, clear, and unspeakably green.

In crossing the ferry a fellow-passenger made many inquiries of the young boatman respecting the battle of Queenstown: he was but a lad, and could remember little about it; but he was a British lad, and his answers smacked strongly of his loyal British feeling. Among other things, the questioner asked if many American citizens had not been thrown from the heights into the river.

" Why, yes, there was a good many of them; but it was right to show them there was water between us, and you know it might help to keep the rest of them from coming to trouble us on our own ground."

This phrase " our own ground " gave interest to every mile; or I believe I should have shut my eyes, and tried to sleep, that I might annihilate what remained of time and space between me and Niagara.

But I was delighted to see British oaks, and British roofs, and British boys and girls. These latter, as if to impress upon us that they were not citizens, made bows and courteseys as we passed, and this little touch of long unknown civility produced great effect. " See these dear children, mamma! do they not look English ? how I love them!" was the exclamation it produced.

Chapter Thirty-Three

Niagara—Arrival at Forsythes—First Sight of the Falls
    —Goat Island—The Rapids—Buffalo—Lake Erie
    —Canandaigua—Stage-Coach Adventures

At length we reached Niagara. It was the brightest day that June could give; and almost any day would have seemed bright that brought me to the object which for years I had languished to look upon.

We did not hear the sound of the Falls till very near the hotel, which overhangs them: as you enter the door you see behind the hall an open space, surrounded by galleries, one above another, and in an instant you feel that from thence the wonder is visible.

I trembled like a fool, and my girls clung to me, trembling too, I believe, but with faces beaming with delight. We encountered a waiter who had a sympathy of some sort with us; for he would not let us run through the hall to the first gallery, but ushered us up stairs, and another instant placed us where, at one glance, I saw all I had wished for, hoped for, dreamed of.

It is not for me to attempt a description of Niagara; I feel I have no powers for it.

After one long stedfast gaze, we quitted the gallery, that we might approach still nearer, and in leaving the

336

house had the good fortune to meet an English gentle-man,[1] who had been introduced to us at New York; he had preceded us by a few days, and knew exactly how and where to lead us.* If any man living can describe the scene we looked upon, it is himself, and I trust he will do it. As for myself, I can only say, that wonder, terror, and delight completely overwhelmed me. I wept with a strange mixture of pleasure and of pain, and certainly was, for some time, too violently affected in the *physique* to be capable of much pleasure; but when this emotion of the senses subsided, and I had recovered some degree of composure, my enjoyment was very great indeed.

To say that I was not disappointed is but a weak ex-pression to convey the surprise and astonishment which this long-dreamed-of scene produced. It has to me something beyond its vastness; there is a shadowy mystery hangs about it, which neither the eye nor even the imagination can penetrate; but I dare not dwell on this, it is a dangerous subject, and any attempt to describe the sensations produced must lead direct to nonsense.

Exactly at the Fall, it is the Fall and nothing else you have to look upon; there are not, as at Trenton, mighty rocks and towering forests, there is only the waterfall; but it is the fall of an ocean; and were Pelion piled on Ossa, on either side of it, we could not look at them.

The noise is greatly less than I expected; one can hear with perfect distinctness every thing said in an ordinary tone, when quite close to the cataract. The cause of this I imagine to be, that it does not fall im-mediately among rocks, like the far noisier Potomac, but direct and unbroken, save by its own rebound. The colour of the water, before this rebound hides it in foam and mist, is of the brightest and most delicate green; the violence of the impulse sends it far over the precipice

[1] The accomplished author of *Cyril Thornton*.

before it falls, and the effect of the ever varying light through its transparency is, I think, the loveliest thing I ever looked upon.

We descended to the edge of the gulf which receives the torrent, and thence looked at the horse-shoe fall in profile; it seems like awful daring to stand close beside it, and raise one's eyes to its immensity. I think the point most utterly inconceivable, to those who have not seen it, is the centre of the horse-shoe. The force of the torrent converges there; and as the heavy mass pours in, twisted, wreathed, and curled together, it gives an idea of irresistible power, such as no other object ever conveyed to me.

The following anecdote, which I had from good authority, may give some notion of this mighty power.

After the last American war, three of our ships, stationed on Lake Erie, were declared unfit for service, and condemned. Some of their officers obtained permission to send them over Niagara Falls. The first was torn to shivers by the rapids, and went over in fragments; the second filled with water before she reached the fall; but the third, which was in better condition, took the leap gallantly, and retained her form till it was hid in the cloud of mist below. A reward of ten dollars was offered for the largest fragment of wood that should be found from either wreck, five for the second, and so on. One morsel only was ever seen; and that, about a foot in length, was mashed as by a vice, and its edges notched like the teeth of a saw. What had become of the immense quantity of wood which had been precipitated? What unknown whirlpool had ingulfed it, so that, contrary to the very laws of nature, no vestige of the floating material could find its way to the surface?

Beyond the horse-shoe is Goat Island, and beyond Goat Island the American fall, bold, straight, and chafed to snowy whiteness by the rocks which meet it; but it does not approach, in sublimity or awful beauty, to the wondrous crescent on the other shore. There, the form of the mighty cauldron, into which the deluge pours, the hundred silvery torrents congregating round its verge, the smooth and solemn movement with which it rolls its massive volume over the rock, the liquid emerald of its long unbroken waters, the fantastic wreaths which spring to meet it, and then the shadowy mist that veils the horrors of its crash below, constitute a scene almost too enormous in its features for man to look upon. "Angels might tremble as they gazed"; and I should deem the nerves obtuse, rather than strong, which did not quail at the first sight of this stupendous cataract.

Minute local particulars can be of no interest to those who have not felt their influence for pleasure or for pain. I will not tell of giddy stairs which scale the very edge of the torrent, nor of beetling slabs of table rock, broken and breaking, on which, shudder as you may, you must take your stand, or lose your reputation as a tourist. All these feats were performed again and again, even on the first day of our arrival; and most earthly weary was I when the day was done, though I would not lose the remembrance of it to purchase the addition of many soft and silken ones to my existence.

By four o'clock the next morning I was again at the little shanty, close to the horse-shoe fall, which seems reared in water rather than in air, and took an early shower-bath of spray. Much is concealed at this early hour by the heavy vapour, but there was a charm in the very obscurity; and every moment, as the light increased, cloud after cloud rolled off, till the vast wonder was again before me.

It is in the afternoon that the rainbow is visible from the British side; and it is a lovely feature in the mighty landscape. The gay arch springs from fall to fall, a fairy bridge.

After breakfast we crossed to the American side, and explored Goat Island. The passage across the Niagara, directly in face of the falls, is one of the most delightful little voyages imaginable; the boat crosses marvellously near them, and within reach of a light shower of spray. Real safety and apparent danger have each their share in the pleasure felt. The river is here two hundred feet deep. The passage up the rock brings you close upon the American cataract; it is a vast sheet, and has all the sublimity that height and width and uproar can give; but it has none of the magic of its rival about it. Goat Island has, at all points, a fine view of the rapids; the furious velocity with which they rush onward to the abyss is terrific, and the throwing a bridge across them was a work of noble daring.

Below the falls, the river runs between lofty rocks, crowned with unbroken forests; this scene forms a striking contrast to the level shores above the cataract. It appears as if the level of the river had been broken up by some volcanic force. The Niagara flows out of Lake Erie, a broad, deep river; but for several miles its course is tranquil, and its shores perfectly level. By degrees its bed begins to sink, and the glassy smoothness is disturbed by a slight ripple. The inverted trees, that before lay so softly still upon its bosom, become twisted and tortured till they lose their form, and seem madly to mix in the tumult that destroys them. The current becomes more rapid at every step, till rock after rock has chafed the stream to fury, making the green one white. This lasts for a mile, and then down sink the rocks at once, one hundred and fifty feet, and the enormous flood falls after them. God said, Let there be a cataract, and it was so. When the river has reached its new level, the precipice on either side shows a terrific chasm of solid rock; some beautiful plants are clinging to its sides, and oaks, ash, and cedar, in many places, clothe their terrors with rich foliage.

This violent transition from level shores to a deep ravine, seems to indicate some great convulsion as its cause; and when I heard of a burning spring close by, I fancied the volcanic power still at work, and that the wonders of the region might yet increase.

We passed four delightful days of excitement and fatigue; we drenched ourselves in spray; we cut our feet on the rocks; we blistered our faces in the sun; we looked up the cataract, and down the cataract; we perched ourselves on every pinnacle we could find; we dipped our fingers in the flood at a few yards' distance from its thundering fall; in short, we strove to fill as many niches of memory with Niagara as possible, and I think the images will be within the power of recall for ever.

We met many groups of tourists in our walks, chiefly American; but they were, or we fancied they were, but little observant of the wonders around them.

One day we were seated on a point of the cliff, near the ferry, which commands a view of both the falls. This, by the way, is considered as the finest general view of the scene. One of our party was employed in attempting to sketch, what, however, I believe it is impossible for any pencil to convey an idea of to those who have not seen it. We had borrowed two or three chairs from a neighbouring cottage, and amongst us had gathered a quantity of boughs, which, with the aid of shawls and parasols, we had contrived to weave into a shelter from the mid-day sun; so that altogether I have no doubt we looked very cool and comfortable.

A large party, who had crossed from the American side, wound up the steep ascent from the place where the boat had left them; in doing so their backs were turned to the cataracts, and as they approached the summit our party was the principal object before them. They all stood perfectly still to look at us. This first examination was performed at the distance of about a dozen yards from the spot we occupied, and lasted about five minutes by which time they had recovered breath, and acquired courage. Then they advanced in a body, and one or two of them began to examine (wrong side upwards) the work of the sketcher, in doing which they stood precisely between him and his object; but of this I think it is very probable they were not aware. Some among them next began to question us as to how long we had been at the falls; whether there were much company; if we were not from the old country, and the like. In return we learnt that they were just arrived; yet not one of them (they were eight) ever turned the head, even for a moment, to look at the most stupendous spectacle that nature has to show.

The company at the hotel changed almost every day. Many parties arrived in the morning, walked to the falls, returned to the hotel to dinner, and departed by the coach immediately after it. Many groups were indescribably whimsical, both in appearance and manner. Now and then a first-rate dandy shot in among us, like a falling star.

On one occasion, when we were in the beautiful gallery, at the back of the hotel, which overlooks the horse-shoe fall, we saw the booted leg of one of this graceful race protruded from the window which commands the view, while his person was thrown back in his chair, and his head enveloped in a cloud of tobacco smoke.

I have repeatedly remarked, when it has happened to me to meet any ultra-fine men among the wilder and more imposing scenes of our own land, that they throw off, in a great degree, their airs, and their " townliness ", as some one cleverly calls these *simagrées*, as if ashamed to " play their fantastic tricks " before the god of nature, when so forcibly reminded of his presence; and more than once on these occasions I have been surprised to find how much intellect lurked behind the inane mask of fashion. But in America the effect of fine scenery upon this class of persons is different; for it is exactly when amongst it that the most strenuous efforts at elegant *nonchalance* are perceptible among the young exquisites of the western world. It is true that they have little leisure for the display of grace in the daily routine of commercial activity in which their lives are passed, and this certainly offers a satisfactory explanation of the fact above stated.

Fortunately for our enjoyment, the solemn character of the scene was but little broken in upon by these gentry. Every one who comes to Forsythe's Hotel (except Mrs Bogle Corbet) walks to the shanty, writes their name in a book which is kept there, and, for the most part, descends by the spiral staircase which leads from the little platform before it to the rocks below.* Here they find another shanty, but a few yards from the entrance to that wondrous cavern which is formed by the falling flood on one side, and by the mighty rock over which it pours on the other. To this frail shelter from the wild uproar, and the blinding spray, nearly all the touring gentlemen, and even many of the pretty ladies, find their way. But here I often saw their noble daring fail, and have watched them dripping and draggled turn again to the sheltering stairs, leaving us in full possession of the awful scene we so dearly loved to gaze upon. How utterly futile must every attempt be to describe the spot! How vain every effort to convey an idea of the sensations it produces! Why is it so exquisite a pleasure to stand for hours drenched in spray, stunned by the ceaseless roar, trembling from the concussion that shakes the very rock you cling to, and breathing painfully in the moist atmosphere that seems to have less of air than water in it? Yet pleasure it is, and I almost think the greatest I ever enjoyed. We more than once approached the entrance to this appalling cavern; but I never fairly entered it, though two or three of my party did. I lost my breath entirely; and the pain at my chest was so severe, that not all my curiosity could enable me to endure it.

What was that cavern of the winds of which we heard

of old, compared to this? A mightier Spirit than Æolus reigns here.

Nor was this spot of dread and danger the only one in which we found ourselves alone. The path taken by "the company" to the shanty, which contained the "book of names", was always the same; this wound down the steep bank from the gate of the hotel garden, and was rendered tolerably easy by its repeated doublings; but it was by no means the best calculated to manage to advantage the pleasure of the stranger in his approach to the spot. All others, however, seemed left for us alone.

During our stay we saw the commencement of another staircase, intended to rival in attraction that at present in use; it is but a few yards from it, and can in no way, I think, contribute to the convenience of the descent. The erection of the central shaft of this spiral stair was a most tremendous operation, and made me sick and giddy as I watched it. After it had been made fast at the bottom, the carpenters swung themselves off the rocks, by means of ropes, to the beams which traversed it; and as they sat across them, in the midst of the spray and the uproar, I thought I had never seen life perilled so wantonly. But the work proceeded without accident, and was nearly finished before we left the hotel.

It was a sort of pang to take what we knew must be our last look at Niagara; but "we had to do it", as the Americans say, and left it on the 10th June for Buffalo.

The drive along the river, above the falls, is as beautiful as a clear stream of a mile in width can make it; and the road continues close to it till you reach the ferry at Black Rock.

We welcomed, almost with a shout, the British colours which we saw, for the first time, on Commodore Barrie's pretty sloop, the *Bull Dog*, which we passed as it was towing up the river to Lake Erie, the commodore being about to make a tour of the lakes.

At Black Rock we crossed again into the United

States, and a few miles of horrible jolting brought us to Buffalo.

Of all the thousand and one towns I saw in America I think Buffalo is the queerest looking; it is not quite so wild as Lockport, but all the buildings have the appearance of having been run up in a hurry, though every thing has an air of great pretension; there are porticoes, columns, domes, and colonnades, but all in wood. Every body tells you there, as in all their other new-born towns, and every body believes, that their improvement and their progression are more rapid, more wonderful, than the earth ever before witnessed; while, to me, the only wonder is how so many thousands, nay millions of persons, can be found, in the nineteenth century, who can be content so to live. Surely this country may be said to spread rather than to rise.

The Eagle Hotel, an immense wooden fabric, has all the pretension of a splendid establishment; but its monstrous corridors, low ceilings, and intricate chambers, gave me the feeling of a catacomb rather than a house. We arrived after the *table d'hôte* tea-drinking was over, and supped comfortably enough with a gentleman, who accompanied us from the falls; but the next morning we breakfasted in a long, low, narrow room, with a hundred persons, and any thing less like comfort can hardly be imagined.

What can induce so many intellectual citizens to prefer these long, silent tables, scantily covered with morsels of fried ham, salt fish, and liver, to a comfortable loaf of bread with their wives and children at home? How greatly should I prefer eating my daily meals with my family, in an Indian wig-wam, to boarding at a *table d'hôte* in these capacious hotels; the custom, however, seems universal through the country, at least we have met it, without a shadow of variation as to its general features, from New Orleans to Buffalo.

Lake Erie has no beauty to my eyes; it is not the sea,

and it is not the river, nor has it the beautiful scenery generally found round smaller lakes. The only interest its unmeaning expanse gave me arose from remembering that its waters, there so tame and tranquil, were destined to leap the gulf of Niagara. A dreadful road, through forests only beginning to be felled, brought us to Avon; it is a straggling ugly little place, and not any of their " Romes, Carthages, Ithacas, or Athens " ever provoked me by their name so much. This Avon flows sweetly with nothing but whiskey and tobacco juice.

The next day's journey was much more interesting, for it showed us the lake of Canandaigua. It is about eighteen miles long, but narrow enough to bring the opposite shore, clothed with rich foliage, near to the eye; the back-ground is a ridge of mountains. Perhaps the state of the atmosphere lent an unusual charm to the scene: one of those sudden thunder-storms, so rapid in approach, and so sombre in colouring, that they change the whole aspect of things in a moment, rose over the mountains and passed across the lake while we looked upon it. Another feature in the scene gave a living, but most sad, interest to it. A glaring wooden hotel, as fine as paint and porticoes can make it, overhangs the lake; beside it stands a shed for cattle. To this shed, and close by the white man's mushroom palace, two Indians had crept to seek a shelter from the storm. The one was an aged man, whose venerable head in attitude and expression indicated the profoundest melancholy: the other was a youth, and in his deep-set eye there was a quiet sadness more touching still. There they stood, the native rightful lords of the fair land, looking out upon the lovely lake which yet bore the name their fathers had given it, watching the threatening storm that brooded there; a more fearful one had already burst over them.

Though I have mentioned the lake first, the little town of Canandaigua precedes it, in returning from the west, It is as pretty a village as ever man contrived to build.

346

Geneva

Every house is surrounded by an ample garden, and at that flowery season they were half buried in roses.

It is true these houses are of wood; but they are so neatly painted, in such perfect repair, and show so well within their leafy setting, that it is impossible not to admire them.

Forty-six miles farther is Geneva, beautifully situated on Seneca Lake. This, too, is a lovely sheet of water, and I think the town may rival its European namesake in beauty.

We slept at Auburn, celebrated for its prison, where the highly-approved system of American discipline originated.* In this part of the country there is no want of churches; every little village has its wooden temple, and many of them two, that the Methodists and Presbyterians may not clash.

We passed through an Indian reserve, and the untouched forests again hung close upon the road. Repeated groups of Indians passed us, and we remarked that they were much cleaner and better dressed than those we had met wandering far from their homes. The blankets which they use so gracefully as mantles were as white as snow.

We took advantage of the loss of a horse's shoe to leave the coach, and approach a large party of them, consisting of men, women, and children, who were regaling themselves with I know not what, but milk made a part of the repast. They could not talk to us, but they received us with smiles, and seemed to understand when we asked if they had mocassins to sell, for they shook their sable locks, and answered " no ".

A beautiful grove of butternut trees was pointed out to us, as the spot where the chiefs of the six nations used to hold their senate; our informer told me that he had been present at several of their meetings, and though he knew but little of their language, the power of their eloquence was evident from the great effect it produced among themselves.

Towards the end of this day, we encountered an adventure which revived our doubts whether the invading white men, in chasing the poor Indians from their forests, have done much towards civilising the land. For myself, I almost prefer the indigenous manner to the exotic.

The coach stopped to take in " a lady " at Vernon; she entered, and completely filled the last vacant inch of our vehicle; for " we were eight " before.

But no sooner was she seated than *her beau* came forward with a most enormous wooden best-bonnet box. He paused for a while to meditate the possibilities—raised it, as if to place it on our laps—sunk it, as if to put it beneath our feet. Both alike appeared impossible; when, in true Yankee style, he addressed one of our party with, " If you'll just step out a minute, I guess I'll find room for it."

" Perhaps so. But how shall I find room for myself afterwards ?"

This was uttered in European accents, and in an instant half a dozen whiskey drinkers stepped from before the whiskey store, and took the part of *the beau*.

" That's because you'll be English travellers, I expect; but we have travelled in better countries than Europe— we have travelled in America—and the box will go, I calculate."

We remonstrated on the evident injustice of the proceeding, and I ventured to say that, as we had none of us any luggage in the carriage because the space was so very small, I thought a chance passenger could have no right so greatly to incommode us.

" Right!—there they go—that's just their way—that will do in Europe, may be; it sounds just like English tyranny, now—don't it ? but it won't do here." And thereupon he began thrusting in the wooden box against our legs with all his strength.

" No law, sir, can permit such conduct as this."

" Law!" exclaimed a gentleman very particularly

drunk; "we makes our own laws, and governs our own selves."

"Law!" echoed another gentleman of Vernon; "this is a free country—*we have no laws here*, and we don't want no foreign power to tyrannise over us."

I give the words exactly. It is, however, but fair to state, that the party had evidently been drinking more than an usual portion of whiskey; but perhaps in whiskey as in wine, truth may come to light. At any rate the people of the Western Paradise follow the Gentiles in this, that they are a law unto themselves.

During this contest the coachman sat upon the box without saying a word, but seemed greatly to enjoy the joke; the question of the box, however, was finally decided in our favour by the nature of the human material, which cannot be compressed beyond a certain degree.

For great part of this day we had the good fortune to have a gentleman and his daughter for our fellow-travellers, who were extremely intelligent and agreeable; but I nearly got myself into a scrape by venturing to remark upon a phrase used by the gentleman, and which had met me at every corner from the time I first entered the country. We had been talking of pictures, and I had endeavoured to adhere to the rule I had laid down for myself, of saying very little, where I could say nothing agreeable. At length he named an American artist, with whose works I was very familiar; and after having declared him equal to Lawrence (judging by his portrait of West, now at New York), he added: "and what is more, madam, he is perfectly *self-taught*."

I prudently took a few moments before I answered; for the equalling our immortal Lawrence to a most vile dauber stuck in my throat: I could not say Amen; so for some time I said nothing, but at last I remarked on the frequency with which I had heard this phrase of *self-taught* used, not as an apology, but as positive praise.

"Well, madam, can there be a higher praise?"

" Certainly not, if spoken of the individual merits of a person without the means of instruction, but I do not understand it when applied as praise to his works."

" Not understand it, madam ?   Is it not attributing genius to the author; and what is teaching compared to that ?"

I do not wish to repeat all my own *bons mots* in praise of study, and on the disadvantages of profound ignorance, but I would, willingly, if I could, give an idea of the mixed indignation and contempt expressed by our companion at the idea that study was necessary to the formation of taste, and to the development of genius. At last, however, he closed the discussion thus: " There is no use in disputing a point that is already settled, madam; the best judges declare that Mr. H——g's portraits are equal to those of Lawrence."*

" Who is it who has passed this judgment, sir ?"

" The men of taste of America, madam."

I then asked him if he thought it was going to rain ?

*   *   *   *   *

The stages do not appear to have any regular stations at which to stop for breakfast, dinner, and supper. These necessary interludes, therefore, being generally *impromptu*, were abominably bad.   We were amused by the patient manner in which our American fellow-travellers ate whatever was set before them, without uttering a word of complaint, or making any effort to improve it; but no sooner reseated in the stage, than they began their complaints: " 'Twas a shame "; " 'Twas a robbery "; " 'Twas poisoning folks "; and the like.   I, at last, asked the reason of this, and why they did not remonstrate.   " Because, madam, no American gentleman or lady that keeps an inn won't bear to be found fault with."

We reached Utica very late and very weary; but the delights of a good hotel and perfect civility sent us in good humour to bed, and we arose sufficiently refreshed to enjoy a day's journey through some of the loveliest scenery in the world.

Who is it that says America is not picturesque ? I forget; but surely he never travelled from Utica to Albany. I really cannot conceive that any country can furnish a drive of ninety-six miles more beautiful, or more varied in its beauty. The road follows the Mohawk River, which flows through scenes changing from fields waving with plenty to rocks and woods; gentle slopes, covered with cattle, are divided from each other by precipices 500 feet high. Around the little falls there is a character of beauty as singular as it is striking. Here, as I observed of many other American rivers, the stream appears to run in a much narrower channel than it once occupied; and the space which it seems formerly to have filled is now covered with bright green herbage, save that, at intervals, large masses of rock rise abruptly from the level turf; these are crowned with all such trees as love the scanty diet which a rock affords. Dwarf oak, cedars, and the mountain ash, are grouped in a hundred different ways among them; each clump you look upon is lovelier than its neighbour; I never saw so sweetly wild a spot.

I was surprised to hear a fellow-traveller say, as we passed a point of peculiar beauty, " All this neighbour-hood belongs, or did belong, to Mr Edward Ellice, an English Member of Parliament; but he has sold a deal of it, and now, madam, you may see as it begins to improve "; and he pointed to a great wooden edifice, where, on the white paint, " Cash for Rags ", in letters three feet high, might be seen.*

I then remembered that it was near this spot that my Yankee friend had made his complaint against English indifference to " water privilege ". He did not name Mr Edward Ellice, but doubtless he was the " English, as never thought of improvement ".

I have often confessed my conscious incapacity for description, but I must repeat it here to apologise for my passing so dully through this matchless valley of the Mohawk. I would that some British artist, strong in youthful daring, would take my word for it, and pass over for a summer pilgrimage through the State of New York. In very earnest he would do wisely, for I question if the world could furnish, within the same space, and with equal facility of access, so many subjects for his pencil. Mountains, forests, rocks, lakes, rivers, cataracts, all in perfection. But he must be bold as a lion in colouring, or he will make nothing of it. There is a clearness of atmosphere, a strength of *chiaro oscuro*, a massiveness in the foliage, and a brilliance of contrast, that must make a colourist of any one who has an eye. He must have courage to dip his pencil in shadows black as night, and light that might blind an eagle. As I presume my young artist to be an enthusiast, he must first go direct to Niagara, or even in the Mohawk valley his pinioned wing may droop. If his fever run very high, he may slake his thirst at Trenton, and, while there, he will not dream of any thing beyond it. Should my advice be taken, I will ask the young adventurer on his return (when he shall have made a prodigious quantity of money by my hint), to reward me by two sketches. One shall be the lake of Canandaigua; the other the Indians' Senate Grove of Butternuts.

During our journey, I forget on which day of it, a particular spot in the forest, at some distance from the road, was pointed out to us as the scene of a true but very romantic story. During the great and the terrible French revolution (1792), a young nobleman escaped from the scene of horror, having with difficulty saved his head, and without the possibility of saving any thing else. He arrived at New York nearly destitute; and after passing his life, not only in splendour, but in the splendour of the court of France, he found himself jostled by the busy population of the New World, without a dollar between him and starvation. In such a situation one might almost sigh for the guillotine, The young noble strove to labour; but who would purchase the trembling efforts of his white hands, while the sturdy strength of many a black Hercules was in the market? He abandoned the vain attempt to sustain himself by the aid of his fellow-men, and determined to seek a refuge in the forest. A few shillings only remained to him; he purchased an axe, and reached the Oneida territory. He felled a few of the slenderest trees, and made himself a shelter that Robinson Crusoe would have laughed at, for it did not keep out the rain. Want of food, exposure to the weather, and unwonted toil, produced the natural result; the unfortunate young man fell sick, and, stretched upon the reeking earth, stifled, rather than sheltered, by the withering boughs which hung over him, he lay parched with thirst and shivering in ague, with the one last earthly hope that each heavy moment would prove the last.

Near to the spot which he had chosen for his miserable rest, but totally concealed from it by the thick forest, was the last straggling wigwam of an Indian village. It is not known how many days the unhappy man had lain without food, but he was quite insensible when a young squaw, whom chance had brought from this wigwam to his hut, entered and found him alive, but totally insensible. The heart of woman is, I believe, pretty much the same every where; the young girl paused not to think whether he were white or red, but her fleet feet rested not till she had brought milk, rum, and blankets; and when the sufferer recovered his senses, his head was supported on her lap, while, with the gentle tenderness of a mother, she found means to make him swallow the restoratives she had brought.

No black eyes in the world, be they of France, Italy, or even of Spain, can speak more plainly of kindness than the large deep-set orbs of a squaw: this is a language that all nations can understand, and the poor Frenchman read most clearly, in the anxious glance of his gentle nurse, that he should not die forsaken.

So far the story is romantic enough, and what follows is hardly less so. The squaw found means to introduce her white friend to her tribe; he was adopted as their brother, speedily acquired their language, and assumed their dress and manner of life. His gratitude to his preserver soon ripened into love; and if the chronicle spoke true, the French noble and the American savage were more than passing happy as man and wife, and it was not till he saw himself the father of many thriving children that the exile began to feel a wish of rising again from savage to civilised existence.

My historian did not explain what his project was in visiting New York, but he did so in the habit of an Indian, and learnt enough of the restored tranquillity of his country to give him hope that some of the broad lands he had left there might be restored to him.

I have made my story already too long, and must not linger upon it farther than to say that his hopes were fulfilled, and that, of a large and flourishing family, some are settled in France, and some remain in America (one of these, I understood, was a lawyer at New York), while the hero and the heroine of the tale continue to inhabit the Oneida country; not in a wigwam, however, but in a good house, in a beautiful situation, with all the comforts of civilised life around them.

Such was the narrative we listened to from a stage-coach companion ; and it appears to me sufficiently interesting to repeat, though I have no better authority to quote for its truth than the assertion of this unknown traveller.

Return to New York

Chapter Thirty-Four

Return to New York—Conclusion

THE comfortable Adelphi Hotel again received us at Albany on the 14th of June, and we decided upon passing the following day there, both to see the place, and to recruit our strength, which we began to feel we had taxed severely by a very fatiguing journey, in most oppressively hot weather. It would have been difficult to find a better station for repose; the rooms were large and airy, and ice was furnished in most profuse abundance.

But notwithstanding the manifold advantages of this excellent hotel, I was surprised at the un-English arrangement communicated to me by two ladies with whom we made a speaking acquaintance, by which it appeared that they made it their permanent home. These ladies were a mother and daughter: the daughter was an extremely pretty young married woman, with two little children. Where the husbands were, or whether they were dead or alive, I know not; but they told me they had been *boarding* there above a year. They breakfasted, dined, and supped, at the *table d'hôte*, with from twenty to a hundred people, as accident might decide; dressed very smart, played on the piano in the public sitting-room, and assured me they were particularly comfortable, and well accommodated. What a life!

Some parts of the town are very handsome; the Town Hall, the Chamber of Representatives, and some other public buildings, stand well on a hill that overlooks the Hudson, with ample inclosures of grass and trees around them.

Many of the shops are large, and showily set out. I was amused by a national trait which met me at one of them. I entered it to purchase some *eau de Cologne*; but finding what was offered to me extremely bad and very cheap, I asked if they had none at a higher price, and better.

" You are a stranger, I guess " was the answer. " The Yankees want low price, that's all; they don't stand so much for goodness as the English."

Nothing could be more beautiful than our passage down the Hudson on the following day. As I thought of some of my friends in England, dear lovers of the picturesque, I could not but exclaim:

> " *Que je vous plains! que je vous plains!*
> *Vous ne la verrez pas.*"

Not even a moving panoramic view, gliding before their eyes for an hour together, in all the scenic splendour of Drury Lane or Covent Garden, could give them an idea of it. They could only see one side at a time. The change, the contrast, the ceaseless variety of beauty, as you skim from side to side, the liquid smoothness of the broad mirror that reflects the scene, and, most of all, the clear bright air through which you look at it— all this can only be seen and believed by crossing the Atlantic.

As we approached New York, the burning heat of the day relaxed, and the long shadows of evening fell coolly on the beautiful villas we passed. I really can conceive nothing more exquisitely lovely than this approach to the city. The magnificent boldness of the Jersey shore on the one side, and the luxurious softness of the shady lawns on the other, with the vast silvery stream that flows between them, altogether form a picture which may well excuse a traveller for saying, once and again, that the Hudson river can be surpassed in beauty by none on the outside of Paradise.[1]

[1] I have since seen both the Rhine and the Danube, but I feel no inclination to retract my opinion. That both these rivers possess sources of interest of which the lovely Hudson can show no trace, is

Return to New York

It was nearly dark when we reached the city, and it was with great satisfaction that we found our comfortable apartments in Hudson Street unoccupied; and our pretty, kind (Irish) hostess willing to receive us again. We passed another fortnight there; and again we enjoyed the elegant hospitality of New York, though now it was offered from beneath the shade of their beautiful villas. In truth, were all America like this fair city, and all, no, only a small proportion of its population like the friends we left there, I should say, that the land was the fairest in the world.

But the time was come to bid it adieu! The important business of securing our homeward passage was to be performed. One must know what it is to cross the ocean before the immense importance of all the little details of accommodation can be understood. The anxious first look into the face of the captain to ascertain if he be gentle or rough; another, scarcely less important, is that of the steward, generally a sable one, but not the less expressive; the accurate, but rapid glance of measurement thrown round the little staterooms; another at the good or bad arrangement of the staircase, by which you are to stumble up and stumble down, from cabin to deck, and from deck to cabin; all this, they only can understand who have felt it. At length, however, this interesting affair was settled, and most happily. The appearance promised well, and the performance bettered it. We hastened to pack up our " trumpery ", as Captain Mirven unkindly calls the paraphernalia of the ladies, and among the rest, my six hundred pages of griffonage.* There is enough of it, yet I must add a few more lines.

I suspect that what I have written will make it evident

---

certain ; but with the exception of the spot immediately under the Lurleyberg on the Rhine, and that beneath the wondrous crags of Dürrenstein on the Danube, I still think that in *natural* beauty nothing in either can equal many points of the Hudson.

that I do not like America. Now, as it happens that I met with individuals there whom I love and admire, far beyond the love and admiration of ordinary acquaintance; and as I declare the country to be fair to the eye, and moſt richly teeming with the gifts of plenty, I am led to ask myself why it is that I do not like it. I would willingly know myself, and confess to others, why it is that neither its beauty nor its abundance can suffice to neutralise, or greatly soften, the diſtaſte which the aggregate of my recollections has left upon my mind.

I remember hearing it said, many years ago, when the advantages and disadvantages of a particular residence were being discussed, that it was the " Who ?" and not the " Where ?" that made the difference between the pleasant or unpleasant residence. The truth of the observation ſtruck me forcibly when I heard it; and it has been recalled to my mind since, by the conſtantly recurring evidence of its juſtness. In applying this to America, I speak not of my friends, nor of my friends' friends. The small patrician band is a race apart; they live with each other, and for each other; mix wondrously little with the high matters of ſtate, which they seem to leave rather supinely to their tailors and tinkers, and are no more to be taken as a sample of the American people, than the head of Lord Byron as a sample of the heads of the British peerage. I speak not of these, but of the population generally, as seen in town and country, among the rich and the poor, in the slave ſtates and the free ſtates. I do not like them. I do not like their principles, I do not like their manners, I do not like their opinions.

Both as a woman, and as a ſtranger, it might be unseemly for me to say that I do not like their government, and therefore I will not say so. That it is one which pleases themselves is moſt certain, and this is considerably more important than pleasing all the travelling old ladies in the world. I entered the country at New

Orleans, remained for more than two years west of the Alleghanies,[†] and passed another year among the Atlantic cities, and the country around them.[†] I conversed during this time with citizens of all orders and degrees, and I never heard from any one a single disparaging word against their government. It is not, therefore, surprising, that when the people of that country hear strangers questioning the wisdom of their institutions, and expressing disapprobation at some of their effects, they should set it down either to an incapacity of judging, or a malicious feeling of envy and ill-will.

" How can any one in their senses doubt the excellence of a government which we have tried for half a century, and loved the better the longer we have known it ?"

Such is the natural inquiry of every American when the excellence of their government is doubted; and I am inclined to answer, that no one in their senses, who has visited their country and known the people, can doubt its fitness for them, such as they now are, or its utter unfitness for any other people.

Whether the government has made the people what they are, or whether the people have made the government what it is, to suit themselves, I know not; but if the latter, they have shown a consummation of wisdom which the assembled world may look upon and admire.

It is matter of historical notoriety, that the original stock of the white population now inhabiting the United States, were persons who had banished themselves, or were banished from the mother country. The land they found was favourable to their increase and prosperity; the colony grew and flourished. Years rolled on, and the children, the grandchildren, and the great-grandchildren of the first settlers, replenished the land, and found it flowing with milk and honey. That they should wish to keep this milk and honey to themselves is not very surprising. What did the mother country do for them? She sent them out gay and gallant officers to guard their frontier; the which they thought they could guard as well themselves; and then she taxed their tea. Now, this was disagreeable; and to atone for it, the distant colony had no great share in her mother's grace and glory. It was not from among them that her high and mighty were chosen; the rays which emanated from that bright sun of honour, the British throne, reached them but feebly. They knew not, they cared not, for her kings nor her heroes; their thriftiest trader was their noblest man; the holy seats of learning were but the cradles of superstition; the splendour of the aristocracy, but a leech that drew their "golden blood". The wealth, the learning, the glory of Britain, was to them nothing; the having their own way every thing.

Can any blame their wish to obtain it? Can any lament that they succeeded?

And now the day was their own, what should they do next? Their elders drew together, and said: " Let us make a government that shall suit us all; let it be rude, and rough, and noisy; let it not affect either dignity, glory, or splendour; let it interfere with no man's will, nor meddle with any man's business: let us have neither tithes, nor taxes, game laws, nor poor laws; let every man have a hand in making the laws, and no man be troubled about keeping them; let not our magistrates wear purple, nor our judges ermine; if a man grow rich, let us take care that his grandson be poor, and then we shall all keep equal; let every man take care of himself, and if England should come to bother us again, why then we will fight all together."

Could any thing be better imagined than such a government for a people so circumstanced? Or is it strange that they are contented with it? Still less is it strange that those who have lived in the repose of order, and felt secure that their country could go on very well and its business proceed without their bawling and squalling, scratching and scrambling to help it, should bless the gods that they are not republicans.

So far all is well. That they should prefer a constitution which suits them so admirably, to one which would not suit them at all, is surely no cause of quarrel on our part; nor should it be such on theirs, if we feel no inclination to exchange the institutions which have made us what we are, for any other on the face of the earth.

But when a native of Europe visits America, a most extraordinary species of tyranny is set in action against him; and as far as my reading and experience have enabled me to judge, it is such as no other country has ever exercised against strangers.

The Frenchman visits England: he is *abîmé d'ennui* at our stately dinners; shrugs his shoulders at our *corps de ballet*, and laughs *à gorge déployée* at our passion for driving, and our partial affection for roast beef and plum pudding. The Englishman returns the visit, and the first thing he does on arriving at Paris, is to hasten to *le Théâtre des Variétés*, that he may see " *Les Anglaises pour rire* ", and if among the crowd of laughers, you hear a note of more cordial mirth than the rest, seek out the person from whom it proceeds, and you will find the Englishman.

The Italian comes to our green island, and groans at our climate; he vows that the air which destroys a statue cannot be wholesome for man; he sighs for orange trees and macaroni, and smiles at the pretensions of a nation to poetry, while no epics are chaunted through her streets. Yet we welcome the sensitive southern with all kindness, listen to his complaints with interest, cultivate our little orange trees, and teach our children to lisp Tasso, in the hope of becoming more agreeable.

Yet we are not at all superior to the rest of Europe

in our endurance of censure, nor is this wish to profit by it at all peculiar to the English; we laugh at, and find fault with, our neighbours quite as freely as they do with us, and they join the laugh, and adopt our fashions and customs. These mutual pleasantries produce no shadow of unkindly feeling; and as long as the governments are at peace with each other, the individuals of every nation in Europe make it a matter of pride, as well as of pleasure, to meet each other frequently, to discuss, compare, and reason upon their national varieties, and to vote it a mark of fashion and good taste to imitate each other in all the external embellishments of life.

The consequence of this is most pleasantly perceptible, at the present time, in every capital of Europe. The long peace has given time for each to catch from each what was best in customs and manners, and the rapid advance of refinement and general information has been the result.

To those who have been accustomed to this state of things, the contrast upon crossing to the new world is inconceivably annoying; and it cannot be doubted that this is one great cause of the general feeling of irksomeness and fatigue of spirits, which hangs upon the memory while recalling the hours passed in American society.

A single word indicative of doubt, that any thing, or every thing, in that country is not the very best in the world, produces an effect which must be seen and felt to be understood. If the citizens of the United States were indeed the devoted patriots they call themselves, they would surely not thus incrust themselves in the hard, dry, stubborn persuasion, that they are the first and best of the human race, that nothing is to be learnt but what they are able to teach, and that nothing is worth having which they do not possess.

The art of man could hardly discover a more effectual

antidote to improvement, than this persuasion; and yet I never listened to any public oration, or read any work professedly addressed to the country, in which they did not labour to impress it on the minds of the people.

To hint to the generality of Americans that the silent current of events may change their beloved government, is not the way to please them; but in truth they need be tormented with no such fear. As long as by common consent they can keep down the pre-eminence which nature has assigned to great powers, as long as they can prevent human respect and human honour from resting upon high talent, gracious manners, and exalted station, so long may they be sure of going as on they are.

I have been told, however, that there are some among them who would gladly see a change; some who, with the wisdom of philosophers and the fair candour of gentlemen, shrink from a profession of equality which they feel to be untrue, and believe to be impossible.

I can well believe that such there are, though to me no such opinions were communicated, and most truly should I rejoice to see power pass into such hands.

If this ever happens, if refinement once creeps in among them, if they once learn to cling to the graces, the honours, the chivalry of life, then we shall say farewell to American equality, and welcome to European fellowship one of the finest countries on the earth.

Editor's Notes

xxxvi In 1836, Mrs Trollope published her fourth novel, *The Life and Adventures of Jonathan Jefferson Whitlaw: or Scenes on the Mississippi*, which has claims to be the first anti-slavery novel. In it she drew upon her recollections of many of the places she had visited. In 1857 it was reissued under the new title of *Lynch Law*. The novel gave considerable offence in the United States, while in England it was generally attacked as being an exaggerated account of slavery.

9 The various Radicals mentioned here were all associated with Fanny Wright: Mary Carroll gave up millinery to open a bookshop for the sale of Radical pamphlets; William Maclure was a Scotsman who conducted the progressive school at New Harmony, Indiana, with the help of a Frenchwoman, Marie Fretageot. New Harmony had been set up to follow the ideas of Robert Owen, including his concept of buildings surrounding a huge, hollow square. Henry Trollope spent a short time at the New Harmony school; the miserable time he had there is reflected in Mrs Trollope's hostile comments.

10 Almack's Assembly Rooms provided the centre of aristocratic social life in early nineteenth-century London. The five lady patronesses decided who was eligible to attend.

15 The victory of Andrew Jackson over John Quincy Adams in the presidential election of 1828 was seen as the triumph of Western democracy against the Eastern élite. The military titles she criticizes were given to militia officers, who were often elected.

24 Plate 5 of Hervieu's twenty-four engravings in the original edition.

Camilla, the younger sister of Fanny Wright, married Richeson Whitby, the manager of the settlement.

Editor's Notes

43 William Bullock, an Englishman, had emigrated to America. He had owned the 'Egyptian Hall', a London museum.

53 Mrs Trollope herself actually arranged the scenes from Dante, with paintings by Hervieu and wax figures by the young American sculptor, Hiram Powers.

56 Phrenology was one of the great crazes of the early nineteenth century. Johann Spurzheim was the great apostle of the movement. Dr Charles Caldwell gave lectures throughout America. George Combe was the most prominent British lecturer. He also wrote a book of American travels, *American Notes*, giving a much more favourable picture than Mrs Trollope.

71 See 'Summer' in James Thomson's poem, *The Seasons*.

76 Mary Russell Mitford, author of *Our Village*, was an old friend of Mrs Trollope's.

99 In the *Quarterly Review*, Basil Hall disagreed with Mrs Trollope's comments about the paucity of private charity. This was his one substantial disagreement with her.

111 Marie Taglioni was the greatest dancer in the period of Romantic ballet.

115 The Shaking Quakers were a religious sect which, under the leadership of an Englishwoman, Mother Ann Lee, settled in America in 1774. They are better remembered as 'the Shakers'.

119 Various scandals about Andrew Jackson's wife had played a part in the recent presidential election.

122 Dr Alexander Campbell founded the 'Disciples of Christ' which often calls itself 'The Christian Church'. Bethany College was a fundamentalist training college in what is now West Virginia. Robert Owen, the British philanthropist and Utopian reformer, eventually became a spiritualist.

132 At the Battle of New Orleans in January 1815, American troops under Andrew Jackson defeated the British army.

158 Henry Clay of Kentucky was one of the leaders of the anti-Jackson forces. Mrs Margaret Botsford is the author Mrs Trollope met.

162 A famous road built by Napoleon in Switzerland.

Editor's Notes

199 Anna Maria Stone was the eldest of the Garnett sisters, an English family who had emigrated to America in the 1790s. Her father had taught Mrs Trollope and it was the Garnetts who introduced her to Fanny Wright.

219 From Edmund Burke's *Reflections on the Revolution in France* (1790).

231 Tortoni's was the most famous café on the Boulevard des Italiens in Paris. It was renowned throughout Europe for its ice-creams. Parisian society gathered there after the opera.

262 An eighteenth-century novel by Frances Brooke, *The History of Emily Montague*, set in Canada.

263 Mrs Trollope does not appear to know that there was a similar law in England where the Stamp Tax required accurate returns of the circulation of newspapers. The crusade against the 'tax on knowledge' was a great radical cause. Mrs Trollope's ignorance of it would indicate that her early learning to 'sedition' did not extend too far.

265 The Duke of Saxe-Weimar published his *Travels Through North America* in 1828. Milledgeville became the capital of the State of Georgia in 1804.

271 Micah Flint was the son of Mrs Trollope's friend, Timothy Flint. He died before the publication of *Domestic Manners*.

295 Joseph Bonaparte, formerly King of Naples and then of Spain, fled to the United States after the final defeat of his younger brother, Napoleon. His elegant home, which then possessed the best art collection in America, was a Mecca for tourists. Fanny Wright had visited him. In 1832 he was titular Bonapartist claimant to the throne of France.

308 This was part of a plan to develop Paterson, New Jersey, as America's industrial centre.

327 Charles Leslie, the artist, records an interesting account of a dispute about American manners and language occasioned by Mrs Trollope's book. Charles Matthews, the English comedian, said he 'had made out a pretty long list [of Americanisms] but had since met with every one of them in England excepting only "slick right away".' Tom Taylor (ed.), *Autobiographical Recollections of Charles Robert Leslie, R.A.* (London, 2 vols., 1860), I. 251.

Editor's Notes

335   Sir Isaac Brock, a British General, killed while defeating the invasion of Canada by United States troops in 1812.

337   Captain Thomas Hamilton was a Scottish novelist whose most famous novel was *Cyril Thornton*. He was travelling in America at the same time as Mrs Trollope and published *Men and Manners in America* in 1833. For his unfavourable views on Mrs Trollope at Niagara see Heineman, *Mrs Trollope*, p. 73.

343   From a novel, *Mrs Bogle Corbet* (1831), by the Scottish novelist John Galt, who had visited Canada.

347   American prisons had a high reputation in Europe for enlightened treatment. Tocqueville was sent to America by the French government to study their methods.

350   It is probably the American artist, Chester Harding, who is here compared to Sir Thomas Lawrence.

351   There were two English MPs of this name, father and son, who owned large tracts of land in New York State and Canada. The father (known as 'Bear' Ellice from his connections with the fur trade) was the brother-in-law of the Whig Prime Minister, Earl Grey.

357   From a character in Fanny Burney's novel, *Evelina* (1778).

Mark Twain's Comments

Mark Twain carried a copy of *Domestic Manners* with him while writing *Life on the Mississippi* (1883). His copy of the New York edition of Mrs Trollope contains numerous comments by him as well as instructions to his publisher on which passages to quote in his own book. This copy is now part of the Arents Collection of the New York Public Library. This collection was formed to show the influence of tobacco in history and Mrs Trollope's book was included because of her frequent attacks upon tobacco spitting. The following are some of the comments made by Twain a half century after Mrs Trollope was published. It is interesting to note that Twain thought Mrs Trollope had married Hervieu.

7   She is very fair and thoughtful

12   This is the boat I saw

15   This was still true in a large measure 25 years ago

21   Island gone, now

39   She hit it

44   A fair shot

45   but your memory was woefully defective as to details

52   True, then, no doubt, but the thing is reversed now

57   This is changed, too

58   It is within the possibilities at any rate

84   Changed now

89   True yet

90   Changed

359   Right [—in] a boarding house

        Mrs T then married a French *valet*.

MORE OXFORD PAPERBACKS

Details of a selection of other Oxford Paperbacks follow. A complete list, including the World's Classics, Twentieth-Century Classics, Oxford Shakespeare, Oxford Authors, Oxford Paperback Reference, Past Masters, and OPUS, can be obtained in the UK from the General Publicity Department, Oxford University Press, Walton Street, Oxford OX2 6DP.

In the USA, complete lists are available from the Paperbacks Marketing Manager, Oxford University Press, 200 Madison Avenue, New York, NY 10016.

ANTHONY TROLLOPE IN THE WORLD'S CLASSICS

ANTHONY TROLLOPE: An Autobiography
Edited by P. D. Edwards

Barchester Towers
With an introduction by James R. Kincaid

Can You Forgive Her?
Edited by Andrew Swarbrick
With an introducion by Kate Flint

Dr. Thorne
Edited by David Stilton

The Duke's Children
Edited by Hermione Lee

The Eustace Diamonds
Edited by W. J. McCormack

Framley Parsonage
Edited by P. D. Edwards

The Kelly's and the O'Kelly's
Edited by W. J. McCormack
With an introduction by William Trevor

The Last Chronicle of Barset
Edited by Stephen Gill

Phineas Finn
Edited by Jacques Berthoud

Phineas Redux
Edited by John C. Whale
Introduction by F. S. L. Lyons

The Prime Minister
Edited by Jennifer Uglow
With an introduction by John McCormick

The Small House at Allington
Edited by James R. Kincaid

The Warden
Edited by David Skilton

The Way We Live Now
Edited by John Sutherland

Martin Chuzzlewit

Charles Dickens

Edited by Margaret Cardwell

Martin Chuzzlewit—hailed as the most ambitious of Dicken's early novels—has frequently been likened to Franny Trollope's book, *The Domestic Manners of the Americans*, for the criticism it aroused by its controversial opinions of the Americans.

This edition, with a new introduction and explanatory notes, includes Dicken's Prefaces and the 1868 Postscript which gave his later views of America, the few working notes which accompany the manuscript, and eight of the original illustrations by 'Phiz'.

THE WORLD'S CLASSICS

English Hours

Henry James

Introduction by Leon Edel

'The great relisher of impressions and nuances turns his attention in these occasional pieces to aspects of English life, metropolitan and provincial, Wonderful.' *Sunday Times*

English Hours is an affectionate portrait, warts and all, of the country that was to become Henry James's adopted homeland. One of the great travel writers of his time, James takes the reader on a series of visits, ranging from Winchelsea to Warwick, taking in abbeys and castles, sea-fronts and race-courses. Though no mere travel guide, the book will certainly enhance any tourist's pleasure.

A Little Tour in France

Henry James

Foreword by Geoffrey Grigson

One rainy morning in the autumn of 1882 Henry James set out on a trip to the French provinces, which took him from Touraine to the south-west, through Provence, and northwards again along the flooding Rhone to Burgundy.

James is a knowledgeable guide. His verbal discussions make no pedantic tourists' handbook: and if, as Geoffrey Grigson points out, they lead the reader round not only France but also the country called Henry James, lovers of both countries, will find that each in this book exerts an irresistible charm.

Travels through France and Italy

Tobias Smollett

Edited by Frank Felsenstein

Whether he describes the French tax system, the culture of silk-worms, or the marbles of Florence, Smollett provides many insights into eighteenth-century taste and into his own cantankerous, perceptive and intelligent personality.

'any reader of this new edition of his *Travels* . . . will be amused, horrified and aghast – aghast at Smollett (sometimes) as well as at the French of the eighteenth century (some of them).' Geoffrey Grigson, *Country Life*.

THE WORLD'S CLASSICS

Lavengro

George Borrow

Now acknowledged as a classic, *Lavengro* is a book in which autobiography is inextricably linked with fiction. Borrow was an inveterate traveller with a taste for the outlandish. The restless spirit of the young hero of *Lavengro* leads him to strange lands and adventures with gypsies, rogues and thieves.

'One of the more remarkable literary oddities of the nineteenth century: an autobiographical fantasy journey.' *Observer*

The Romany Rye

George Borrow

The sequel to *Lavengro* which continues Borrow's adventurous tale of gypsy life.

The Wynne Diaries

The Adventures of Two Sisters in Napoleonic Europe

Edited by Anne Fremantle

These diaries provide one of the most detailed and vivid accounts of the Napoleonic era, as well as a delightful, amusing, and intimate picture of the lives of two young women.

Betsey Wynne was ten and her sister Eugenia nine when they started writing these diaries, which cover the period 1789–1820. Their family—rich, well-connected, and unconventional—travelled round the Continent with an enormous suite at the whim of their charming but irresponsible father. The diaries are full of their accounts of parties, balls, and practical jokes; their opinions of counts, countesses, and ambassadors, interspersed with anecdotes; stories of their romances; and descriptions of life on board the ships of Nelson's navy.

'records in the undisciplined English of educated young women that gives to the slightest and greatest events an unjaded excitement; from the guillotine to the galantine.' *Vogue*

'Of many excellent reprints . . . the one I have picked for your particular attention is *The Wynne Diaries* . . . The sister diarists, Betsey and Eugenia, are very good acquaintances to make.' Marghanita Laski, *Country Life*